CHICAGO PUBLIC LIBRARY

D0083609

CHICAGO
LINCOLN
1150 W.

THE TIME OF THE FRENCH
IN THE HEART OF
NORTH AMERICA

1673-1818

Charles J. Balesi

Alliance Française Chicago

With the support of Mr. Barry MacLean

1992

© 1991 by Charles Balesi
All Rights Reserved
Published by the Alliance Française Chicago
810 North Dearborn, Chicago, Illinois, USA

Design and Production by Tom and Terry Willcockson
Cartography by Tom Willcockson
Printed in the United States of America by the Sheffield Press,
Hammond, Indiana

First Published 1992

Library of Congress Cataloging in Publication Data

Balesi, Charles
The Time of the French in the Heart of North America, 1673-1818

Includes bibliographical references and index.

1. French - History. 2. North America - History.
3. Illinois - History. 4. Great Lakes - History.
5. Indiana - History. 6. Missouri - History.

Library of Congress Catalog Card Number 92 - 071593
ISBN 1-881370-00-3

MAR 2 0 1995

Cover: Detail showing the Upper Mississippi Valley. From Henry Popple, "A Map
of the British Empire in North America," London ,1733. (The MacLean Collection)

To the memory of those anonymous individuals, French and Indian, who lived, fought, and fell together.

CHICAGO PUBLIC LIBRARY
LINCOLN PARK BRANCH
1150 W. Fullerton Avenue 60614

Acknowledgments

One does not make a journey, beginning with only a tentative outline and ending with a finished product on a shelf, without the support of many; an historian is definitively not a *navigateur solitaire*. I must first thank the Newberry Library, the best spiritual home a scholar would ever be privileged to share with colleagues, and with a staff whose collective knowledge remains to me a never-ending source of wonder. I want particularly to single out John Aubrey, whose encyclopedic and analytical mind came to my rescue many a time, and to evoke the memory of Michael Kaplan, who could magically unearth on demand the most obscure publications. Both Helen Tanner and Francis Jennings have been a precious source of information and wisdom-weathered opinions on Indian matters; (case in point, on Helen's advice, I have not given the customary "s" ending to Indian names in a plural context). I cannot leave the Newberrry Library without expressing my deepest thanks to my good friend, David Buisseret, the unflappable Director of the Hermon Dunlap Smith Center for the History of Cartography, who took the time to hunt down mercilessly the gallicisms that escaped my editors. My gratitude also goes to Carl Ekberg at the Illinois State University for his support, and the valuable opinion of a well-seasoned scholar. Writing is a demanding sport, on oneself and one's spouse: I want to thank my wife Myra for her patience, support, and incisive criticism. Noreen Giles served in this project in the thankless role of editor; Tom and Terry Willcockson get my deep feelings of appreciation for their meticulous production work.

I want to thank the Alliance Française of Chicago for its trust in me and in the project, for its daring spirit of innovation, so well demonstrated by Jean Brown, President of its Board; Réal de Mélogue, General Director; and Sonia Adjem, Program Director. It is, I think, fitting that my last acknowledgment goes to Barry MacLean, whose personal interest in the French history of North America has continued to manifest itself throughout the years, and to whose generous support the quality of this book owes much.

Contents

Foreword

Charles Balesi's subject in this book is the French presence in the heart of North America during the colonial era. Any such study must be written with Clarence Alvord's classic *The Illinois Country, 1673-1818,* in the background. Alvord's book is now over seventy years old, however, and Charles has added new and important perspectives on the subject. Rather than limiting the Illinois Country to the east side of the Mississippi (Alvord's book was written as the background for Illinois state history), Charles deals with both sides of the river. This is the correct approach, for in the eighteenth century the Mississippi was not a line of division, but was instead the geographical feature that bound together French-Creole society in the region. French Illinois included both sides of the Upper Mississippi River.

Moreover, Charles has broadened our understanding of French colonialism in the Illinois Country by dealing at some length with subjects, such as slavery and agriculture, that were of little interest to Clarence Alvord. Charles' more comprehensive approach, of course, reflects changes that have occurred in American historiography over the past two generations, but in any case, his larger perspective makes his book richer and more interesting for today's readers.

Finally, it is refreshing to read about French Illinois from a French point of view. Alvord's biases were distinctly Anglo-American; Charles' are passionately French. Given the fact that there is no such thing as unbiased history writing, it is salutary to have French Illinois now interpreted by an historian with French roots.

All of us who have enjoyed Charles' company over the years know that there is always structure and logic and some objective in what he says. Charles speaks (and writes) with a seriousness of purpose, which, even if one does not necessarily agree with him, means that he is always worth listening to. This is true whether the subjects at hand are history, politics, or wine. The book that follows is suffused with Charles' passion and his charm, and it is also a serious contribution to the history of Illinois and the Mississippi River valley.

Carl Ekberg
Normal, Illinois

Preface

Strangely enough this book was born out of a rejection. Though my manuscript on a subject in African History based on my PhD thesis was later published by the African Section of Brandeis University, I had originally submitted it to the University of Illinois Press. Frank Williams, then Assistant Director, did not handle the rejection routinely, however, and took the opportunity to encourage me to write a new history of the French period in Illinois, a subject about which I knew next to nothing at the time; furthermore, fresh out of a five-year intensive study of all facets of African history , my interest was turned towards what I then considered to be a more exalted, glamorous field. But Frank's arguments on behalf of regional history had a convincing ring, and shortly after our conversation in his Chicago campus' office, I began to read materials on the French period at the Newberry Library. As more and more books on Illinois, Indiana, Wisconsin, and other related areas piled up on my carrel, the truly grandiose dimensions of the history of this French colonial empire, once extending all the way from Quebec to the Gulf of Mexico, became evident to me. It was a history of fierce determination, of anonymous heroism, of incredible challenges experienced by a scant handful of individuals. This was a history, which although told before, and often quite well with an abundance of details, nevertheless had been recounted in a fragmentary fashion; in order to acquire an integrated view of the French period between Lake Michigan and the Ozarks, from Green Bay to the Ohio, one had to juggle several works, not to mention the further reading necessary to place events within a context of global European and North American politics. A new treatment integrating the most recent findings as well was justified, particularly a treatment that, while avoiding the excesses of political revisionism, would not be written from the perspective of the nineteenth-century apologists for anything Anglo-Saxon.

As is customary with any research, I have accumulated over the years enough notes and photostats to fill a multi-volume encyclopedia on the subject at hand. In the course of the always painful selection of what should or should not be retained, this cold-blooded triage of documents, I have no doubt sacrificed information that others would have included. But while developing this project, I came early on to change from my original intention of producing one of those monographs throbbing with charts and statistics, very "French school of modern history," very in the genre of the *6ème section du Centre National de la Recherche Scientifique*, to the idea of a general work to appeal to "civilians" who would read, understand, and appreciate this fascinating time.

There are few inhabitants of today's Midwest who are aware that a large part of that land was once a French province. It is unfortunate yet true that the French names of hundreds of localities are for many little more than debris with uncertain origins rather than links with a history that deserves to be known and appreciated. It is my personal belief that if historians want to participate in an effort to conserve the past, whether landmarks, sights, or memories, we must progress more frequently beyond the necessary (and certainly essential) level of addressing each other in scholarly meetings and journals. This book, therefore, was written primarily in response to this concern, along with several specific intentions: to offer a basic text as an aid to teachers and professors dealing with local and regional history; to induce many to travel back in time by visiting the towns and areas mentioned throughout the following pages; and to intrigue some to further satisfy their curiosity by reading more deeply into the subject.

Abbreviations

AJQ	Archives Judiciaires de Québec
ANC	Archives Nationales, Colonies, Paris
ANM	Archives Nationales, Marine, Paris
ANQ	Archives Nationales du Québec
BN	Bibliothèque Nationale, Paris
CA	Canadian Archives, Ottawa
DN	Dépôt Notarial, Québec
IHS	Illinois Historical Survey
MSS	Manuscript
NB	Newberry Library, Chicago
NYCD	New York Colonial Documents

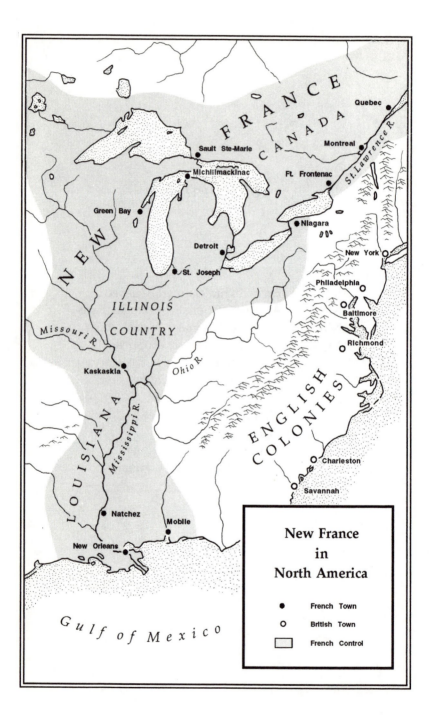

New France
in
North America

● French Town
○ British Town
▨ French Control

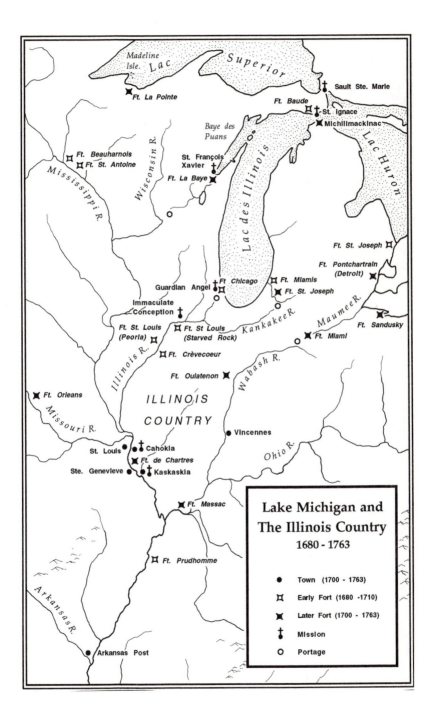

Lake Michigan and
The Illinois Country
1680 - 1763

●   Town   (1700 - 1763)

⊭   Early Fort   (1680 -1710)

✶   Later Fort   (1700 - 1763)

✝   Mission

○   Portage

THE TIME OF THE FRENCH

IN THE HEART OF

NORTH AMERICA

1673-1818

1

French Aspirations in North America

L ouis XIV, King of France, was twenty-two years old when Cardinal
Jules Mazarin, the Prime Minister and most powerful man in France,
died on March 9, 1661. Within minutes after the death of the man who had
taught him all he knew of the art of governing, the young king gathered
the royal council and announced to its bewildered members his intention
to exercise complete authority over all affairs of the nation. Thus the era
of absolute monarchy began in France, an era which innovated both the
notions of supremacy of the state and of centralized government.

Louis XIV was a working king who surrounded himself with working
ministers.[1] The best known of these was Jean-Baptiste Colbert, who was
the son and grandson of provincial cloth merchants. Colbert quickly
realized that a new type of bureaucracy was needed to execute the
grandiose plans that the king was formulating for the glory of France.
Under Colbert's tutelage a corps of competent civil servants responsible
only to the Crown, a new breed of administrators that was willing to
trample feudalistic legalisms, began to grow. They were the first generation of officials, whose spiritual descendants, *les grands commis de l'Etat*
(the "State's high executives"), are still leading France's affairs today.

The king's plans for France called for a powerful professional army to
back up political alliances; in contrast, Colbert's plans envisioned a strong
navy protecting a merchant fleet able to bring back commodities from
colonies yet to be established. Amazingly, during the first years of Louis's
reign, these two costly blueprints for imperialism would be carried out
simultaneously; and, for the first time, France could look seriously overseas.

At the beginning of the seventeenth century, the British, the Portuguese, and, of course, the Spaniards, had already benefited abundantly
from their overseas dominions. Only France had not acquired much from
its ventures in the Americas, with the exception of some profitable sugar
islands in the West Indies. As for the French settlements along the banks
of the St. Lawrence River, everything seemed to conspire against their
growth: poor soil, lack of population, and rigorous winters choking the
harbor of Quebec with ice for three months of the year.

As had other European monarchs who took an interest in overseas expansion, it was the French kings who subsidized the first explorations.
When the new lands did not produce the fabulous riches *à la Mexico* or *à*

Detail from Nicolas Sanson, "Le Canada, ou Nouvelle France", Paris, 1656. (The Newberry Library)

la Peru, they turned them over conditionally to private interests. In 1603, for instance, Henry IV granted a monopoly of trade in North America to Pierre du Cast, *sieur* des Monts. Later, when fishing, fur, and timber attracted more commercial activity, individual investors banded together to ensure a better return on their investments and formed charter companies that in turn bought the exclusive rights for the exploitation of the North American colony from the Crown. New France—or Canada, as it later became known—was still under the régime of a charter company when young Louis XIV took charge of his kingdom. The King, instinctively hostile to any group or institution possibly infringing upon his power, was determined to end this system of indirect colonial government and Colbert, sharing the King's distrust, supported every political move which would lead to the establishment of royal absolutism.

Colbert was searching for expansionist opportunities while the small French community of North America, struggling for survival, was sending distress signals from the banks of the St. Lawrence River. First came a letter from Governor Pierre Davaugour, and later the dispatch of an eloquent spokesman, Pierre Boucher, administrator of the town of Trois-Rivières. In his memoir, Governor Davaugour had presented New France as: "A land of golden opportunities for agriculture, industry and commerce, not to speak of territorial expansion, and a possible solution to the northern mystery [the passage to China]."[2]

The King's curiosity was aroused. He gave a three-hour audience to Boucher before turning him over to Colbert for additional planning to support the colony. Davaugour's long letters and Boucher's visit were, in the words of Father Borgia-Steck, a historian who has looked extensively at the beginnings of French expansion in North America:

> directly responsible for Louis XIV's project and Colbert's ambition to convert North America into a vast French sovereignty. Immense revenues would pour into the royal treasury, as great as those which Spain was amassing from her New World possessions, while the control of a waterway across the continent would secure for France a commercial advantage that her rivals in Europe had long been seeking. Besides, the time would come when a Bourbon would occupy the Spanish throne and in this manner a large share of Spain's colonial revenues become available for the aggrandizement of France on the European continent. . . .[3]

The time was right for French ambitions in North America. France of the 1660s enjoyed a powerful position in the world, a position not held before or since. Within a year after the beginning of Louis XIV's reign, the royal treasury registered a large surplus, and victories to the East and in Flanders brought territorial gains subsequently made permanent by treaty. In short, as wrote William Eccles, one of the most qualified historians of this period: "By 1660, of all the countries in Europe, France was in the best position to avail herself of the latent opportunities in North America."[4]

As expected, in 1663 the administration of New France was removed from the hands of the chartered *Compagnie des Cent Associés* and returned to the Crown. Since the company had never shown a profit, its members were not disappointed by this outcome. In May, Canada was made a royal province and the governing of all French possessions in North America entrusted to a lieutenant-general who was to reside in Quebec,

Portrait of Louis XIV, King of France and Navarre. Unknown Artist. (Musée National du Château de Versailles)

though his authority would extend all the way to the West Indies. The administration of New France proper was to be divided between a governor and an *intendant,* both also to reside in Quebec. Never did such a small capital have to contend with so many officials.

On June 30, 1665, the first of these officials arrived; Lieutenant-General Alexandre de Prouville, Marquis de Tracy. A full regiment of infantry, the regiment of *Carignan-Salières,* which included a thousand men, came with him as reinforcement against Iroquois attacks. On September 12, both the new governor, Daniel de Rémy, Seigneur de Courcelles, and the new *intendant,* Jean Talon, arrived together after a stormy crossing. Their tribulations on the high seas were compensated for by the warm welcome from the tiny population, relieved that the king had finally remembered his subjects in North America.[5]

The position of *intendant* was new in the hierarchy of the French royal administration, having been created by Louis XIII's formidable minister,

Portrait of Jean Talon by
Claude François. (Monastère
des augustines de l'Hotel-
Dieu de Québec)

Cardinal Richelieu. Ostensibly, the role of the *intendant* was to assist the
governors of the provinces in the discharge of their duties, and through
this innovation, the Crown was able to exert control over local governments. Disputes between provinces and central government were
remnants of feudalism, the likes of which the small, new settlements of
French North America had never known. In New France, an *intendant*
and a governor had a fresh start without concern for political precedent.
Royal power was absolute from the beginning, in contrast to the system
in the thirteen English colonies where local rule was the established
order.[6]

At the time of the arrival of these new French officials, New France was
in danger of disappearing altogether, partly because of decades of royal
neglect, but also from the continual threat presented by the only American Indian people solidly allied to the British—the Iroquois. Peace may
have prevailed in Europe between France and England, civilities may
even have been exchanged between the Court of St. James and the Louvre,
but the silent, smoldering rivalry between the French and British colonists
of North America had never entirely ceased. It was fortunate for the
French colony that the administrators it received were capable and
devoted men.

The most effective administrator among the three would prove to be *intendant* Jean Talon. Born in 1625 to a family belonging to the *noblesse de robe*, he had received the usual solid education that the Jesuits provided to the children of the upper-and middle-classes. In 1653, thanks to an older brother who worked for Cardinal Mazarin, Talon entered the military administration, where his eye for detail, his talent for organization, his love for work, and above all, his deep sense of loyalty, quickly attracted the Minister's attention, and two years later, he was appointed *intendant* of the Hainaut, a vital province guarding the northern border. There, Talon's administrative talents emerged in such an evident manner that when Colbert sought the right man for that other sensitive frontier, French North America, he immediately sent for this promising young official.[7]

Talon remained *intendant* of New France for seven years, from 1665 to 1672 (including one year on leave in France). During his administration he worked feverishly in an attempt to transform Colbert's blueprints into reality. His task was complicated by the fact that while the settlements along the St. Lawrence needed administrative organization, the territories to the west and to the south still had to be brought under French control before the British or the Spaniards could reach them and claim de facto sovereignty. In his letter of October 10, 1670, Talon informed the king that:

> Since my arrival here I have dispatched persons of resolution, who promise to penetrate farther than has ever been done; one to the west and to the northwest of Canada; and the other to the southwest and to the south. The adventurers are to keep diaries in all instances and on their return, answer to the written instructions given to them; in all cases they are to take possession, display the king's arms and draw up an affidavit to serve as title.[8]

Another important element in the pursuit of French expansion in North America during the late 1600s, was the possible existence of a large waterway believed to be somewhere to the west of the Great Lakes. The French had been looking for this river for forty years; they hoped that it would prove to be more than an Indian myth, and moreover, that it would flow in a westerly direction toward China, providing direct passage to the coveted wealth of Asia.

Indians who came to trade in Montreal and Albany freely talked about Miss-i-sipi or Mitchi-sipi, the "great water."[9] The Spaniards had been the first Europeans to hear of it during their attempts to take possession of the entire shore of the Gulf of Mexico. In the early part of the sixteenth century, Cabeza de Vaca and Hernando de Soto did in fact cross the lower Mississippi, but Spain's resources were already spread very thinly over the North American continent and she was not able to investigate any further. Samuel de Champlain,[10] the "creator" of New France, had sent his most trusted agent, Jean Nicolet, on a long-range westward exploration. (Nicolet entered the waters separated by a peninsula from the main body of northern Lake Michigan and, impressed by the dense vegetation, named it *La baye verte*, today anglicized as Green Bay, Wisconsin.) There is some reason to believe that Nicolet continued even farther west and reached a point within two or three walking-days from the Mississippi. During the same period, two remarkable figures of early French Canadian history, Pierre Esprit Radisson and his brother-in-law, Medart Chouart des Groseillers, had come across the headwaters of the Mississippi during their second trip west.

In 1665, after the French had temporarily destroyed the hostile grip of the Iroquois on the western shore of the St. Lawrence River with the renewed strength brought by the Regiment of *Carignan-Salières*, dozens of young men from Montreal and Quebec sought their fortune, by travelling west with the flotilla of Indian traders. They were attempting to enter the fur trade and, not surprisingly, their efforts were supported by the royal authorities. One of these men, Nicolas Perrot, is reputed to have come very close to finding the actual location of the Mississippi. On another occasion, a missionary priest, Claude Alby, during an expedition to the Ottawa Nation, went as far as Lake Superior and subsequently recorded that the Sioux lived "to the west of the place [Chequamegon Bay] towards the great river named Mesippi." [11] Yet another cleric, a Jesuit, Jean Claude Allouez, who from 1665 to 1669 had served as a missionary in what is now Wisconsin, mentioned the river in one of the *Jesuit Relations*.[12] These were pamphlets regularly published and distributed to potential financial supporters of overseas missions; their accounts were meant to inform as well as to entertain and inspire. Finally, Cavelier de La Salle, the most famous of the French adventurers in North America, probably also came close to the Mississippi while following the course of the Ohio River during his exploration of 1669. No doubt, there were more independent souls searching for their fortunes who came close to the Mississippi, but left no records.

From the day of his arrival in Quebec, *intendant* Talon knew that it was only a question of time before someone was going to claim the west for his king and Talon had resolved that this person would be a Frenchman. With much of the administrative reorganization accomplished, he was able to gather a strong expedition for spring 1681. Again, writing to the king on the progress of the preparation, Talon announced that an army

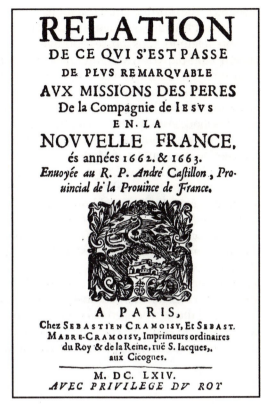

Page from the *Jesuit Relations*
(The Newberry Library)

officer, Simon Francois Daumont, *Sieur* de Lusson, had instructions to find a waterway that would link the "sea of the south which separates this country from China."[13] The choice of an officer rather than a civilian indicates Talon's desire to give the Crown's mark and authority to French expansion. Until this time, France's sovereignty had been extended by missionaries and fur-traders, but their efforts were at the whim of either their spiritual or commercial priorities. Neither the missionaries who penetrated the continent in search of those Indian nations most easy to separate and convert, nor the fur-traders who went only where trade led them, could have been expected to be true agents of French expansion.

Ironically, Lusson was far less adventurous than the *intendant* had expected; he progressed no farther than the most western French outpost, Sault Sainte-Marie. To be fair, it must be said that he did put on an impressive show of strength. On June 14, 1681, in full-dress uniform, with soldiers, drums, banners, flags, and the few traders who had joined in with their best accoutrements, Lusson presided over a large assembly of delegates from fourteen Indian nations. Four Jesuit priests said a *te deum* mass beneath a huge wooden cross, and then, in the fashion of the times, Lusson solemnly took possession over: "Sainte Marie du Sault, Lake Huron, Lake Superior, Manitoulin Island, and all the rest of the country with its rivers, lakes, the rivers and lakes contiguous and adjacent, and the tributaries, as well as those discovered as those to be discovered, bounded on the one side by the north and western seas and on the other by the South Sea, this land, in all its length and breadth."[14]

Having explored and conquered with a stroke of the pen, Lusson returned to the comfort of Montreal, leaving behind a dozen frustrated traders who had been willing to push much farther west. Instead, they had been limited to the role of witnesses to the claim. Among them was a young man by the name of Louis Jolliet.[15]

When *intendant* Talon had left for New France in 1665, his instructions included territorial expansion as one of his major tasks. Now, perhaps, the time had come. Already, the western limits of the colony had been pushed quite far. Sault Sainte-Marie was at the entrance to Lake Superior; the Jesuit mission of Saint Ignace overlooked the strategic Straits of Mackinac; and another mission had been installed at the southern extremity of Green Bay. All of these promised to become important bases for the eventual conquest of an empire. The time was ripe for a deliberate, methodical exploration of the territory which lay west and southwest of New France.

NOTES

1. On King Louis XIV, see John B. Wolf, *Louis XIV*, 1968, the best volume in English about the French monarch's character and ideas.

2. Francis Borgia-Steck, *The Jolliet-Marquette Expedition 1673*, Quicy, 1928, p. 54.

3. Borgia-Steck, *The Jolliet.*, pp. 105-106; Boucher's observations on New France were published in Paris in 1663 in the form of a pamphlet entitled *Histoire véritable et naturelle des moeurs et productions du pays de la Nouvelle France.* Davaugour's memoir to the King which include arguments in the defense of Quebec similar to Boucher's have been published by Brodhead in *Documents Relative to the Colonial History of the State of New York* (Albany, N.Y., 1856-1887), vol. IX, pp. 13-17; see also Rev. Edward D. Neill, "Discovery along the Great Lakes," in *Narrative and Critical History of America*, Justin Winsor ed., 1884, vol. IV, p. 171.

4. William J. Eccles, *Canada Under Louis XIV: 1663-1701*, Toronto, 1964.

5. On November 19, 1663, Alexandre de Prouville, Marquis de Tracy, was appointed "Lieutenant-General of all the lands of our obedience situated North and South America and the islands of America." Daniel de Rémy, *Sieur* de Courcelles and Jean Talon were both appointed, respectively, governor and *intendant* of the same colony on March 23, 1665.

6. A definition of the roles of the two chief representatives of the royal power was needed to avoid conflict. To the *intendant* went: "The actual administration of the colony, financial matters, police protection, criminal proceedings and development of material resources—all this was in the hands of Talon," while "the governor's military role was not to be a sinecure. . . . In New France. . . . there was a governor-general, always a professional soldier, a qualification of a major importance since, starting with 1669, he would be entrusted by the King to form the habitants between the ages of sixteen and sixty into military companies." See William J. Eccles, *France in America*, Harper and Row, (New York, 1972), pp. 68-69.

7. On Talon, see Thomas Chapais, *Jean Talon, Intendant de la Nouvelle France: 1665-1672*, Paris, 1904.

8. Talon to the King, in Pierre Margry, *Découvertes et établissements des français dans l'Ouest et dans le Sud de l'Amérique Septentrionale, 1614-1754, Mémoires et Documents originaux*, Paris, 1876, Extract letter to King, October 10, 1670, 1, 82; also in Brodhead, *Documents Relative to the Colonial History of the State of New York*, Albany, 1851-1887, IX, p. 64, and in Borgia-Steck, *Jolliet-Marquette.*, pp. 117, 131.

9. The name Mississippi, although spelled in different ways according to various Indian as well as European pronunciations, is a compound from *mechac*, meaning "big," and *seebe*, meaning "water", from the Ojibway (Chippewa) language. See H.W. Beckwith, ed., *Collections of the Illinois State Historical Library*, (Springfield, 1903), vol. 1, p. 4.

10. Samuel de Champlain, 1567-1635, appointed geographer to a French expedition sent to North America in 1603, returned several times to the new continent and was finally given two vessels with which he carried the expedition that founded Quebec on July 3, 1608. In 1628, Champlain was one of the *Cent-Associés* appointed by Cardinal Richelieu to run the colony of New France.

11. John Gilmary Shea, ed., *Establishment of the Faith by Father Christian LeClerq*, New York, 1881, vol. 1 p. 399, F.N.; Reuben Thwaites, *The Jesuit Relations and Allied Documents: Travel and Exploration of the Jesuit Missionaries in New France*, Cleveland, 1896-1901; also in Joseph P. Donnelley, S.J., *Jacques Marquette S.J.: 1637-1676* Chicago, Loyola University Press, 1968, pp. 106-07.

12. "These people (Miami) are settled in a very attractive place . . . their river (Fox) leads by a six-day voyage to the great river named Messi-sipi and it is along the same river that the other nations are located." In "Journal of Father Allouez," excerpt from the *Jesuit Relations, 1669-1670*, published in Paris in 1671 and translated in Thwaites, vol. LIV, pp. 197-214; also quoted in Louise Phelps-Kellog, *Early Narratives of the Northwest*, Charles Scribner & Sons, New York, 1917, p. 156; see also Donnelley, *Marquette*, pp. 103-107.

13. *Mémoire Succint, Talon à Colbert*, November 10, 1670, *Archives Nationales* in Margry, *Découvertes.* , 1, 86; also in Donnelley, *Marquette*, p. 174, quoting the *Rapport de l'Archiviste de la Province de Québec pour 1930-31*, p. 112.

14. *Procès-verbal de la prise de possession des pays vers les lacs Huron et Supérieur, le 14 juin 1671, Sainte-Marie du Sault*, in Margry, *Découvertes.*, XC Vol. 1, 96-99.

15. Jolliet indifferently spelled his last name with one or two l's; I have selected the latter form which he used increasingly towards the end of his life.

2

Explorations: 1673 - 1678

On June 25, 1673, two canoes with seven white men on board glided down-current along the western bank of a river whose existence had fascinated explorers of the North American continent for a century, the Mississippi.

A few days before, these seven men had left the easy waters of the Wisconsin River and were now hugging the cliffs of what we know today as the state of Iowa. One of the seven men, history has not retained his name, spotted a path that led away from the water's edge straight up the wooded bluff. Perhaps an impulse, an intuition, or an educated guess inspired the trader Louis Jolliet and the missionary Jacques Marquette to land at this spot and then go on to explore the unknown world at the other end of the trace.

After about a mile of cautious and arduous progression, all the while gripped by a mixture of anxiety and anticipation, as they would later recall, Jolliet and Marquette came in view of the huts of three villages clustered within a mile of each other. They waited a few minutes to compose themselves and then, as demanded by the etiquette of the North American plains in those times, when it was difficult to distinguish between friend and foe, called out to signal their presence.

> At this cry the Indians rushed out of their cabins, and having probably recognised us as French, especially seeing a black gown or at least having no reason to distrust us, seeing we were but two, and had made known our coming, they deputed four old men to come and speak to us. . . . They marched slowly, lifting their pipes toward the sun. . . . I spoke to them first, and asked them who they were; they answered that they were Illinois and, in token of peace, they presented their pipes to smoke.[1]

On this day, these two obscure subjects of the Sun King began the building of a French North American empire. If, as Jolliet believed, the waters flowing under the bark of their canoes mixed with those of the Gulf of Mexico (and not, as some still hoped fervently, with the Pacific Ocean), then a long-range plan for bringing about French aggrandizement could emerge: a French Mississippi would link Canada with the border of Texas and would permanently hem in the British colonies to the East and the Spanish possessions to the South.

The expedition led by Jolliet and Marquette was not the sort of random attempt that has been popularized in nineteenth century accounts. The French were well-acquainted with the existence of a major waterway somewhere west of their settlements. Besides the missions, commercial expeditions and officially-sponsored explorations, the intercourse which existed between Indians who freely entered French towns and Frenchmen who enjoyed the same privilege in Indian villages, had contributed to the accumulation of information in Quebec, information that would finally find its way to the King's desk. It had taken more than ten years for all this intelligence to be translated into an effective move westward, ten years during which the French presence in North America had slowly improved in quality and size thanks to a small, but steady, transfer of capital and manpower.

Whether the course of the Mississippi "was the burning question of the day,"[2] it was the river's strategic implications as understood in Quebec that had determined Jolliet and Marquette's westward voyage.

Although Louis Jolliet was a man of modest background and limited experience as an explorer, his selection by *intendant* Talon was a logical decision. Born in 1645, in New France, Jolliet was only twenty-seven years old at the time of the expedition. The education he had received from the Jesuits was the highest possible available this side of the Atlantic Ocean and even included the successful defense of a philosophical dissertation before a jury involving *intendant* Talon himself. A trader who had learned his metier alongside his older brother Adrien, Louis Jolliet was reported to have shown a gift for Indian languages. While engaged in business activities with his brother, he had spent a year in France where he took courses in hydrography. Jolliet's educational and professional background offered the basic ingredients that made him an acceptable leader in the eyes of the *intendant*. It must be remembered that New France of the 1670s was an extremely small community where the authorities knew everyone and in turn were known by everyone on a personal basis.[3] As we have seen, Talon had previously tried to extend France's control to the west by using an army officer, the *sieur* de Saint-Lusson, and had failed. Jolliet himself had witnessed the impressive but vain display of force and pageantry at Sault Sainte-Marie. Now, reasonably confident that he would succeed through a low-key approach, he seized the opportunity to lead an expedition even though it was to be at his own expense.

Enjoying the trust of his fellow traders, Louis Jolliet had no difficulty in gathering funds or men. Furthermore, as a former pupil of the newly-founded Jesuit college of Quebec, he benefited from the support of the church in New France, a church essentially made up of Jesuits. *Intendant* Talon, who still hoped to crown his tenure of office in North America with the glory of having enabled the discovery of the "large water" for France, had not been successful with expeditions funded by the royal treasury.[4] This time there would be no risk of financial loss: Louis Jolliet received only a *congé*, a royal license with trading rights attached; nonetheless he was expected to advance the interests of France with the Indian nations that he would meet along his way. Jolliet reduced his own financial risks by taking partners: the *Archives judiciaires* of Quebec hold a document dated October 1, 1672, that carefully establishes the financial responsibilities of each of the investors who joined with Jolliet to form a society for the discovery of new territory and the exploitation of its potential trading possibilities: "Before Gilles Rageot, notary ... were present the *Sieur* Louis Jolliet, François Chavigny, *écuyer*, *Sieur* de la Chevrotière, Zacharie Jolliet, Jean Plattier, Pierre Moreau, Jacques Largilier, Jean Tibergé, all now in this town, who of their own free will have entered into partnership and society to make together the voyage of the Ottawa country [to] trade with the Indians as profitably as possible...."[5]

The expense of the expedition amounted to 3,000 *livres*; half of this amount was provided by Louis Jolliet and the other half by his partners. While Jolliet was in the process of making his preparations *intendant* Talon was preparing to leave New France for the last time, the King having finally granted his wishes to return to France. In marked contrast, the next "strong man" of the colony would be the new governor, Count Frontenac, rather than the new *intendant*.

Louis de Buade, Count Frontenac, was born in 1620, the offspring of a family richer in glory than in material wealth (whatever had remained, he had helped dissipate). His grandfather had been a long-term aide to King Henry IV, and his father, as a child, had been Louis XIII's playmate. Now, Frontenac was in New France, not only to escape his creditors but, in addition, to rebuild his fortune.[6]

Talon, in his recommendations to the new governor, had suggested that Jolliet be retained as leader of the planned expedition to the West. Frontenac followed Talon's advice without question.[7]

On December 8, 1672, just before the beginning of winter, Jolliet, his

Portrait of Father Marquette
by John A. Nielson. (Mar-
quette University)

partners, and the hired hands beached their canoes in front of the cabins
of the Mission Saint Ignace, an outpost founded by the Jesuits at the Straits
of Mackinac, the door to Lake Michigan. They had travelled two months
to reach Saint Ignace where they were about to be joined by a member who
would have been a worthy adjunct to any expedition: Father Jacques Marquette.

The Jesuit priest had arrived at Saint Ignace only the preceding year,
leading a band of Christianized Chippewa fleeing Sault Saint-Marie and
the threat of extermination by the Sioux.[8] Father Marquette first settled
his protégés on Mackinac Island, (the Island of the Great Turtle, a site
occupied over the centuries by different branches of the Algonquin
speaking people) then moved them back to the mainland when safety was
assured.

Born on June 1, 1637, into a prominent family of Laon, a small town in
eastern France, Father Marquette had shown a precocious interest in
religion. As a child of nine he had entered the college of Jesuits in Reims,
where he took his vows in 1656, at nineteen, and was fully ordained ten
years later. He then left for New France where his arrival brought the total
number of Jesuit *missionaires* to thirty-two, a considerable figure.[9]

At the time of his arrival in St. Ignace, Louis Jolliet carried a letter from the Superior of the Jesuits of New France ordering Father Marquette to join his expedition for the discovery of the Mississippi. In exchange for the Jesuit experience in dealing with Indian nations, a missionary was to be allowed to follow the expedition. This was an order that filled the missionary with joy; he had wanted all along to proselytize farther than the shores of Lake Michigan. Yet, appearances covered the existence of a deep conflict between the royal power and the Society of Jesus in North America that would eventually lead to the expulsion of the latter. The conflict was, to be sure, not indigenous to New France, but had originated years before.

After the long and costly religious wars ended with King Henry IV's conversion to Catholicism, in 1593, France had decisively rejected the Reformation but just as assiduously opposed political interference by the Holy See. In this milieu, the Society of Jesus, the self-confessed militant arm of the papacy, was looked upon as an agent of a foreign power. Ministers and administrators of the King and even many members of the French clergy mistrusted the French Jesuits. Yet the Jesuits continued to educate the young élite as well as hear the confessions of the most powerful, including the members of the royal family, a paradox less difficult to understand when placed within the context of an age where loyalties of all kinds overlapped.

From the first days of European colonization, France as well as Spain and Portugal, had attached clerics to all overseas expeditions; the royal charters given to private colonial companies always required supporting the missions. Even when the last company to date, the Company of the *Cent-associés*, failed to live up to the promises of its royal charter, its economic problems did not affect the growth of the Church in New France, a Church almost entirely represented by the Jesuits beginning in 1632, when Cardinal Richelieu, then France's prime minister "... selected [the Jesuits] as spiritual directors of the colony ..." [10]

The mismanagement of New France's affairs was regarded with unspoken satisfaction by the Jesuits who harbored the secret ambition to transform the land into a new "Paraguay," the South American colony turned over to their direct rule by the Spanish monarchy at the beginning of the seventeenth century. Although the French Jesuits always hotly denied such an intention, an examination of their Indian policy from the 1670s to the end of the century supports the view of those historians who read unspoken territorial ambitions into their missionary work. The rise of Colbert and the interest shown by the King for the colonies would nullify their expectations. Colbert's appointment of royal administrators to replace the functionaries of the *Cent-associés* signaled the end of the political and military abandonment of Canada. Since the administrators were given the task of redirecting New France from a "mission land" to a "royal domain," conflicts between Jesuits and representatives of the royal authority were bound to arise. Initially, the crown was careful to avoid direct confrontation with the Bishop of Quebec, Monsignor François-Xavier de Laval.[11] Nevertheless, it was clear from the start that the new royal administrators intended to affirm their authority over all, clerics included, and that:

> . . . the duties of Talon qualified by the aims of Louis XIV were by their very nature at variance with the duties and aims of the Jesuits. To appropriate as government property lands near Quebec in order to establish towns was to deprive the Jesuits of a valuable and long-standing concession. To increase the number of colonists, to form new settlements and to encourage trade with the Indians meant increasing the risks of reviving the liquor traffic. To make the Indian sedentary, to bring them in closer touch with the whites, to teach them the language and customs of the French, to stress the allegiance they owed to the King—all this was equivalent to withdrawing them from the control of the missionaries . . .[12]

Yet, in a colony with so few human resources as New France—in 1672, the total population reached only 7,000—the contribution of all, including the Jesuits, was needed. Driven by insatiable missionary zeal, they planned on expanding farther west, and, through a system of interviews had obtained much information from Indians. It was this body of knowledge that would prove useful for the Jolliet expedition.

When Father Marquette arrived at Sault Sainte-Marie, there were two strong-minded Jesuits sharing the spiritual responsibility of the far Northwest: Father Claude Allouez and Father Claude Dablon. During the summer of 1669, Father Dablon had become the superior for all the western Jesuit missions. The following year, he was appointed Superior of the Order for all of New France, a position obliging him to reside in Quebec but which did not diminish his burning interest for missionary work in the west. It was in one of his *Relations* published in 1671, that the first mention of the Illinois Indians appeared. "These people are situated in the midst of that beautiful region mentioned by us, near the great river named Mississippi. . . ."[13]

The life of a missionary perforce embodied much more than the task of convincing the Indians to adopt Catholicism. Whether mediating the continual warfare between nations inhabiting the Lake Superior and Lake Michigan areas, or attempting to persuade strongly individualistic Frenchmen to behave within the accepted moral code, the missionary represented a major political force. Father Marquette, by then well acquainted with the diverse Indian nations roaming the Northwest—the Sioux, the Ottawa, the Chippewa, the Creek, the Miami, and the Illinois— had acquired such an influence.

On May 15, 1673, Louis Jolliet, the trader, and Jacques Marquette, the missionary, along with five other Frenchmen, pulled away from the beach of Saint Ignace in two canoes for what would become one of North America's foremost historic trips.

The route that the little expedition followed was the well-beaten path of the farthest French penetration; first the northern shore of Lake Michigan, then to the western shore of Green Bay up to the Jesuit Mission (DePere, Wisconsin). We look to Father Joseph Donnelly for his precise description:

> Leaving Saint-Ignace, the travellers rounded Groscap and followed the northern shore of Lake Michigan to Point Detour, averaging about thirty miles a day. Rather than risk the sixteen miles of open water at the mouth of Big Bay De Noc, they probably headed southward, island-hopping from Point Detour to Washington Island at the mouth of Green Bay. Coasting along the eastern shore of Green Bay to Eagle Harbor, they could easily cross westward to Strawberry Island thence to Chambers Island, and reach the western shore of the great bay without facing more than seven miles of open water at any point. About two weeks after leaving Saint-Ignace Marquette and his party reached the Menominee River where they stopped briefly to visit the *Folle Avoine* or Menominee to whom Allouez and Dablon had preached in the summer of 1670. On learning the objective of the journey the Menominee strove to dissuade the French, warning that the country to which they were bound was inhabited by people ". . . who never show any mercy to strangers . . ." Thanking them for their advice, the missionary explained that he could not follow it ". . . because the salvation of souls was at stake . . ." Reaching the end of [Green] Bay, the *voyagers* pushed up the lower Fox River to the first rapids near where the Mission of Saint-Francois-Xavier stood, arriving on about May 27. Father Andre

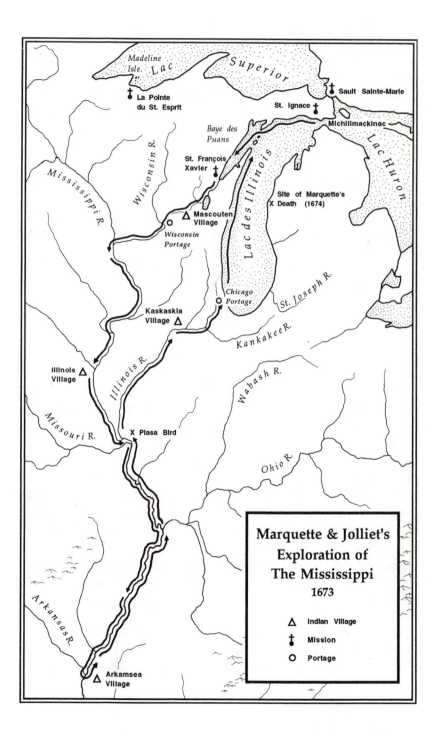

Marquette & Jolliet's
Exploration of
The Mississippi
1673

△ Indian Village

✝ Mission

○ Portage

was absent . . . but Father Allouez was home to welcome the callers . . . The
sixty-year-old Allouez had important information for the explorers. Some
Illinois Indians, calling themselves the Kaskaskia, who had been frequenting the mission . . . informed Allouez that in their country there was a
tributary of the Mississippi [the Illinois River] which greatly shortened the
distance between the mission and their homeland. . . . The next thirty miles
of their outward journey were the most difficult which the travelers would
meet: the lower Fox River, from Lake Winnebago to its mouth at Green
Bay, falls 169 feet, rushing over five dangerous rapids, Rapid des Peres at
DePere, Petit Kakalin at Little Rapids, La Croche at Kimberly, Grand Chute
at Appleton, and Winnebago Rapids at Doty's Island where Lake Winnebago drains into the lower Fox. . . . Emerging at last on broad, shallow, odor-
iferous Lake Winnebago, the voyagers followed the western shore south-
ward for twenty miles to the marshy entry of the Upper Fox and continued
up that pleasant stream forty-nine miles to the great village of the Mas-
countens. . . .[14]

Though they obtained the services of two Miami guides there, from
then on, it was a journey into the unknown. They continued via the
portage linking the narrow Fox to the wider waters of the Wisconsin, and
one month and 30 miles after their departure from Saint Ignace, on June
15, they finally emerged on the Mississippi. Ten days later, they came
across the camp of the Illinois, two miles from the confluence of the Iowa
River with the Mississippi. It was a pleasant, even a joyous meeting as
many warriors had travelled to the missions of Saint Xavier and Saint
Ignace and were familiar with the ways of the "black robes," as the French
priests had been nicknamed.[15]

Marquette and Jolliet smoked a peace pipe in the first of their three
villages, which were only separated from each other by a short distance
and which all together comprised a temporary home for the Illinois. In
the second village, the Great Captain of all the Illinois led a ceremony that
began with an exchange of speeches and gifts. Jolliet was given a ten-year-
old slave boy and a calumet. Then, all dignitaries proceeded to attend a
great feast:

consisting of four dishes which had to be partaken of in accordance with
all. . . . The first course was a great wooden platter full of *sagamité*, that is
to say meal of Indian corn boiled in water and seasoned with fat. The

Drawing of an Illinois Indian. (Thomas Gilcrease Institute of American History and Art)

Master of ceremonies filled a spoon with *sagamité* three or four times and put it to my mouth as if I were a little child. He did the same to Monsieur Jolliet. As a second course, he caused a second platter to be brought on

which were three fish. He took some pieces of them, removed the bones
thereupon, and after blowing upon them to cool them, he put them in our
mouths as one would give food to a bird. For the third course, they brought
a large dog that had just been killed; but when they learned that we did not
eat its meat, they removed it from before us. Finally, the fourth course was
a piece of wild ox [buffalo], the fattest morsels of which were placed in our
mouths.[16]

These Illinois on the western bank of the Mississippi were the latest
victims in the struggle being waged by Indian nations for control of the
fur-rich lands surrounding Lake Michigan. The French had first met them
in 1670, when they began coming to *La Pointe du Saint Esprit*, (Bayfield,
Wisconsin) to trade their furs. They had begun to migrate annually
beyond the safety of the great river to escape total destruction at the hands
of the Iroquois who, by the end of the seventeenth century, had already
reached this far east in their quest for trapping grounds. The Illinois had
been the dominant power of the region until the preceding century, but
had dwindled in number, and far worse, lost confidence in their ability to
withstand their adversaries. Their military weakness vis-à-vis the Iroquois threat probably accounted in part for the enthusiastic welcome extended to Jolliet and Marquette. The presence of the black robes and their
reputed "strong medicine" was obviously desired, but the Illinois also
coveted the firearms that fur trading would make accessible.

The first village the French visited was inhabited by the Peoria branch
of the Illinois. There, Jolliet and Marquette counted about 300 cabins
sheltering a population of a thousand persons. Multiplying by three—the
three villages—and using the observations of the two travelers, even the
most generous estimate points to a sparsely inhabited Illinois, a land as
empty of people as it was rich in game, which of course, meant furs and
pelts, destined to remain North America's most important commodity for
the next one hundred years.

After having spent the night in the cabin of the Great Sachem—the title
borne by the chief of the Illinois confederation, an expression common to
the Algonquin-speaking people—the next afternoon, Jolliet and Marquette were escorted to their canoes by "nearly six hundred persons." [17]
Promising to return, they resumed their voyage downriver. After a few
days of hugging the western side of the Mississippi, they reached the
portion of the river lying between the mouths of the Missouri and the
Illinois, and came within view of two large colored paintings, red, green,

and black, high on the rocks of the opposite cliff (near the present city of Alton, Illinois). These petroglyphs were the *Piasa* monsters, *Piasa* (or *Piesa*) an Illinois word meaning man-devouring bird, "a fabulous animal of the Indian mythology which is supposed to be the Thunderbird," the guardian of the passage to the south.[18] Jolliet and Marquette were sufficiently impressed that they stopped to make a sketch of the drawings. So absorbed were they in their task that, oblivious to the turbulent waters of the Mississippi, they almost capsized. The sketch unfortunately has never been found.

After another month of traveling, on July 15, they reached the village of Akamsea on the eastern bank of the Mississippi, thirty-five degrees latitude south, and there among the villagers found a young man who understood the Illinois language. Through him, the Arkansas chiefs told the French not to pursue any farther south because of the hostile Indians they were bound to encounter. Jolliet and Marquette decided to heed their advice:

> We were not far from the Gulf of Mexico, the basin of which is at the latitude of thirty-one degrees forty minutes; we judged that we could not be more than two or three days journey from it. . . . We further considered that we exposed ourselves to fall into the hands of the Spaniards who, without doubt, would at least detain us as captives. . . . All these reasons induced us to decide upon returning.[19]

On July 17, they turned their canoes around, this time facing the powerful Mississippi prow first. Although they had not descended its entire course, Jolliet and Marquette were now satisfied that the river disgorged its waters into the Gulf of Mexico and was not at all the hypothetical passage to the China seas. After fighting the fast current for a month, and following the eastern bank for fear of missing the entrance to the Illinois River, they finally entered the latter's calmer waters during the first days of August. Originally, they had planned to retrace their route up the Wisconsin River. We can only assume that Jolliet and Marquette knew that by the time they arrived back north, the Illinois (Kaskaskia and Peoria) would have left their refuge near the Mississippi and returned to their usual locations along the river bearing their name. Since Marquette had promised to instruct them in the Christian religion, it was a propitious time to begin. For Jolliet, this change of route would have been an additional opportunity to learn more about the Illinois country and its

people. Later, in a letter to Father Dablon, he wrote lyrically about the
area. In fact, his is the first recorded description of central Illinois:

> The river which we have christened St. Louis rises near the lower end of the
> Lake of the Illinois [Lake Michigan], and seemed to me the most beautiful
> and most suitable for settlement. At the place where we entered the lake
> is a harbor, very convenient for receiving vessels and sheltering them from
> the wind. The river is wide and deep, abounding in catfish and sturgeon.
> For a distance of eighty leagues, not a quarter of an hour passsed without
> seeing game which is abundant in those parts; cows [*buffaloes*], stags, does
> and turkeys are found there in much greater number than elsewhere.
> There are prairies three, six, ten and twenty leagues long and three wide,
> surrounded by forests of the same extend. Beyond these, the prairie begins
> again so that there is as much of one sort of land as of the other. Some of
> the grass is very short, but some grows as high as five or six feet; hemp
> grows wild here and reaches a height of eight feet. A settler would not have
> to spend ten years in cutting and burning trees; on the very day of his
> arrival he could put his plow into the ground.[20]

And, as Father Dablon would subsequently record for the *Jesuit Relation* of 1674, "Our *voyageurs* counted more than forty villages, the majority of which consisting of sixty to eighty cabins, some of three hundred. . . ."[21]

The village of three hundred cabins mentioned above was the village of the Peoria. There, and in all the communities along the Illinois River, Marquette exercised his ministry. He founded the first Catholic parish, the *Mission de l'Immaculée Conception*, in the largest Illinois agglomeration, called by the French both the "Great Illinois Town" and the "Great Illinois Village," and which will be referred to hereafter as "Illinois Town." The home of the Illinois confederation, it was originally located just west of the present-day small town of Twin Bluffs, and later moved east of where Utica stands today. The population of Illinois Town was estimated by Jolliet and Marquette to be about 8,000, large for an Indian settlement.[22] Before leaving Father Marquette promised to return soon.

The French were escorted from Illinois Town all the way to the Chicago portage by one of the Kaskaskia chiefs along with dozens of young warriors. The existence of the portage was probably known to Jolliet and Marquette. There are some indications that another well-known trader, Nicholas Perrot, had reached the Chicago landing the preceding year; its location had become the semipermanent settlement of a small band of

Miamis and was a natural trading point.

Jolliet made a careful notation of the physiography of the area, which leads us to believe that he and his companions spent several days there. The Chicago portage had two variations: the first took the travellers to the Des Plaines River and the second, which they probably used, connected directly to Lake Michigan. It was the second that fascinated Jolliet. He seemed to have been the first to recognize the potential implications of a direct maritime link between the Gulf of Saint Lawrence and the Gulf of Mexico. The distance between the Chicago and the Des Plaines Rivers was short and France had the technology to build canals (it was precisely during the reign of Louis XIV that the *Canal du midi* linking the Atlantic Ocean to the Mediterranean Sea was dug). Jolliet communicated all these observations to Father Dablon who, naturally, integrated them into his next *Relation*:

> The fourth remark which concerns an advantage, very considerable and which will hardly be believed by one, is that we should be able quite easily to go as far as Florida in a bark and by very pleasant navigation. There would have to be made but one canal intersecting only half a league of prairie in order to enter from the foot of the lake of the Illinois into the river of St. Louis which discharges into the Mississippi; being there the bark would navigate easily as far as the Gulf of Mexico.[23]

Jolliet, Marquette, and their party left Chicago by canoe at the end of August 1673, following the western shore of Lake Michigan. They reached the Mission Saint Francis Xavier—their departure point—during mid-October. While Marquette remained in the relative comfort of the mission, Jolliet continued to Sault Sainte-Marie where he spent the winter months. During Spring of 1674, he made a brief stop at Saint Francis Xavier from where he continued with two men and the young Indian boy given to him. Jolliet stopped at Fort Frontenac, just completed by La Salle during the preceding summer. Circumstantial evidence provided by the comparison of dates and routings suggests that Jolliet met with La Salle at the Fort. If they did meet, La Salle, no doubt, received precious intelligence from Jolliet.

On Saturday July 21, near Montreal, Jolliet chose to risk shooting the last rapids before the city, the Rapids of La Chine (near La Salle's first property in Canada), usually avoided by the *voyageurs* using a portage nearby. His canoe overturned causing the death of his crew—including

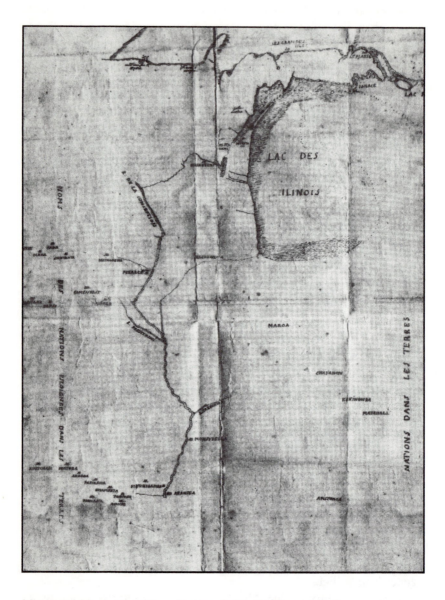

Marquette Manuscript Map showing Lake Michigan and the
Mississippi River (Rivière Colbert).   (Service Historique de la
Marine, Vincennes, France)

the Indian boy—the loss of his equipment, mementos and documents. It was thus only from memory, but with the details of his explorations still fresh in his mind, that he wrote an account of the expedition for Governor Frontenac.[24] Also from memory, Jolliet drew a map that he entitled *Nouvelle Découverte de plusieurs Nations dans la Nouvelle-France en l'année 1673 et 1674*. In keeping with the practice of the time, Jolliet renamed all rivers and lands; the Mississippi became *Riviere Buade* to honor Governor Frontenac whose family name was Buade, and the region between the river and Lake Michigan, *La Frontenacie*. A few days later, Jolliet met with Father Dablon and dictated to him the account that constituted the essential part of the *Jesuit Relation* of August 1, 1674.

Also in 1674, Father Marquette travelled back to Illinois (with the authorization of his new superior, Father Nouvel). It took him forty days to reach the south branch of the Chicago River; he had with him two veterans of the previous trip, Pierre Porteret and Jacques Largillier. They had left the Mission Saint Ignace during the last days of October, late in the year for a long canoe trip on the waters of Lake Michigan, which can get very rough in the fall. Fortunately, they travelled in the company of fifty Illinois and Potawatomi Indians manning a flotilla of nine canoes. Together, they used the portage between Sturgeon Bay and Lake Michigan (Door County, Wisconsin). The weather was poor. Stormy conditions on the lake during most of November often limited their daily progress to no more than five miles. On December 4, they reached the mouth of the Chicago River. Marquette had maintained a positive outlook all along as shown in his journal:

> We started to reach Portage River [Chicago River] which was frozen half a foot thick. There was more snow there than anywhere else, and also more tracks of animals and turkeys. The navigation of the Lake from one portage to the other is quite fine, there being no traverse to make and landing being quite feasible all along providing you do not obstinately persist in travelling in the breakers and high winds. The land along the shore is good for nothing except on the prairies. You meet eight or ten pretty fine rivers.[25]

After several days of waiting at the Chicago portage for an improvement in the weather, it became obvious that Father Marquette's failing health would prevent them from traveling the remaining sixty miles to Illinois Town (Utica). On December 14th they moved to a spot between the Chicago and Des Plaines rivers, four miles inland from the lake and decided ". . . To winter here, as it is impossible to go further since we are too much hindered and my ailment did not permit me to give myself much fatigue."[26]

The Illinois party stayed with them until the following day and then moved on. Before departing they did a little sharp trading, leaving the French with three buffalo robes in exchange for a large quantity of tobacco.[27]

That winter was particularly hard; Father Marquette was in such poor health that he often could not even attend to his religious duties. Because they relied only on the supplies they had brought along, Marquette's two assistants remained close to the hut they had built for shelter. However, during one of his short hunting trips around the camp, Largillier learned about another Frenchman wintering in the area. A message was relayed to him and soon Pierre Moreau, known as "Le Mole," accompanied by his partner, remembered only by his nickname of "Le Barbier," appeared at the hut. They had traveled fifty miles to bring some blueberries and corn to Marquette.[28] Besides the obvious respect that Father Marquette commanded among the traders, this anecdote also suggests that French trade was beginning to expand throughout Illinois, an area which had only been travelled by Jolliet and Marquette barely a year before. We know of Moreau and "Le Barbier" being in Illinois only through fortuitous circumstances, but there probably were a few more traders who did not leave behind any signs of their presence; the first wave of French penetration in the future American Midwest, men who did not bother to obtain permission from Quebec before venturing into the woods and who left no trace in archives, no memoirs for posterity.

Towards the end of winter some Illinois appeared at the camp to trade, and soon after, on March 31, 1675, Marquette and his two companions resumed their trip first down the Des Plaines River, and then down the Illinois. On April 10, they arrived at the Illinois Town where the *robe noire* (the black robe of the Jesuits) was welcomed "as angel from heaven." [29]

Marquette counted 500 to 600 families living in the town, including about 1,500 men, whom he began to evangelize immediately. On April 14, he celebrated Easter Mass with all the solemnity he could muster. But soon after, Marquette again fell ill and felt that he had to return home to his mission in the North. Once again, a large group of Illinois warriors escorted the Frenchmen part of the way. Marquette this time took another route north using the portage "between the Kankakee and the St. Joseph rivers, a carrying place of between four and five miles,"[30] near What is now South Bend, Indiana. This same portage would be used extensively Seven years later by La Salle and his men.

Father Marquette's health was deteriorating rapidly. By mid-May, he was unable to go much further, and on May 18, 1675, he died on the shore of Lake Michigan near the point where the town of Ludington, Michigan now stands. He was thirty-eight years old.[31]

The death of Father Marquette did not stop the missionary work begun by the Jesuits in Illinois. The Jesuits, like soldiers, replaced fallen comrades, and Father Claude Allouez was ordered to replace Marquette and embarked ". . . about the close of October, 1676, in a canoe with two men to endeavor to go and winter with the Illinois"[32] Again, the winter of 1676 was difficult. It was months before Father Allouez and his men were able to navigate on Lake Michigan (which Father Allouez promptly renamed Lake St. Joseph in honor of the patron Saint of Canada). On March 23, Father Allouez wrote that they: ". . . had much to do with ice, through which we had to break a passage. The water was so cold that it froze on our oars, and on the side of the canoe which the sun did not reach."[33]

On a parallel course, Jolliet's impetus would also be followed by other traders. We have seen how some Frenchmen had already preceded Father Marquette's second return to Illinois. Jolliet also was eager to return but, unfortunately, the fact that he was a protégé of the Jesuits played against his commercial ambitions. Two years after his return to Montreal, he applied to Colbert through *intendant* Jacques Duchesneau's office for authorization to found a settlement in Illinois with twenty men. The exact date of Louis Jolliet's letter of application (by then married, father of a son, and a merchant in Quebec), is not known, but we have the answer from Colbert to Duchesneau, dated August 26, 1677. "His Majesty is unwilling to grant the leave asked by *Sieur* Jolliet to go to the Illinois country with twenty men to begin a settlement there. The number of settlers in Canada should *be* increased before thinking of settlements elsewhere. This should be your guiding principle regarding newly made discoveries."[34] One year later, Governor Frontenac granted La Salle what had been refused Jolliet.

Frontenac's flamboyant personality was the perfect choice to advance the king's glory, but, on the other hand, he was unable to resolve the conflicts between royal power and Jesuit power, the latter more often political than spiritual. Frontenac reacted tempestuously to any action that he perceived to be an encroachment of the prerogatives of the Crown, but his perceptions were often exaggerated. Nevertheless, it was clear that more

Portrait of La Salle. From *Narrative and Critical History of America*, Vol. 4, Justin Winsor, ed., 1884. (The Newberry Library)

than ever the Society of Jesus opposed any extension of contact between the French and Indians. The Jesuits were concerned about losing the control they exercised in their far-flung missions. They had hoped to see these western outposts of Christianity become the foundation of a Christianized Indian society free from the corrupting influence of French soldiers and traders, but now, once again, the prospect was disappearing.

Back in France, Colbert, still troubled by a territorial expansion that was too rapid considering the small French population in Canada (in 1664, the French population of Canada numbered only 6,705), was firmly opposed to the propagation of Jesuit missions to the West.

In spite of Colbert's reservations and, of course, Jesuit opposition, Governor Frontenac remained committed to conquest. To avoid accusations of insubordination, he used Colbert's directives to justify the acquisition of new territories when they could be used to develop trade, or when these territories might be in danger of falling into the hands of other nations. To carry out his policies, Frontenac needed a reliable person: he found such a man in the the the young, ambitious, Robert Cavelier de la Salle.

Born in Rouen, Normandy, in 1643, into a wealthy merchant family, La Salle had entered the Jesuit seminary in 1658. In 1660, he took minor religious vows and entered the Royal College of La Fleche where he took classes in mathematics and physics, and later taught. Unhappy over religious discipline, he asked permission to leave the Order, which was granted on January 28, 1667. La Salle's experience at the College of La Fleche had left him bitter and suspicious towards the Society of Jesus. Ironically, his very career in New France was to give him many occasions to rekindle these feelings.[35]

La Salle was twenty-three years old when he arrived in Canada where his older brother, Jean Cavelier, was a Sulpician monk. He first tried farming a piece of land given to him by the Sulpicians and located just outside Montreal. He named this property *La Chine*, underscoring his early hopes of discovering the mysterious passage said to connect North America to the Orient, a passage that many still believed to originate south of the Great Lakes. Three years later, La Salle, unsuccessful at farming, left on his first exploration in the company of two Sulpician missionaries also attempting to discover the passage. This first journey was not a great success, but it did whet La Salle's appetite for more traveling, an endeavor he pursued all the while acquiring an understanding of the Iroquois culture and a command of the Iroquois language. His skills and knowledge led to a rapid change of fortune. In 1673, when Governor Frontenac went to the north of Lake Ontario to meet with the Iroquois chiefs, La Salle suddenly found himself indispensable as an interpreter and advisor. It was during this trip that he convinced the governor of the necessity of building a permanent settlement at the very place of their meeting with the chiefs. This location, called by the Indians "Catarakoui," became the site of a new fort built without the King's approval, Fort Frontenac (presently, Kingston, Ontario). A year later, when the King and Colbert learned that they had unwittingly acquired a new fort, Governor Frontenac dispatched La Salle to the Court to defend the enterprise. Carrying with him a letter of introduction from the governor, he was well received and made such an excellent impression that a year later he returned from France with both the patent for the *"seignory* of Fort Frontenac" and fresh capital easily raised among relatives and friends. There is some indication that Governor Frontenac became La Salle's silent partner with the launching of the first enterprise. While Frontenac gave La Salle the full backing of his authority, La Salle brought to the endeavor capital, expertise, and the actual direction of the operations, a formula to be followed as long as Frontenac remained governor.

Frontenac and La Salle had in mind better and bigger things than Fort Frontenac—which, incidentally, was strategically important for New France in the face of the permanent threat of the British and their Iroquois allies, but before larger projects could be planned, more financing was necessary. La Salle, who would later prove himself inept at keeping accounts and calculating budgets, had to return once again to France. He left Quebec in November 1677, and by the following spring, had not only managed to obtain new subsidies but also gained the full support of the crown as well. On May 12, 1678, La Salle received from the king *Lettres patentes* which authorized him: "To work at discovering the western parts of our country of New France and, in order to implement this enterprise, to build forts in locations where you deem them necessary; we want that you enjoy in these forts the same rights and conditions in existence at Fort Frontenac. . . . "[36]

The era of exploration was now over. French expansion in North America was ready to start in earnest.

NOTES

1. *Récit Des Voyages et Des Découvertes Du P. Jacques Marquette De la Compagnie de Jésus en l'annee 1673 et aux suivantes*, Archives du Collège de Sainte-Marie, Montreal, MS, translated by Francis Borgia-Steck in *The Jolliet-Marquette Expedition, 1675*, p. 155.

2. Louise Phelps Kellog, *Early Narratives of the Northwest, 1634-1699*, p. 223.

3. For a detailed history of Louis Jolliet, see Jean Delanglez, *Life and Voyages of Louis Jolliet (1645-1700)*, Institute of Jesuit History, Chicago, 1948; it is worth noting that in Quebec, in 1635, the Jesuits had established a college to educate the colonists of New France, spending 64,000 livres, quite a large sum for the time. As William J. Eccles has remarked: "Classes began that year, a year before Harvard was established;" see *France in America*, Harper and Row, New York, 1972, p. 41.

4. *Intendant* Talon had advanced 1400 livres to Adrien Jolliet—Louis' older brother—for the cost of an exploration in the Great Lakes region with the goal of discovering copper mines. Adrien and his partner came back with nothing but vague information.

5. This long document was drawn the day before the departure of Louis Jolliet and his partners; Louis Jolliet bound himself to provide trade goods as well as supplies. He was to receive in addition to his share—one-seventh—a share which corresponded to his expenses. See *Archives Judiciaires de Québec*(AJQ), *Greffe Rageot*, No. 939; the translation into English used here is from Joseph P. Donnelly, *Jacques Marquette*, Loyola University Press, Chicago, 1968, p. 202.

6. See William D. LeSueur, *Count Frontenac*, Toronto, 1906.

7. Frontenac to Colbert, Letters in Pierre Margry, *Découvertes et établissements des Français dans l'ouest et dans le sud de l'Amérique septentrionale, 1614 à 1754, mémoires et documents originaux*, Paris 1876-1886, 6 vols., Vol 1, p. 255.

8. The Jesuits had sent Father Marquette to Sainte Marie du Sault in 1668 where the French fur traders, no more than twenty, had subsequently opened a trading post.

9. On Jacques Marquette see the book by Father Joseph P. Donnelly, *Jacques Marquette*, the most complete work in English to date.

10. Borgia-Steck, *The Jolliet-Marquette Expeditions*, p. 52. In addition to the Jesuits, the Order of Saint-Sulpice was also represented in the colony in small number.

11. In 1608, King Philip II entrusted to the Jesuits the conversion of the Indians of Paraguay. There, they built establishments they called *réductions*, large missions which ruled directly over Christian Indians. The Jesuits were finally expelled from Paraguay in 1767.

12. Francis Borgia-Steck, p. 68; much research has been done on the question of Jesuit influence in the French North America. Memoranda written to Minister Colbert by *intendant* Talon and Governor Frontenac as well as the memoirs and instructions sent back by Colbert to them and other royal administrators leave little doubt about the dimensions of the problems caused by Jesuit influence and activities. On this subject see particularly the *Extrait d'une lettre du Comte de Frontenac à Colbert, 2 Novembre, 1672*, quoted in Margry, vol. 1, pp. 247-50, and *Frontenac à Colbert, 14 novembre, 1674; Colbert à Frontenac, mai 1, 1674*. For further reading, see Borgia-Steck, *The Jolliet.*, Chapter 1, "New France in the Middle Seventeenth Century," pp. 48-10; see also Camille de Rochemonteix, *Les Jesuites et la Nouvelle-France au XVIIeme siecle*, Paris, 1896.

13. *Jesuit Relations and Allied Documents*, Vol. 55, p. 207; Thwaites translated from French into English all the *Relations* concerning a period from 1610 to 1780, a total of seventy-three volumes.

14. *Jacques Marquette.*, pp. 209-11; the Menominee Indians received the nickname of *folle avoine*, or "wild oats," because of the swamp grass common in the area of their major settlement. The Mascoutens' name means the "fire nation" in their own idiom which is a part of the Algonquin family of languages.

15. During spring of 1666, Father Claude Allouez "had occasion to question Potawatomi, Foxes and Illinois" at Chequamon Bay; the Illinois travelled north regularly to trade nearby the Mission Saint Ignace. *Puants* or "stinking," was a name given by the French to a group of Indians because the Algonquin word *ouinipeg* means "smelly water," which is what the sea was for them, or *"puant"* in a literal French translation. See Margry, vol. 1, p. 48, FN 1, quoting *Relation de la Nouvelle France*, 1646, Chapter X. On the Illinois, see Hiram W. Beckwith, *The Illinois and Indiana Indians*, Chicago, 1844; all Illinois belonged to the same Algonquin-Lenape linguistic family, which did necessarily mean close kinship ties. The Illinois Metchigamies were originally a foreign clan from the western side of the Mississippi who had been adopted by the Illinois Confederation.

16. *Récit*, MS, pp. 18-19, trans. in Borgia-Steck, p. 156; L.G. Weld, in his book

Jolliet and Marquette in Iowa, Iowa City, 1903, claimed that the three Illinois villages were located along the Iowa River.

17. *Récit de voyages,* MS, translation in Borgia-Steck, p. 157

18. Thwaites, *Jesuit Relations and Allied Documents,* pp. 139-142; until 1847, some traces were still visible: see Garrick Malley, *Picture Writing of the American Indians,* in the *Annual Report of the Bureau of Ethnology,* Washington, 1888-89, also quoted by Borgia-Steck, FN 5-6, p. 158 and by John G. Shea in *Discovery and Exploration of the Mississippi Valley,* New York, 1852, p. 30; by Clara K. Bayliss in "The significance of the Piasa." *Transactions of the Illinois Historical Society for 1908,* pp. 114-23.

19. *Récit.,* pp. 33-36, translation in Borgia-Steck, p. 163.

20. *Relation,* M.S., *collection Renaudot,* Vol. 30, trans. Borgia-Steck, p. 184.

21. *Relation,* sent by Father Dablon on August 1, 1674, translation in Borgia-Steck, p. 175.

22. On the location of the Great Illinois Town, see Marion A. Habig, "The Site of the Great Illinois Village," *Mid-America, An Historical Review,* Vol XVI, July 1933, Number 1, 3-13.   This article refers to several previous studies by Thwaites, Parkman, Margry, the most important for the subject being the article written by Gilbert J. Garraghan, "The Great Illinois Village: a Topographical Problem," *Mid-America, Vol XIV, New Series III,* 141-151, October, 1931, also reprinted as a pamphlet.

23. Borgia-Steck, p. 178-9 and Delanglez, p. 217 quote this *Relation.* A complete study of the location of the Chicago portage has been made by Robert Knight and Lucius H. Zeuch: *The location of the Chicago Portage Route of the Seventeenth Century,* Chicago, 1928.

24. "Le Sieur Jolliet . . . est de retour depuis trois mois, et a decouvert des pays admirables et une navigation aisee par de belles rivieres...Je vous envoye par mon secretaire la carte qu'il en a faite et les remarques dont il s'est souvenu, ayant perdu tous ses memoires et ses journeaux dans le naufrage qu'il fit a la veue de Montreal. . . . Il avait laisse dans le lac Superieur, au Sault de Sainte-Marie, chez les Peres, des copies de ses journeaux que nous ne scaurions avoir que l'annee prochaine . . ." *Détails sur le voyage de Sieur Jolliet,* sent to Colbert by Governor Frontenac to Colbert, November 11, 1674, in Margry, Vol. 1., pp. 257-262; see also *Relation de la découverte de plusieurs pays situés au midi de la Nouvelle-France, faîte en 1673* pp. 262-270.   The official report on the exploration of the Mississippi was twofold: one part embodied in a letter sent to Frontenac by Louis Jolliet, and the other part consisted of the account given by Father Marquette to his ecclesiastic superior, Father Claude F. Dablon, in Quebec. Dablon transmitted this account in 1678 to the Jesuits in Paris. This account was co-annotated and co-translated by Benjamin French and John Gilmary Shea, then published by Shea in 1852, in *Discoveries and Explorations of the Mississippi,* Part IV, French Historical Collection. As previously mentioned, the Jesuits published the *Relations* to obtain public support for their missionary work. These *Relations* were widely read, and even translated into English. The original printing of the account of the Jolliet and Marquette travels in Illinois is found in the *Relation de ce qui s'est passé dans les Missions Des Pères de la Compagnie de Jésus en la Nouvelle France l'année 1673 Envoyée par le Réverend Père Jean Pinette, Provincial de la même Comp. en la Province de France.*

One copy can be seen in the Jesuit Archives of the Province of France, *Fonds Brotier*, 155, Canada 1, 1-5; this copy was published by Father Jean Delanglez in "The 1674 Account of the Discovery of the Mississippi," *Mid-America* 26, 1944, pp. 324-27. However, it must also be noted that the details of the exploration were also published in 1681, in Paris, by Estienne Michallet in a pamphlet entitled: *Recueil de voyages de Mr. Thevenot, Découverte de quelques pays et nations de l'Amérique septentrionale*. This pamphlet of forty-three pages was based on the 1673 Dablon manuscript. We must also mention that several translations of this account were published at the turn of the century, adding to the confused body of secondary sources on secondary sources; in H.W. Beckwith, ed., *Collections of the Illinois State Historical Library*, Springfield, 1903, vol. 1, Chapter 1, pp. 8-40. This publication referred to an abridged translation included by Jared Sparks in *Life of Father Marquette*, 1844, and to a full *Collections of Louisiana*, part II, Philadelphia, 1850. The most definitive translation from the French original was published in Thwaites, *Jesuit Relations* l, LIX, pp. 87-163, 1899. Finally, we should mention that "The autograph manuscripts of his (Marquette) account of his two voyages were kept for a century and a half with the Jesuit convent (sic) at Montreal." Louise Phelps Kellog, ed., *Early Narratives*.

25. *Relations*, translation in Donnelly, p. 173.

26. Ibid.; the winter camp of Father Marquette was probably located where now Damen Avenue crosses the Sanitary and Ship Canal in Chicago.

27. *Relation*, translation in Donnelley, p. 175 and p. 245.

28. *Relation*, LIX, Trans. in Donnelley, p. 175.

29. Ibid., p. 161

30. Ibid.,

31. The exact location of the death site of Father Marquette has been recently determined as the south bank of the north channel connecting Pere Marquette Lake with Lake Michigan, in Ludington. See David D. Nixon, "New Findings about the Marquette Death Site," paper read at the 1982 meeting of the French Colonial Historical Society, at Northwestern University, Evanston, Illinois. One of Marquette's two companions, Jacques Largillier, forty-one years old when Marquette died, became a Jesuit lay brother and returned to Illinois where he died at age eighty, on November 14, 1714.

32. *Relation du Rv. P. Claude Allouez de son voyage aux Illinois*, trans. in Shea, *Discovery and Explorations*, p. 70.

33. Ibid., p. 71

34. *Colbert à Duscheneau, intendant du Canada*, April 28, 1677, AC, B 71: 76; also in *Lettres de Colbert*, Vol. lll, p. 618; translation in Delanglez, *Life and voyages of Louis Jolliet*.

35. Robert Cavelier, son of Jean Cavelier and Catherine Gest, was baptized in the Church of St. Herbland, on November 26, 1643. La Salle's associations with the Society of Jesus are found in the archives of the Order. For example on his separation: "Exivit Mag, Robertus Ignatius Cavelier e Collegio Flexiensi de 28 Mardii 1667," quoted in Rochemonteix, vol. 3, p. 48. The first document to show his presence in New France is his signature as a witness to the marriage of Sidrac Dugue de Bois Briant, in November 1667, where he signed as "R. de la Salle."

36. Ibid.

3

La Salle's Illinois, 1670 - 1683

T he boldness of La Salle's character has been described so extensively (and appropriately) in other works that no more than a mention is required here. La Salle exhibited a strength in many ways comparable to that of the Conquistadors, the single force responsible for Spain's domain encircling the globe. The circumstances of North America in the seventeenth century were different, however, from those of Mexico or Peru at the time of the Spaniards' arrival. Cortès and Pizzaro conquered with naked steel; La Salle, for the most part, extended French power without unsheathing his sword.

From its first days, the expansion of the French establishment in North America demanded strong financial backing. This backing could only come from private sources since the king's purse was already considerably taxed by its subsidy of emigration to Canada and the costliness of its defense. But, these investors had to have had some hope for a return on their investment before they consented to risk it on an American adventure which could not inflame the imagination as could gold or silver, no matter how attractive the fur trade sounded.

In these circumstances, La Salle's ability to raise considerable funds during each of his trips to France speaks well of his talent for communication even though most of the backing received in 1678 came from relatives. They must have had at least as much faith in the business potential of New France as in family ties. The opportunity to ride the crest of success was tempting though the risks were high. Potential investors had to take into account the fact that the cost of skills and supplies in New France ran twice as high as in metropolitan France. Distances, hardships, limited manpower, the high prices of goods such as nails, cloth, powder and brandy, considerably raised the outlay of necessary capital. A good illustration of this economic conjuncture is presented by the records of the expenditures incurred by La Salle during the 1677 reconstruction in stone of Fort Frontenac (now Kingston, Ontario). It shows that a carpenter was paid 300 livres annually and a smith 310, salaries equal to the pay of the surgeon assigned to the garrison. Masons commanded 480 livres a year, which compared handsomely with the 600 livres paid to the lieutenant in charge of the military detachment. Obviously, in New France even more than in France, income and social status were not necessarily linked. All in all, before any profit, the rebuilding of Fort Frontenac cost La Salle the respectable amount of 37,340 livres, an indication of what sort of expenses he could expect for his next venture.[1]

The scarcity of currency, a continuing problem in French North America, added to the cost of commercial transactions. Suppliers from France were nervous: "Coin would not remain in the colony . . . it went back on the returning ships . . . " and to remedy this situation the *intendant* adopted the drastic measure of coining a Canadian livre "one-fourth less in value than that of France."[2] Yet, even this measure was not enough to stop the flight of currency. Devalued Canadian livres had such an "urge" to find their way to the coffers of the French port of La Rochelle and beyond, that the authorities of the colony were obliged to make legal tender out of such unorthodox forms of money as moose skins (in 1674) or wheat (in 1699). They also used beaver skins or—the most original— playing cards cut in four, each quarter duly signed by the governor, the *intendant* and the clerk of the treasury. Worthless except in Canada, this last system was begun in 1685 as a way of paying the soldiers. It reached such proportions that when converted into bills of exchange for the first time in 1774, the quartered cards totaled a phenomenal two million livres.[3]

La Salle, never attentive enough in accounting matters and always impatient with those who questioned the ultimate economic value of North American exploration, fared badly in this uncertain financial climate. The money he had raised at a high price (forty percent interest on one loan, all his properties as collateral on another) was primarily used to pay for exhorbitant recruiting costs.[4]

He had addressed the problem of recruiting an adequate number of skilled workers with his usual haste, leaving himself little bargaining room, but it was to his credit that in planning for the penetration of North America he consistently showed more interest in mustering skilled workers than swashbucklers. Though not a timid soldier himself, he had concluded early in his travels that Europeans obtained more from Indian nations through negotiation than through the artifice of war. Recruiting qualified hands was difficult and demanded time, because French people of the 1600s cared little for emigration, even to overseas lands belonging to the king. Conditions, as difficult as they were for France of the pre-Revolution days, were never as bad as in England where the enclosure

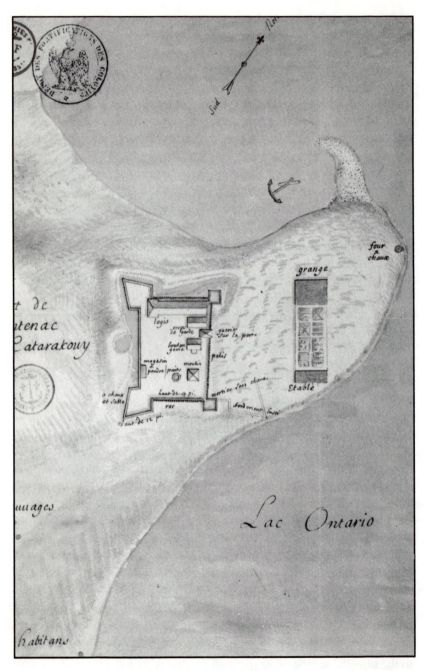

Map of Fort Frontenac in 1685. (Archives Nationales, Paris)

movement and uncertain climate led many peasants to welcome the opportunity to escape their living conditions even at the price of indenture. In fact, with the exception of a few thousand destitutes sheltered in the poor-houses of Paris and the provincial cities, both rural and urban populations had a relatively good standard of living. An important factor in the economic boom of the period was the expected construction of the palace of Versailles. It would start in earnest in 1679 with an annual budget of 500,000 livres. It attracted craftsmen from all over France and beyond, thus making skilled workers less available and more expensive for the rest of the nation.[5] Thanks to Colbert's policy, shipyards and arsenals were active again, and harbors and fortifications were also being expanded. This conjuncture of prosperous conditions made it more difficult for La Salle to recruit able men. Not one of the least difficulties was to guarantee safe and comfortable working conditions to artisans without a taste for adventure. A vivid illustration of this situation was an instance where in order to secure the services of a ship's carpenter by the name of Roussel, "dit La Rousseliere," La Salle was obliged to pay off all the man's creditors first, a total of 1,800 livres.[6] La Salle was more fortunate in recruiting assistants and two joined him in La Rochelle. These were both professional soldiers in search of employment: La Motte de Lussière and the man who would become his most loyal officer, Italian born Henry de Tonty.

On July 12, 1678, after some final difficulties necessitating costly bribes to soothe the port authorities, La Salle and his men sailed from La Rochelle. Their ship reached Quebec on September 15th, and from there, almost immediately, everyone moved on to Fort Frontenac.

The winter months of idleness at Fort Frontenac helped the civilian members of the expedition to adapt to the new, harsh environment. While not Quebec, Fort Frontenac was rather comfortable; between the garrison, the few settlers and the Indian families, it offered a warm, lively atmosphere. Meanwhile, La Salle was busy securing additional loans, never quite able to find enough money to pay off old debts while he was incurring new, larger ones. To secure these Canadian loans, he used properties and anticipated profits for collateral that he had already pledged for the funds he received in France. With every passing day, the increasing weakness of his financial structure threatened to end the expedition before it started. Finally, though, La Salle made his first move during spring 1679, sending a party of sixteen men to the *Sault de Conty* (Niagara Falls) under the command of La Motte. This party included

Veue du Saut de Niagara.

Niagara Falls in 1715. Detail from the *Cartes Marines*.
(The Newberry Library)

several carpenters and a Recollect priest, Father Louis Hennepin, whose writings would later became a great source of information as well as of controversy. From then on, Recollect priests would always be part of La Salle's journeys.[7]

The Falls were then within the land belonging to an off-shoot of the Iroquois Indians, the Sonnontoutan, or Seneca band. The Seneca, like all other Iroquois, were allies and trading partners of the Dutch and the English. They looked at French western expansion as a threat to their access to the fur-producing regions and to their communication with the markets of Albany. The Seneca, however, were not at the time involved in active warfare against the French, and La Motte and Hennepin, once at the Falls, resolved to travel overland an additional five days to meet with their Great Council, and negotiate the right to construct a fort and a shipyard. Although the move was wise, and the presents they brought were appreciated, nothing was concluded. But, La Salle, who had been alerted to the difficulties, arrived directly from Fort Frontenac and reopened the negotiations as La Motte and Hennepin were on their way back to the falls. La Salle, a master of Indian psychology, was at his best in this sort of situation. The parley was moderately successful; the Iroquois maintained their opposition to a full-fledged fort, but finally accepted the erection of a fortified house with a simple stockade around the grounds.

What concerned La Salle was not so much the Seneca's grudging cooperation but the presence among them of two Jesuit missionaries. Always suspecting the worst, La Salle insisted that they both attend his parleys "In order to remove from them the means to destroy all what I would have accomplished."[8] The Seneca were fearful that the large quantities of arms and ammunition that the French carried were intended to supply their enemies, the Illinois. However, with the Jesuit missionaries "silenced", La Salle felt free to move up to the Falls to join the expedition. He immediately assembled an advance party with the land of the Illinois as the final destination. Incredibly, this party made up of a few *voyageurs* and artisans from France was sent to set up winter quarters for the entire expedition with no officer in charge. We can only conclude that an easy navigation was expected for them, that the route was known, and the Indians friendly.

While this advance party was paddling west, others were building what would become the first vessel to navigate the western lakes (the Great Lakes): the *Griffon*, of forty-five tons burden, completed in the record time of a month-and-a-half under the personal care of Tonty.

News of La Salle's enterprise had reached the British who kept a wary eye on its development. They had been informed of La Salle's efforts by a letter from the governor of New York which stated:

An Indian Sachem reports that ye French of Canada intend this year to send a Garrison or setlem into one of their towns where these Xtian captives were at this ye lake wer being of import ile endeavor to present but if effected will not only endanger all ye indian trade, but expose all ye king's plantations upon this contingent where they please they pretending no bounds that way. [9]

Meanwhile, La Salle, exhausted, fell ill and had to return temporarily to Fort Frontenac. As if the problems of the hour were not already awesome, news came to him at Fort Frontenac of the wreck on the Canadian coast of a ship from France with the total loss of its cargo. She had carried

Top: An 1891 photograph of the probable location of the *Griffon*
shipyard: the Angevine Farm, on the east bank of the Little
Niagara, opposite Cayuga Island. Note the remarkable similarity
between the channel as it appears above, and in the Lower image
depicting the *Griffon's* construction. The engraving is from
Hennepin's *Nouvelle Decouverte* of 1704. The photograph is from
Kingsbury Remington's book, *The Shipyard of the Griffon*, Buffalo,
1891. (The Newberry Library)

25,000 livres worth of La Salle's additional supplies. As Father Hennepin appropriately wrote, this was news that "would have made anybody but him give up the enterprise." [10]

There were rumors in Montreal and Quebec about La Salle's difficulties at the Falls. The rumors created a climate of apprehension among his Canadian creditors who moved quickly to seize his properties. Time was now running out on the whole project. On August 7, resolutely turning his back to adversity, La Salle embarked on the *Griffon* with all of his men plus three Recollect fathers, and sailed west. [11]

On the 27th of August, the *Griffon* arrived at Michilimackinac, France's strongest and most western Canadian outpost. Here were the buildings of the Jesuit Mission, plus a sizable number of cabins belonging to French traders and their Indian wives, as well as both the Huron and Ottawa villages. Bad news awaited La Salle's arrival: more than half of his advance party had deserted, even La Rousselière, the man whose debts he had settled while in France. Four of the deserters had remained in Michilimackinac where they had joined local traders "for a bit of a good time." They were promptly arrested by La Salle. Six others had already left for Sault Sainte-Marie, taking along 4,000 livres worth of supplies. La Salle sent Tonty after them. Too late, he now saw his mistake: sending ahead a motley crew of craftsmen and voyageurs, already less than fired with enthusiasm, without any sort of leadership. The traders of Michilimackinac, hostile to the competition they feared La Salle's arrival would mean for them, had provided the little encouragement that these men needed to desert.

Next, La Salle had to search for the loyal members of the advance party trading for furs in the vicinity of Michilimackinac. Sailing on the *Griffon*, he found them north of Washington Island (Door County, Wisconsin), on an island then called Pouteouatami (Rock Island), the home of a very small pro-French Indian village. [12] The *Griffon* was quickly loaded with 12,000 livres worth of furs and sent to the *Sault de Conty* under the pilot's command. La Salle, discouraged by his fresh experience, had abandoned his original intention of taking the ship back himself.

On September 19, La Salle, the three Recollect priests and eleven men began their voyage south on Lake Michigan in four canoes. [13] They carried an incredible load of merchandise and tools, including an 80 pound anvil which they had brought on the more spacious *Griffon*. They encountered difficulties from the start: extremely bad weather, rough open waters, and a scarcity of food. Staying close to the Wisconsin side of the lake,

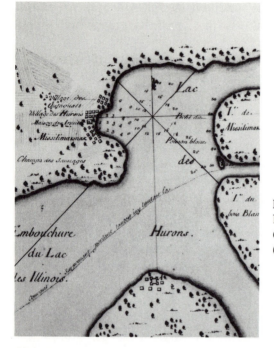

Michilimackinac in 1717.
Detail reproduced from the
Cartes Marines.
(The Newberry Library)

progressing at a slow pace, on November 1st, after a month and a half of
navigation under bad conditions, they finally reached the mouth of the
Miami River (now the St. Joseph River flowing through Michigan and
Indiana). La Salle had expected to find Tonty already there since he was
scheduled to return from Sault Sainte-Marie along the more direct route
of the eastern shore of the lake. Tonty had more paddlers, twenty men,
and little equipment to slow him down, but he was still nowhere to be
seen. The days were dark and gloomy. Anything approaching civilization had been left far behind. La Salle's men were exhausted and the
immediate future looked uncertain.[14]

Winter was at hand, and the stream would soon be frozen. The men
clamored to go forward, crying that they would soon starve if they could
not reach the villages of the Illinois before the tribe scattered for the
Winter hunt. La Salle was inexorable. If they should all desert, he said,
he with his Mohecan hunter and the three friars would still remain and
wait for Tonty. The men grumbled but obeyed; and, to divert their
thoughts, he set them to building a fort of timber on rising ground at the
mouth of the river.

La Salle named the strong house they built *Fort des Miamis*, a simple construction of hewn logs surrounded by a palisade, on top of a sandhill "that skirted the southern shore of the river mouth." [15]

Tonty finally arrived a few days later. He had not come across the *Griffon*, whose fate was becoming increasingly worrisome to La Salle, as she carried much of what he needed to build another vessel for the downstream journey on the Mississippi, but he could not postpone departure any longer. On December 3, he began the long trip toward the Gulf of Mexico, paddling upstream on the St. Joseph River with his thirty companions. The first goal was a portage they knew to be only about twenty leagues (sixty miles) away. Only four men had been left behind: two at the *Fort des Miamis* and two who were dispatched back along the eastern coast of the lake with the mission of finding and guiding the elusive *Griffon* to the safe anchorage that La Salle had prepared for her at the mouth of the river.

The expedition covered 69 miles in two days. Snow was falling heavily when they reached the portage and food supplies were low. La Salle sent the Mohecan hunter on a short tracking trip. He also went to look for game, quickly finding and shooting a deer, but unable to return to the camp before dusk, he had to spend the night alone, causing anxiety for Tonty and everyone else by his failure to return on schedule. Eventually daylight brought both La Salle and the Mohegan back to the little flotilla. They quickly found the portage path leading to the bluff and began to walk with their charges and their canoes. The distance between the St. Joseph and the Theakiki (Kankakee) [16] Rivers was short, about five miles, but, " the portage was across a vast plain, a part of which was a quaking, oozing bog ... the source of the Kankakee was in the midst of a quaking, saturated soil, all around which were pools or ponds of glistening water." [17]

Along the path, on the western side, were the deserted huts of a large village (now South Bend, Indiana), normally occupied by a grouping of Miami, Mascounten, and Ouyatanon. The bogs, the deserted village, the heavy sky of winter, the silhouettes wrapped in their great *capotes*, [18] curbed under loads, weapons and canoes, composed a pessimistic *tableau vivant*. But La Salle was impervious to this sort of scene; unlike other men, he only knew arrogant self-confidence where fear would have been understandable, while he took comfort in the immense solitude that surrounded him and his companions. The success of his plans depended in part on the Indians being out of their villages and dispersed into small

groups for the winter hunt. La Salle calculated that with 30 men he made
enough of a show of strength to insure respect from bands of as great as
300-400 warriors, (the maximum number that could hunt together effectively during the winter). His calculations proved correct. His men
progressed slowly because they had trouble finding game (over a 120-
mile distance they killed only two buffaloes) but they remained undetected and unchallenged. On January 1, 1680, they reached a second
deserted agglomeration: Illinois Town, which then "counted 460 cabins,
built like long cradles and covered by a double matting made of flat reeds
so well stitched together that neither snow, wind or rain could penetrate.
Each cabin shelters four to five hearths and each hearth serves one or two
families." [19]

The French had by now exhausted their meat and La Salle reluctantly
agreed to take some food, about thirty *minots* or approximately 255
gallons of corn, out of the cache that each Indian town maintained for
"rainy days." [20]

On January 4th, La Salle and his expedition emerged on the widest
segment of the Illinois River known as Pimiteoui (Peoria) Lake. [21] Five
miles farther down the Peoria Lake narrows, and at

> about nine in the morning, we saw on both sides of the river, a great number
> of canoes and about eighty huts, full of Savages who saw our boats only
> after they had passed a peninsula behind which they had their encamp-
> ment, at about half-musket range. The French, their eight canoes progress-
> ing all on the same line, weapons ready, let the current carry them down. [22]

The Illinois were totally surprised. Panic and confusion overcame
women, children and warriors. Tonty recorded: "They were alarmed,
mistaking us for Iroquois." [23] The French jumped onto the beach, facing
the main part of the village, arms in hand, but La Salle had strictly forbidden the firing of any weapon, and on the other side, the Illinois chiefs
managed to calm their own men before arrows could fly. There would be
no battle between the Illinois and the French. When everyone settled
down enough to talk, La Salle told the Indians about taking the corn from
their caches and paid generously for it with trade goods. The Illinois appreciated the gesture and offered more corn. La Salle proceeded to speak
about the need for peace between the Illinois and the Iroquois, and how
it could be better insured by the French building a fort, and with more
French people present. He told the Illinois that he also was going to build

"a large canoe to go down river all the way to the ocean, and how he would bring them all sorts of merchandise through that way [being] much shorter and easier."[24]

Coincidentally, Father Allouez, the Jesuit priest who served at the mission of the *Immaculée Conception* with the Illinois since the death of Father Marquette, had left only a few days before the arrival of La Salle and his men. Later, La Salle, whose suspicion of the Jesuits at times colored his perspective with an element of paranoia, explained Father Allouez's departure as a gesture of hostility towards his enterprise. However, how Allouez would have known of his arrival while the Illinois would not, taxes credence.

Now, La Salle had brought his expedition to the midpoint of an arc that extended north to Quebec and south to the mouth of the Mississippi River. This point, the center of the *Pays des Illinois,* was then the lush confluent of several navigable waterways and the dividing line "between the grand prairie and the timber land."[25] This Illinois prairie has not been better described than by Clarence Alvord, a regional historian who in his youth had seen the country still virtually unchanged:

> Most of the open prairie was covered with high beard grass, usually inter-spersed with tall-growing flowers, such as prairie arch, cup plant and compass plant, a number of gaudy sunflowers, several species of osage, and large purple patches of ironweed, often mixed with various thorohwoks, asters and ragweed. Indian plantain, leafcup, horseweed and lujssop were abundant while dragonhead, prairie clover, blazing star milkweed, orange lillies and wild roses added to the gorgeous blackeyed Susans, purple coneflowers and bright fur marigolds. . . . In the Spring, strawberries bearing abundant scarlet fruits, were scattered far and wide; wild phlox added gay splash of blue and pink, the blue phlox, the Greek valerian and the bluebell were usually found in the more moist areas. Wild garlic was abundant. The blue Iris made a rich spot of color and the unicorn plant and the bendtongue occasionally grew in great patches. For acres at a stretch the Summer fields glowed with vivid goldenrod.[26]

When La Salle retired on the night of his arrival, the prospects for his ambitions looked fairly bright. He had charted a course grandiose yet quite simple: he was going to claim for France the title to the entire course of the Mississippi River, and establish at its mouth a colony that would parallel, or even rival, that of Canada. The land of the Illinois had to be secured: it was the key to the very success of this enterprise. Here, La Salle would build his headquarters which would anchor a line of posts eventually stretching from Fort Frontenac to the Gulf of Mexico, to act as a collection center for the untapped reserves of furs from the West. But dawn came quickly and brought to La Salle a new herculean task. One of the Mascouten chiefs, known by the name of Monso, had arrived from the East during the night with gifts and a secret message for the Illinois: "Beware of La Salle, he is a friend of the Iroquois." [27]

Again, La Salle's ability in dealing with the Indians paid off: his newly made Illinois friends promptly informed him of both Monso's arrival and of the contents of his message. Now, he had to confront the messenger. A feast had been prepared for the following night in honor of La Salle and his companions, and the French and Indians were sitting together, regaled with choice venison, when the host rose and began a long harangue. He painted a frightening picture of the dangers of the Mississippi River, and advised the French to go no farther. La Salle listened patiently. When his turn came to rise and speak, he dramatically denounced those who tried to thwart his project, particularly those who believed he and his men to be Iroquois spies. La Salle's speech impressed the Illinois, but not two of his French, *voyageurs* who understood the exchange. That same night, they easily convinced four other Frenchmen that the dangers of the Mississippi were not for them and all six deserted. The next morning La Salle was faced not only with a blow to the morale of all, but to his ability to carry out plans based on the building of a boat; the deserters included the pit-sawyers who, alone, knew how to saw a tree trunk in its length. La Salle's first concern was maintaining the now diminished group intact: under a pretext of safety, he convinced the remaining men to move half a mile down from the Indian village. On January 15th, taking advantage of a sudden thaw, La Salle and his remaining men began building a fort on: "a knoll about two hundred feet from the river . . . two wide and deep gullies protected from the sides and part of the back that the *Sieur* de La Salle improved with a connecting ditch." [28] A palisade made of twenty-foot stakes reinforced with a dirt parapet, having semi-underground lodgments at each corner, completed the construction of Fort Crevecoeur. [29]

As Fort Crèvecoeur rapidly became more habitable, La Salle's main concern was again with resuming his progress down the Mississippi. Even without news of the *Griffon* and her supplies, and without his pit-sawyers, La Salle had not given up the idea of building a craft to carry his

Artist's reconstruction of Fort Crèvecoeur. (Illinois State Historical Library)

entire expedition downriver. Explaining this to one of his carpenters, he found a responsive chord in the man's pride and soon, with "a little good will and some time" was able to get them all to work.[30] On March 1st, a hull forty-two feet long and twelve feet wide stood on the south bank of the Illinois River, quite an achievement for men without experience in naval construction.

Until then, everything seemed to indicate La Salle's willingness to make do with the means he had at hand. The day before the completion of the hull of his new boat, on February 29th, he sent a trade expedition to the upper Mississippi with a mission of establishing trade links with the Sioux. With this action, La Salle obviously had decided that risking the wrath of the Michilimackinac traders was worth the profits to be made with the Sioux, profits which assuredly would help the financial survival of Crèvecoeur. This trade expedition was as small as it was heavily laden. La Salle entrusted its command to a capable man with a good knowledge of the Illinois language, Michel Accault; it included only two other volunteers and the Recollect, Father Hennepin. The four of them had to man a canoe carrying a 1,200 pound load. On March 7, they reached the encampment of the Tamaroa on the western side of the Mississippi, a few miles south of the mouth of the Illinois River. This tribe of about two hundred families were the most friendly among the Illinois. Accault and his party spent several days of welcome rest among them before pushing on north, up the Mississippi. Disaster struck on April 11th, when they encountered and were captured by a Sioux war party. Freedom came three long months later, and then only because their misfortune was discovered by another famous French explorer, Greysolon Du Luth, who happened to be dealing with the same Sioux near the *Sault de St. Antoine* (St. Paul-Minneapolis). Accault would later make his way back to Illinois, where he established family roots, while Father Hennepin continued on to Quebec and returned to France in 1682. In 1683, Hennepin published a book which made La Salle's expedition famous. His subsequent publications, however, of doubtful accuracy, gave rise to heated controversy.[31]

On March 10th, while Accault was just starting north on the Mississippi and the hull stood completed, La Salle handed over Fort Crevecoeur to Tonty and began the long trek back to Fort Frontenac. To abandon the Mississippi River descent at that time was a difficult decision. However, La Salle had finally realized that he had too few men available to maintain the fort and arm a boat at the same time, a boat moreover which lacked the necessary sails and ropes. He knew that:

> Summer was near and that if he waited a few months unnecessarily, his enterprise would be delayed perhaps by a year and even two or three because being so far away he could not organize his business and order what he needed, he decided for a solution as difficult as it was extraordinary, that is to walk back to Fort Frontenac which is more than 500 leagues away [from Peoria].[32]

La Salle could have sent Tonty, his second-in-command, to their home base, instead of going himself and leaving behind a precariously established beachhead. But La Salle never liked waiting for situations to develop. For him, movement was too often synonymous with progress. His feat of crossing the enormous distance separating Fort Crevecoeur from Fort Frontenac with five men in two months time, almost entirely on foot and with little food, was a remarkable display of courage and determination. At the same time, however, events of far-reaching consequence were taking place in Illinois.

Soon after La Salle's departure, Tonty had to face a volatile atmosphere among the French and an unsettled political climate among the various groups which combined to make the Illinois Indian confederation. The French of Fort Crèvecoeur suffered from low morale. They had seen Accault disappear over the western horizon; they had seen La Salle and his escort disappear over the eastern horizon. Food was scarce and the unknown looked more fierce by the hour. An unexpected message from La Salle a few days after his departure made the situation seemed even worse: the *Griffon* was confirmed lost, a loss for La Salle of probably 40,000 livres. Tonty's men were now convinced of the hopelessness of their situation. In the same letter, La Salle demanded that everybody move to a rocky promontory directly overlooking the Illinois River, and two miles south of the Illinois Town, *Le Rocher*, a site known now as "Starved Rock." Carrying out La Salle's orders, Tonty set out with the two Recollects,[33] the Sieur de Boisrondet, and two remaining soldiers, to examine the new emplacement and make preliminary arrangements. They left the workers behind to watch the fort, their security insured by the Illinois warriors. Tonty and his group faced an unpleasant surprise on their return: all the French workers had deserted with the tools. Whatever supplies they had not stolen had been purposely spoiled. The deserters had left a message summarizing their feelings: "*Nous sommes tous des sauvages, Ce 15 A. . . .* 1680.*" 'We are all savages', in other words, claiming that they had chosen freedom over the constraints of civilization to follow an Indian life-style. In fact, they made it back to Lake Erie and were well on their way to Montreal when they were intercepted by La Salle who, by then, had been forewarned by Tonty's messengers. Two of the deserters were killed in a firefight and the remainder captured and brought back to Montreal. The most adamant rebel among them, a ship's carpenter named Moyse Hillaret, when taken before *intendant* Duchesneau, justified his and his companions' desertion as a result of the back pay La Salle owed them. These were French peasants whom La Salle had foolishly dressed as knight-errants and for whom unpaid glory had no value and commanded no loyalty.

Tonty and his companions found themselves in an extremely grave situation at Fort Crèvecoeur. The Illinois, bewildered witnesses to this strife among the French, began to believe all the negative rumors that were reaching their ears: that Tonty was not a Frenchman and should not be trusted; that La Salle was dead; that these Frenchmen were Iroquois allies.[34] The origin of these rumors was uncertain. In Tonty's mind, they came from the Jesuits. They might also have been spread by some of the Illinois and Miami chiefs whose power plays were upset by the arrival of the French. At any rate, Tonty sent two messengers to La Salle with the improbable task of reaching and informing him of this new disaster. As incredible as it might seem, the two, Jacques Messier and Nicolas Laurent, did join La Salle before the deserters could reach Montreal, a feat which led finally to their interception.

At Crèvecoeur, Tonty was now in command of a miniscule force practically without ammunition. In the face of the persistent rumor of La Salle's death, he decided that the wisest course was to retreat to Michilimackinac. On September 18th, Tonty and his retinue—two priests, one officer, and two men—reached Illinois Town. There, they found a surly population whose council of elders accused them of being friends of the Iroquois. As luck would have it, the day the French were to continue on their journey, a warrior ran into town with the astonishing news of a large Iroquois party lurking on the southern side of the Aramoni (Vermilion) River, a few miles away. For Tonty and his party, leaving was no longer possible. Immediately surrounded, insulted, threatened by angry Illinois, they could do only one thing: offer to fight along with them.

The Iroquois made no secret about coveting the fur-rich lands of the Illinois. The rapid disappearance of furs in the East and the constant pressure of the British and Dutch merchants combined to make their expansion towards Lake Michigan just a question of time. If the Iroquois established a foothold in Illinois, they would make it difficult if not impossible for the French to move south and west of Michilimackinac and Green Bay. The Illinois, divided and demoralized, were no match for the Iroquois; their very survival depended on what the French would be able to do militarily to stem the relentless aggressors from the East. Unfortunately for the Illinois, on the morning of September 18, 1680, French power was represented by only six men.

The situation was grave. The Illinois had sent half of their warriors, their best, on a pre-winter hunt. Tonty had attempted, in vain, to dissuade them from taking such a risk since the hunters were given the best weapons and most of the available ammunition. On that morning, the Illinois could only line up a hundred men with muskets, each with just about three to four shots, supported by 400 others with bows and arrows. Challenging these defenses were 500 Iroquois hunters, all armed with firearms, sabers, shields, and well provisioned with powder and balls. More important, the Iroquois were animated with confidence in their invincibility. Across the river, the Illinois hurriedly sent their families away towards the Mississippi under escort and, in doing so, further depleted their ranks. To Tonty, the situation presented all the ominous signs of defeat. Negotiation, he decided, was the only recourse. In an attempt to bluff them into retreating, Tonty crossed the river and the fields to meet face to face with the surprised Iroquois. Recognizing a Frenchman, they expressed their anger, but did not dare to kill him outright. Until Tonty's appearance, they were confident of achieving an easy victory. Now, their frustration increased as they listened to his tales of large numbers of French soldiers across the river. The palaver was stormy. While Tonty urged the Iroquois to accept a gift and return east, one of their young warriors stole his hat and paraded around with it in full view of the Illinois. Believing Tonty dead, Boisrondet in desperation led the Illinois in a vigorous surprise charge. His action was almost fatal to Tonty who, in the meantime, had finally reached some form of agreement. Both Iroquois and Illinois would withdraw a few miles, and the Iroquois would eventually return to their homes. This settlement bought the Illinois a little time. For the Iroquois, the suspension of hostilities was meant to be only a temporary delay.

During the following days, the Iroquois moved along the eastern side of the Illinois River, maintaining constant pressure against the Illinois warriors who kept on falling back towards the Mississippi. Tonty saw that he had failed to do any better than slow down the Iroquois. By remaining, he would only expose himself and his party to unnecessary danger; therefore, he gave the signal to return to Michilimackinac. The French began their journey back "without provisions, food or anything in a wretched bark canoe." [35]

The Iroquois kept moving deeper and deeper into Illinois land. The Kaskaskia, Cahokia, and Peoria opted for retreat all the way to the safety of the Mississippi. The Tamaroa were slower in realizing the true nature of the danger and were caught off guard. The consequences were terrible: the Iroquois captured 700 of their women and children, burned half of them slowly on spits and carried the other half into slavery.

Tonty's journey was another of those incredible feats of courage and determination, examples of which abound in the tales of early North American exploration. His small group was made even smaller by the early disappearance of Father de la Ribourde, who one morning had walked away to read his breviary in solitude, never to come back.[36] At first, the French tried to follow the waterways but:

Our canoe failed us and leaked on all sides. After some days' travel we had
to leave it in the woods and make the rest of our journey by land, walking
barefoot over snow and ice. I made shoes for my companions and myself
with Father Gabriel's cloak. As we had no compass, we frequently got lost,
and found ourselves in the evening where we had started in the morning
without any other food than acorns and little roots . . . The *Sieur* de Bois
Rondet . . . had a pewter cup that he melted to make balls for his gun which
had no flint. By firing it with a coal he killed some turkeys. . . .[37]

The pathetic group was finally met in northern Wisconsin by a small
rescue party during early spring 1681 and, with this help, reached Michilimackinac on June 4th. A day later, Tonty and his companions were
reunited with La Salle and the rest of the expedition returning from the
fort at the St. Joseph River. The meeting was charged with emotion when
Tonty and his companions learned the details of La Salle's frustrated
attempts to rescue them.

As soon as La Salle had reached his fort at Niagara Falls he had sent one
of his officers "*sieur* Jacques d'Autray a young man wise and courageous,
the son of the first Attorney General of Quebec," [38] with four men in two
canoes loaded with supplies, with orders to reach Tonty and the five other
Frenchmen left behind in Illinois. From Niagara, La Salle then traveled on
to Fort Frontenac where he relieved the garrison's commander, Mr. de la
Forest, sending him with four more men to rescue Tonty. Unfortunately,
both rescue parties first came across the group of deserters, who told them
that Tonty and his companions were dead and that everything in Illinois
was lost. Believing their story, d'Autray returned to Michilimackinac
where he found to his surprise that La Salle had already intercepted the
deserters. On October 4th, somewhat regrouped, La Salle and twelve
men (including d'Autray and a surgeon in addition to soldiers, builders,
and carpenters) left Michilimackinac for Illinois for a third attempt. Wind
and rain delayed them considerably and they reached the St. Joseph River
only one month later. La Forest was supposed to be there with the balance
of the supplies and the remainder of the men, but he had misinterpreted
his orders. La Salle, now quite anxious about the fate of Tonty, (who was
at the time in northern Wisconsin trying to find his way either to St. Ignace
or to Michilimackinac) waited no more than a few days and forged ahead
with only six Frenchmen and one Indian. On November 15th, he reached
the site of the deserted Miami village, and the next day, the portage of the
Theakiki (Kankakee River). On December 1st, he entered Illinois Town,

"where he found only traces of fire and of the rage of the Iroquois."[39] Three days later, he was at Fort Crèvecoeur. The cold was already severe but even more depressing was the way the entire area, fort and village, had been devastated. The French found "heads and entire bodies of women and children skewered and roasted."[40] La Salle found more desolation towards the Mississippi. Once there, the men offered to continue all the way down to the Gulf of Mexico and complete the exploration. Deeply moved, but concerned over the guard left at Illinois Town and Tonty's fate, La Salle declined and they began retracing their steps. Not finding any trace of French bodies or equipment, they now were confident that Tonty and his companions had survived the Iroquois onslaught. By the end of January 1681, they were back at the mouth of the St. Joseph River.

The diminished military force of the Illinois, even though merely temporary, had changed the political situation. The French could not prevent invasions by the Iroquois, and consequently, English infiltration, without the help of Indian allies. To correct the situation, La Salle opened conversations with the Miami. Although related to the Illinois, they had until then maintained a prudent, almost frightened neutrality. Two events helped La Salle change their minds. First a band of fifty Indians from New England (Mohecan and Abenaki) who had lost their land to the encroaching American farmers, reached the Miami River seeking a new home. La Salle convinced the Miami to make room for their eastern brethren, who were warriors with great military experience and who could become precious reinforcement.[41] The Miami agreed. The second event involved the Iroquois.

On its way back east the Iroquois war party, slowed down by the 400 captured Tamaroa women and children, was surprised by an early snowfall. In their inimitable way, they appropriated all Miami supplies found in caches, accepted Miami gifts, and gave nothing in exchange. Then, the impossible occurred: a party of 100 Kaskaskia warriors led by Chief Paessa, hunting when the raid took place, attacked the intruders. Although they succeeded in inflicting serious losses on the Iroquois, the impact of their action was mainly felt by the Miami who, impressed by this renewed vitality shown by their Illinois cousins, decided to cast their lot with La Salle. La Salle's ability in dealing within the complex domain of Indian diplomacy had been once again quite extraordinary. His fortunes were taking a turn for the better. His men, responding to his infectious enthusiasm, substantially improved the material conditions at the fort and, with the arrival of spring, began to sow. On May 25th, La Salle resolved to return to Michilimackinac to organize a total resupplying of the expedition to the Mississippi and ten days later, on June 5th, stepped ashore into the friendly arms of his comrade Tonty.[42] The vicissitudes of yesterday were instantly forgotten and those of tomorrow ignored. As wrote Father Membré: "Anyone else would have thrown up his hands and abandoned the enterprise; but far from this, with firmness and constancy that never had equal I saw him more resolved than ever to continue his work and push forward his discovery."[43]

La Salle again had to return to Fort Frontenac before he could do anything else; he had to put a semblance of order into his hopelessly entangled financial affairs. He made it quickly, paddling the thousand miles of lake waters which separated Michilimackinac from his home base as if it were a pleasure outing. From Fort Frontenac, he had to go even farther, to Montreal, where he took time to write his will, making Francois Plet, his cousin and one of his principal financial backers, his sole heir. No morbid thoughts were involved in this instance; to raise capital, La Salle at this point had little to use for any collateral but his own life. In fact, optimism permeated his correspondence: "I hope to write more at leisure next year and tell you the end of this business which I hope will turn out well for I have Mr. de Tonty who is full of zeal; thirty Frenchmen, all good men without reckoning such as I cannot trust, and more than a hundred Indians some of them Shawanoes, and others from New England all of whom know how to use guns."[44]

La Salle left Michilimackinac on October 4th and a month later, on November 3rd, landed at the Miami village by the St. Joseph River. His expedition counted 23 Frenchmen, 18 Mohican and Abenaki Indians (plus 10 of their wives) selected from among those who had recently arrived from the East to settle with the Miami clan. On December 21st, Tonty, Father Membré, and an advance party left by canoe down the St. Joseph River, then up along the western shore of the Lake Dauphin (Lake Michigan), reaching the mouth of the Checagou (Chicago) River where they were joined on January 4, 1682, by La Salle and the rest of the men.

La Salle never favored the Chicago portage because of its difficulties. It was not uncommon for canoes to have to be carried over a distance of four to six miles between the Chicago River and the waters of the Des Plaines River.[45] However, this time the rigors of a particularly harsh winter made the frozen waters of the Chicago, the Des Plaines, and the Seignelay (Illinois) rivers [46] an easier route for the sleighs on which canoes

Portaging at Mud Lake on the Chicago River. (Chicago Department of Development and Planning)

and supplies were loaded. On January 27th, La Salle and the expedition passed through Illinois Town, which was totally deserted, and a few days later arrived in Peoria, where all the Illinois Indians had moved for the duration of winter. They camped with the Illinois for a short time and resumed their journey on the Illinois River, which was ice-free south of Peoria. On February 6, when they reached the Mississippi, which La Salle promptly renamed *Fleuve Colbert*, they found so much floating ice that they had to stop for a few days. On the 14th, they came across the deserted Tamaroa village and left the customary gifts. From then on, every mile downriver brought them out of the winter weather. Food became abundant and although some Indian populations along the way showed hostility, the size of the French party rendered it immune to any real danger.

On April 6th, La Salle's canoes arrived at a point where the Mississippi opened into three broad channels. La Salle, Tonty, and d'Autray each followed one, and a few miles farther each found the open waters of the Gulf of Mexico. On April 9th, the entire party reassembled on top of a small elevation. They had finally reached their goal: they had followed the course of the Mississippi all the way to the ocean. A cross was erected, banners unfurled, and La Salle read a proclamation by which he claimed in the name of Louis XIV, King of France, the land which later would be called the Louisiana Territory. The royal notary of Fort Frontenac, Jacques de la Metairie, who had accompanied the expedition for this specific purpose, made it all official. On April 9, 1682, France had acquired an empire, the magnitude of which she never quite understood.[47]

La Salle's return was difficult. The men had to paddle hard against a rapid current, their physical condition deteriorated, and food was hard to find. Only occasional alligator flesh provided the necessary nutrients. Some of the Indian groups who had been reasonably friendly on the downriver voyage, seemed to experience a change of heart. Their open hostility obliged the little expedition, already quite exhausted, to expend much needed energy in repeated defensive formations. As if fatigue, starvation and hostile populations were not enough, La Salle fell gravely ill. On June 4th, he had to let Tonty go ahead while he spent the summer at "Fort" Prudhomme, a fortified cabin that the French had built at the Chickasaw Bluffs (Arkansas) on their way down. When La Salle was finally able to resume his journey, it took him fifteen days to reach the Tamaroa village at the confluence of the Mississippi and Illinois rivers, and 15 more to ascend the Illinois River to the site of Fort Crevecoeur where he found everything burned or destroyed. Leaving a small garrison of nine men, he pushed on to Illinois Town, which he reached on July 15th. This town was also totally deserted. All along the Illinois River fear and desolation seemed to have settled in. Perturbed, but determined, La Salle kept on. He was at Fort Miami by the end of September, and from there went quickly to Michilimackinac where he joined Tonty.

Crèvecoeur was to be rebuilt and the task would be entrusted to Tonty, as the fort was destined to anchor the supporting role of Illinois in the development of a French Mississippi, "a colony of French and Indians to answer the double purpose of a bulwark against the Iroquois and a place of storage for the furs of all the Western tribes; and he hoped in the following year to secure an outlet for this colony and for all the trade of the valley of the Mississippi, by occupying the mouth of that river with a fort and another colony."[48]

But New France's political leadership was changing and La Salle was about to lose his patron, Governor Frontenac. In what was an unusually prudent decision for him, he remained in Michilimackinac to give the news of his discovery of the mouth of the Mississippi and annexation of half of North America time enough to reach Versailles.

It was vital that his numerous backers in France maintain faith in the eventual repayment of their investments with future riches. For this reason, La Salle, although now committed to the idea of returning to the

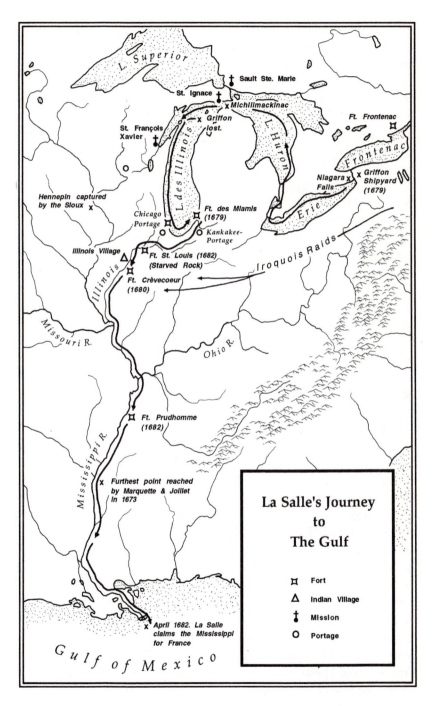

L. Superior

Sault Ste. Marie

St. Ignace

x Michilimackinac

x Griffon lost.

Ft. Frontenac

St. François Xavier

L. des Illinois

L. Huron

Frontenac

Niagara Falls

x Griffon Shipyard (1679)

Hennepin captured by the Sioux x

Erie

Chicago Portage

Ft. des Miamis (1679)

Kankakee-Portage

Iroquois Raids

Illinois Village

Ft. St. Louis (1682) (Starved Rock)

Ft. Crèvecoeur (1680)

Illinois

Missouri R.

Ohio R.

Ft. Prudhomme (1682)

Mississippi R.

x Furthest point reached by Marquette & Jolliet In 1673

x April 1682. La Salle claims the Mississippi for France

Gulf of Mexico

**La Salle's Journey
to
The Gulf**

⌂   Fort

△   Indian Village

✝   Mission

O   Portage

mouth of the Mississippi directly by ship from France, was concerned with the transformation of Illinois into a self-sufficient and profitable entity. To this end, Tonty arrived at Fort Crèvecoeur with men and supplies, joining its small garrison. However, during the same period at Michilimackinac, La Salle received many reports of a possible new Iroquois attack. Always loyal to his men and anxious to avoid a repetition of the tragedy of 1680, he returned to Illinois to join Tonty at Fort Crèvecoeur. Promptly determining it vulnerable to a large-scale assault, he ordered all to *Le Rocher*.

Le Rocher, renamed *Fort Saint Louis des Illinois*, possessed infinitely better military qualities than Crèvecoeur. It became a theater of frenzied activity: warehouses, cabins and palisades were erected, improving the already formidable natural defenses. With its front towering above the water (the highest part reaching 125 feet), and its two sides protected by ravines, then as now, the top of the rock was "accessible only from behind where a man may climb up, not without difficulty, by a steep and narrow passage."[49] It was here that the French spent the winter of 1682-83 in relative comfort, with hundreds of Indians camped nearby. For the French, the only serious problem in the fort's installations was its lack of protected access to water. Water had to be stored, a weakness which counted for little at the time. The general appearance of *Fort Saint Louis des Illinois* attracted the Illinois, the Wea, the Shawnee, the Miami, and others who gradually began to settle in large numbers in close proximity. The population of Illinois Town grew to about 20,000 people, including 4,000 warriors. Corn was planted, more huts were erected. Under La Salle's guidance, an alliance was formed between the Illinois, Miami, Chaouanon, and Mascouten. Once more, the Iroquois threat seemed to have been removed. This development of a French establishment along with a large Indian settlement was another demonstration of La Salle's ability to inspire. La Salle's talent was above all evident when dealing with Indians, as he "often failed in his dealing with his equals and inferiors among his countrymen, but with the Indians, his arrogance and his love of solitude and silence made him a hero whose advice they eagerly accepted."[50]

Fort Saint Louis des Illinois with its increasing popularity among the Indians, and trade goods flowing from Montreal, was sure to become a major center of French influence in the West. *Saint Louis* was "the first French fort of a permanent character in the upper country and here was signed the first patents to land ever made in Illinois."[51]

Unfortunately for La Salle, the arrival of a new governor for New France, a Navy officer, Le Fèvre de la Barre, was to deliver a serious blow to the whole enterprise.

NOTES

1. All the documents regarding La Salle are well known and have been cited by his numerous biographers. The most important documents on La Salle were originally published in Pierre Margry, *Découvertes et Etablissements des Français.* , Vol. 1; the details of La Salle expense for Fort Frontenac are found in pp. 292-95.

2. Francis Parkman, *France and England in North America*, Part 4, *The Old Regime in Canada*, Boston, 1884, p. 299.

3. *Intendant Meules au Ministre, 24 septembre, 1685*, in Parkman, *The Old Régime*, p. 300.

4. La Salle raised a total of 45,483 livres and 4 sols.

5. On this period of French history, see John B. Wolf, *Louis XIV*, New York, 1968, particularly the chapter entitled "The Cult of the King," 357-358.

6. *Relation des descouvertes et des voyages du sieur de la Salle Seigneur et gouverneur du fort de Frontenac, au delâ des grands lacs de la Nouvelle-France, faite par l'ordre de Monseigneur Colbert, 1679-80-81*, in Pierre Margry, Vol. 1, 435-544. This document is the official report presented to the Minister.

7. The Recollects were a reformed branch of the Franciscan Order, inroduced in northern France in 1592; they were part of the first French colonization of New France until Cardinal de Richelieu decided to give the spiritual guidance of this overseas province to the Jesuits. When, in the eyes of the Crown, the Jesuits became too powerful in New France, the Recollects were permitted to return. See the *Memoire faict en 1637 pour l'affaire des Pères Recollectz de la Province de Sainct-Denis, dicté de Paris, touchant le droit qu'ils ont depuis l'an 1615 d'aller en Quanada*, in Margry, Vol. 1, 4-33.

8. ". . . Je fis assister a cette negotiation deux peres jesuites afin de leur oster les moyens de destruire par la suite ce que j'aurois avance . . .," *Lettres de Cavelier de La Salle et correspondance relative à ses entreprises, 1676-1685, lettre du 29 septembre 1680*, in Pierre Margry, Vol. 2, p. 35.

9. See Cyrus Kingsbury Remington, *The Shipyard of the Griffon*, Buffalo, N.Y., 1891, 28-30.

10. Father Louis Hennepin, *Description de la Louisiane*, 1683, in Parkman, Vol. ll, 129.

11. The two Recollect Fathers in addition to Louis Hennepin were: Father Zenobe Membré and Father Gabriel de la Ribourde. Father Membre, a cousin of of Father Le Clercq, was born at Bapaume in 1645 or about; he came to New France in 1675 and returned to France after the end of La Salle's expedition on the Mississippi. Once more, Father Membré joined La Salle, this time for his ill-fated attempt to annex the coasts of Texas.

12.   Professor Ronald J. Mason of the Department of Anthropology of Law-
rence University, Appleton, Wisconsin, published a detailed article on the loca-
tion of the *Griffon*'s landing with La Salle on board, in "Aspects of Upper Great
Lakes Anthropology," *Papers in honor of Lloyd A. Wilford*, Minnesota Historical
Society, St. Paul, Minnesota, 1974; also, see the last chapter of his book, *Great Lakes
Archæology*, Academic Press, New York, 1981.

13.   Lake Michigan, originally called *Lac des Illinois* was renamed *Lac St. Joseph*
by the Jesuit Father Allouez and *Lac Dauphin* by the Recollect Father Membré, a
difference of names which illustrated the contrasting political views between the
two religious orders.

14.   Parkman, Vol. 1, 149.

15.   "Il y avait a l'embouchure de la riviere une eminence plate et naturellement
fortifiee; elle estoit haute et escarpee, de figure triangualaire, fermee des deux
costez par la riviere, et de l'autre par une profonde ravine. Il fit abbattre les arbres
dont elle estoit couverte et netoyer toutes les broussailles a beux portees de fusil
du coste des bois. Il fit ensuite faire une redoute de 40 pieds de longueur sur 30
de largeur, fortifiee de poutres et de solives esquarries et a l'epreuve du mousquet,
posees en traverse, l'une sur l'aure. Il fit fraiser les deux faces qui regardoient la
riviere et planter en tenailles des pieux de 25 pieds de hauteur du coste de la terre."
*Relation des descouvertes et des voyages du sieur de La Salle . . . Faite par l'ordre de
Monseigneur Colbert*, in Margry, Vol. 1, 460-61. The Jesuit Pierre Charlevoix who
travelled in Illinois in 1721—forty-two years later—and who passed through the
St. Joseph River, does not mention any fort. The site was never used for defense
purposes after La Salle and must have rapidly returned to its original state. It was
known as the Saranac and Newberryport by sailors of the 1830's and, ". . . in March
1834, the little settlement was incorporated as the village of St. Joseph . . ." George
Baker, *The St. Joseph-Kankakee Portage*, Indiana Historical Society, South Bend,
Indiana, 1899, 42, note 1.

16.   Father Charlevoix who travelled in these parts when oral tradition
regarding Indian history was still alive and well (1721), explained the origin of the
name of the river as such: "Theakiki, which, by corruption our Canadians name
Kiakiki, *Theak* means a wolf, I no longer recall in what language, but the river bears
the name because the Mahangans who are also called wolves, formerly took
refuge there." in Baker, 44; an identical explanation is also given in the *History of
Peoria County*, 272, Footnote 2.

17.   Baker, 33: the complete course of the portage was intact when visited in
1848 by Francis Parkman. Today, the landing at the River St. Joseph has remained
probably intact being a part of the River View Cemetery of South Bend, Indiana;
the Kankakee landing has suffered considerable modifications: three ponds
marking its start have been drained and the course of the Kankakee River, still
extremely narrow, has been straightened by an improvement project.

18.   *Capotes* were great blue coats that the French Canadians wore during the
winter; the term has survived today in French military parlance.

19.   *Relation*, in Margry, Vol. 1, 466, trans. by this author. In 1675 Marquette had
estimated that the number of families equalled 600 (2500 people); in 1677, Father
Allouez counted 351 cabins and three years later, in 1680, Father Membré

estimated the population to 3,000 people in all of Illinois. "This great Illinois village . . . the village of the Kaskaskias proper was two leagues below the mouth of the Postgouki proper or Fox, and six leagues above the Great Village," Margry, Vol. II, 175; Shea, Le Clercq, Vol. 2, 117. On the location of the site of Illinois Town (or Illinois Village), see footnote above.

20. *Relations.*, in Margry, Vol. II, 36-37.

21. Pimiteoui in Illinois language means "That there are plenty of fat beasts in the spot." Vol. 2, 118, Shea trans. Le Clercq, *First Establishment*.

22. *Relation.*, Margry, Vol l, 467.

23. *Relation ecrite de Québec, le 14 novembre 1684 par Henri de Tonty*, in Margry, Vol l, 573-615.

24. *Relation.*, in Margry, Vol. l, 470.

25. Ridgley, *The Geography of Illinois*, 92, quoted in the *Inventory of the County Archives of Illinois*, Peoria County, Illinois, Historical Survey carried out by the WPA, Chicago, January 1942.

26. Clarence Walworth Alvord, *The Illinois Country, 1673-1818, The Centennial History of Illinois*, Chicago 1922, 1-2.

27. Monso or Monceau, a name close to the Illinois *Mousoa*, meaning "deer." See Parkman., Vol. 3, *La Salle and the Discovery of the West*, and Shea, Le Clercq, Vol. 2, 121.

28. *Relation des descouvertes.*, in Margry, Vol. l, 476; trans. by this author.

29. The name of Crèvecoeur was given to the Fort in honor of a French victory in the Flanders, near the town of Crevecoeur, and not, as some have written as a symbol of La Salle's feelings, taking the translation a little too literally—Broken Heart. Shea, Vol 2, 123, FN quoting H.A. Rafferman, *Deutsche Pionier*, Aug-Oct., 1866, who wrote a series of articles on Father Hennepin; Rafferman claimed that Tonty had taken part in the capture of a Dutch town of Crevecoeur, referring to the *Tegen Woordige Staat der Vereinigte Nederlanden*, Amsterdam, 1740, 11,57. Although a small park and a monument marks an area southwest of Peoria, in the town of Crevecoeur, the exact emplacement of the Fort has been a subject of discussion. A citizen from Peoria, Richard M. Phillips, published findings on the site of the first fort, Fort Crevecoeur, and the second fort built by the French near Peoria, Fort St. Louis, in *Iliniwek*, Vol. 13, No 4, October-December 1975, which seem much closer to the reality than what was previously considered.

30. *Relation.*, in Margry, Vol. l, 477.

31. Father Louis Hennepin, *Relation des descouvertes et des voyages du sieur de La Salle avec la Carte du pays: Les Moeurs et la maniere de vivre des Sauvages*, Paris, 1683; several translations were made of this work. A second book entitled *Nouvelle Decouverte d'un tres grand Pays situe dans l'Amerique*, a book full of plagiarisms and doubtful observations, was published at Utrecht in 1697 by Father Hennepin and dedicated to the King of England. By then, Father Hennepin *persona non grata* in France, had changed allegiance.

32. *Relation des découvertes.*, in Margry, Vol l, 483-84.

33. Father Gabriel de la Ribourde, sixty-three years old, and Father Zénobé Membré. Father de la Ribourde belonged to an old prominent Burgundian family; he had come to New france during the Summer of 1670 and was among the first

Recollects authorized to establish a mission. Father Zenobius Membré, born in Bapaume, in northern France, was a cousin of Father Christian Le Clercq (who later published Membré's travel account in the *Etablissments de la foi*); Father Membré came to New France in 1675 and was assigned in 1678 to Fort Frontenac. In 1681 he accompanied the ill-fated La Salle expedition to the Gulf of Mexico and died in Texas in 1689 at the hands of the Indians who destroyed the mission.

34. *Relation de Henri de Tonty, ecrite le 1er novembre 1689,* in Margry, Vol. l, 584.

35. *Narrative of the Adventures of La Salle's party at Fort Crevecoeur, in Illinois, from February 1680, to June 1681,* by Father Zenobius Membré, *Recollect,* English version, published by Isaac Joslin Cox in *The Journeys of Rene Robert Cavelier Sieur de la Salle,* New York, 1905, Vol, l, 106-130, and in Shea, *First Establishment.,* Vol. II, 102-197.

36. Father Gabriel de La Ribourde was surprised by three Kickapoo warriors out looking for Iroquois scalps and who decided to return to their village claiming the priest's as proof of their prowess. La Ribourde was sixty-nine years old at the time of his death. A street in South Bend, Indiana, commemorates his sacrifice.

37. Membré's narrative translated by Cox in *The Journeys.*

38. *Relation . . . des descouvertes.,* in Margry, Vol, l, 502; Jacques Bourdon, *Sieur* d'Autray, was the son of Jean Bourdon, *Sieur* de St. Francis. Bourdon's father was public prosecutor when his son joined La Salle in 1675. Autray, St. Francis, were names of Canadian seigneuries. D'Autray had served in the Marine infantry in Canada with the rank of lieutenant; he sailed on the *Griffon,* and was one of the men who accompanied La Salle in search of Tonty; (Andre Henault, Pierre You and the Mohecan hunter made the balance). In 1682, D'Autray will be at the discovery of the Mouth of the Mississippi with La Salle. In 1687, he will again accompany Tonty against the Iroquois. D'Autray was killed in 1688 by a party of Iroquois on his way back to Montreal.

39. *Relation.,* 516.

40. *Relation.,* 521

41. These Indians belonged to "seven or eight different nations originally from the vicinity of Bristol, Manhattan or New Amsterdam.," in Margry, Vol. l, 533.

42. The *Relation officielle de l'entreprise de Cavelier de La Salle de 1679 à 1681,* erroneously indicates Fort Frontenac as the meeting point of La Salle and Tonty; the *Relation de Henri de Tonty* as well as the narrative of Father Zenobius Membré give Michilimackinac, which is logical for travellers lost in Wisconsin.

43. Father Zenobius Membré's Relation in Le Clercq, Vol. II, 208, and in Parkman, *France and England,* Vol. III, 272, fn. 1.

44. *Relation de découvertes,* trans. in Parkman, Vol, III, 273.

45. See Robert Knight and Lucius H. Zeuch, *The Location of the Chicago Portage Route of the Seventeenth Century,* Chicago Historical Society, Chicago, 1928.

46. The Illinois River had been renamed "Seignelay" in honor of a minister of Louis XIV.

47. "In the name of the most high, mighty, invincible, and victorious Prince, Louis the Great, by the Grace of God, King of France and Navarre, fourteenth of that name, I, this ninth day of April, one thousand six hundred and eighty-two, in virtue of the commission of his Majesty, which I hold in my hand, and which may be seen by all whom it may concern, have taken and do now take, in the name

of his Majesty and of his successors to the crown, possession of this country of Louisiana . . .within the extend of the said Louisiana, from the mouth of the great river St. Louis, otherwise called the Ohio . . . as also along the river Colbert, or Mississippi, and the rivers which discharge themselves thereinto, from its sources beyond the country of the Nadouessioux . . . as far as its mouth at the sea, or Gulf of Mexico." Francis Parkman, trans. excerp from the *Procés verbal de la prise de possession de la Louisiane*, published in his *La Salle And the Discovery of the Great West*, Boston 1886, pp. 286-7. The map drawn by Franquelin in 1684 which is now at the *Dépôt des cartes de la marine* in Paris shows the magnitude of La Salle's claim. As Parkman wrote: "On that day, the realm of France received on parchment a stupendous increase: the fertile plain of Texas; the vast basin of the Missisippi; from its frozen northern springs to the sultry border of the Gulf; from the woody ridges of the Alleghanies to the bare peaks of the Rocky Mountains." Vol. 3, p. 238.

48. Parkman, *La Salle and The Discovery* .,p. 292.

49. Parkman, La Salle., 293.

50. Clarence W. Alvord, *The Illinois Country, 1673-1818*, Illinois Centennial Commission, Chicago, 1921, p. 89.

51. Clarence W. Alvord, *The Illinois.*, 89.

4

The Perilous Transition

F rom his first days in New France, the actions of the new governor, La
Fèvre de la Barre, clearly revealed him to be La Salle's implacable
enemy. Although La Salle's instinctive reactions, and those of his friends
and associates as well, led him to read into the governor's ill will yet
another manifestation of Jesuit evil, the truth was that La Barre's motiva-
tions stemmed from simple greed. The governor had easily found partners among the many fur traders who resented La Salle's intrusion. With
his power to grant government privileges, La Barre had only to collect
his clandestine profits in Quebec where all fur harvests eventually arrived
to be stored and counted.

In the meantime, from the top of his *Rocher*, La Salle remained unaware
of this new development. He had dutifully written a letter to Governor
La Barre stating among other things that:

> My losses in my enterprises here exceeded forty thousand crowns. I am
> now going four hundred leagues southwest of this place to induce the
> Chickasaws to follow the Chawanoes and other tribes, and settle, like
> them, at St. Louis [des Illinois]. It remains only to settle French colonists
> here, and this I have already done. I hope that you will not retain them as
> *coureurs des bois* [unlicensed traders] when they come down to Montreal to
> make necessary purchases.[1]

But this was exactly what came to pass: the men that La Salle sent to
Montreal for supplies were all detained. La Barre justified his action on
the basis of instructions that Versailles had sent to him and to *intendant*
Jacques de Meulle on May 10, 1682, although these instructions only sus-
pended explorations and were not applicable to La Salle. On June 4, 1683,
La Salle sent a new letter from the Chicago portage to Governor La Barre,
a letter in which he stated his predicament and its consequences quite
bluntly:

> I have postponed going to Michilimackinac because if the Iroquois strike
> any blow in my absence, the Miami will think that I am in league with them;

whereas, if I and the French stay among them, they will regard us as protection. But, Sir, it is in vain that we risk our lives here, and that I exhaust my means in order to fulfill the intentions of His Majesty, if those who go down to buy ammunition without which we cannot defend ourselves, are detained under pretexts trumped up for the occasion. . . . I have only twenty men with scarcely a hundred pounds of powder and I cannot long maintain the country without more. The Illinois are very capricious and uncertain. . . . I trust that you will put it in my power to obtain more, that this important colony may be saved.[2]

La Salle still did not know at this point that Governor La Barre had resolved to destroy him. To this end the Governor had already sent several letters to Versailles in which he tried at length to demonstrate the explorer's lack of honesty.[3] La Barre's administration, however, was endangering more than the French presence in Illinois: the whole French establishment in North America would soon be in peril. La Barre's venality would not have been such a major sin if it had not been accompanied by incompetence, a definite contrast with his predecessor, Frontenac. Coinciding with La Barre's arrival in Quebec, a new Iroquois offensive, inspired by the Dutch and English traders of New England, was about to begin. The goal of the Iroquois was the elimination of all the western Indian nations from participating in the fur trade. Years later, when La Barre was finally recalled by the minister, he would be accused of having suggested to the Iroquois chiefs who came to Montreal for peace parleys, that they confine their belligerence to the Illinois, while the governor was secretly offering La Salle's domains as spoils of war in exchange for peace on the St. Lawrence River,[4] an accusation that he would vehemently protest. At any rate, Indian diplomacy was complicated and required skills that the new governor did not possess. Alternating between crude dealings and brutal exercise of force, La Barre was playing dangerous games that he would eventually lose.

When La Barre seized Fort Frontenac under the pretext that La Salle did not maintain a sufficient garrison there, La Salle's position at Fort St. Louis became untenable. His only alternative was to return to the Court at Versailles, present his case directly to the minister and, if possible, to the king himself.[5] In August 1683, leaving Tonty in command, he began what would be his last journey out of Illinois. He traveled lightly in his usual fashion, in only one canoe with two of his most trusted Chaouanon Indians.

Leaving Illinois was a timely decision. Fourteen leagues (forty-two miles) east, on the Illinois River, La Salle suddenly met with an imposing convoy heading towards Fort St. Louis: thirty canoes carrying one hundred traders plus twenty soldiers, all led by Mr. de Baugy, an officer in the king's Dragoons, who had been ordered by the governor to take over the command of Illinois and send La Salle back to Quebec. [6] La Salle confronted the hostile action with his usual calm. He stopped at the fort built in Chicago only a few months before to write a farewell note to the inhabitants of Fort St. Louis, asking them to obey Tonty and respect Baugy's authority.

The construction of the fort in Chicago had been underwritten by the Jesuits in their efforts to steer fur trade away from Fort St. Louis. Fort Chicago, commanded by an officer appointed by Governor La Barre, was the first real permanent establishment built on the site of the future metropolis, a fact that seems to have escaped all recent accounts on the history of Chicago. [7]

La Salle continued on his journey back to Quebec and to France, landing at La Rochelle on January 7, 1684. [8] While La Salle's régime in Illinois ended in a summary manner, he had brought France to Illinois, building on the fragile footsteps of Marquette and Jolliet. But, to borrow once again from one of his greatest admirers, nineteenth century historian Francis Parkman, La Salle:

> was very indifferent trader; and his heart was not in the commercial part of his enterprise. He aimed at achievement and thirsted after greatness. His ambition was to found another France in the West. . . . His misfortune was that, in the pursuit of a great design, he was drawn into complications of business, with which he was ill fitted to grapple. He had not the instinct of the successful merchant. He dared too much, and often dared unwisely; attempted more than he could grasp; and forgot, in his sanguine anticipation, to reckon with enormous and incalculable risks. [9]

The orders of Mr. de Baugy were to take over Fort St. Louis from La Salle, and while La Salle was gone, Tonty remained. The governor had overlooked Tonty in his orders. Now, Tonty and Baugy settled down into an uneasy *de facto* co-direction of the fort.

Henry de Tonty, probably born in 1649 or 1650, was the son of Isabelle di Lietto and Lorenzo Tonti, a banker who had joined the leaders of the Neapolitan revolt against the Spanish occupation. The Neapolitan rebels,

Portrait of Henri de Tonty. Painted from life by Nicolas Maes.
(Illinois State Historical Society)

the *lazzaroni,* (scoundrels) as they were soon nicknamed, did not long
enjoy the sudden success they had first met. Lorenzo had been made
governor of Gaeta by the revolutionaries but had to flee for his life along
with his family with the return in force of the Spanish army. They found
shelter in France where, luckily for them, power lay in the hands of Italian-
born Cardinal and Prime Minister Jules Mazarin. Soon employed by the
cardinal, Mr. Tonti would be remembered for a system of life insurance
that he created, the *tontine.* In 1668, his son Henry (who later gallicized
the spelling of his family name), at age eighteen was given a cadet's commission in the French navy. From the start of his career, Tonty distinguished himself by his calm courage under fire; losing a hand in action
against the Spanish fleet at Libisso, off the Sicilian coast, he is reported to

have severed the mangled limb himself. The hand was later replaced by a prosthesis which Indians and *voyageurs* claimed was made of silver, but was probably copper. Tonty's proverbial quick use of this "iron hand" to settle disputes long remained part of Illinois folklore. [10] When he returned to France as part of a prisoners' exchange, he received a *gratification* of 300 livres from the king's treasury. The peace treaty of 1678 left him unemployed, not an unusual situation for professional soldiers during the eighteenth century when large standing armies were too expensive to be maintained in idle times. But Paris and the Court were the center of many worlds and it was not long before another of the powerful protectors of the Tonti family, the Prince of Conti, recommended the young soldier to the young adventurer who had just received a commission from the King to open the western marches of Canada to France: Robert Cavelier de la Salle. Both men took an instant liking to each other and, on July 12, 1678, Tonty was on the vessel departing La Rochelle with the bulk of La Salle's expedition.[11]

Now, five years later, Henry de Tonty was standing alone in the defense of La Salle's most important fruit of his travails. His concern was increased by the presence, along with Baugy, of two known rivals of La Salle: Greyloson Du Luth and De la Durantaye. Ironically, Du Luth was Tonty's second cousin and would later play a vital role in the development of French influence in that part of the Northwest which is now the State of Minnesota. La Durantaye was a career officer in command of Michilimackinac when ordered to join Baugy. Like many army officers, he was deeply involved in fur trade.[12] Baugy came from a long line of soldiers and magistrates from the province of Berry; educated not only in the metier of arms but in the humanities as well, he was very much the proverbial young noble without resources who looked for employment in the service of the King. When, in 1682, he arrived in Canada, he was quickly recruited by Governor La Barre, as officers were always in short supply. On July 7, 1683, he wrote from Michilimackinac to his brother in France: "I must soon leave to spend Winter in the country of the Illinois, a large people whose country is very beautiful, where one can see quantities of wild oxen. . . . I have to go soon because I have orders to send down [to Quebec] Mr. de la Salle who must give account of his actions."[13]

Baugy, although not personally involved in the dispute, was bound to execute orders that Tonty was just as determined to oppose. Tonty, in spite of the difficulty of his position, still attempted to carry out some trade. Without any funds, surrounded by numerous competitors, he offered to give the *habitants du Fort St. Louis* 300 *livres tournois* each at the end of the season if they would in exchange grant him the 400 livres worth of merchandise they were due to receive from Montreal as payment for their services to La Salle.[14] This transaction went beyond the discussion stage, and was written in the form of an agreement. But Tonty was not in a position to obtain any supplies from the merchants of New France to send back to Illinois, and his bold scheme did not materialize.

It is no small irony that Governor La Barre's efforts to remove La Salle proved beneficial for the solidification of the French presence in Illinois. While La Salle had given only twenty-five passports to maintain control over the business transacted in his seigniory, the waters of the Illinois and Kankakee Rivers were now becoming crowded with canoes. The majority of these *voyageurs* had never been seen south of Michilimackinac until La Barre encouraged large numbers of men to descend upon Illinois. La Salle had left Tonty a command of about twenty soldiers with as many traders. Even if we count a few extra people such as a missionary or two, and some unlicensed traders, we can reasonably assume that in 1683 fewer than sixty men made up the French population of Illinois. In contrast, Baugy brought with him thirty canoes loaded with traders. Since each canoe required a crew of at least three to four men and the *canots de maître* (a much larger craft) could carry ten to eighteen *voyageurs*, even by using a low average of six men per canoe, we can estimate the total number of traders who arrived that year at Fort St. Louis to be about 180. Including the twenty *soldats de marine* of the escort, there were now more than 200 more Frenchmen at the fort. It was only the beginning as, in addition, La Salle, while on his journey back to Quebec and France, had encountered a second convoy of sixty canoes heading for Illinois, suggesting another 400 men. Farther along, La Salle came across—and fed—the starving crews of still eight more canoes so heavily loaded with trade goods that there was no room for supplies.

Adding all these figures we reach a total of 600 traders, a commercial force which represented half the "brigades" of *voyageurs* plying their trade in the back country of Canada. The word was out: Illinois was the Eldorado of furs. The budding Canadian merchant class had always looked upon La Salle as an intruder and was glad to seize the moment, and volunteers for the journey had been easily recruited. Most of these canoes, however, were not individually owned and belonged to syndicates of investors (two among them, Le Bert and La Chesnaye, jointly owned 100 canoes). Although Canadian investors were not shifting all their man-

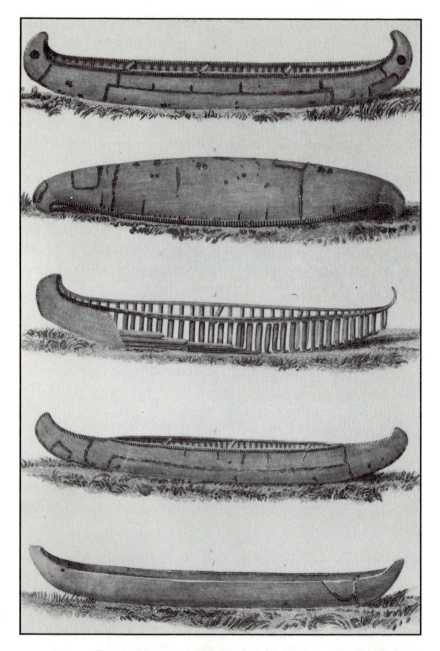

Four bark canoes and a wooden dugout canoe. By Seth Eastman.
From Schoolcraft, *History of the Indian Tribes of the United States.*
(The Newberry Library)

power to Illinois, and although the majority of the men would return to Michilimackinac and Montreal before winter made the rivers impracticable, some of the *voyageurs* were bound to remain. These would disperse and penetrate more deeply, perhaps beyond Peoria towards the Mississippi, where winters are milder, some establishing a more permanent presence. They would trap with Indian partners, marry Illinois women, sink foundations for homes next to Indian dwellings, and watch their numerous offspring grow.

Almost overnight, the impact of the new governor's policies had changed the Illinois conjuncture. The sudden upsurge of French population accelerated the acculturation of the Illinois people. The process, as in other parts of New France, was facilitated by the French traders' adaptability to the Indian way of life. As the number of mixed unions increased (although only a small proportion was recorded on parish registers) the number of children with family ties to Indian populations also increased. The new Indian generations, in turn, would retain a "trading-post" mentality, seeing furs as the source of all the necessities and life's luxuries, and the French military as the sole arbiters of all conflicts. Regularly, the royal authorities would issue statements from Quebec deploring this state of affairs while at the same time pursuing a policy that fostered it.

Governor La Barre had made secret arrangements with the Iroquois to insure that Frenchmen without passports would be divested of their trading goods. It was an effective means of guaranteeing that any competitors would be driven out of business very quickly. The arrangement, however, backfired. The Iroquois, who were only too happy to oblige the governor, made little distinction between Frenchmen whether they were bearing passports or not. On March 8, 1684, a contingent of 200 Iroquois on their way to attack Fort St. Louis detained and robbed a French party of eighteen men they encountered on the Kankakee River. The French protested to no avail that they had the governor's passports: the Iroquois took all they had including their supplies, leaving them with only two firearms. This party was fortunate as they were rescued by a band of Mascouten a few days later.[15]

Eventually, the strange actions of Governor de la Barre reached the minister who sent him a reprimanding note. Ironically, as La Barre dictated replies protesting his innocence, the Iroquois raiding party we saw pillaging French traders was making its way towards Fort St. Louis des Illinois reaching it on March 30.[16] The fact that La Salle was no longer in control of that fort had no meaning for the Iroquois. As they had been asked by the governor's emissaries to destroy La Salle's establishment, nothing would stop them now. Forewarned of the Iroquois' attack, Baugy sent a messenger asking for help to La Durantaye back to his command in Michilimackinac. On the day following the departure of the messenger, Fort St. Louis was totally surrounded. For one week, the Iroquois vainly attempted to rush the defenses, then finally disappeared as quickly as they had come.[17] Durantaye had received Baugy's message, however, and on May 21st arrived in *St. Louis des Illinois* with a party of sixty soldiers and volunteers. Father Allouez was with them; his return to Illinois at the very time La Salle's interests were being liquidated might have been more than coincidental. La Durantaye also carried Governor La Barre's orders for Tonty to leave immediately and report to Quebec. Another order from the governor directed Baugy to proceed with the seizure of all goods belonging to La Salle. This order had been issued on July 20, 1684, but it referred to La Salle's stay in Quebec during November 1683, when he borrowed 4,000 *livres* from the governor to continue his journey. La Barre saw the loan as an opportunity to get rid of the adventurer for good. He was now repaying himself by confiscating an empire.[18]

Meanwhile, La Salle had not remained inactive. His friends at the Court had rallied behind him, supporting his project to land an expeditionary force directly at the mouth of the Mississippi and then to link it with a party from *St. Louis des Illinois*. Information on alleged misdeeds by Governor La Barre and his suspected collusion with the Jesuits continued to reach the minister's desk and made the King impatient with the state of affairs in New France. On April 10, 1684, he signed a stern letter to the governor. Four days later, a *lettre de cachet*, probably the strongest form of official communication existing under the *Ancien régime* in France, was entrusted to M. de la Forest. Addressed to *intendant* de Meulle, it ordered the return to La Salle of all his properties, including the seigniories of Frontenac and Illinois to be placed in the care of La Forest. *Fort St. Louis des Illinois* was returned to Tonty's command along with a company of *infanterie de marine*.[19] The choice, intentional or not, of La Forest as the bearer of bad news to the governor, pointed to an early end of his tenure.[20]

On April 12, 1684, La Salle finally received the King's commission to govern all North American lands "from Fort St. Louis on the Illinois River all the way to New Biscaye" with the right to appoint local governors and commanders along with rights to all profits, revenues, franchises, and more, "as long as it shall please the King." [21]

La Forest's instructions were to gather all La Salle's disbanded men who were in Canada, and lead them down to the mouth of the Mississippi where they were to join forces with a naval expedition led by La Salle. Tonty was to leave New France and join La Salle at La Rochelle. This elaborate plan never materialized. Both Tonty, gravely ill, and La Forest, immobilized by the frozen St. Lawrence River, remained in Montreal until June 1684, when they joined their detachment in Fort Frontenac.[22] La Forest reorganized Fort Frontenac and Tonty, with whom he had entered a business partnership, took the road to Illinois with 20,000 livres of supplies and merchandise, carrying an order for Baugy to return Fort St. Louis to him, signed by the governor. La Barre, practical to the end, had however ordered Baugy to take back to Quebec anything not at the fort at the time of his arrival, "even the war ammunition."[23] Baugy was also to take along furs from the fort for the equivalent of 4,000 livres still owed to the Governor by La Salle. On June 26, 1685, the transfer of command at Fort St. Louis was marked by an exchange of notes between Baugy and Tonty, Tonty certifying that he had received everything in order, or at least "in the same state as I left it on last May 22, 1684, having been obliged to go to Kebec on order of the said M. de la Barre."[24]

On this receipt, Tonty takes great care to list all of his titles in a most high-hat manner: "Henry de Tonty, First Lord of the Island of Tonty, Captain of a company of marine infantry; Sub-delegate of M. de Meulle, *Intendant* of New France. . . . Governor of Fort Saint Louis in Louisiana."[25]

His listing is embarrassingly pompous, but Tonty can hardly be blamed for taking advantage of a moment of revenge. Interestingly, in Tonty's phraseology, Illinois is changed to Louisiana. It does appear that Tonty was trying to get in step with the wording of La Salle's commission, and trying to establish some distance between the administrative structures in Canada and those that he expected La Salle to build at the mouth of the Mississippi.

During the same year, the King finally dismissed La Barre from his post of governor and lieutenant general, replacing him with a colonel of cavalry: Jacques René de Bressay, Knight, *Marquis* de Denonville, *Seigneur* d'Avesnes.

The final blow to La Barre's career was probably a *mémoire* that the Jesuits had forwarded to Minister Seignelay (Colbert's son). In this mémoire the Jesuits offered to take responsibility for the exploration of the land immediately adjacent to the Misissippi River, and determine its navigability all the way to the Gulf of Mexico, even to make use of Tonty, "who is in charge of Fort Saint Louis." It showed the king that La Barre had not only endangered the colony with his own business schemes but had also become a tool of the Jesuit expansionist policies rather than remaining the appointed instrument of the Crown.[26]

Denonville took over New France armed with strong, clear orders from the king: "the principal object he ought to have in view is the re-establishment of the tranquility of the colony by means of a firm and lasting peace; but in order that this peace may be lasting he must humble the pride of the Iroquois, give assistance to the Illinois and the other Indian allies whom the Sieur de la Barre has abandoned."[27]

Tonty was unaware of all these events until the fall of 1684, when, still without news of La Salle, he decided to return to Montreal. Upon his arrival at Michilimackinac, he learned of the dismissal and replacement of La Barre, and found a letter from Governor Denonville informing him of La Salle's landing in the Gulf of Mexico and his rumored difficulties. Denonville also asked Tonty to make preparations for a campaign against the Iroquois. Instead Tonty decided to postpone these preparations and to put together a support expedition for La Salle, which he would take down the Mississippi route.

Tonty found a fast-freezing Lake Michigan while making his way back to Illinois. He and his escort had to abandon their canoe and walk the last 240 miles to the Chicago portage where they stopped at Fort Chicago. Wrote Tonty: "I arrived at the Fort of Chicago where M. de la Durantaye commanded and from there [went] to the Fort Saint Louis where I arrived during mid-January 1685."[28]

Tonty would now emerge as the new leader in the foremost western marches of New France, an officer who would slowly come into his own as French Illinois began to take shape.

NOTES

1. *Lettre de La Salle à M. de la Barre, Gouverneur et Lieutenant-general pour le Roi en Canada, du fort Saint-Louis, le 2 Avril dernier, 1683*, in Pierre Margry, *Découvertes et Etablissements.*, vol. 2, 312-317; trans. in Francis Parkman, *France and England in North America*, Part 44, *The Old Regime in Canada*, Boston, 1884, 299, FN. 1.

2. *Seconde lettre de La Salle à la Barre, Portage de Chicagou, 4 juin 1683*, trans. in Parkman, *France and England*, 301, FN 1.

3. *La Barre au Ministre, 14 novembre 1682; 30 avril 1683; 4 novembre 1683*, in Margry, vol. 2, 329-36.

4. *Mémoire pour rendre compte à Monseigneur de Seingnelay de l'estat ou le sieur de La Salle à laissé le fort de Frontenac pendant le temps de sa découverte*, in Margry, III, 25; trans. in Parkman, II, 304, footnote 1.

5. *Mémoire pour rendre compte.*, Margry, III, 35.

6. *Relation de Henry de Tonty*, in Margry, I, 613. The *Chevalier* Louis Henry de Beaugis also spelled "Baugy," seigneur de Villevion, and Villevalier, belonged to an ancient and prestigious noble family of Berry. The *Baugy Papers*, published first by Ernest Serrigny under the title: *Journal d'une expédition contre les Iroquois en 1687, rédigé par le Chevalier de Baugy*, Ernest Leroux, Paris, 1883; this work was ranslated into English by Nathaniel S. Olds as *Journal of Chevalier de Baugy*, Publication Fund Series, IX. The Rochester Historical Society, New York, 1931. The Baugy papers were kept by the descendants of the Baugy family when they were first read by Professor Serrigny. The Chevalier de Baugy served as aide-de-camp to Governor Denonville during the Iroquois campaign. He spent four years in New France before returning to his h ome in 1689. He rceived before leaving an Honorable discharge on November 1, granted by Governor Frontenac; the discharge read: ". . . We permit the Sieur de Baugis, Captain commanding a detachment of the marines consisting of seven reorganized companies, to return to France, accompanied by one Dupayrous, his valet, in whatsoever ship may seem convenient to him. . . ."Appointed Captain-Major in 1696, he retired in Paris where he died on February 19, 1720.

7. "The Jesuit fathers had said several things to stop La Salle's enterprise and had even wanted to detach several Indian nations which had entrusted themselves to M. de la Salle. They even went to the extend of being willing to destroy Fort Saint Louis by building a fort in Chicago where they had attracted a part of the Indians since they could not capture the first." *Relation, Henri Joutel*, in Margry, III, 500; trans. this author.

8. *Relation de la descouverte que Mr. de La Salle à faite de la rivière de Mississippi en 1682, et de son retour jusqu'a Québec*, by Nicolas de la Salle, in Margry, I, 540-570. Nicolas de la Salle was not related to the explorer. We will find him as a commissioner in Louisiana, from 1701 to 1709. His father was a high official of the navy.

9. Parkman, 310-11.

10. "The Chevalier de Tonty in an engagement in Messina, received a sabre-stroke on the fist and was taken prisoner. He, himself, cut off the hand with a knife without waiting for a surgeon to perform the operation. . . . The Indians greatly feared it; they called him Iron-Arm," Bacqueville de la Potherie, 1722, translated and quoted by Frank Severance in *An Old Frontier of France, The Niagara and adjacent lakes under French control*, New York, 1917, I, 77.

11. See Edmund Robert Murphy, *Henry de Tonty, Fur trader of the Mississippi*, Institut Francais de Washington, Hopkins Press, Baltimore, 1941. Little of any consequence has been written on Tonty; what is known about him and his career emerges from the various *Relations* penned by himself and contemporaries who participated in La Salle's expeditions. One of France's eighteenth century historians, Bacqueville de la Potherie, mentioned him in a book published in 1724. An article of little value was published in the *Parkman Club Papers*, by Henry E. Legler,

"Chevalier Henry de Tonty," Milwaukee, 1896, 37-57. Some of the same information can also be found in a book by Tonty's enthusiastic apologist:, Frank H.
Severance, *An Old Frontier of France,* V.

12.   Olivier Morel, *Sieur* de la Durantaye, (1641-1727), ensign in 1662, was
commissioned captain in 1665 in the regiment of Carignan-Salières the year of his
dispatch to Canada.   From 1683 to 1690, he commanded the Ottawa country.   In
1684, he was sent to Saint Louis des Illinois to help Beaugis carry out the Governor
La Barre's orders.   In 1687 he campaigned against the Iroquois under Governor
Denonville.   From 1690 on, although retaining his military ranks, he devoted the
essential of his attention to his *seigneuries;* although he had amassed very large
land holdings, he returned to France in 1699 and was awarded an annual pension
of 600 livres.   In March 1703, he was appointed to the Sovereign Council.   *Jesuit
Relations,* 63:271, 303; *Transactions,* Royal Society of Canada, 1893, section I, 10-11,
20-21, 22-23; *Canadian Archives,* 1899, supplement, 26, 105, 352; *New York Colonial
Documents,* 9:300, 337-340, 346.13.

14.   Theodore Calvin Pease, *The French Foundations, 1680-1693,* XXIII, French
Series, Springfield, 1934, Vol. 1, 45.

15.   See *Relations d'un voyage dans le pays des Illinois par Mr. Beauvois,* in Margry,
II, 339-44; see also *Extrait du Mémoire Insructif de l'état des affaires de la Nouvelle-
France depuis la campagne dernière, 1687, adressé au marquis de Seignelay,* in Margry,
II, 346-47.

16.   *Extrait du Mémoire adressé au Roy par Mr. de la Barre en réponse à la dépêche
du 30 Avril; le 13 Novembre 1684,* in Margry, II, 611.

17.   On April 23, 1684, the Jesuit missionary Father Nouvel had sent a letter to
Governor de la Barre, from the Mission Saint Francois Xavier, on the Baie des
Puans, to inform him of the Iroquois attack on Fort Saint Louis des Illinois; in
Margry, II, 334-35.

18.   "La Salle advanced several false statements, as when he claimed having left
at the Fort Saint Louis des Illinois enough beaver for the repayment of the said
amount of 4,000 livres, which has not been found to be true. We order the *chevalier*
de Baugy being presently at the Fort to seize all effects which belong to the said
La Salle up to the same value." *Baugy papers.*

19.   A *lettre de cachet,* literally a sealed letter, was a private communication of
the king applied to the affairs of state, signed by the king and countersigned by
the secretary of state.

20.   *Mémoire pour représenter à Monseigneur le Marquis de Seignelay la nécéssité
d'envoyer le sieur de la Forest en diligence pour la Nouvelle-France;* Margry, II, 370-73.
ANC BI:2 v-10 C., copy and translation in Theodore Pease, *The French Foundations;*
also in Parkman, *La Salle and the Discovery of the West,* II, 330.

21.   *Mémoire pour représenter . . .;* also in Baugy papers.

22.   See the *Relation écrite de Québec, le 14 novembre 1684 par Henry de Tonty,*
Margry, I, 573-614.

23.   *Ordre au Chevalier de Baugy de remettre à M. de Tonty le fort de Saint Louis
restitué à Cavelier de la Salle,* in *Baugy papers.*

24.   Copy of the exchange of command of Fort Saint Louis, in *Baugy papers.*

25.   Copy . . . *Baugy papers.*

26. *Mémoire sur la proposition à faire par les Rev. Pères jésuites pour la descouverte des environs de la rivière du Mississippi et pour voir si elle est navigable jusqu'à la mer* Margry, II, 611-12.

27. The King to Denonville, March 10, 1685, at Versailles (A.N.C. B11:6v 18-C), also in N.Y.C.D. French Foundations, 9:271 and in Pease, *French Foundations*, 68-78.

28. "... *j'arrivay au fort de Chicagou ou M. de la Durantaye commandait et de là, au fort de Saint-Louis ou j'arrivay à la my-janvier 1685.*" in *Dernières découvertes dans l'Amérique Septentrionale de M. de la Salle mises au jour par le M. le Chevalier de Tonty, gouverneur du Fort Saint-Louis aux Illinois*, Paris, 1697, in Margry, Vol. I, 23.

5

Tonty takes Charge

On February 13, 1685, Tonty and Jacques d'Autray, his lieutenant, left *Fort St. Louis des Illinois* with a group of volunteers: twenty-five Frenchmen and eleven Indians from the Illinois and Shawnee nations. Thirty men had been left behind to defend the fort. First on sleds on the frozen Illinois River, then in canoes, Tonty and his men carried 6,000 livres worth of gifts for the Indians, following a route that was familiar to most of them by now. Travelling quickly, they arrived at the mouth of the Mississippi on April 9th, but found no trace of La Salle. Tonty left a letter with an Indian chief in case somebody from the expedition arrived after them. Fourteen years later, this chief handed over the letter to Lemoyne d'Iberville, the next French officer he met.

On the way back to Illinois, ten of the Frenchmen asked Tonty for permission to settle along the Arkansas River. This land had been deeded to him by La Salle as a *Seigneurie*, and, according to feudal laws in effect in Canada, Tonty was obligated to open it to settlers. This system meant very little economically as Canadian feudality was an extensively revised, even gutted, version of the French one, essentially retaining only its social, military and ceremonial aspects. Nevertheless, Tonty selected six of these supplicants and duly granted them the right to settle on the "land of Arkansas" provided that they would immediately build a strong house and a chapel. The site later became the Fort of Arkansas, received a permanent French garrison and became an important stopover for French commerce moving up and down the Mississippi.

Tonty was back at *Saint Louis des Illinois* on June 24th. However rudimentary the fort's quarters were, they must have been the epitome of luxury for anyone who had just spent 120 nights in the swamps of the Mississippi Valley. Yet, almost immediately, Tonty was on his way to inform the governor of the details of the journey. Traveling with great speed, he arrived on July 24th in Montreal where he wrote his report and also sent a letter to a family friend in France, one of the rare personal documents which has survived.[1]

Tonty did not have the sanction of Governor Denonville when he chose to attempt a liaison with La Salle instead of preparing for the

Iroquois campaign. Indeed, he bypassed the governor, even going to the extent of writing directly to the minister, to explain that upon learning of La Salle's arrival on the coast of Florida and of his difficulties, he: "believed that in such circumstances it was of the service of the King and for the pleasure of your Highness that I gave him help."[2]

One year earlier, the governor also had written a letter to the minister, asking for clarification on the nature of his authority over La Salle and his men: "I have been advised that Monsieur de la Salle claimed that the commander of his fort in Illinois was not under my orders. I beg you to let me know the King's intentions in this matter."[3]

The governor was cautious in his wording, knowing the support that La Salle had at the Court. Uncertain about the terms of La Salle's commission, he added: "In the meantime, I will manage things so as not to commit myself in any way.... Nevertheless, should you decide in my favor or not, it is desirable in the present circumstances that you inform the Sieur de Tonty it is the King's intentions that he has the Illinois marching and that he places himself at their head under my orders."[4]

In the opinion of an eminent nineteenth century French Canadian historian, Benjamin Sulte, if La Salle had been successful, he would have asked for the right to be appointed governor for Louisiana, including Illinois, thereby becoming an officer on equal footing with the governor of New France,[5] an ambition which Denonville must have known. The continuous danger that the Iroquois presented to Canada was a good argument to support his wish for control of Illinois' commanders. The minister agreed and sent a letter to Tonty on May 31, 1686, stating that the: "King was surprised ... he instructs me to inform you that it is his intention that you accept and execute without evasion all orders which you may receive from him [the governor] ... and also that you march with the Sieur de la Forest at the head of the Indians which obey you, whenever he may order."[6]

The minister's words sounded harsh and impatient, but Tonty had already left by the time this letter reached *St. Louis des Illinois*. Denonville had sent a letter to La Forest—in command in Tonty's absence—urging him to make the preparations: "You are sufficiently aware of the importance of engaging your people of the Illinois to put themselves in condition to march when the time comes; you ought to put yourself in condition to march at their head when the Reverend Father tells you...."[7]

Father Jean Enjalran, the missionary referred to by Denonville, was a Jesuit attached to the Ottawa nation, French allies in this campaign.

Father Enjalran maintained the liaison with Michilimackinac and would play an important role in France's control in the eastern part of the Great Lakes.

The letter was long and detailed. It was meant to encourage, to let La Forest know that he would receive support: in early spring 1687, Du Luth was to move with fifty men to the strait between Lakes Erie and Huron and wait for the Illinois. The Illinois were to receive muskets that the governor would ship to Michilimackinac as soon as they arrived from France. These muskets, incidentally, never reached the Illinois, although the request had been personally approved by Louis XIV. They were, instead, distributed to the Canadian militia.[8] The letter shows a mixture of frustration, concern, and hope that marked Denonville's actions during his tenure as Governor: "If Tonti is able to march at their head [the Illinois], as he is known to them, it cannot but have a good effect, and, in the event that the poor man has perished on his journey, it is for you to find the man most capable of conducting this affair. . . . "

The whole episode is an interesting commentary on the cherished, but false, popular notion of French royal absolutism. In their correspondence with North America, the King and ministers asked, wished, expected, instructed, but rarely ordered something be done. And often they were not obeyed as promptly or as faithfully as one might expect. Limited by a slow and difficult system of communications, they had to rely on "the man on the spot." To be carried out, the will of the King of France had to be shared. Each civil or military officer, regardless of how lowly his position, strongly felt that he embodied the will of the state. Reading a proclamation to a handful of *habitans*, signing a treaty with an Indian band or taking possession of some wilderness, took on a religious solemnity in New France. Within such a structure many power plays could and did take place, expressed in their final form in long reports and memoirs addressed to Versailles. However, this Versailles cared little for those who failed and Denonville did not intend to be among them. To insure his sucess he had to keep the Iroquois out of French lands and the French inside them, both tasks equally difficult.

They are a number of our French, among the Ottawa who claim to have orders from Monsieur de la Barre to go to the Mississippi. . . . I know that it is not your intention to permit so many of our French to roam and I will do my best to have them return. . . . I have been told that Monsieur de Tonty does not desire to permit our French to trade among the Illinois. If the King has granted the country to Monsieur de la Salle exclusively it would be well that you be so good as to inform me in order that I may conform to His Majesty's orders.[9]

The constant pressure brought about by the Iroquois threat reached the farthest limits of the French establishment in North America. After Tonty returned from his fruitless search for La Salle and from his visit to the governor with his campaign orders, he threw himself into preparations that took the better part of winter. These preparations consisted of what we would call the "morale build-up" of the Indian allies, mainly the Illinois and the Miami, since the Shawnee hardly needed encouragement.

On April 17, 1687, Tonty left Fort St. Louis with only sixteen soldiers and two officers, Lieutenant Jacques d'Autray and Ensign Pierre De Liette, his nephew. Tonty had entrusted the fort to the two other officers who completed his staff: Mr. de Bellefontaine, and Mr. de Boisrondet, the latter entrusted with the important task of supervising the warehouse. Between them they disposed a small but cohesive force of twenty soldiers to see to the safety of people and goods. On the first night, Tonty set his camp only one mile from the fort to wait for the Indian volunteers. During that night and the next day, fifty Shawnee joined, then eighty Miami arrived led by their chief, Michitonka. By the third day, 149 Illinois and several French voyageurs completed the expeditionary force. Although the total was far below the 700 warriors Tonty had expected to gather— a rumored Sioux attack had retained most of the Illinois braves close to their camps—it was nonetheless an impressive number.[10] On May 19th, after a 400-mile march northeast overland, the Illinois contingent and Tonty caught up with the rest of the French troops at Fort Detroit.

We must now leave Tonty and New France to find out what happened to La Salle.

On July 24, 1684, when La Salle sailed from La Rochelle, France's main naval base on the Atlantic coast, he headed an expedition of one hundred soldiers; thirty volunteers who came from all walks of life, and five Recollect priests, including his own brother, Father Cavelier de La Salle. The naval force carrying the expedition was modest although sufficient for the task ahead: the *Joly*, a man-of-war of thirty-six guns, accompanied by two smaller vessels. The voyage from France to the West Indies and then to the Gulf of Mexico was fraught with a succession of problems made much more acute by the conflict between La Salle and the naval commander, Mr. de Beaujeu. From the start, Beaujeu had been at odds with La Salle; the division of command and responsibility being a source of conflict. As they came closer to their expected goal, the mouth of the Mississippi River, the conflict intensified. Beaujeu strongly disagreed on the actual location of the mouth of the river; La Salle's opinion was based on little actual knowledge. As the days went by, the whole affair was increasingly acquiring the characteristics of a "quixotic daring" rather than a well-directed and organized operation.[11] After courting disaster almost continuously, the expedition finally landed in March 1685, on specific orders from La Salle. Beaujeu would be proven correct: La Salle had led his men to the shores of Texas, having missed the mouth of the Mississippi by 400 miles.

What followed has been well reported by several participants who managed to survive the ordeal.[12] La Salle, and his soldiers and colonists who were quickly becoming dispirited, tried at first to set up a foothold on the eastern shore of the Matagorda Bay, which he had mistaken for one of the branches of the Mississippi. They built a fort by the ocean and, naturally, named it Fort St. Louis. After two years of struggle against hostile Indians, rattlesnakes and low morale: "La Salle . . . embraced a resolution which could be the offspring only of a desperate necessity. He determined to make his way to the Mississippi and the Illinois [River] to Canada. . . . This attempt was beset with uncertainties and dangers. The Mississippi was first to be found."[13]

La Salle selected his brother, Father Cavelier, a young cadet named Moranget, another friar, Father Anastase Douay,[14] and twenty more men to constitute the party that he sent to reach Illinois while he remained at the fort with the survivors.

A few days later Cavelier returned: he had lost his way, twelve men, and, worse, all hope. This time La Salle decided that he himself would lead the party to find help. On January 7, 1687, while twenty men remained behind to protect the women and children, he led a small group in a northerly direction.[15] This would be his last command. On March 19, at the south branch of the Trinity River, forty-three years old Robert Cavelier de la Salle, *seigneur* of Fort Frontenac, was shot in ambush by the surgeon of the expedition.[16] Several other members of the party were also killed by the small group of mutineers who sided with the surgeon. The remaining loyal members of the expedition were kept in semi-captivity for two months in a village of Cenis Indians at the hands of the plotters, then finally set free.

The pitiful little group resumed its travel to Illinois. Fortunately, it

Globe gore showing the Great Lakes and the Mississippi Valley as they were known in 1688. Vincenzo Coronelli. Gore from the Globe of 1688, Venice. (The Newberry Library)

included an old soldier, Henri Joutel, who was an experienced and capable man. Joutel would later write his memoirs, a precious tool for the history of these events. Father Cavelier, Father Douay, two young boys, Moranget and another cadet also named La Salle (but not related to the explorer), a repentant plotter named Tessler, and Barthélémy, a young man, constituted the whole group. With six horses and two Indian guides, they proceeded on a northeastern course for two months before reaching the confluence of the Arkansas and Mississippi rivers. Then suddenly, the worst of their tribulations was over: on July 24th:

> beneath the forests of the farther shore they saw the lodges of a large Indian town; and here, as they gazed across the broad current, they presently described an object which nerved their spent limbs and thrilled their homesick hearts with joy. It was a tall, wooden cross and near it was a small house, built evidently by Christian hands. . . . Two men, in European dress, issued from the door of the house and fired guns to salute the excited travellers who, on their part, replied with a volley. Canoes put out from the farthest shore and ferried them to the town where they were welcomed by Couture and Delaunay, two followers of Henry de Tonty.[17]

These two were the only men who had remained from the original six whom Tonty had authorized to settle in Arkansas; the others, having had a change of heart, had returned to Illinois.

On July 27th, Father Cavelier and his travelling companions, with the exception of the young Barthélémy who had decided to remain with Couture and Delaunay, embarked on canoes and, escorted by a large group of friendly Indians, two days later: "entered on the river Colbert or Mississippi which we had hoped to reach."[18] On August 19th, they were at the mouth of the Wabash River; on September 1st, they passed the Piasa paintings and, on the 3rd, entered the Illinois River. They reached Peoria on September 11th, where they met with the first Illinois Indians, and arrived after three days in view of *Fort St. Louis des Illinois*. To them, it was Versailles and Jerusalem rolled into one.

Three years had elapsed between La Salle's sailing from France with a small flotilla carrying soldiers, artisans and their families, and the arrival in Illinois of this small band of stragglers. Thousands of livres had been wasted, three vessels of the King's navy wrecked,[19] dozens of lives lost, but, worst of all, a great dream seemed to have disappeared like snow on fire.

Before they reached Illinois, Father Cavelier had convinced Joutel and the rest of their party to keep secret the death of his brother, even from Tonty. They would pretend that La Salle had escorted them part of the way and would try to evade further questioning. The rationale for this subterfuge was that the King should be informed first of the disaster that ended an enterprise he had personally approved. Subsequent behavior of Father Cavelier tends to support a different motive. One of La Salle's historians claimed that he was: "fearing lest he and his party would lose the advantage they might derive from his character as representative of his brother."[20]

On his return to France, Father Cavelier was accused of having hidden the news of his brother's assassination in order to insure material support—mainly from Illinois—along the way on their return. Hiding the truth during the first hours of the effusive welcome by the French and Illinois at fort and village was made easier by Tonty's absence, (he was still campaigning against the Iroquois). Boisrondet and Bellefontaine expected the weary travelers to remain with them until Tonty's return, but Father Cavelier insisted that they would stay only a few days before continuing their journey westward; Father Cavelier immediately went to pray in the chapel, while outside much powder was spent in a joyous musketry. After singing *Te Deum*, both Father Cavelier and Joutel rendered visit to Father Allouez, sick in bed in his quarters. Father Allouez inquired with much interest—or, at least, so it seemed to Father Cavelier and Joutel—about La Salle's expedition in Texas. Joutel observed that the Jesuit missionary, upon learning that La Salle would soon return to Illinois, was "troubled."[21] A few days later Father Allouez left Fort St. Louis, reportedly concerned by the prospect of coming face to face with La Salle.

On September 17th, Father Cavelier, Joutel, their companions, plus three French volunteers from the fort, embarked in a large canoe bought from Boisrondet. On the 25th, they were at Chi-ca-gou, noting: "which, as per what we have been able to learn, has taken this name from the great quantity of garlic which grows in this area, in the woods."[22]

The weather had already turned for the worse. With the exception of the volunteer escort of *voyageurs*, none among them was able to handle the canoe well on the rough, short waves of Lake Michigan. After they managed to progress approximately thirty miles in eight days food became scarce and everybody, all but Joutel, concerned with the real prospect of starving to death, favored a return to Fort St. Louis before the first

Shawnee Indian. Taken from Victor Collot, *Voyage dans l'Amérique du Nord*, Paris, 1826. (The Newberry Library)

snow. Majority opinion prevailed: on October 7th, to the great surprise of the occupants of Fort St. Louis, Father Cavelier, Father Membré, Joutel, and their men, were once more at the gate. Room was made; Father Cavelier was given private lodgings while Henri Joutel, Father Douay and the three other Frenchmen were housed by M. de Boisrondet in the warehouse.

On October 27th, Tonty and his war party also arrived. For them, Father Cavelier repeated his sanitized version of the disastrous events of Texas, a version that Tonty accepted without question. The general excitement which met the return of the Illinois contingent from the Iroquois campaign helped distract attention from La Salle's fate, and probably helped Father Cavelier to maintain the fiction that he had worked so hard to establish.

The Iroquois campaign had been only partially successful. Officially launched on May 23rd, it began by a demonstration of strength with, as we have seen, Denonville gathering all the available reserves in addition to the 800 regular troops which were the backbone of New France's defense. Denonville had lined up the Canadian militia, 1,000 men led by the local nobles; the Indian contingent from the St. Lawrence valley, another 300 men, and Tonty's western contingent joining with the soldiers commanded by La Durantaye, La Forest, Du Luth and his lieutenant, De Beauvais de Tilly; all in all, an additional 376 Frenchmen and 423 Indians.[23] Few among them were "green" soldiers. Many of the regular troopers and the volunteers had hardened their skills through encounters with Iroquois and by those long journeys across land and water which were the lot of the French of New France. Among them were Claude Grisolon de la Tourette, Du Luth's brother, who came alone in a canoe all the way from Michilimackinac, and the notorious Baron de La Hontan.

The western reinforcements linked up with the bulk of the French troops at a place called *Le grand marais*, north of Niagara, where the French had a fort. Continuously harassed by bold Iroquois scouts, the French and their allies—a total of 2,132 officers and men—proceeded to open a temporary camp. They burned a few Seneca villages and a few cornfields, and captured some prisoners; but by and large, two weeks later, the operation was over and the Iroquois force remained intact. As if to prove it, the Iroquois ambushed a column returning from Iroquois-held territory. The ambush failed mainly because of the personal courage shown by Tonty who happened to march on avant-garde with his Illinois company. Tonty and his men rushed the Iroquois in a furious counterattack, putting them to flight at the cost of only one officer and seven other men killed.[24] The most tangible result of this rather large military action (aside from an impressive display of force which had a certain psychological effect on the Iroquois), was the fortuitous capture by La Durantaye of two English convoys of traders and soldiers near Niagara. These convoys, coming all the way from Albany in the colony of New York—fifty-eight and thirty men respectively—and having the incredible audacity to navigate in what was a fairly well-traveled French territory, were a good illustration of the constant pressure the British colonies exercised on New France. Loaded wih English-made goods and brandy, they were on their way to Michilimackinac guided by a French *voyageur* who had deserted a few years before, and led by an officer, Major Patrick McGregor. The *voyageur*, incidentally, was shot on Denonville's specific orders.[25]

Meanwhile in France, re-emphasizing the communication delays between mother-country and colonial possessions, the minister, Seigne-lay, was still without any news on the whereabouts of La Salle, and had written to Governor Denonville for information. The governor had talked to Tonty during the Niagara expedition, and wrote back on August 25, 1687, with the meager news he had obtained.

Tonty had returned to Illinois from Niagara, marching part of the way with Du Luth and Juchereau, La Durantaye's lieutenant, and their men. The disputes generated by former Governor La Barre were forgotten. That Du Luth and Tonty were cousins might have helped the situation but Tonty's generous nature, quite different in this respect from La Salle's, was mostly responsible for the change of atmosphere. Even Father Allouez returned to Fort St. Louis. Tonty had invited Juchereau to St. Louis for some winter hunting, since game was becoming rare in the Michilimackinac area. He arrived on December 20th, with good and bad news. The good news was that at the Chicago portage he had overtaken the men sent from Illinois to Montreal for re-supplying. They were on their way back with their three canoes loaded with powder and musket balls when they were delayed by a completely frozen Illinois River. Tonty hired a Shawnee chief and thirty of his men for a handsome price to retrieve the load and bring it overland to the fort (Tonty made no secret of the fact that he trusted Shawnee honesty over the Illinois). The bad news was that another convoy of French canoes had been attacked by a large party of Iroquois at Cataracouy, near Fort Frontenac. These were French traders who had been careless and paid dearly for it with the loss of twelve of their number. The incident showed that the effects of Denonville's military demonstration were shortlived. For all intents and purposes, regular communication between the Great Lakes forts and Montreal was now once again cut. Only military escorted convoys would be allowed until the situation changed.

Everybody settled down to spend winter at Fort St. Louis in the best fashion possible. Henri Joutel used his leisure time to observe and write. Thanks to his initiative, as well as to the fortuitous circumstances which kept him and the rest of Father Cavelier's party in Illinois, we have an insight into the life of one of France's farthest outposts in seventeenth century North America.

Looking at the surface of Starved Rock today, overgrown with vege-tation and devoid of any trace of construction, it is hard to imagine that it was at one time the site of Fort St. Louis, a miniature establishment of the French crown, with flags, uniforms, fife and drum calls, and the rest

Aerial photograph of Starved Rock in April of 1987. (Photograph by David Buisseret)

of the apparatus. Officers and guests dined together and early; we can only regret that their table conversations were not recorded.

Meat was plentiful around the fort. Father Cavelier mentioned in his report that he had hired two Indian hunters who brought in all the game that was needed. The game was fat and good that winter due to an abundance of nuts and fruit. The country was rich-looking, and Joutel noted there were lots of apple trees, and that the apples when cooked made excellent applesauce. There were vineyards, some hemp, all sorts of berries, hazelnuts, lots of corn, oak trees, and walnut trees, and the dirt was reported to be black with a good six-foot fertile layer. There were coal mines in the vicinity of the fort, important to the smith who had to repair tools and weapons. There were quarries, lead mines and all sorts of natural wealth, described by Joutel:

The commodity of wood and coal is not a small advantage; the trees are good for the building of boats which would go up and down in all these rivers supporting a very considerable commerce and the traffic of furs and skins which are found here in great abundance. The only missing element needed to extract from this country great riches is people who could live here much better than in many other lands where enormous expense is made for little return.[26]

Wheat, a very important commodity for French people whose diet included—and still does—much bread, was beginning to take. In that year eight *minots*, each *minot* being a little more than a bushel, were harvested, and thanks to a small iron grinder, bread was made in Illinois for the first time. The winter of 1687-1688 was harsh. The river remained frozen solid for five weeks. Nevertheless, neither the French nor the Indians were immobilized. Joutel wrote: "We have little hooks to walk better on ice," [27] and there were sleds as well. The fort had an imposing appearance; however, it lacked a direct, protected access to water. For this reason, "Mr. de Tonty had four big beams placed [on the edge of the cliff] in order to draw water in case of attack." [28] Probably a system of pulleys and buckets was engineered to circumvent the lack of a cistern at the top.

A palisade linking the outside walls of the houses built on the edge of the drop over the Illinois River completed the fortification. The houses were built of beams and stakes and were nothing more than comfortable large-size cabins. A few more houses and the cabins of several Indian families, along with the warehouse, the chapel, and the commandant's lodgment, were built inside the enclosure. The total surface of the fort was a little more than two acres. Immediately outside were more Indian cabins, although the bulk of the Indian population was installed across the river. There were perhaps as many as ten thousand Indians camping on both banks of the Illinois River: Kaskaskia and Peoria, living in Illinois Town, and Miami who lived with the Shawnee, four miles upriver from the fort, "in a strong position which could easily become the site of a powerful town, being on a hill with steep slopes, almost surrounded by the river like Fort Saint Louis." [29]

Attending mass was an important part of the daily routine. Father Allouez and Father Cavelier said Mass alternately in the chapel. The liturgy suffered from lack of an adequate supply of wine, but a vineyard had been planted. Every day, Indian women brought gifts to the fort: watermelons, pumpkins, nuts, firewood. Joutel noted that whether in the villages or at the fort they did all the work.

The picture of life in Fort St. Louis which evolves from Joutel's descriptions is of a comfortable settlement, run with a mixture of conventional and ceremonial daily routine. This was a King's garrison, with a certain relaxed atmosphere that the French call *bonhommie* or "good-nature," not unlike the style to be found again and again in most of the French military outposts that mushroomed in Africa and in the Orient during the nineteenth century.

On March 17, 1688, Father Cavelier and his party bid farewell to *Fort Saint Louis des Illinois* for the second and last time. They were not traveling alone; with them was Juchereau returning to his command at Michilimackinac, and Boisrondet, returning to France. Four Indians—two Illinois and two Shawnee—were also going to France, sponsored by Father Cavelier who thought that they might be useful if an expedition were sent to rescue the French left behind in Texas. (Father Cavelier could not know of their unhappy fate.) Years later one of these Indians was reported to be living near Versailles. Henri Joutel, who was short of funds (he was owed large sums of money by La Salle) had engaged himself as one of Mr. de Boisrondet's crew, as few *voyageurs* were available for this journey. Father Cavelier did not have financial woes: he carried a letter of credit from his dead brother that he had cashed at the fort for 4,000 livres worth of beaver and other skins and, of course, he had his own "four good rowers." [30]

On March 29th, they arrived at the Chicago portage where they had to remain for more than a week as the bad weather was unsuitable for navigation. As others before him, Joutel saw the importance of Chicago as the connecting point between Canada and the Mississippi Valley: "It would be easy to connect the two rivers because the land is quite flat... However, a large settlement would be necessary to support such an expense." [31]

Hunting was particularly poor at the portage and they had to subsist on *sagamité* (boiled corn), much improved, however, by the syrup provided by the abundant maple trees which grew in the area. When they resumed their navigation along the western shore of the lake, for their subsistance they had to steal freshly killed prey from the wolves roving the beach. [32] They also bought corn at inflated prices from the Potawatomi they occasionally saw on the bank. After several weeks of travel, they finally reached Michilimackinac where the prospects were not bright either. As mentioned before, not a single canoe had come west from Montreal since the beginning of winter because of the Iroquois. Father Cavelier and his party maintained their silence about the real fate of La Salle, although they did not find there the same credulity. Baron de La

Hontan, then an officer, later better known as an adventurer, wrote: "Mr. Cavelier arrived here on May 6th, being accompanied with . . . a sort of party-coloured Retinue. These Frenchmen . . . give out, that they are sent . . . with some Dispatches from Mr. de la Salle to the King: But we suspect that he is dead, because he did not return wih them. "[33]

Father Cavelier could not find any French, Ottawa, or Huron to volunteer as escort to Montreal. At last, on June 14th, four canoes under military command arrived, but before they could return to Montreal, two were bound for the Baye des Puants and two for Sault Sainte-Marie. Cavelier and his party had no choice but to join the last two and add an additional voyage to their already long trip. Finally, in Montreal on July 17th, they met Governor Denonville with whom they still maintained the deception about La Salle's fate. In Quebec on the 29th, they boarded a vessel which had completed its cod fishing season off the coast of Canada. They landed in La Rochelle on October 15th; it had taken them six months to get from Fort St. Louis to France. By then, Tonty had learned the truth about La Salle's fate.

Back on September 7th, Jean Couture had arrived from Fort Arkansas and told Tonty all the details of La Salle's death. At the same time Tonty had received an advance notice from Governor Denonville that a second military campaign was being planned. Tonty lost no time in writing back that he was first going to attempt to rescue the French who might have survived on the Texas coast. Once more, on December 3rd, he left for the lower Mississippi with only five Frenchmen and three Indians. They arrived in March 1689, on the Red River, where conditions were so difficult that only two Frenchmen and one Indian continued the trip with him. They reached a point 250 miles from La Salle's fort on the Gulf of Mexico, St. Louis of Texas, but could not progress any further because of heavy rains which had flooded the area for hundreds of miles. The painful, slow return, took from May to July:

> We crossed fifty leagues of flooded country; the water, where it was the least deep, reached half-way up the legs; and in all this area we found only one little island of dry land where we killed a bear and dried its flesh. It would be difficult to give an idea of the troubles we had to get out of this miserable country where it rained night and day. . . . In short, I never suffered so much in my life as in this journey to the Mississippi which we reached on the eleventh of July.[34]

Tonty was back at *Fort St. Louis des Illinois* sometime in September. He had remained a tower of strength throughout the ordeal and now faced two alternatives: clinging to the impossible dream, there, in Illinois, or returning to Canada, even to France. Remaining in Illinois, he opted for La Salle's legacy although it consisted of little else but the crushing weight of an accumulated ten-year debt of a half-million livres to private creditors. It was, however, preferable to returning to France with neither income nor position. At this moment and in the face of these circumstances, the chances of survival of La Salle's claim to all the lands east of the Allegheny Mountains in the name of Louis XIV were limited.

There had been another change during Tonty's absence: Governor Denonville had been recalled following new setbacks at the hands of the Iroquois. The King had resolved to send back to Canada the only man who seemed able to face and overcome the problems which beset the French: the Marquis of Frontenac.

NOTES

1. *Procés-verbal du voyage de Henry de Tonty à l'embouchure de Mississippi à la recherche de M. de la Salle*, Tonty wrote on August to M. Cabart de Villermont, answering a letter from his father.

2. Tonty to Minister Seignelay, August 24, 1686, in Margry, 1, 553-562.

3. Denonville to Seignelay, November 13, 1685, ANC, C 11 A 7:88-89; also in Pease, 78-80.

4. Ibid.

5. Benjamin Sulte, *La Mort.*, 8.

6. From Versailles, Minister to Tonty, May 31, 1686, ANC, B 12:20 v C.

7. Denonville to La Forest, June 6, 1686, ANC, C11 A 8:57-57 v-C; also in Benjamin Sulte, *La mort de Cavelier de La Salle*, Société Royale du Canada, Deuxieme Serie, Section 1, Ottawa, 1898, 8-9.

8. ANAM, Col. C.A. 8:243; March 1687, ANC, B 13:16-34-C; also in NYCD, 9:322.

9. Ibid.

10. Charlevoix, *Histoire de la Nouvelle France*, I, 512-13.

11. Parkman, III, 341.

12. See *Henri Joutel, Journal historique*, in Margry, III.

13. Parkman, III, 381-82.

14. Father Anastase Douay would return to North America in 1699 with the Iberville expedition which first implemented a successful French presence at the mouth of the Mississippi. Father Douay left a narrative which is one of the major sources of information on La Salle's 1687 attempt to ascend the Mississippi.

15. Fort Saint Louis was destroyed and all its occupants killed by hostile Indians. A Spanish ground expedition led by Don Alonzo de Leon reached its location in 1689. See *Ensayo cronologico* published by J.G. Shea in *Discovery and Exploration of the Mississippi Valley,* 208, footnote.

16. Among the killers were Liotot, a surgeon, and Duhaut; both men had invested money in the expedition and were understandably bitter about its outcome. Also involved in the plot were a German buccaneer, Hiens, nicknamed "Gemme l'Anglais" or "English Jammes." Three separate narratives, all published, cover La Salle's last journey: Father Douay's, Cavelier de La Salle's and Joutel's. One of the reasons for La Salle's failure may have been that his unpublished, secret intentions were to go beyond the establishment of a permanent settlement in Louisiana; that he wanted in fact to reach Northern Mexico through Texas and establish a French claim to a region rumored rich in mines. This theory espoused by the nineteenth century historian John Shea—ed. Le Clerq, *Establishment of the Faith,* 202, footnote—because of the series of documents existing in the French Archives which would explain La Salle's apparent hesitations.

17. *Relation de Henri de Joutel,* integral version in Margry, III, 91-534; Parkman, III, 247-48.

18. *Relation de Henri Joutel,* in Margry, III, 457.

19. The *Saint-Francois,* the *Belle,* and the *Aimable.*

20. Parkman, III, 431.

21. Joutel, in Margry, III, 480; also in Shea, ed. Le Clerq, *First Establishment.,* II, 274.

22. . . .*qui suivant ce que l'on a put apprendre a pris ce nom de la quantite d'ail qui croit dans ce canton, dans les bois.* . . . Joutel, in Margry, III, 485; trans. by this author.

23. See *Baugy* papers; also the *Jesuit Relations,* 63:287, 371; Denonville's orders to DuLuth, Tonty, and La Durantaye in NYCD, 9:283-84, 309, 345, 365, 553, 562.

24. *Relations et Mémoires,* Joutel, in Margry, III; the fight is also mentioned in Baugy's papers but not described as an ambush. The July *Ordre de marche* written by Denonville is a good example of French colonial fighting style which can be found throughout the French colonial campaigns down to the 19th century, particularly in regard to the fire plan: "Do not open fire until being at close range; open fire only line by line; wounded must be carried back."

25. Letter of Callières de Chatauvillain, October 12, 1687, B.N. Clairambault, 1016:483-483-C; *Baugy* papers; NYCD, III, 287, 297, 486; *Relation.,* Joutel, in Margry, III, 89-534; Parkman, 151; Alvord, 94-95; Charlevoix, *Histoire.,* 2:352-353. The French deserter guiding the English convoys to Michilimackinac was named Marion.

26. *Relations de Henri Joutel,* in Margry, III, 492; this author translation.

27. Joutel, in Margry, III, 493.

28. Joutel, Margry, III, 493.

29. Joutel, Margry, III, 482.

30. *Journal de voyage du Sieur Cavelier* . . . *présenté à Monseigneur de Seignelay,* published by Jean Delanglez in *The Journal of Jean Cavelier,* Chicago, 1938.

31. Joutel, Margry, III.

32. Joutel described how the wolf packs would corner deer in the water of the lake until fatigue made them easy prey; in Margry, II, 511.

33. A.L. de L'Om Darce, Baron de La Hontan, *Nouveaux Voyages de M. le Baron de La Hontan dans l'Amérique Septentrionale*, La Haye, 1703, 121. Also, *Mémoires de l'Amérique Septentrionale, ou la suite des Voyages de M. le Baron de La Hontan*, La Haye, 1703. On La Hontan, see a bibliographical note included by Justin Winsor, ed., in *Narrative and Critical History of America*, IV, New York, 1884.

34. *Mémoire envoyé en 1693 sur la découverte du Mississippi et des nations voisines par le Sieur de la Salle en 1678 et, depuis sa mort, par le Sieur de Tonty*, in Margry, III, 35-36; trans. in B.F. French, *Historical Collections of Louisiana*, Wiley & Putnam, New York, 1856, 52-78; also in Parkman, 55. The narrative of Tonty's life ends with this entry; it was sent to Paris in 1693. Four years later, the same narrative was used as the basis of a spurious work by an anonymous writer, work which was later repudiated by Tonty.

6

A Lonely Command

F rontenac landed in Quebec on October the 14th, 1689. He was seventy years old, an advanced age even to attain in the eighteenth century, let alone to carry the responsibilities of government. The situation he found was quite serious, almost desperate. Danger was mounting from all directions. From Michilimackinac, a message sent by La Durantaye informed the governor that the Indians there were convinced the French were thinking about seeking alliance with the Iroquois. This was bad news: communications between Michilimackinac and the rest of Canada were already extremely difficult since Denonville had made the mistake of removing the garrison at Niagara, dismantling Fort Frontenac and pulling the troops back to Montreal. But Frontenac immediately showed the brio which had earned him the nickname of Montio, the "Beautiful," from the Indians.

In the spring of 1690, he sent Captain Louis de Louvigny [1] to Michilimackinac with a large detachment to replace La Durantaye. Louvigny brought a message from Frontenac to all the Indian nations of the area who were gathered especially by Nicolas Perrot, the legendary *coureur des bois*. Perrot also acted as the interpreter for the governor's message: "I am astonished to learn that you have forgotten the protection that I always gave you. . . . I am strong enough to kill the English, destroy the Iroquois and whip you, if you fail in your duty to me." [2]

The West taken care of, Frontenac followed words with action and sent a powerful force which penetrated deeply into what is now the state of New York, and burned the town of Schenectady. His moves paid off almost immediately. The Indians' renewed confidence in the French ability to stand up to the English and their Iroquois allies manifested itself with the unscheduled arrival in Montreal of 110 canoes loaded with furs and manned by young warriors representing all the nations west of Michilimackinac. [3]

It was as if the clock had been turned back a few years when ideas were new, projects bold, and men ready to follow their dreams. But Frontenac's age and, perhaps, the lack of a leader like La Salle among the protagonists, made a great deal of difference. There were still several old hands around;

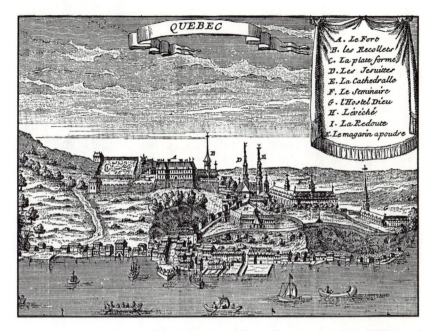

Quebec in 1722. Reproduced from *Narrative and Critical History of America*, Vol 4, Justin Winsor, ed., 1884. (The Newberry Library)

their visions, however, were now framed in down-to-earth boundaries. Tonty, the most prominent among them, was no longer interested in the building of empires, but rather in the revenue of his Illinois land. He and La Forest, who since July 27, 1688 had been Tonty's full partner for the Illinois concession, were wasting their talents. They were storekeepers wearing the king's uniform, a role forced upon them by lack of adequate resources. One of the last administrative acts by Denonville was the signing of a certificate for both Tonty and La Forest confirming that they had not received any money since 1687, when they were given their pay and then only for the year 1684![4] This neglect could have only harmful consequences for New France. Officers who had to maintain their standards without regular remuneration could hardly be reproached for their extra-curricular activities. Yet, the same Governor Denonville could not reconcile himself to the spectacle of officers openly involved in commercial transactions. A year before he had sent a lengthy report to the minister in which he complained about the perennial problem created by the constant flight of the young and adventurous toward the fur country.

In this report, he indirectly accused La Salle and Tonty of ill-advised decisions which encouraged this exodus. The expected answer from Versailles was not long in coming: "Regarding the [land] concessions around Fort Saint Louis given by the said Sieur de La Salle, since they have caused such a disorder as these which you indicate, His Majesty permits to revoke them as well as all the other concessions."[5]

The letter included a simple solution to the confusion created by the presence of too many *voyageurs*: no issuance of new trading licenses and a two-year duration of those allocated the previous season. Of course, these instructions required time before they could begin to be implemented, and were more often than not contradictory.

La Forest had gone to France to petition the king on his and Tonty's behalf for the transfer of La Salle's grant to them. Coupled with the return of Governor Frontenac, their request could have been the signal of the beginning of real development for Illinois. A partnership, although not without its problems, would allow for more ability to oversee trading, the conveying of the furs and their sale. Tonty's historian, Robert Murphy, claims that Frontenac was a silent partner in Illinois fur trade, as he was rumored to have been with La Salle.[6] Although we lack proof to substantiate the existence of such an arrangement with both Illinois commanders in succession, there is much evidence of Frontenac's support of Fort St. Louis over the vehement objections of intendant Champigny.[7] Silent partner or not, Frontenac's support should have been a guarantee of success.

On July 14, 1690, an *arrest du Conseil d'Etat du Roi* signed by the Minister Colbert made this success even more of a real possibility when he stated that:

> . . . the petition presented to His Majesty by Sieur de La Forest and Sieur Tonty, praying that it may please him to grant them the establishment erected by Sieur de La Salle at Fort St. Louis des Illinois which they have maintained at much expense and care since the latter's death; it is his Majesty's desire to confirm the said grant in order to give the peaceable and perpetual possession thereof to the above mentioned persons, their heirs and assignees. . .[8]

This ordinance effectively annulled the letter sent two years before in which Governor Denonville was told to put the lid on Tonty's and La Forest's activities. The news of the grant traveled slowly, reaching Tonty in September of the following year, at Michilimackinac, where he had gone on business. Pierre de Liette, his nephew, had been left in command of Fort St. Louis, ("De Liette" was the gallicized version of the patronym of Tonty's mother, Di Lietto). In his memoirs, De Liette described the circumstances of Tonty's departure from the Fort, another rare vignette of seventeenth century Illinois: "[Tonty] had assembled all the principal Illinois and told them that he was leaving me in his place and that in case any matter turned up regarding the service of the King and the well-being of the village, they had only to apply to me—he would approve whatever I might do." [9]

De Liette spent at least ten years in Illinois and we find him not only at Fort St. Louis, but also in command of the warehouse in Chicago, and later in Michilimackinac. In 1691, his capacity as acting commander of St. Louis was tested: some corn had been found cut near the fort, and two Iroquois scouts were subsequently captured; all indications pointing to a large raiding party nearby. Effectively, three hundred warriors were detected within one day's march. With only four Frenchmen including the Jesuit missionary, Father Gravier, and 250 Illinois, De Liette was still able to mount a convincing show of force. He had captured four more Iroquois by the time their band returned East. Illinois could expect better protection the following year: a letter from Tonty arrived in September with the news that La Salle's royal grant had been transferred and that he was returning to St. Louis with a large number of *engagés*. These were Canadians who had "engaged" themselves to work in Illinois for at least a year. Tonty also asked De Liette to: "sound out the Illinois regarding the abandonment of this village [Fort Saint Louis] . . . because firewood was so remote and because it was so difficult to get water up on the rock if they were attacked by the enemy." [10]

De Liette followed Tonty's instructions:

> I assembled the chiefs and, having learned that they had not changed their minds, I bade them to choose such places as suited them best. They chose the end of Lake Pimitoui [Peoria] which means "fat lake," so called because of the abundance of game there. This is where the Illinois are at present and where I was for seven years [1692-99]. Monsieur de Tonty arrived in the Winter and started the building of a large fort to which the savages might return in case of alarm. The following Spring Monsieur de la Forest arrived also with a considerable number of *engagés* and of soldiers who completed the work.[11]

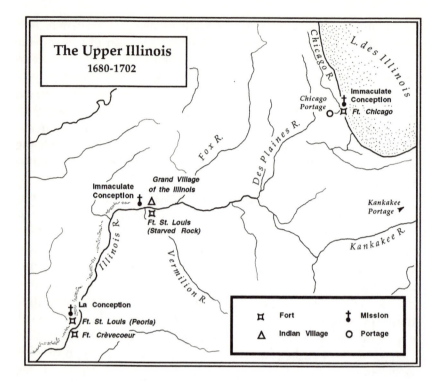

This was a return to an area close to the original site of French implantation, Fort Crèvecoeur. The change could have been very beneficial for the future of Illinois, as the country where the city of Peoria now stands was far more favorable to urban development than Fort St. Louis. For one, *Fort St. Louis de Pimitoui* sat at the point where the Illinois River begins to be ice-free all year around.[12] This was a wood and earth structure whose construction was facilitated by the availability of timber. The outside wall was made up of 1800 vertically planted pickets, or, as the French called them: *poteaux en terre.* It enclosed four large log houses, barracks and warehouses, plus a chapel and a huge cross. The development of settlements was a main concern in Versailles. At the same time the king was signing the *lettres patentes* extending to Tonty and La Forest the privileges previously held by La Salle, the minister was reminding the governor of New France that: "The King has awarded the post of Fort St. Louis of the Illinois to the Sieur de la Forest and to the Sieur de Tonty on condition that they develop it to the fullest extent and conform to the terms of the concession made in favor of the late Sieur de La Salle. . . . Do see that these orders be carried out." [13]

"Develop to the fullest extent," meant facilitating the settlements of *habitans* who would till the soil rather than run the rivers. This part of the agreement was difficult to implement and would be effective only in isolated circumstances—such as a man growing tired of paddling canoes for a living and deciding to take up sedentary life. While there is not a single record of anyone having applied for working the land, we have the records of a series of engagements from *voyageurs* who signed one-year and two-year contracts with either Tonty or La Forest. An ordinance enacted on May 2, 1681 and then still in force, limited the total number of *passeports*, the annual trading licenses granted to Canadians, to twenty-five a year. It must be kept in mind, however, that this allocation was not for Illinois alone and included the traders operating out of Michilimackinac. Since there were always more young men interested in adventure than twenty-five passports could accommodate—each passport was valid for a canoe with a crew of two or three men—it is easy to understand why it was nearly impossible for the administration of New France to prevent clandestine departures and the rising numbers of *coureurs de bois* plying their illicit trade west of Lakes Michigan and Superior. Tonty and La Forest were concerned with the illegal trade as well since it impinged upon their own enterprise. Their best defense was to maintain their trade business for which they pursued the recruitment of *voyageurs*. For 1690 alone, we have the records of the engagement of eleven men. In 1691, twelve men, an overseer and a surgeon signed or made their marks on engagement contracts with Tonty and La Forest. There are no records for 1692, and only six engagements recorded for 1693. [14] Even if incomplete, the figures show that during these three years Illinois received a substantial share of the legitimate fur trade. The terms of engagement were generally quite simple: the employer provided canoes, trade goods, food and other supplies, plus a salary payable in beaver skins. The salary for the men going to Illinois varied between 200-300 livres annually, in some cases going as high as 500, depending on experience. [15] The *voyageurs* agreed not to trade goods for themselves and to remain in Illinois either one or two years. Their ages varied only between the early twenties and late thirties, reflecting the physical demands of their profession. Governor Denonville had eased their burden somewhat in 1696, by enacting new regulations for the fur trade, making compulsory a crew of three men for each canoe. [16]

Neither Governor Frontenac's open protection nor the support of a network of bases (the warehouse in Chicago that De Liette commanded when not at Fort St. Louis, the king's warehouse in Michilimackinac commanded by Alphonse de Tonty, Henry's brother, and Fort Frontenac) would make it possible for Tonty and La Forest to achieve commercial success.[17] Frontenac had even allowed their trade activities to continue after the King had ordered its prohibition, an extraordinary advantage over the competition, but to no avail. Although we would need to know a good deal more about Tonty and La Forest's trading operation to understand its failure, we can nevertheless pinpoint its major flaws.

To begin with, Tonty's major responsibility was military service for the King. But his duty as military commander was in conflict with his ability to oversee trade, and equally interfered with the Illinois warriors' ability to trap the best furs at the most propitious periods of the year: since he had taken command of *Fort St. Louis des Illinois*, Tonty was almost always absent from the fort, often campaigning hundreds of miles away. As a case in point, in the last year of Denonville's government, Tonty was sent north, near the source of the Mississippi River, to fight hostile Sioux. He brought back eighty prisoners who were later burned at the stake by his Illinois warriors as per the brutal practice of Indian warfare of the time.[18] During these absences, the day-to-day business of the fort, his only source of revenue, had to be entrusted to assistants and good fortune. We must also add, however, that what we know of Tonty the soldier, and Tonty, the entrepreneur, leads us to believe that his business sense, although better than La Salle's, was his least effective quality. The Notarial Archives of Montreal contain a protest sworn by a Quebec merchant against La Salle for the nonpayment of a letter of exchange valued at 150 livres. It was served on La Forest while on his way to Versailles. It is a good illustration of Tonty's chaotic financial situation that La Forest was almost prevented from continuing his journey to Versailles to obtain a valuable grant, by a default that amounted to about half of a *voyageur's* yearly pay.[19]

Precisely during the period when Tonty and La Forest were struggling to survive economically, trade operations also suffered from the competition of British traders able to offer much more for good beaver skins than could merchants in Montreal and Quebec. For example, Indians who received four pounds of gunpowder for each beaver skin brought to Albany, needed four skins to receive the same quantity from Montreal. In Albany one skin could be traded for a variety of choices: four shirts; six pairs of stockings; six quarts of rum; one white blanket or one blanket of red cloth. With the exception of the rum—the French gave twelve quarts—two skins were needed in Montreal for any of the same items.[20]

As if these negative conditions were not sufficient obstacles to success, during this precise period the fur trade in Canada was experiencing a crisis brought on by an unsold surplus. France's fur market was overloaded (often with low-grade pelts) and, consequently, Quebec's warehouses were filled to capacity, with furs even rotting for lack of adequate storage. Voyageurs continued to gather pelts that the crown continued to buy knowing perfectly well that the market in Europe was completely saturated. Only the fact that the economy of New France was so interlocked with the fur trade prevented its elimination. With a conjuncture of economic factors so unfavorable, financial failure was the logical conclusion for Tonty's and La Forest's enterprise in Illinois.

For the two new *seigneurs* of Illinois signs of failure began to appear rather soon. On April 19, 1692, La Forest was forced to sell half of his concession to Michel Accault for 6,000 *livres*. The amount was to be paid in beaver skins, "which the aforesaid Accault shall give me at Chicago."[21] The contract was signed at the *Fort St. Louis des Illinois*, in Peoria. (This was the same Accault sent by La Salle to accompany Father Hennepin on the exploration of the Upper Mississippi; he had married Aramepinchone, daughter of Rouensa, the most powerful Illinois chief.)[22] On September 13, 1693, La Forest and Tonty, "acting for themselves and Sieur Accault," paid off "6,966 *livres*, 19 *sols*, 1 *denier*" for merchandise furnished by a thirty-eight year old fellow officer in the marine troops, Charles Juchereau de St. Denis, also actively involved in trade. At the time, Juchereau was also assuming the functions of lieutenant general for the district of Montreal.[23] This curious crisscross of professional, business and even blood ties here gets even more complicated: on the same day, Tonty and La Forest obligated themselves for an additional 695 *livres* for equipment and goods to Juchereau's fifteen year old bride. This young woman was the heiress to the estate of a merchant who had advanced 46,000 *livres* of merchandise to La Salle. There are indications that Tonty and La Forest's payment to Juchereau was made with funds advanced by Accault, clearly fast becoming the business power broker of Illinois. Still, on the same day—September 13th—Tonty signed a bond to La Forest for 3,892 *livres* for the payment of accounts due to Accault and Juchereau. The agreement stipulated that this amount was not to be included in another 5,440 *livres* that Tonty acknowledged owing La Forest.[24] And, again on

September 13th, Tonty petitioned the minister of the navy, the Count of Pontchartrain, for the command of a company:

> As he now finds himself without employment, he prays that in consider-
> ing his voyages and heavy expenses, and considering also that during his
> service of seven years as captain he has not received any pay, Your
> Highness will be pleased to obtain for him from His Majesty a company [in
> order] that he may continue his services in this country where he has not
> ceased to harass the Iroquois by enlisting the Illinois against them in His
> Majesty cause.[25]

To this petition, Governor Frontenac added:

> Nothing can be more true than the account given by the *Sieur* de Tonty in
> this petition and, should His Majesty reinstate the seven companies which
> have been disbanded in this country, there will be justice in granting one
> of them to him, or some other recompense for the services, that he had
> rendered and that he is now rendering by returning to *Fort St. Louis des
> Illinois.*[26]

All these transactions, concluded within a day, point to Tonty having given up on building a commercial empire and hoping to fall back essentially on income that his service to the King would provide. He would now continue to be involved in the fur trade only on a much smaller scale. At this point in his life, he was theoretically without resources since his was one of the seven companies of marine infantry which had been disbanded as the result of the reorganization of the French colonial army in North America. Because the royal treasury had not paid the officers serving in New France for several years, Tonty's financial loss as the result of this disbanding would seem purely academic. However, the unpaid monies and the merchants' advances for the service of the king were recorded. Officers and administrators who used their personal income were eventually compensated by gifts of lump sums (the *gratifications*), or by lucrative and honorific positions, or by pensions.[27] In New France, they were encouraged to marry and settle down in the colony with land grants. Many second lieutenants without command, assigned the half-pay of fifteen *sols* a day, would consider this alternative, founding families in-between campaigns. Even when not paid, an officer could live on his credit as he was himself a creditor of the crown. It would be erroneous to pictureTonty as "destitute." First, he remained the commander of *Fort St. Louis des Illinois* with a garrison which had to be maintained; and secondly, he continued to be routinely involved in every campaign fought against the Iroquois—and occasionally against the Sioux. As such, he could count on the necessities of life that French and Indians under his administration would provide him, besides the fur trade licenses he still received periodically.

From the various bits and pieces of evidence to which we have access, it is reasonable to conclude that Illinois as a French possession (one can hardly use the term "colony") did more than survive during these years which preceded the second—and this time successful—French attempt at colonization in Louisiana. Demographic and economic growth between 1690 and 1700 was limited in Illinois because growth was limited in Canada. The picture of trade conditions in Illinois for this period remains murky: on the one hand, for half a decade Tonty and La Forest, joined later by Accault, seemed to have been the undisputed major business entrepreneurs of the region. Yet, their commercial domain was restricted, their operation small-scale and their profits at best insufficient. Nonetheless, they did stimulate trade in Illinois and stir interest for the Mississippi Valley even if they would not profit from the eventual results.

Henri de Tonty paid a price much greater than apparent financial embarrassment for his unsuccessful efforts to build Illinois economically. Despite his talents as a loyal and brave leader, he became the sort of hero who was praised by all but constantly passed over for each important new position. His plight is even clearer if we look at his own career in juxtaposition to the fortunes of others.

In 1694, Antoine de Lamothe Cadillac, then commanding at Michilimackinac, was made the chief administrator of the Western territories, including Illinois, although he had neither Tonty's experience nor his seniority and certainly not his honesty. Even Tonty's responsibility in Illinois was reduced when Frontenac sent a lieutenant, M. de Manthet, to command in Chicago with orders to report directly to the officer in charge in Michilimackinac. Also during the same period, Nicolas Perrot was authorized to build a trade fort at Malamel (Marameg), among the Miami, on the Fox River of Illinois. Tonty was slowly being cast into the role of the "old officer," the veteran whose time has come and gone and whose future was linked only to whatever he could make out of his St. Louis fort. Was Frontenac aware of some limitations in his protégé that cannot easily be understood today? It would seem likely, since Tonty was never given the opportunity to indulge in the accomplishment of any "grand design" of his own. In 1695, following a truce with the Sioux, he solicited and was granted the authorization to embark on a long expedition in the Assiboin country, near Lake Superior, to find new sources of better quality furs. It was, however, a small expedition. Tonty scouted the area with only an escort of two soldiers from the Michilimackinac garrison, "with the hope to make bigger profits, this nation [the Assiboins] having not done any business with us yet."[28]

For his expenses, he received one additional trading license for Illinois, a small reward with overtones of charity. Yet, perhaps it was merely a reflection of the changing times. The King was no longer an ardent supporter of expeditions in the western marches of Canada; they cost money and brought little in return, generally not even enough to cover the expense of initial investments. While Governor Frontenac had always been, and continued to remain, an ardent supporter of a policy of expansion through trade, the *intendant*, Jean Bochart de Champigny, was just as firmly opposed. Champigny observed the fur trade between Montreal and the West and saw a monopoly in the hands of a small, almost "incestuous" group of men who, "have but one and the same mind and but one interest, tending solely to trading."[29] Champigny was in total agreement with the Jesuits when it came to the recall of all French traders, although for reasons other than the spread of immorality. For him, to continue the issuance of trade licenses, mainly in those days of fur glut, was not justified as it profited only this little group:

> They will also, under other pretexts, directly or indirectly, enjoy alone the favor of the twenty-five licenses which were worth 20,000 livres of income to the poor families of Canada, for whom they were designed; those permits will be worth infinitely more in their hands, as they can have no competitors who can form an obstacle to their trade, upon whatever footing they may care to put it, even including brandy.[30]

To complicate matters even further, Louis XIV had "found religion" again since his secret marriage to his old favorite, Madame de Maintenon. Unfortunately for France's political interest, it was a religion of the worst kind, encouraged by a new Jesuit confessor, Father La Chaise. Through his offices, the Jesuits of New France begged the King to put a stop to the development of the colony, accusing voyageurs and soldiers in the outposts of ruining their missionary work with the Indians. Their opinion had acquired more weight since the bevy of great ministers who had steered France and her King towards expansion—the Colberts, Louvois, and Seignelays—were now dead. The Jesuits firmly believed:

> that the best policy towards the West was to withdraw all troops and to prohibit all traders from going among the Indians. They represented to the court that the western posts were places of debauchery where the innocent natives were demoralized, an accusation which was not far from the truth; but certainly, such a policy would have cost France an empire in the beginning of its career.[31]

The Jesuits succeeded, and on May 26, 1696, and again on April 27, 1697, Governor Frontenac was ordered by the Minister "to abandon Fort Frontenac which had been restored, to recall all Frenchmen from the West and to make peace with the Iroquois even if it were necessary to exclude from its terms the western [Indian] allies."[32]

The order applied to all except Tonty and La Forest; they still had a few friends in Versailles. Frontenac tried to parry the blow to Canada by delaying the implementation of the order as long as he could. Indeed, the new ordinance could not be, and was not effective. The Indians protested its application and the French traders ignored it.

On November 28, 1698, seventy-year old Governor Frontenac died in Quebec and, with him, the informality and the rough directness of an administration which had been more successful than many had wished. Although the King had provided the government of Canada with very little means, he could now think only of the hopes it had failed to fulfill. By October 24th of the same year, a four-ship expedition had sailed from the port of Brest for a second attempt to colonize Louisiana, which would become the promised land of the next century as Canada had been for the preceding. This change of emphasis would have a radical impact on Illinois.

The Mississippi Delta had been claimed but still needed to be brought under effective French control. Over the years, since the death of La Salle, several petitioners, many undoubtedly seeking an opportunity to associate their own fortunes with those of France, had written memoirs attempting to convince the King of the urgency of the task. Among them was Father Jean Cavelier, La Salle's brother, who had presented the minister with a document emphasizing very cogent points: 1) the beaver trade with the Western Indians was necessary to the economic health of

Canada; 2) the Illinois as a nation and under French leadership were an effective deterrent against the Iroquois' encroachment, and consequently vital to the protection of the Canadian settlements; and 3) that maintaining Illinois and securing the Mississippi would cut off the British colonies from any possible extension of their own fur trade. Father Cavelier added that four voyages per year could be made between the mouth of the Mississippi River and Illinois while the long winter season froze all the water to the north, rendering communication with Canada extremely tenuous.[33]

In 1687, Governor Denonville had written to Minister Seignelay to make a case for an expedition to the mouth of the Mississippi to be led by Tonty and financed by the crown.[34] In 1693, Tonty sent a memorandum and a map on the same subject which analyzed the problems of navigation on the Mississippi and specified the supplies that he deemed necessary for such an expedition and their estimated cost. Two months, fifty men, twelve canoes and 4,000 francs to cover supplies and gifts for the Indian nations, were all that he claimed he needed to bring about an effective French presence at the mouth of the Mississippi. Considering Tonty's experience and knowledge of the area, the king would probably have been well-advised to accept Tonty's proposal.[35] In 1697, the *Sieur* d'Ailleboust de Manthet, who had served as commander of the Chicago post, offered a plan in cooperation with another officer, Captain La Porte de Louvigny, which, they guaranteed, would cost little to the royal treasury. Coincidentally, during the same year an old friend of La Salle, Mr. de Remouville, and a well-known personality in the scientific world, the *Sieur* Argoud, sent a memorandum on the urgency of establishing a durable French presence in Louisiana.[36]

The petitioners may not have been responsible for the final decision on the matter but their impact cannot be discounted. Since information from the local administrators was often insufficient, additional sources were always sought. Many factors contributed to the decision of King Louis XIV and his ministers to occupy the mouth of the Mississippi.

First of all, the Lower Mississippi Valley was considered a potentially rich area which could supply France and the French West Indies with agricultural products, and in exchange, absorb much sugar from the Islands and manufactured goods from the Metropole. The King had long deplored the fact that the Canadian economy was built on furs, but now the Lower Mississippi was looked upon as offering all the ingredients for a successful commercial colonization, the likes of which the French had not found in the northern part of the American continent where harbors were shut almost half the year by winter ice. Economic considerations alone would not, however, determine that the French move from the planning stage to realization: as often would be the case in French colonial history, it was precipitated by the decisions that London was about to make.

An English physician and entrepreneur of means and vision, Daniel Coxe, had bought the license to colonize the territory of Carolina from the British crown. He had been previously involved with the development of trade routes west of New Jersey. These trade routes, he had claimed, extended west all the way to the Great Lakes region, and his commercial operations were a challenge the French had already been forced to combat. For the British, the colony of Carolina included all the lands from the Atlantic Ocean to the Mississippi, and Coxe:

> Having imagination to see the potential wealth of the territory, began immediately to bombard the British government with memorials which stressed the strategic position of his proposed colony. For his propaganda he found an able and not too scrupulous assistant in Father Hennepin, quondam friend and associate of La Salle, who now printed the famous modification of his journeying in which he claimed for himself the honor of discovering the Mouth of the Mississippi River.[37]

The preparations of Doctor Coxe, although handicapped by the death of King William III, nevertheless accelerated at a pace and with a magnitude sufficient to greatly alarm French observers in London. The intelligence gathered by the French ambassador (intelligence gathering was already one of the diplomatic corps' major roles) was most conclusive: there could be no doubt about the seriousness of the British intentions. In France, the Jesuits, greatly concerned by the British plans in the Mississippi Valley to make good use of hundreds of French Huguenots who had sought refuge in Charleston, Carolina,[38] suddenly reversed their stand against further penetration in North America and joined the "imperialist party" lobbying for prompt colonization.[39] Ironically, Father Louis Hennepin whose unfounded claims in his publications had made him a *persona non grata* in France, was now an appreciated source of information for the British. It was important for the French to act, and the occupation of the Mississippi Valley became a matter of urgency. The conjuncture of all these events had weighed heavily on the mind of Louis XIV. As a result of his concern, strict instructions were sent to the French envoys who were negotiating the peace treaty of Rijswijk (which in 1697 brought an end to the War of the Grand Alliance between France and Britain and its ally, Holland). It also ended the dispute over the rights to the Mississippi Valley.

By 1698, the decision had been made: France was to take possession of her Louisiana claim. To achieve this goal, the navy would carry troops directly from Brest to the Mississippi. The Québec-Illinois route had been rejected as impracticable; thirty-six portages would have meant a difficult journey for a large expedition. This time a single command would be held by a navy officer. The navy was fast becoming the growing military and administrative power of colonial France, a charge it would assume until the turn of the nineteenth century. Tonty, who could have claimed the honor, was far from where decisions were made; it is doubtful that his name was even advanced. Instead, the responsibility was given to a young Canadian-born navy captain who had acquired a well-founded reputation in several engagements with British ships and who happened to be at Versailles: Pierre Le Moyne, *Sieur* d'Iberville, Knight of the Military Order of St. Louis.[40]

The instructions Iberville received from the Minister of the Navy, the Count of Pontchartrain, on July 23, 1698,[41] were to scout the mouth of the Mississippi, build a fort, search for pearls, obtain buffalo wool, look for mulberry trees (for the silk industry) and, naturally, discover mines—not a small agenda!

At Brest, October 24, 1698, the sails were hoisted on board the frigate *La Badine* and with the firing of the signal gun, the squadron commanded by Iberville, the newly commissioned Governor-General of *la colonie du Mississippi*, was on its way.[42]

Much preparation had gone into this new effort. All possible sources of intelligence were gathered from France; the minister had even sent for Henry Joutel and Father Cavelier.[43] Along with Iberville, dozens of other Canadians were part of the expedition. Their experience with wilderness and Indians was expected, quite justifiably, to be of great value. Joutel had been offered passage but declined. One of the survivors of La Salle's attempt, Father Anasthase Douay, did accept and was on board. There were no plans, however, to launch even a simple simultaneous reconnaissance from Illinois.

The first to grasp the implications of the lower Mississippi under the control of the French monarchy was the Catholic Church, or, more to the point, the Jesuits, who were always concerned with expansion.

The Bishop of Quebec, Saint-Vallier,[44] happened to believe in an even-handed repartition of religious responsibilities. Consequently, with the support of Governor Frontenac, on May 1, 1698, he appointed priests of the *Missions étrangères* to the spiritual lordship of the Upper Mississippi Valley, which then meant southwest Illinois and Arkansas.[45] This appointment unleashed a crisis. It was one thing for the missionary priests to assume the teaching responsibility at the Quebec seminary and quite another to venture into the field when the Jesuits considered the whole of North America as their own spiritual domain. They had tolerated the presence of a few dozen Recollects in Quebec, but were not about to accept any additional encroachment of their monopoly—this time by secular priests—without a fight. The whole affair would eventually end up in the King's Council when the vicar general travelled down the Mississippi and embarked for France from Louisiana. The King found an easy way out by turning over this hornets' nest to a committee of French bishops who, on June 7, 1701, would wisely settle for the status quo.[46]

The three missionary priests who left Quebec for the Mississippi were indeed fortunate to join forces with two gentlemen of great experience: Jean-Baptiste Bissot de Vincennes, Canadian-born and a nephew of Louis Jolliet, on his way to take command of the *Fort des Miamis* (Fort-Wayne, Indiana), and Tonty.[47] This was not a chance encounter for Tonty, who had been looking for a new patron as he correctly expected Governor Frontenac's days to be numbered. Very diplomatically, from Michili-mackinac where he had accompanied the canoes loaded with Illinois furs during their annual voyage, Tonty wrote to the bishop in Quebec, lauding the mission to the Mississippi and offering his services.[48] Ironically, almost at the same time, Father Gravier, obviously well-informed, had also written to the bishop, warning him against Tonty. Close association with him, in Gravier's opinion, would have a negative effect on the Indians of the Mississippi Valley.[49] Both letters reached them simultaneously, so the missionary priests hesitated before answering Tonty's offer to escort them all the way to their destination. There were disturbing rumors of "debauchery" about him. Back in 1694, Tonty's nephew, Pierre de Liette, had allegedly insulted Father Gravier in front of French and Indians, and the Jesuit had then complained that: "when he [Tonty] left [De Liette] in command of *Fort St. Louis des Illinois* during the two years he was absent [he] did more by his debauchery and impious talk to disparage the truth of the Gospel than can be imagined." [50] Four years later, Father Gravier had not forgotten.[51]

Although no evidence exists or has survived to support the Jesuits' accusations, it must have been a rare French outpost where occasional bouts of wild behavior did not occur. Commanding such outposts required a mixture of discipline and free hand. The rigors of a narrow Catholic orthodoxy were bound to confront the realities of garrison life. For the soldiers, *voyageurs, coureurs des bois,* and gallicized Indians who endured the rigors of winter with few creature comforts, to occasionally drink from a cask of brandy, make love to Indian women, or gamble, was what made life bearable and, at times, even pleasurable. Tonty was himself an able card player; Henry Joutel observed him winning a large part of Boisrondet's pay during the winter of 1687. De Liette had also acquired quite a reputation at the card table.[52] Little else has been recorded about the sins of the officers in Illinois, except that La Salle had probably lived together with a lady of noble birth while at Fort Frontenac. All in all, the Frenchmen who served for years, in uniform or in buckskin, in seventeenth century North America often lived outside the values taught by the church. If heathen of a sort, these men were still the most experienced, a factor which in the end counted much in the decision made by the three priests—Francois de Montigny, the designated Superior; Antoine Davion, and Jean-Francois Buisson de Saint-Cosme—to politely ignore the Jesuits' warning and accept Tonty's offer.[53] Along with a deacon, Thaumur de la Source, three lay brothers and two blacksmiths, they joined forces with Vincennes and Tonty in Michilimackinac and left on September 14th, eight canoes hurrying down Lake Michigan before the bad weather set in.

On September 18, 1698, they were at the *Baie des Puants* (Green Bay), and on October 7th, they camped on the shores of Melwarik (Milwaukee). On October 10th, they passed Kipikawi (Racine) where Vincennes took his four canoes directly across the lake to St. Joseph. By then the weather was very poor; for five days a high wind grounded Tonty and the missionaries only twenty miles from the mouth of the Chicago River. They continued on foot the short distance to the Mission of the Guardian Angel, also known as the Chicagua (Chicago) Mission. This mission, a group of about 150 cabins, had been founded in 1696, by two Jesuits, Father Pinet and Father Binneteau, to serve the Weas and the Miamis. From a letter sent later by Father St. Cosme, the site of the mission appears to have been between the lake shore and the forks of the Chicago River, north of its mouth.[54] The mission had been closed for a year on direct orders of Governor Frontenac, anti-Jesuit to the end, but was reopened after the bishop's strong protest. [55] At any rate, the missionary priests and Tonty were cordially received. Father Montigny later wrote a letter to the superior of the Canadian Jesuits expressing his deep thanks.[56] The voyage continued and on November 19th, the whole group arrived at Fort St. Louis. Once again, the priests were the guests of the Jesuits. Father St. Cosme commented approvingly of their installation and work in a letter to the bishop. This letter gives some additional glimpses into the life of Illinois at the turn of the seventeenth century:

> The Illinois mission seems to me the finest that the Jesuit fathers have up here . . . there are many grown persons who have abandoned all their super-stitions and live as perfectly good Christians, frequenting the sacraments and who are married in the Church. We had not the consolation of seeing all these good Christians for they were all dispersed going down the bank of the river for the hunt. We saw only some Indian women married to Frenchmen who edified us by their modesty and by their assiduity in going several times a day to the Chapel and pray.[57]

Regarding these marriages, we know only of a few, such as Accault's and the soldier La Violette's, in whose house the missionary priests said Mass and baptized a child. Father Gravier, during a trip to Quebec in 1696, however, claimed that in six years he had baptized 2,000 Illinois "who live in the simplicity of the first Christians;"[58] a large number which, if accurate (the Jesuits were given to exaggerate), would naturally include many wives.

At each step of the way Tonty was present, facilitating the journey. He introduced the priests to Chief Rouensa. They spent a few nights in his care while Tonty went on ahead to visit the Cahokia and settle some obscure dispute they were having with French traders. On December 5th, they reached the Mississippi, and on the 15th camped a couple of miles below the Ohio River (called the *Ouabache* by the French). On Christmas Day, 1698, mass was started late "because we had to wait for an Indian boy that M. de Tonty had, who went into the woods the day before to look for fruit and got lost. . . . we were quite glad to see him come back next morning."[59]

St. Cosme later wrote to his bishop: "I cannot *Monseigneur* express our obligations to him . . . he guided us . . . he facilitated our course . . . he has not only done the duty of a brave man, but also discharged the function of a zealous missionary . . . He is the man that best knows the country . .

. he is loved and feared everywhere."[60]

When they arrived at the Arkansas post, Tonty and his men found a dismal situation. The Indians of the area—the Tonica, the Quapaw, the Yazoo—all had been decimated by smallpox or hostile raids, and Tonty's agent, Jean Couture, a veteran *voyageur*, had deserted to the English.[61] On January 2, 1699, Tonty returned north, carrying the missionaries' mail, which contained many flattering comments about him. He would need them all under the administration of the *Chevalier* Louis-Hector de Callières, the new governor. In April of that year, St. Cosme also returned north, and founded a mission at Cahokia that rekindled the dispute with the Jesuits.

NOTES

1. The Biography of Louis de la Porte, Sieur de Louvigny, can be found in L.C. Draper, *Wisconsin Historical Collection*, 108.

2. *Parole de M. de Frontenac qui doit être dite à l'Outanouais pour le dissuader de l'alliance qu'il veut faire avec l'Iroquois et l'Anglois*, Parkman, V, *Frontenac*, 704.

3. Alvord, *The Illinois Country*, 96.

4. ANC, C 11 A 10; 206-200v-C, October 15, 1689.

5. King to Denonville and Champigny, March 8, 1688, ANC, B 15:11-7v-C.

6. Murphy, *Henry de Tonty*.

7. Murphy, *Henry de Tonty.*, 78-79.

8. *Lettres patentes de Sa Majesté, Versailles; Edits . . . Canada*, 1 262-63.

9. De Liette has left memoirs known as the "DeGannes Memoirs," but as Theodore Pease remarked in his introduction for his book *French Foundations*, IX, ". . . the signature 'Degannes' is quite inexplicable unless it be the name of the secretary or transcriber or the usurpation of someone seeking to gain its credit for himself. The things which the author tells us about himself, his own experiences . . . point unmistakably to the Sieur Deliette, nephew of Henri de Tonti, as the author . . . He writes very much from the point of view of the modern anthropologist, quite conscious of such things as racial psychology, sociology and habits of life." The *De Gannes Memoirs* are deposited at the Newberry Library, in Chicago.

10. *DeGannes Memoirs*.

11. Ibid.

12. The site of the Fort Saint Louis on Lake Peoria has been the subject of a vigorous controversy among local amateur historians. I tend to agree with one of the most distinguished and erudite, the late Richard M. Phillips, publisher of the *Illiniwek*, who in the issue of Winter 1975, identified the Sections 14, 22, 23 and 27 of Fond du Lac township of Tazewell County as the location of the new fort built by Tonty and La Forest.

13. King to Frontenac and Champigny, ANC, B 16:17-29-C.

14. These engagement contracts are kept in the Notary files of A. Adhemar, *Palais de justice*, Montréal, DNS.

15. Agreement between Jean de Broyeux and La Forest, August 19, 1687, Notarial File, A. Adhemar, Montreal.

16. January 29, 1686; Canadian Archives, Supplement 83, 1899.

17. Alphonse de Tonty, born in 1650, married in 1689 Anne Picote de Belestre from Montreal with whom he had eight children. Commander of Fort Frontenac in 1706, of Detroit in 1717, he died on November 10, 1727.

18. Tonty to M. Cabart de Villermont, *du Fort Saint Louis de la Louisiane*, March 29, 1689; Margry, 228-30.

19. The protest was from Francois Pachot (1628-1698), who was much involved in the fur trade. His wife, Charlotte-Francoise, was the sister of Charles Juchereau de St. Denis; later, after the death of Francois Pachot, she remarried La Forest. In New France business ties were often criss-crossed with family ties. In May 1690, La Forest had left Quebec for France; in his haste, he forgot to sign the power of attorney for his Illinois business that he had entrusted to Boisrondet. The mistake was repaired when the power was legalized on May 12, 1690, at Boisrondet's request.

20. N.Y.C.D., 9:408-409; Margry, *Mémoires.*, 98-99.

21. April 16, 1692, C.H.C., Schmidt Collection, D.S.

22. Sidney Breese, *The Early History of Illinois from its Discovery by the French in 1673 until its cession to Great Britain in 1763*, Eugene Myers, Chicago, 1884, 141; Breese, a law student of Edward Kane, had come to Kaskaskia in 1818. See also Schlarman, *From Quebec to New Orleans*, Belleville, 1929.

23. Notary Files, A. Adhemar, Montreal. Juchereau, born on December 2, 1655, died in Illinois in 1703 from an epidemic of unspecified nature.

24. Notary file, A. Adhemar.

25. Letter to M. de Pontchartrain, September 13, 1693, in Margry, *Relations et Mémoires inédits*, 1-36.

26. Letter to M. de Pontchartrain.

27. A military engineer and former student of Vauban, the Sieur de Villeneuve, drew in 1687 all the fortification plans for the Canadian cities and received a gift of 600 livres from the King.

28. Intendant to Minister, Québec, November 6, 1697; quoted in Margry, V, 65-66, and in Alvord, 102.

29. Champigny to the Minister, October 13, 1697, in C.M. Burton's "Cadillac papers," *Michigan Pioneer and Historical Collections*, XXXIII, 75.

30. Champigny to the Minister, October 14, 1698, *Wisconsin Historical Collections*, XVI, 175.

31. Parkman, *Frontenac*, 441.

32. Parkman, *Frontenac.*,

33. *Mémoire de l'abbé Jean Cavelier.*, Margry, V, 586-596.

34. Denonville to Seignelay, August, 27, 1687, NYCD, IX, 343.

35. *Relation de la découverte de Mississippi commencée par M. de la Salle en 1678 et de celle faîte depuis par le Sr. Tonty, tant de cette rivière que des pays voisins jusqu'en*

1690, avec la lettre du Sr. Tonty du 12 Mars 1693, ANC, C13C3:142-143-L.S., trans. in Pease, *French Foundations,* 276-282.

36. *Mémoire adressé au Conte de Pontchartrain sur l'importance d'établir une colonie en Louisiane,* par M. de Remonville, Paris, December 10, 1697, trans. in Benjamin F. French, *Historical collections of Louisiana* , New York, 1869.

37. *The Illinois Country,* 1922, 124.

38. Baron Marc de Villiers, *La Louisiane, Histoire de son nom et de ses frontières successives, 1681-1819,* Paris, 1929, 45-48.

39. The Edict of Nantes signed in April 1598 by King Henry IV giving religious freedom to the Protestants had been revoked on October 18, 1685.

40. "The illustrious Pierre Le Moyne d'Iberville, first Royal Governor of Louisiana, was the third of eleven sons of the brave Charles Le Moyne, Seigneur of Longueil, Lower Canada, all of whom distinguished themselves in the wars of France with England, Spain and Holland. He was born at Montreal, July 20, 1662, and at an early age entered the naval service of France. In 1685, he took part in the expedition commanded by M. de Troyes to Hudson Bay and captured Fort Rupert and Monsonis. In 1687, M. d'Iberville was promoted to the rank of Captain of a ship of war and ordered to Quebec. On his way to that port, he captured an English ship of war with the British Governor and suite on board, and took them prisoners to Quebec. In 1689, he was sent to take command of Fort St. Ann which he nobly defended against the combined attack of a British fleet and repulsed, with a large loss to the enemy. He continued in command of this fort for more than a year when he sailed for France with dispatches for the government, where he was graciously received by the King and Court. In 1692, he returned to Canada in command of a squadron and captured Fort Nelson . . . .In this attack he lost his gallant brother, M. de Chateauguay, in leading an attack on one of the bastions of the fort. In concert with M. de Brillon, they afterwards destroyed the fortress and town of St. John's, in Newfoundland. At the close of the war with England and Holland, in 1697, and while in command of the ship *Pélican,* of fifty guns, he fought one of the most unequal and decisive battles in naval history. . . . attacked by three English ships of war: the *Hampshire,* of fifty-two guns, which surrendered; the *Hudson,* of thirty-six guns, which he sank; and the *Dehring,* of thirty-two guns which he put to flight." *French Historical Collections of Louisiana.*

41. Louis Phelypeaux, Count of Pontchartrain.

42. The name *Louisiane* which was quite popular in 1683, disappeared from the official parlance after the disaster suffered by La Salle in 1683, and will not be used again for a long time. See Baron Marc de Villiers, *La Louisiane, Histoire de son nom et de ses frontières successives, 1681-1819,* Paris, 1929.

43. "There is in Rouen a gate keeper called Jointel who has an accurate relation of the voyage made by the late Sieur de La Salle to the Gulf of Mexico in 1684. Kindly call this man and ask him for his relation and send it to me. You may assure him that I shall return it in a month or six weeks; I only want to satisfy my curiosity." Minister Pontchartrain, Navy, to La Bourdonnaye, Intendant of Normandy, AM, B2, 132:374; also in Margry, IV, 50; trans. by Delanglez, *The Journal of Jean Cavelier,* Institute of Jesuit History, Chicago, 1938, 11.

44. Jean-Baptiste de la Croix de St. Vallier, replaced the first Bishop, Francois

de Montmorency-Laval, after his resignation in 1688. Laval died in 1708 and St. Vallier in 1727.

45. ASQ, Missions, 61; a seminary to train priests for foreign missions had been created in 1663 in Paris by friends of Bishop Laval, opposed to the Jesuit monopoly.

46. See Charles Edwards O'Neill, *Church and State in French Colonial Louisiana,* Yale University Press, New Haven, 1966.

47. Jean-Baptiste Bissot de Vincennes would be killed thirty-two years later while leading Miami warriors in a campaign against the Chicachas, a nation then threatening French Louisiana.

48. Tonty to the Bishop of Quebec, September 13, 1698, ASQ, *Missions,* No.50.

49. Gravier to Bishop, September 20, 1698, ADQ, N. 132; also in R.G. Thwaites, *Jesuit Relations.,* v. 65, 58-62. On the question of Church politics in New France during the end of the seventeenth century, see also Charles Edwards O'Neill, *Church and State.,* Yale University Press, New Haven, 1966.

50. See Gravier to Villermont, March 17, 1694, BN ff 22804 F 59-60 v; Delanglez, *Mid-America,* 21, 217-19; *Lettre du Pere Jacques Gravier...aux Illinois,* February 15, 1694, BN ff/453, F-30-43 v.

51. Father Jacques Gravier arrived in Canada on June 16, 1672; assigned to Illinois in 1693, recalled, he was killed by Iroquois in 1710.

52. Henry Joutel, *Remarques,* 16.

53. Acts of May 1, July 14, 1698, *Archives, Université Laval, Quebec;* Father Saint-Cosme was born in Quebec on November 26, 1660; he died in Natchez, killed by Indian Chicachas on May 15, 1712. See Monsignor Cyprien Tanguay, *Répertoire general du clergé canadien,* Montréal, 1893.

54. There is no little controversy on the site of the Mission; Frank R. Grover, *Father Pierre Francois Pinet, S.J. and his Mission of the Guardian Angel, A.D. 1696-1699,* Chicago, 1907, claimed Ridgeland Avenue, near the present church of St. Mary in Wilmette as the probable location. Milo Quaife, in *Chicago and the Old Northwest, 1673-1835,* 42, and Garraghan in "Chicago under the French Regime," *Transactions of the Illinois State Historical Society,* 1930, both placed the Mission not far from the Mouth of the Chicago River on the basis of St. Cosme's letter. The Wea, after they moved away from Illinois Town in 1692, went to Chicago, Racine (Wisconsin), and St. Joseph.

55. September 17, 1697, Father Gravier's letter to Bishop Saint Vallier protesting Governor Frontenac's decision to close the Jesuit missions of Chicago and Ouatanon, on the Wabash River. See John Shea, ed., *Relation des Affaires du Canada en 1696,* reprint, New York, 1865.

56. Montigny to Rev. Father Brayas, April 23, 1699, in Shea, *Relation.*

57. Trans. in John G. Shea, *Early Voyages Up and Down the Mississippi,* Sibana, New York, 1861, 47.

58. *Relation des affaires du Canada en 1696.,*

59. Shea, *Early Voyages.,*60. St. Cosme to Bishop, Jan. 2, 1699, ASQ, Lettres, R 26, 7-8.

61. See Stanley Faye, *The Arkansas Post of Louisiana: French Domination,* LHQ, Vol. 26, 3, July 1943.

7

Illinois Enters Modern History

I t was at Michilimackinac that Henri de Tonty learned of the landing of the French at the mouth of the Mississippi. The news had reached Canada through a letter sent from Biloxi by one of Iberville's brothers. Details were sketchy, but for Tonty they composed a clear picture.[1]

Iberville had reached the western coast of Florida near the Spanish establishment of Pensacola on January 24, 1699. On March 2nd, after spending several weeks building a fort near the home of the Bilochi Indians, Fort Maurepas (Biloxi, Mississippi), he entered the muddy waters of the Mississippi with some of his smaller craft. It was during a reconnaissance of the Delta's main waterways that his brother and second-in-command,Mr. de Bienville,came acrossthe village of Bayougala,[2] meeting the chief who was still wearing: "a hooded great-coat of blue serge from Poitou which, he told me, Tonty had given him as a present when he passed by."[3]

Tonty was the last European whom the chief of the Bayougala had seen. That was fourteen years before, when Tonty had entrusted him with a letter for La Salle. The chief handed over the precious document to Bienville, its seal still intact. There could no longer be any doubt that the expedition had reached the mouth of the Mississippi River. The first objective, occupation, had been achieved and Iberville left for France to give Versailles a first-hand account of his success. Unknowingly, he had beaten the British by only five months: on August 29th, a vessel chartered by Dr. Coxe was almost one hundred miles upstream on the Mississippi when it was turned back by Bienville.[4]

If Tonty wished to play a role of consequence in the expansion of colonial France, about to unfold in the very backyard of Illinois, he had to act quickly without waiting for an official invitation, or soliciting authorization. At this point in his career he had exhausted his good will credit in France; Pontchartrain, the King's minister, had left unanswered the petition sent by La Forest on his and Tonty's behalf in which the two associates claimed that: "the commerce of the Mississippi is one attribute of the said concession [La Salle's] which they have always been prepared to excercise."[5]

The minister's marginal notes on the petition hint at his displeasure: "When orders were given to oblige the return of all Frenchmen from the interior, they [Tonty and La Forest] were always excepted."[6]

Nothing more was heard on the subject. The document is undated, but La Forest probably wrote it while in France at the end of 1698 or the very beginning of 1699. During the same period, Tonty, who was at Michilimackinac waiting for the missionary priests' arrival from Quebec, had sold half his share of the Illinois concession to his brother Alphonse. With the money of this sale he had bought enough merchandise to supply both Fort St. Louis and the Arkansas outpost, determined to maintain his position at the core of all dealings up and down Illinois.[7]

As news of Governor Frontenac's death the previous fall finally filtered down to Michilimackinac, it was more important than ever for Tonty to continue nurturing the moral and political support he had received from the priests of the *Missions étrangères*. To this end, he wrote to the bishop in Quebec, bringing him up-to-date on the conflict with the Jesuits, commenting harshly on the bad effect that this Jesuit-fomented disturbance had on the Illinois.[8]

The roots of the disturbance, as usual, laid with the rivalry between the two orders, *Missions étrangères* and *Jésuites*. Only a few weeks after the completion of the missionary priests' church the Jesuits sent Father Julien Binneteau to Cahokia where, in spite of his poor health, he immediately proceeded to establish a rival community. Father Binneteau died on Christmas Day, 1699, in Peoria, and Father Pinet came from the Chicago mission to take up where he had left off, finishing the construction of the Jesuit sanctuary. The fact that he had left behind a young and less experienced fellow missionary, Father Jean Mermet, to run the Chicago mission underlines the importance given by the Jesuits to their running conflict with the priests of the *Missions étrangères*. At stake was the control of spiritual matters in the whole Mississippi Valley. In spite of the conflict, both Jesuits and the priests of the *Missions* in Cahokia behaved in a very civilized way; only the Illinois Indians were left trying to understand why two groups of "black robes" competed for their souls.

Tonty naturally sided with the priests of the *Missions* in this conflict but he had greater concerns than the rivalry of clerics: returning to Fort St. Louis from Michilimackinac, Tonty was now organizing his journey to the Lower Mississippi in a semi-clandestine fashion. He could not invite a mass departure of *voyageurs*; he knew that would unleash the wrath of the governor in Quebec. His precautions, nevertheless, would be of little

Portrait of LeMoyne de Iber-
ville. Reproduced from
*Narrative and Critical History
of America*, Vol 5, Justin
Winsor, ed., 1884. (The
Newberry Library)

avail for when the news of Tonty's departure reached the capital of New
France, Governor Callières promptly requested that "the rebels be arrested, claiming that Tonty had taken along with him eighty-four deserters," a gross exaggeration.[9]

Tonty, twenty woodsmen, and a smaller number of Illinois arrived in
Bayougala at the end of January, 1700, a full year after the landing of
Iberville's expedition. From Bayougala, the farthest point of his fruitless
search for La Salle, Tonty continued with only one canoe to Biloxi, where
he arrived on February 16th, and was greeted by Iberville who had
returned from France just five weeks earlier.

This was an historical encounter if ever there was one. Several eye-
witnesses recorded the momentous event. A soldier of fortune, Bernard
de la Harpe, wrote with a hint of sarcasm that: "M. de Tonty arrived from
Canada in a canoe with seven Canadians, after having left others in Bay-
agoula; they came down for the sole curiosity of knowing if the Mouth of
the River was settled." [10] The Jesuit Paul du Ru, chaplain of Iberville's
expedition, recorded in his journal the great joy which greeted Tonty, the
Canadians and the Tamaroa Indians: "Much clamor, much musketry,
much rejoicing! Monsieur de Tonti has come!" [11]

As for Iberville, he gave a more limited meaning to Tonty's journey in his own diary:

The 16th, M. de Tonty arrived toward evening in a boat with eight men, having left fourteen at the Bayougalas along with their baggage and canoes. The men with him are *habitans*, most of them from the Illinois and Tamaroas who came on their own initiative to see what there might be to do here, in response to the letter M. de Sauvolle sent up there, [saying] that if men came from upriver they would find work and would be welcomed here.[12]

Iberville's rather cold assessment is poignantly reflected in Tonty's correspondence:

Although I could have felt some jealousy seeing another in a country where I had the right to hope for everything after the expenses I underwent for the service of the king, I came down here and I am well pleased I made 900 leagues for such a purpose. When M. d'Iberville told me he was going to the Cenis [Hasinai], I made him offers of service, having formerly visited these people. . . . As he has long been a friend of mine, he told me the following in confidence. When he was ready to leave for this country, since it was necessary that a number of Frenchmen should come from Canada to meet him, he mentioned me to M. de Latouche [first clerk of the Ministry of Navy]. The latter replied that I would not do, that I was a debauchee. I don't know who they are who painted such an ugly portrait of me. I have had a few quarrels with the Jesuits about matters which had nothing to do with debauchery. I can only accuse them of the bad services rendered me, directly or indirectly, in the [colonial] office, or M. the Intendant of Canada who has always opposed us.[13]

Iberville also raised the question with Tonty of an account of his travels recently published in France, and filled with all sorts of fables readily apparent to the experienced observer. Tonty was able to prove to Bienville that he had nothing to do with the printing of the pirated version of his *Relation*. Nevertheless, it was obviously a publication injurious to him and, in the same letter quoted above, Tonty asked his brother's help: "I am very sorry to see a *Relation* under my name to which much has been added and in which the memoirs I sent you were not followed point by point. It is disagreeable to pass for a liar. It would please me if you could retrieve my memoirs and exhibit them when necessary." [14]

Tonty was in the difficult position of having to convince Iberville of his usefulness. Much of his future role could be determined by the degree of effort Iberville would want to invest in extending into the northern hinterland. Gaining a strong foothold farther inland would only be important to Iberville if he wanted to establish good communication between the Gulf and the Upper Mississippi. Then Tonty's expertise would be very precious. Another factor at play to Tonty's advantage was Iberville's keen business sense. He had every intention of exploiting all money-making possibilities by buying the heavy loads of furs brought by Tonty's canoes and reselling them for a 7,000 livres profit (in total disregard of the minister's orders forbidding trade in beaver pelts between Upper and Lower Mississippi). Tonty's arrival then did play a small but positive role in Iberville's schemes. However, the *seigneur de l'Illinois* was also an anachronism, a character à la Cervantes, tolerated by Versailles but cursed by Quebec. Iberville could justify further use of Tonty's services, and trample the feelings of the governor of New France in the process, but probably could not have done much more without running afoul of the minister. He certainly would not share responsibilities or give him a command of major importance. At first, Tonty believed that his seniority and experience would earn him the position he considered his due. Father du Ru noted in his diary for February 17th, the day after Tonty's arrival, that: "M. de Tonty is giving us much information by which we shall profit. M. d'Iberville will do what he can to persuade him to go back up the river with him." And, the next day's entry: "M. de Tonty has already engaged fourteen of his men to accompany us." [15]

Soon, however, the climate changed. In a second letter to his brother in Paris, Tonty explained an abrupt change in plans by pointing (this time an unfounded accusation) to his *bête noire*, the Jesuits:

> I wrote you a letter [last] month in which I informed you that I was to accompany M. d'Iberville to the Cenis. When I arrived at the Quinipissa village, I found everthing changed. M. d'Iberville told me that he wished me to go to the Chicachas [Chickasaw] to arrest an Englishman who has settled among them . . . it was known that I was to accompany him [Iberville], since, should something happen to him, the [leadership of the] voyage he was about to undertake would fall upon young men. I thought this change could only come because of a letter he received from a Jesuit who is in the Illinois country. . . . I think that, being entirely devoted to those

people [the Jesuits] he did not wish to offend the Company [of Jesus] who is very angry with me because I accompanied the Gentlemen of the *Missions étrangères* to the Mississippi. Since M. d'Iberville is a great friend of mine, I did not want to ask for an explanation as to the cause of his change; I was satisfied with telling him that when it was question of the king's service, I cared very little about what the whole of Canada would say. Since he believed it was to be of service to the king to fetch an Englishman, I would do my best to arrest him, but since I had only eight men, if I caught the Englishman, I would send him back with five men commanded by the *garde-marine*, M. de la Ronde; afterwards I would continue my journey with the rest [of the men] to join La Forest who must have arrived in the Illinois country.[16]

In the same letter, Tonty included a series of recommendations to his brother on how to remind the King, on his behalf, of his many services. Tonty added a detailed description of the course of the Mississippi from its mouth to Illinois, with a wealth of observations on the hydrographic conditions and on the character of the population inhabiting its banks. This was a barely disguised attempt at demonstrating once more his intimate knowledge of the area. But the letter also shows his obvious discouragement. Holding on to the king's service seemed to be the last and only sure solace for his hurt dignity: "All the voyages I made for the success of this country have ruined me. I hope the Court will take it in consideration having given satisfaction. Even if you do not obtain what I am asking, if troops are sent to this country as M. d'Iberville tells me they will, at least, secure a company for me." [17]

At the end of February, 1700, Tonty was already on his way back to Illinois, having spent a fews days vainly looking for the English slave trader. By then he had been in the Gulf area two weeks and his status was still not clear. Meeting with Iberville had not brought the concrete results that he expected. He would soon be even more disappointed.

On March 1st, Tonty arrived at the camp set up by Pierre-Charles Le Sueur, a cousin of Iberville, who had joined his expedition. A trader and an entrepreneur, veteran of the Sioux country, he was also on his way up the Mississippi charged with the mission of discovering and developing mines.[18] He had with him a party of thirty miners from France, and this large contingent moved slowly in several canoes and one felucca. The latter was a broad-beamed vessel with a flat bottom and shallow draft, one or two masts rigged with a lateen sail, the craft of excellence of the Nile

River; it was then being introduced on the Mississippi for the first time. If successful, Le Sueur's experimentation would greatly affect commercial development.

On March 2nd, while Tonty was still at his camp, Le Sueur wrote in his log that he had received a letter from Iberville warning him of possible attacks in Illinois country by the Tamaroa as "this could happen following the instigation of people who have interest that nobody come close to their business; [the letter] advised me to move ahead of M. de Tonty . . ."[19]

Le Sueur's log, like many papers of this period concerning North America, was copied in France by Claude Delisle, a renowned geographer of the time who had access to many other documents which since have disappeared. A somewhat mysterious figure who may have played the role of a "secret agent" under the cover of his profession, he also routinely interviewed participants when they came through Paris. In this case he made a rather curious note on the margin of the document: "It seems that M. d'Iberville suspected M. de Tonti." Today, from our vantage point, and from all that we know of his record and character, Tonty appears to have been above suspicion. Even when he was disgruntled we would not have expected him to instigate attacks on fellow *serviteurs du roi*. However, Iberville noted that among the *voyageurs* who came down with Tonty ". . . all but four," were going back to Illinois, disappointed. They may have been even apprehensive about an uncertain future. Several had relatives among the Tamaroa and the Kaskaskia whom they could have easily recruited for some concerted harassment of Le Sueur's party. By then Tonty may have lost his grip on their actions,[20] as he was in fact heading for Fort St. Louis des Illinois. There, once more, and for the last time, he joined La Forest in writing a petition to the minister, Mr. Pontchartrain, this time asking for a concession in Arkansas with the right to erect a new trading post along the Ohio River.

On Friday, June 25, 1700, at nine in the morning, having ignored the warnings of Iberville and of some *voyageurs* (who had suggested bypassing the area completely), Le Sueur pulled his canoes onto the beach of *le village Tamarois (et) des Casaquias*, "residence of two Jesuit missionaries (plus four Missionary priests), this village is composed of three nations. . . the Casaquia, Tamarois and the Metchigamia. The first housed in sixty cabins, the second only thirty and the third, nine or ten."[21]

At the time, Cahokia was the forced temporary home of three groups: a large band of Illinois-speaking Missouri, very unhappy about their new conditions; of hostile *voyageurs* who had just returned from the gulf ahead of Le Sueur; and Illinois Indians, made uneasy by the arrival of a new, large group of unfamiliar Frenchmen. All this diverse and unsettled population added to an already tense environment. Le Sueur, however, like La Salle, was a man who confronted situations. He called a parley of all the available warriors and chiefs. Standing at his side was Tonty, who had returned from Fort St. Louis for the occasion, the two Jesuits, and the four missionary priests. It was in keeping with Tonty's character that in spite of the bitterness he might have harbored, he once again "rallied the flag," thereby giving credit to Le Sueur's *parole* to the Illinois. The *parole*, or harangue, was long; slowly translated into Illinois from the French by Father Pinet it included twelve points, each dealing with specific problems.

The essence of Le Sueur's harangue was that the King, "our master and yours," wanted them to be better instructed in the ways of God; that M. de Tonty would keep them informed of the king's intentions; that they should ignore the bad example of a few Frenchmen; that they should not be concerned by the large number of Frenchmen going through their town. The customary gifts were exchanged; Le Sueur gave six axes, two rifles, sixty pounds of powder, the Illinois gave him eighteen deerskins.

On July 12, 1700, Le Sueur left with his felucca and two canoes for the Upper Mississippi passing: "the River of the Missouris which means "canoe", from the name of the Indians who are called "people of the canoe," or Emessourita . . . " [22]

When Le Sueur returned to Cahokia almost a year later (May 25, 1701), a major change had occurred in Illinois: the Kaskaskia had become new neighbors, having arrived from Fort St. Louis des Illinois accompanied by their many French relatives. Together, they had begun a long trek which they expected to end somewhere on the Gulf of Mexico, near the new French establishments created by Iberville. The Peoria had not joined, remaining in sole possession of fort and church. Although the numbers involved were small, this was still a major move as it involved the largest concentration of population in Illinois. Tonty's role in this affair is unknown, as he had already left Fort Saint Louis for the Gulf of Mexico to join Iberville's staff when the move of Illinois and voyageurs to the south began. On the other hand, Rouensa, the Chief of the Kaskaskia (and Michel Accault's father-in-law), greatly stirred his little nation with promises of a land of milk and honey farther down on the Gulf, with Iberville. This sequence of events meshed too well with Iberville's plans for the aggrandizement of Louisiana, at the expense of Canada, to have been only coincidence. Possibly Tonty, in exchange for finding employment with Iberville, had a hand in persuading the Illinois and the French to move south. (The transfer of jurisdiction over Illinois from Canada to Louisiana was part of Iberville's plan.) We are only surmising as there are no traces of such instructions, but the timing and circumstances make the possibility of such an arrangement logical. At any rate, as one of Illinois' most prominent nineteenth-century historians wrote:

> Iberville had conceived far-reaching plans for Illinois. In 1702 he set forth his ideas in an elaborate memorial which makes clear the significance of many happenings in the north. In spite of vociferous protests from New France, Iberville treated the Illinois country as lying within his jurisdiction and proceeded to dispose of its future. His policy, like that of La Salle, contemplated an extensive rearrangement of the native tribes. He planned to move the Illinois Indians from the Illinois river to the Ohio, which he asserted was uninhabited. The places thus left vacant should be occupied by the Mascouten, the Kickapoo, and the Miami tribes. The Sioux he proposed to locate on the lower Missouri, and certain of the Missouri tribes on the Arkansas river; he even contemplated uprooting the Assiniboin far to the north. "In four or five years," he writes, "we can establish a commerce...of sixty to eighty thousand buffalo skins and more than one hundred and fifty thousand skins of bucks, stags and deer, which it will be necessary to have prepared on the spot and which will produce, delivered in France, a return of more than two million five hundred thousand livres yearly.[23]

It almost worked but for the Jesuits' intervention.

The Jesuits had maintained their mission in Peoria. In 1697, Father Marest had taken over from Father Gravier. Both knew the Illinois language, particularly Father Gravier who had "made clear the principle of this language and who adapted it to the rules of grammar."[24] When the Kaskaskias began their move, Father Marest followed them tenaciously, arguing day after day against their intentions to go to Louisiana. By the time they reached the Mississippi, he finally persuaded them to stop on the western bank "opposite Cahokia at the mouth of the Des Pères River, in St. Louis."[25]

Father Gravier, who had hastened from Michilimackinac to help his colleague, wrote in his *Relation* that the Peoria (who had remained behind) had promised him that they would protect the church at St. Louis des Illinois, but that he doubted their word. "God grant that the road from Chicagou to Peoria not be closed . . . or the whole Illinois mission would suffer greatly." [26]

The abandonment of *Fort St. Louis des Illinois* (Starved Rock) probably took place in 1702, when La Forest was recalled to Canada. The loss of population in Cahokia, and the movement fifty miles farther south of the Kaskaskia village, considerably changed the French line of communication between Canada and Louisiana. Although the fort of Chicago was maintained under De Liette for several more years, and Fort St. Joseph remained in use, a new line developed on the broader Ohio River.

As precarious as the French presence in Illinois was then, it remained vital to France's interest. All sorts of indications point to the essential role of Illinois during the initial development of Louisiana. After spending a month *aux Tamarois*, Le Sueur returned to the Gulf of Mexico, in July, 1701, and noted the presence of thirty Canadians from Illinois. They had been hired the previous year by Iberville to manufacture dugout canoes from cypress trees. Le Sueur bought one of these canoes for eighty *livres*, and used it to send five of his men back to the Sioux country. During the same month, three *voyageurs* arrived at the Gulf from Illinois with a boatload of pelts for sale. In February, 1702, Le Sueur again returned to the Gulf from Upper Mississippi, this time with 2,000 pounds of blue and green dirt which he wrongly believed to be minerals. [27] No doubt much more traffic than was recorded was taking place on the Mississippi. Much of this activity with Illinois was generated by the newly established posts of La Mobile and Biloxi. French activity of any sort on the Mississippi was urgently needed to stem the inroads made by English traders from the Carolinas. These traders boldly floated down the Ohio River to meet voyageurs from Illinois, not above selling their peltries to the enemy. In fact, some Frenchmen traveled to British-held territory knowing that they would get a better price for their pelts there. Iberville used this argument in his correspondence with the minister to support the request made by another officer of fortune—Charles Juchereau de St. Denys, then lieutenant-general for Montreal—for the right to build a tannery on the banks of the Ohio, near its confluence with the Mississippi River.

By building a tannery, Juchereau hoped to treat buffalo robes that he would then ship to France via the new ports opened on the Gulf. Thanks to Iberville's support, Juchereau received a grant that also included a trade license for three canoeloads of furs a year, a *largesse* much protested by the government in Quebec. Juchereau began by recruiting a large party of tradesmen in Canada, but things went wrong almost from the start: leaving Michilimackinac during the early part of 1701, he selected the Wisconsin and Fox Rivers route which was faster than others. It turned out to be a costly decision; he was stopped by the Fox Indians to whom he had to pay a *toll* of 1,000 *écus*. The Fox, made nervous by a rapprochement between the French and their enemies, the Sioux, were becoming increasingly dangerous to French commerce. The Fox menace, in time, would become just as great a threat as the Iroquois raids. Finally, Juchereau succeeded in building a post on the Ohio River, Fort St. Vincent. A chaplain was appointed, the Jesuit Mermet from the Illinois Mission, underlining the importance given to the new establishment. (His stipend and provisions were apparently overlooked, to his understandable indignation.) Fort St. Vincent was hardly completed in 1702, when an epidemic struck the French as well as the Mascouten who had been hired as trappers and hunters. It killed off half of the population including Juchereau.[28] Juchereau's lieutenant, Mr. de Saint-Lambert Mandeville, survived and sent word of the disaster to Iberville asking for instructions. Iberville, always practical, dispatched back a ship's carpenter who built enough crafts to load the 12,000 buffalo skins that Juchereau had accumulated. With Saint-Lambert in command and a thirty-man escort, they were shipped to La Mobile. By 1704, the few French traders who had chosen to remain behind gave up and abandoned the post. Father Mermet returned to his missionary work with the Kaskaskia.[29]

In 1701, Tonty had left Illinois for the Gulf of Mexico navigating down the Mississippi for the sixth time; unbeknownst to him, it would be his last. The next trace that we have of Tonty is in an entry of March 19, 1702 in the log of *La Renommée*, where Iberville routinely mentioned him as serving under his command.[30] Tonty, sometimes identified as lieutenant and other times as captain, assumed an important but subaltern role. From September, 1702, to January, 1704, he campaigned against the Alibamon in the hinterland,[31] and all reports showed him to be his usual reliable self. In 1704, he was in command of La Mobile (which then counted 195 inhabitants, including forty Canadians) when the vessel *Le Pélican* not only brought a cargo of marriageable young ladies but, unfortunately, also the yellow fever virus. Along with thirty soldiers, another officer and a Jesuit, Tonty caught the disease and died. Records indicate that his death occurred around the 6th of September of that year. Thus ended the exploits of one of the least known—yet most important— figures of the French conquest of North America.

The Kaskaskia—or Kats, as they were familiarly called—and their Tamaroa cousins had remained at the Des Pères location for three years after their move from Peoria. But Des Pères was inconveniently located on the western side of the Mississippi and consequently lay exposed to Sioux raiding parties. The danger led the Illinois to move again, this time to the site which would become known as "Kaskaskia" and, some 115 years later, the first capital of the State of Illinois. The exact date of this move was recorded on the register of baptisms, probably by Father Marest: "1703, 25 avril, Ad ripam Metchigamiam dictam venimus," immediately below the entry of the baptism performed on April 13th, of Pierre, son of a Pierre and Marie Therese Bizaillon. The River Michigamea, referred to in this entry, was identified by early scholars as being the same as the Kaskaskia or the Okaw.[32]

Illinois was about to settle down.

NOTES

1. Sauvole, from Fort Biloxi, Margry, IV, 459. There were altogether eleven LeMoyne brothers, four of them involved with the expedition to Lower Mississippi.

2. Jean-Baptiste LeMoyne, Sieur de Bienville; Tonty had given the name of Quynypassa to this village; the multiplicity of unfamiliar names confused Iberville considerably.

3. *Journal du voyage fait par d'Hiberville à la coste Méridionale de Floride en 1699*, entry of February 14, AN, Marine: Serie 4 JJ, log of *La Badine*; the three logs kept by Iberville and sent to the Minister of the Navy have been translated and edited by Richebourg Gaillard McWilliams, *Iberville's Gulf Journals*, The University of Alabama, 1981. Charles B. Reed, in *The First Great Canadian, Sieur d'Iberville*, Chicago, 1910, placed the village of Bayougala thirty-eight miles southwest of New Orleans, 191.

4. On August 29, 1699, Bienville turned back Captain Bond telling him that the country was already solidly occupied by the French.

5. La Forest and Tonty to Pontchartrain, AN, Colonies, C11, A120, fols. 50-51-v.

6. La Forest and Tonty to Pontchartrain,

7. Transfer of M. Henry de Tonty to M. Alphonse de Tonty, October 27, 1698, *Louisiana Historical Quarterly*, VI, 578-579.

8. Tonty to St. Vallier, July 14, 1699, from Missilimaquina (Michilimackinac), in M.B. Palm, *The Jesuit Missions of the Illinois Country, 1673-1763*, Cleveland, 1931, 4.

9. Callières to Pontchartrain, October 16, 1700, in NYCD, IX, 1712; a document

kept at the Bibliothèque Nationale in Paris seems to indicate that one of Iberville's brothers had left Montreal to join Tonty before his departure: *Nouvelles du Mississippi apportées par Sargères*, 1701, BN, *Fonds français*, 22801, 147.

10. Bernard de La Harpe, *Journal Historique de l'Etablissement des Français à la Louisiane*, Paris & La Nouvelle Orleans, 1831, 26. A French historian disputed the authorship of this diary, claiming that it was instead, "...the work of the Chevalier de Beaurain;" see Baron Marc de Villiers, *La découverte du Missouri et l'Histoire du Fort d'Orleans, 1673-1728*, Librairie H. Champion, Paris, 1925. Iberville had returned from France on January 9, 1700.

11. *Journal of Paul du Ru, Missionary Priest to Louisiana*, trans. Ruth Laphan Butler, Caxton Club, Chicago, 1934. The original manuscript is kept at the Newberry Library, in Chicago. Du Ru was born in Vernon, France, on October 6, 1666; his journal covers a short period: from February 1 to May 8, 1700. Chaplain at Fort Biloxi and at Fort Mobile, he was recalled to France in 1702 after a dispute with the administration and died in Rouen in 1741.

12. *Journal du Voyage du Chevalier d'Iberville sur le vaisseau du Roi La Renommée en mil six cent quatre dix neuf, depuis le Cap Français jusqu'à la côte du Mississippi et son retour*, BN, MSS. fr., trans. Richebourg G. McWilliams, *Iberville's*,

13. Tonty's two letters, from February 28 and March 4, left from France by the same ship, on March 30. They were addressed to his brother in Paris who had them "deciphered" first, as they were written with a tortured penmanship, before they would be circulated and read by the many people interested in the affairs of North America. Two men, Claude Delisle, a geographer, and Father Leonard de Sainte-Catherine de Sienne, a Discalced Augustinian who collected archives, books, and correspondence, were communicated these letters by M. Cabart de Villermont, Tonty's influential Parisian protector. The English translation used here is from Father Jean Delanglez, "Mid-America", July 1939, 21, No. 3.

14. The text being referred here is the *Dernières découvertes dans l'Amérique Septentrionale de M. de la Salle; Mises au jour par M. le chevalier Tonti gouverneur de Fort Saint Louis, aux Illinois*, Paris, 1697. Tonty, letter, February 28, 1700.

15. *Journal of Paul du Ru.*, 12.

16. M. de Tonty to his brother, March 4, 1700.

17. Ibid.

18. Pierre-Charles Le Sueur was born in Notre Dame de Heden, Artois, France, in 1657; he came to New France probably in 1679, as an unpaid voluntary servant or *donné* to the Jesuits. Sent to Sault Ste. Marie, he gave up religious vocation for the adventures of the fur trade. In 1681, he was already a known *coureur des bois* and fined. Operating among the Sioux in 1689, when Upper Mississippi was annexed to France, was a talented amateur diplomat named Perrot. He was responsible for establishing peace in 1695 between Chippewa and Sioux, bringing their chiefs to a conference with Governor Frontenac. Having received permission to exploit a mine he claimed to have discovered in Upper Mississippi, he joined Iberville's expedition to the Mouth of the Mississippi in 1700. He built Fort l'Huillier—L'Huillier being the name of a *Fermier général*, his financial sponsor— on a branch of the St. Pierre River (Minnesota). In April 1702, Le Sueur travelled

back to France for new grants. He died on March 1, 1707, in Canada. He left a widow in Louisiana, Marguerite Messier, a girl he had married in 1690 in Canada. For more information on Le Sueur see the *Bulletin des Recherches Historiques*, March, 1904; his voyages on the Mississippi are found in Bernard de la Harpe, *Journal Historique de l'Etablissment des Français à la Louisiane*, Paris, 1831, trans. in J.G. Shea, *Early Voyages Up and Down the Mississippi*, Albany, 1861.

19. *Mémoires de M. LeSueur*, AN, Marine 2JJ 56, Colonies, C A 12, ff 290, 440-45.

20. *Journal de d'Iberville. . . . La Renommée . . . Second Voyage.*

21. *Mémoire de Mr. Le Sueur*, trans. this author.

22. *Mémoires de M. Le Sueur . . . Suite du Mississippi depuis les Tamarois*, MS transcribed by Claude DeL'Isle; trans. this author.

23. Alvord, *The Illinois Country.*, 129.

24. *Jesuit Relations*, LXVI, 549.

25. Sister Mary Borgia Palm, *The Jesuit Missions of the Illinois Country, 1673-1763*, The Sisters of Notre Dame, Cleveland, 1931, 36; Sister Palm quotes abundantly from the letter written from Cahokia on April 13, 1701, by M. Bergier, priest of the *Missions étrangères*.

26. *Relation ou journal du voyage du R.P. Jacques Gravier de la Compagnie de Jésus, en 1700*, trans. by John G. Shea, *Early Voyages Up and Down the Mississippi*, Albany, New York, 1861, 3.

27. Le Sueur returned to France in 1702 and died on his way back to Louisiana.

28. Charles Juchereau de Saint Denys, born in Quebec, December 6, 1655, had been appointed First Royal judge of Montreal in 1694. He received *Lettre patentes* to establish a Tannery—Fort St. Vincent—on June 4, 1701. Juchereau's young widow remarried three years later in Montreal, Louis Lienard de Beaujeu; one son from this union would become the *abbé* Louis de Beaujeu, the confessor of Louis XVI.

29. Pénicaut, *Relation*, in Margry, V, 438-39.

30. *Journal du sieur d'Iberville depuis le 15ème décembre 1701 jusqu'au 27ème avril 1702*, AN, Marine: Serie B 23; this was the journal of Iberville's third voyage to the Gulf.

31. "Ce fut au commencement de septembre que nous partimes tous ensemble pour aller contre les Alibamons....Nous avions pour officier de ce parti MM. de Bienville, de Saint-Denis, de Tonty, ancien capitaine du Canada;" Pénicaut, *Relation*, in Pierre Margry, *Découvertes et établissements des français*, V, 429. Also translated in B.F. French's *Historical Calendar of Louisiana and Florida*, N.Y. Sabin, 1869, as the *Annals of Lousiana from 1698 to 1722 by M. Pénicaut*, 81-82.

32. *Extrait des registres des baptèmes de la Mission des Illinois sous le titre de 'Immaculée Conception de la Sainte Vierge*, St. Louis University.

8

The Growing Years

I llinois began the eighteenth century in a state of confusion and neglect: confusion, because Iberville was behaving as though Illinois fell within the boundaries of Louisiana, while it was still—and would remain so for several more years—an integral part of Canada; and neglect, because neither Quebec nor La Mobile was exercising any kind of serious or effective administration. La Forest had been recalled from Illinois to Montreal in 1702, after he wrote to both the governor and the *intendant* of New France (respectively, Mr. de Callières and Mr. de Champigny) requesting instructions regarding Fort St. Louis. He hinted that he might abandon the fort if not reimbursed for his past expenses in the service of the King.[1] Since La Forest's complaint was grounded in fact, the hint was taken and he was compensated with a captain's commission, on the condition that he remain in the King's service in Canada.[2] De Liette replaced La Forest as the *commandant* of Illinois and a modicum of continuity of French authority was maintained, although the real conditions of the early 1700's were much different from the image of stability and order that the dispatches projected.

In 1704 the significant French population of Illinois—its male element eroded by a small but constant migration to the Gulf—[3] was concentrated in Kaskaskia, around a handful of Jesuit fathers acting as temporal and spiritual leaders. While not the farthest outpost of France in North America, Kaskaskia was certainly very remote. On the route to Quebec, the nearest French establishment from which it could possibly draw support, Fort Pontchartrain, was four hundred miles northwest as the crow flies.

We must say a word here about Fort Pontchartrain. Along with the adjacent village, it became the city of Detroit (a French word meaning "the straits," the location between two lakes, Huron and Erie), the fruit of Antoine de La Mothe-Cadillac's ambition and foresight.

In 1699, La Mothe-Cadillac had written to the King arguing in favor of the gathering "of all the Savages who are our allies, in a single community in the area between Lake Erie, Lake Huron, and Lake Illinois [Lake Michigan]."[4] In spite of much skepticism from Canada's governor and *intendant*, La Mothe-Cadillac was able to persuade the Minister, the Count de Maurepas, of the feasibility of the project. La Mothe-Cadillac assured him that within ten years missionaries and nuns would be teaching the French language and Christianity to the Indians, making them the King's good subjects, and that they would blend with the French into one race. "It is evident that the Indians will become civilized when their houses or their cabins will be next to those of the French, mainly when theirs and ours will be permanent constructions . . . removing from them the belief that we want to abandon them and that we only come here to collect beaver skins."[5]

Further, Cadillac argued, such a concentration of Indians would help eliminate much of the fur trade that accounted for the social disorder fomented by the *voyageurs*, and consequently appease the missionaries. Eliminating the fur trade as the principal activity of the colony would remove the burden that plagued the metropolitan economy: "As it is a matter of removing the cause of the problem being that Canada provides a merchandise for which the *fermiers* (tax collectors) state they have neither outlet nor sufficient demand because of quantities that are too great and of poor quality."[6]

Cadillac built the fort and settlement with fifty soldiers and fifty *habitans* and their families. For assistants, he had several capable lieutenants who were veterans of many adventurous enterprises—Alphonse de Tonty (Henri's brother), Dugué de Boisbriant, and De Charconacle—along with the inevitable clergy, in this case both a Jesuit and a Recollet, in a laudable attempt at maintaining religious peace among the two rival orders. La Mothe-Cadillac began gathering Ottawa, Huron, Potawatomi, Miami, and other Indian nations and, on July 24, 1701, Fort Pontchartrain *au détroit des lacs Erié et Huron* was officially in operation.

The new fort and settlement were expected to check Iroquois pretensions more effectively and facilitate the use of the Ohio and Miami Rivers as a means of communication between Canada and Louisiana. However, the establishment of this new French stronghold created a serious backlash: it drove the Iroquois confederation to make a formal request for British protection, which meant recognizing British sovereignty over what the Iroquois claimed was their own territory. They also claimed that the western limits included Lake Michigan and Lake Superior, foretelling more harassment of the Great Lakes Indian nations.[7] The Iroquois were determined to be the only middlemen between British traders and the Indians living in the still mostly untapped, fur-rich lands of the West.

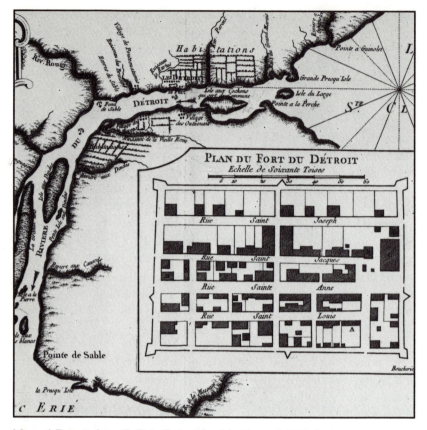

Map of Detroit from Bellin's Petit Atlas Maritime of 1764. Inset
shows the plan of the fort. (The Newberry Library)

Ironically, the new fort was also anathema to the French and Indian
residents of Michilimackinac who saw it as a rival to their own older
settlement.[8] A few Ottawa residing in Michilimackinac went as far as
inciting the Peoria to stage a raid against the Indians who had settled in
Detroit; fifteen Peoria warriors answered the call. Forewarned, but not
taking the threat very seriously, La Mothe-Cadillac simply ordered these
Peoria to be whipped and sent back to their village.

It is hardly surprising that following this questionable choice of
punishment, the Peoria began to engage in all sorts of hostile acts towards
the Kaskaskia, the Miami, the French, and even the "black robes." In 1705,
a soldier was killed and De Liette, then commanding the Illinois territory,

was ordered to bring several Peoria chiefs back to Canada to account for the murder. They came as far as Michilimackinac, where local Ottawa convinced the Peoria Chief, Mantouchensa, to ignore De Liette and the summons and return home. Their return so excited the village of the Peoria that a group of young braves shot several arrows at the resident Jesuit missionary, Father Gravier. Badly wounded in the arm, he was rescued by some friendly Peoria and taken by canoe all the way down to Biloxi, subsequently returning to France for better medical care. He never completely recovered, and died two years later in Mobile after his return from France.

All this petty unrest led the governor to order the Indian allies from Detroit to Illinois on a mission to punish the Peoria. For good measure, he also closed Peoria to all traders. However, his decision was rescinded a year later before it could be put into effect, as a new campaign was about to begin against the Iroquois.[9] This provided to be a fortunate delay not only for the Peoria, but even more so for the French, who had little need to get involved in an additional conflict. The Peoria could be quarrelsome but they were never a serious threat. Their disputes with the French were more akin to family disputes as, like all the other Illinois, they had many relatives among this French "floating population." [10]

Change was in the air; the stability first found only in the Jesuits' and missionary priests' establishments was beginning to spread. Although information on these early days is fragmentary (the *Jesuit Relations* are about the only source), there are indications that *voyageurs* continued to marry Illinois Indian women and add a second layer to the French-Indian population that had begun to develop a generation before. Human roots were growing deeper along the banks of the Mississippi. Kaskaskia's parish records between 1701 (a year before the move to the final site) and 1713, show that of twenty-one French infants baptized, eighteen of them had Indian mothers. Cahokia, the seat of the missionary priests for the same period, sheltered between forty and fifty fur traders (none of whom could have produced a trade license), most with temporary female companions and, we can assume, offspring.

There were also signs that many French had begun to turn away from the fur trade and explore other occupations. An increasing number of men took up mining.[11] Agriculture was also becoming more popular. In 1712, a windmill was already functioning in Kaskaskia and two more were added a few years later, signs of growing grain production, an important commodity for the French. Agriculture and mining were two activities that the Jesuits encouraged heartily. In all the colonies around the world where the Jesuits were free to operate, the little islands of economic prosperity that developed around their churches were certainly the most positive, tangible effects of their work, although they would have thought otherwise. In 1711 the Jesuits had even returned to Peoria, where they rebuilt the mission in a show of faith.[12]

Though agriculture and mining brought a new measure of stable employment, Illinois should not be envisioned as quite the paradise lyrically described by publicity writers of the day for the benefit of potential investors in the Mississippi venture. In addition to mosquitoes and uncontrollable spring floods bringing malaria and yellow fever, the early inhabitants had to deal with their own internal intrigues as well as those of the Illinois Indians, with whom most had family ties.

In 1708, a coterie of *coureurs des bois* attempted to foment local Indian wars with the idea of selling the potential prisoners as slaves to the British. Illinois was still under the jurisdiction of New France, yet help came from the Governor of Louisiana, Bienville, who responded to the pleas of the missionaries with the dispatch of six *soldats de marine*. The small detachment arrived in Illinois led by Mr. d'Eraque, who was familiar with the area having served as Le Sueur's second-in-command during his expedition to the Upper Mississippi. D'Eraque warned the Canadians, talked to the Indians (distributing the customary gifts), delivered letters to the Jesuits, and returned to Mobile a few months later, leaving Kaskaskia calm for the moment.[13]

Disturbances flared once more in 1711, while De Liette was absent on a special mission for Governor Vaudreuil. Again, the missionaries sent for help, asking that: "... an officer with soldiers be sent to prevent the disorders created by several Canadian mechants, who, under the pretext to trade, commit openly the most scandalous crimes, debauching the daughters and the wives of the Illinois, swerving them from conversion to the faith of our religion."[14]

A sergeant and twelve soldiers were sent to Illinois in two canoes. Among them was Jean Pénicaut, a man whose memoirs we have already seen. After weeks of arduous navigation, the squad finally beached near Kaskaskia. Leaving canoes and men behind, the sergeant proceeded alone to the house of Father Marest, who:

> ... advised him to wait until early next morning to surprise these Canadian libertines in their beds. During the night, the sergeant sent word to us to

come over the Illinois. . . . We arrived two hours before daybreak, but, either because they were informed or for other reasons, the Canadians had left the day before and we did not find any. Our sergeant decided to remain for a while in Illinois either because he wanted to wait for their return or perhaps acting on orders as food supplies were much diminished in Mobile. We remained four months with the Illinois and we maintained ourselves by exchanging our mechandise for their victuals which are very good and inexpensive.[15]

Meanwhile, far away on the other side of the Atlantic Ocean, the mother countries of North America had sent their plenipotentiaries to the little Dutch town of Utrecht to decide on matters which would be of great interest to their expatriate subjects. In Utrecht, on April 11, 1713, France, ruled by an aging Louis XIV, concluded peace treaties with England, Holland, Prussia, Portugal, and Savoy, putting an end to the War of the Spanish Succession begun twelve years before (also known as Queen Ann's War after Britain entered the conflict on May 4, 1702). Twelve years of European wars had brought fame to a few soldiers such as Marlborough and Eugene of Savoy, but had emptied the coffers of France and other nations. Louis XIV had begun the war to secure the Spanish throne for his grandson, Philip; at its conclusion, the Bourbons were indeed secure on the Spanish throne, but France, in addition to great financial losses, had suffered a considerable reduction of her North American holdings. To Great Britain, France had surrendered not only the Hudson Bay and New Foundland, but also *l'Acadie*, which the British renamed Nova Scotia. Losing Acadie meant more than a change of name; it marked the beginning of the diaspora of the Acadians whose descendents, the Cajuns, now live in the bayous of Louisiana. What is perhaps most amazing, when looking back at the effects of the War of the Spanish Succession on the Mississippi Valley, is that the French managed to hold on to their claims with practically no regular troops, with weakened Indian allies, and with so few men that one hesitates to call them settlers.[16]

Increasingly, the major threat of British expansion to French North American possessions originated more from the British colonies than from Britain herself. In 1712, Spotswood, Governor of Virginia, had written to London pointing out the French establishment of a line of communication between Canada and Louisiana and vainly suggesting a march through the passes of the Alleghenies, in order to thwart further French expansion.

Indeed, ever so slowly, the French were finally beginning to realize the great design conceived of by Colbert four decades earlier. But, the disappointing results were still far disproportionate. After one and a half decades of tribulations, Louisiana had not even come close to the expectations held on her account by Iberville when he sailed from Brest. The total French population in Lower Louisiana for 1713 numbered only 400! Although glowing reports of Louisiana's riches still circulated in Paris and Versailles, the King's ministers knew well of the stagnant state of affairs affecting the colony. In today's business parlance, a "white knight" was needed. It was found in the person of Mr. Antoine Crozat, *marquis* de Chatel, a gentleman who had accumulated a huge fortune from the East India trade, and who was willing to refinance the development of the new colony, realizing a profit in the process.

Crozat received a Royal Charter which gave him a monopoly of trade and the total profit from the mines—less one quarter set aside for the King's revenues—for fifteen years. In addition, he had the exclusive right to import annually one shipload of African slaves and 100 girls from Paris's charitable institutions and hospitals. French women were few in Louisiana and Africans even fewer until that time. In 1712, there were only twenty blacks in the colony and none in Illinois, where the French population numbered 320.[17] Crozat also received a series of commercial advantages which insured his economic control of the colony. By the terms of the charter, the royal treasury was to pay the governor, officers and troops for the next nine years, considerably reducing the risks of this operation. As was customary, the *Coutume de Paris* as well as royal decrees constituted the law, in part administered by a *Conseil civil*. Established on December 18, 1712, this became the first civil institution established in Louisiana. The northern boundaries of Louisiana were still ill-defined and Illinois remained in a curious political "no man's land;" Ohio and Illinois mines and furs were included in the description provided by La Mothe-Cadillac (who had attached his political future to the financier), although they were not located within the limits of the grant.[18]

La Mothe-Cadillac, who had been recalled to France in 1710, following accusations of financial misappropriations, had been instrumental in convincing Crozat to make this investment in the future of North America. His success washed him of his sins. Chosen by Crozat to head Louisiana, he was quickly appointed governor by the King. In June 1713, La Mothe-Cadillac landed in Mobile and took over for Bienville (Alphonse de Tonty had replaced La Mothe-Cadillac as *commandant du détroit Pontchartrain des deux lacs*). Bienville remained in Louisiana, inactive until February 1716, when he was posted to Natchez as the commanding officer of the Upper Mississippi region. La Mothe-Cadillac, however, refused to release the two companies of soldiers assigned to Bienville, who left for Natchez with only thirty-five soldiers, apparently having accepted the limitations of his new position with grace.[19]

The monopoly given to Crozat's commercial venture had an immediate detrimental effect on Louisiana: "For a bearskin delivered at the port, wild traders had been receiving 60 sous; the new price was 40 sous. Buckskins, later to give the English language a synonym for a dollar, dropped from twenty-five to fifteen sous [a livre was equal to 100 sous]. Traders among the Indians protested these changes and threatened to bring no more furs to French posts."[20]

The traders, forced to sell their peltries at low fixed prices, began to turn to British markets through ready and available agents, mainly Cherokees. With this situation in mind, in 1714, La Mothe-Cadillac made an eight-month trip to Illinois.[21] Very little resulted from his inspection, although, during the same period, some unfounded reports of Illinois mineral wealth were received in France via Canada. Returning to Mobile in October 1715, La Mothe-Cadillac remained very prudent in his correspondence with Versailles, denying any truth in the gold and silver stories coming out of Illinois. He may not have been responsible for these rumors, but they could only be useful to him, as they did calm the impatient shareholders, allowing them more time to find the reported gold and silver mines.

Well-written accounts alone could not convince Crozat, whose losses in this affair grew daily, and by December 1716, his investment showed a deficit of 1,250,000 livres. He did what any good businessman would do: he called it quits. In his case, it was complicated because he had to petition the King to be released from all his obligations. This was accomplished in January 1717, and, once again in his career, La Mothe-Cadillac was recalled.

Meanwhile, a major event had taken place in France: the death of Louis XIV, on September 1, 1715. The "Sun-King" had survived not only his son, but also his grandson. His great-grandson was only five years old on the day of his accession to the throne as Louis XV. The government of the kingdom went to the child's great-uncle and "first prince of royal blood," Duke Philippe d'Orleans, who became Regent of France.[22] This political change would have a great impact on French enterprises in North

Portrait of John Law. Taken
from *Narrative and Critical
History of America,* Vol 5,
Justin Winsor, ed., 1884.
(The Newberry Library)

America, where commercialism would now be given an even freer reign.
On January 1, 1718, Crozat's privileges were turned over for twenty-five
years to the *Compagnie d'Occident,* also known as the Mississippi Company.

The new company was the creation of John Law, a financial wizard
from Scotland who had taken the souls and the trust of France by storm.[23]
Born in Edinburgh, Scotland, he had studied economics and commerce in
London, and banking in Holland. The publication of his theories on the
use of paper money broadened his reputation. Introduced at the court in
Versailles, he was given permission by the Regent to apply his principles
in France where there was an urgent, even desperate, need for a solution
to the 3,000,000,000 *livres* public debt left by Louis XIV. Given a virtual
free hand by the Regent, Law merged his two creations, the *Compagnie
d'Occident* and the Royal Bank, with the East Indian Company. His
personal finances, as well as the investments of thousands, became
closely intertwined with the finances of the kingdom.

In North America, the East Indian Company had a much larger

territory to develop since the Illinois Country had been formally incorporated into Louisiana as of September 27, 1717.[24] The same year, Bienville, vindicated again, was reappointed governor. One of his first tasks was to reorganize Louisiana into nine military districts, one of which was Illinois. This was an Illinois with limits extending south to the Ohio River and north to the Missouri, and an undefined line between the Wisconsin and the Illinois Rivers.[25] In 1718, De Liette transferred the command of Illinois to his old comrade Canadian-born Pierre Dugué, *sieur* de Boisbriant, forty-seven, a cousin of Iberville and a veteran of La Salle's campaigns. He had just been made a knight of St. Louis and was eager to do more. His intimate knowledge of Illinois made him an excellent choice for the post. This was a year of important decisions, not only for Illinois but also for lower Louisiana, where Bienville selected the site for a new city that he would name *La Nouvelle Orléans*, in honor of the Regent of France.

Until the involvement of John Law's *Compagnie d'Occident*, the great schemes plotted in the bureaus of Versailles and in the forts of Louisiana had had no measurable impact on Illinois. Traffic was growing on the Mississippi and on the adjacent northern tributaries, as increasing numbers of Canadians brought their goods to Biloxi and La Mobile, or moved permanently south. For all travelers, Kaskaskia was a vital halt and as such benefited from the traffic. With the change of administrative boundaries in 1717, Illinois officially ceased to be part of Canada, its "mother-colony". But, in fact, as would be dramatically demonstrated with the growing danger presented by the hostility of the Fox Indian nation, Illinois' destiny remained more closely associated with the geopolitics of the Great Lakes region than with those of the area around the Gulf of Mexico.

The magnitude of the investment by John Law's company in the Mississippi Valley was expected to eliminate these threats and to guarantee a safe colony to the new settlers arriving from the metropole. Under the new régime, Illinois received not only a commander backed by a permanent garrison and a judge, but also a council, insuring a broader administrative basis. The word "council" should not mislead; it had nothing to do with the type of local bodies in existence throughout the thirteen British colonies. The Illinois council was composed of the military commander, the officers of the garrison, the royal functionaries, and the employees of the *Compagnie d'Occident*.[26] There cannot be a better example than this difference of approach in government to illustrate the opposing characteristics of British and French mentalities in North

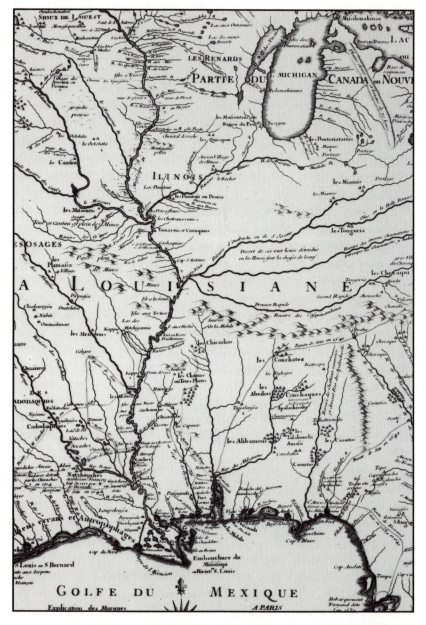

Detail showing the Mississippi Valley.   From Guillaume Delisle,
"Carte de la Louisiane," Paris, 1718.   (The Newberry Library)

America. While the British relied on "caucus of the village green," the French trusted the simple and direct decision of the officer in command or of the captain of the militia.

The slow convoy of the King's *bateaux* which ascended the Mississippi River during the summer of 1718 was imposing. In addition to Boisbriant, it carried Marc Antoine de La Loere Des Ursins, the head clerk; Nicolas Chassin, the keeper of the royal store; and Captain Pierre d'Artaguiette (the younger brother of Diron d'Artaguiette, Louisiana's *intendant*), commanding officer of the one hundred soldiers of marine infantry and four lieutenants of the new garrison. The convoy also included several new settlers from France along with their families. This was implantation in earnest, meant to grow and last.[27] No group of this size lands on a tiny community without affecting all facets of its life. For three years, Boisbriant and a large part of his entire force were lodged in the houses of the *habitans* of Kaskaskia, while the remainder built a new stronghold which was expected to anchor French presence between Louisiana and Canada: Fort de Chartres (named in honor of the son of the Regent, the Duke of Chartres), sixteen miles upriver. Prosperity, security and, for the first time, the trappings of an aristocratic society brought by the officers, gave Kaskaskia a new look. Illinois was the last stop on the route opened by the French speculators. Mining was on their minds and, like Crozat before them, the investors backing John Law and the *Compagnie d'Occident* expected quick profit. No sooner was Boisbriant installed in Kaskaskia than he dispatched teams to survey the upper country for mines. The first consequential French inroads west of the Mississippi date from this period. In 1719, Captain Du Tisné visited Missouri and Osage villages west of the Mississippi.[28] In 1721, Bernard de la Harpe, an officer posted on the Gulf coast, was sent to Arkansas with sixteen soldiers and one ensign on a mission to go west as far as possible to find mines. In the spring of 1723, the French, pushing further west, explored the course of a tributary of the Missouri to which they gave the name *La Plate*, and, during the fall of the same year, they built a fort about fifteen miles up from the mouth of the Missouri, the *Fort Orléans*.[29]

Although the fort was eventually abandoned, the explorations had not been in vain, for by the early 1730's, Missouri would be annexed to Louisiana, replacing Illinois as the western frontier of the French North American empire. Closer to Kaskaskia and Fort de Chartres several mines had been opened a few miles up the *Merameg*, a temperamental small stream flowing from a chain of medium-range mountains (Today's

Ozarks) to the western bank of the Mississippi. To find silver the company had recruited a bona fide smelter, the *sieur* de Lochon. But "he extracted fourteen pounds of a rather bad quality lead, at a cost of 1400 francs. Discouraged by these unrewarding labors, he returned to France."[30] Unwilling to accept defeat, the company then dispatched to Merameg a former Spanish prisoner who claimed experience in the Mexican silver mines. He dug the rock along the Merameg longer and deeper with no better results. He was followed by a *Brigade de Mineurs du Roi*, directed by a *Sieur* La Renaudière. Since none among them had any experience in the building of smelting facilities, their disorganized efforts were also useless. Finally, an able man and former banker, Philippe François Renault, arrived in 1720, as the commissioned director general of mines for the company. He had with him professional miners and a force of two hundred African slaves. Within two years he found large quantities of lead along the Merameg, and coal along the Illinois. He explored the Illinois all the way up to the former site of *Fort St. Louis des Illinois,* which by then was simply known as *le Rocher.*[31] None of the mining operations led to the discovery of silver, either in Illinois or in Missouri. The investment in money and men, nevertheless, had been massive, considering the means available at the time and how far Illinois was from France.

Aside from the much-hoped-for mines, the directors of the *Compagnie d'Occident* expected the valley of the Mississippi to produce a variety of merchandise and, like their predecessors, published a tariff fixing the prices they would pay to the *habitans*. These prices, not surprisingly, were very low. For instance, for one hundred pounds of good-quality wheat flour, fifteen *livres*; for one hundred pounds of oats, four *livres*; for four large deerskins, one *livre*; for good beaver pelts, three *livres* each. All prices quoted were for goods delivered either to Biloxi or Mobile.[32]

The Company paid low prices for Illinois products while it simply doubled the cost for the merchandise *coming* from France. In 1722, as authorized by its charter, the Company began to sell Black slaves, most of whom came from Senegal via Saint Domingue (Haiti). Male laborers were priced at 660 *livres* each and buyers given three years to pay. Costs and conditions were too high for settlers, considering the low return they were allowed on their grain and other farm products. The slaves sold in Illinois (a few hundred within the first two or three years of the company's existence) worked for most part either in the lead mines, or for the only agricultural enterprise able to afford them, the Jesuit house of Kaskaskia;

or, they became house servants for the officers of the garrison.[33]

The officers' salaries, in fact, underline the harshness of the financial conditions that the company imposed on the colonists: Boisbriant received an annual salary of 3,000 *livres,* Des Ursins received 2,000; Mr. de Bourrion, the officer put in charge of an outpost on the Missouri, 1,800. Eventually, prices would circumvent edicts and be dictated by the laws of the marketplace. The Canadians—including the old Illinois hands— were leaders in this domain, having never been easily impressed by tariffs, decrees, or licenses; they had made an art of ignoring these for at least a century. La Harpe recorded in his journal how on his way north he came across several Canadians going down the Mississippi with a load of 5,000 pounds of salted beef (buffalo meat) that they were going to sell in New Orleans. Lower Louisiana was too much in continuous need of food supplies to haggle with willing suppliers; the administrators would just have to go along.

When Fort de Chartres, a log construction, was completed in 1721, government and garrison moved to the new location, while a village appropriately named *La Nouvelle Chartres* was built outside the bastions to accommodate the families. In 1723, Diron d'Artaguiette toured Illinois, keeping a daily log where we find a first-hand description of the original Fort de Chartres and nearby developments:

> Fort de Chartres is a fort of piles the size of one's leg, square in shape, having two bastions, which command all the curtains. . . . There is church outside the fort and some dwellings a half league lower down on the same side as well as half a league above as far as a little village of the Illinois where two Jesuit fathers, missionaries, who have a dwelling and a church. This is a little village which is called Mechiquamias and numbers perhaps 200 warriors. From there one goes through a large and vast prairie a league and a half to the northwest where Mr. Renaut, director of the mines, is established with two scores of Frenchmen, all laborers. This place is a quarter of a league distant from the Mississipy. There is a fort, with stakes the size of a leg. The shape is that of two horse shoes, one turning in and the other turning out, with two square bastions. There are in this fort a church, four frame houses and one stone house.[34]

By then, the man whose vision had much to do with the impetus given to French Illinois, John Law, had long fled France, a victim of his own genius and the speculation fever dooming sound economic innovation.

Millions of *livres* had been lost to many; but the magnitude of the *Compagnie d'Occident's* holdings and organization prevented its disappearance. Reorganized, the Company remained in operation and maintained its impetus on Louisiana, including Illinois. The Company's initiatives were matched by Canada's efforts to shore up communications. This was the sort of cooperation between the two colonies that the ministry had encouraged. In 1719, the Marquess de Vaudreuil, Governor of Canada, ordered the establishment of two new posts, both on the Wabash River: one at the village of Chipkawkay, at first simply called the "Fort on the Wabash," later known by the name of its most famous commandant, Vincennes; and, farther upriver, *Fort Ouatanon*, near the present city of Lafayette, Indiana.[35] Both of these fortified posts filled the void left by the disappearance of Juchereau's enterprise fifteen years before.

On Sunday, June 27, 1723, Diron d'Artaguiette, having completed his inspection of Illinois, left Kaskaskia with the feeling that the danger represented by hostile actions of the Fox Indians, a small nation whose ancestral lands lay south of Green Bay, had been exaggerated. He was to be proven wrong. On the other hand, from a passing indication in his journal, we see that already Illinois was well on its way to becoming the food supplier to Lower Louisiana: d'Artaguiette was going downriver with two boats, he noted, one for himself, and the second, a Company's craft loaded with corn to supply the Arkansas post.[36] In a quiet way this routine notation illustrates well Boisbriant's dilemma when later, during his short tenure as governor of Louisiana, his task was to continue developing Illinois' much-needed potential riches on the Company's reduced budget.

Skirmishes with the Fox resumed after D'Artaguiette's departure, however it probably was only a coincidence; as adept as the Fox were at guerrilla warfare and inter-tribal communications, attributing to them the sophistication of our times would be absurd. Nevertheless, trivial as they appeared in nature, the continuous hostile actions by the Fox Indians during a period of eighteen years—from 1712 to 1730—had a disproportionate impact on the French North American empire. In the following chapter, the ramifications of the Fox wars will be examined in more detail.

The company that Law created remained, and in spite of its obsession with fast profits, provided the structure necessary to any development. The "burst of the Mississippi bubble," as this early version of a Wall Street crash came to be known in France, would seriously affect future growth in Louisiana but could not reverse the dramatic progress made in Illinois during the preceding decade. Short of abandoning the territory completely, whoever was to carry on with Law's unfinished project, the Crown or the Company, would have to continue to maintain Louisiana's garrisons and trade as well as subsidize its clergy. Within this general state of affairs, both economic growth and strategic importance were still in Illinois' future. However, the hostility of the Fox Indian nation, a danger that Diron d'Artaguiette had judged negligible, was about to escalate from a level of insidious guerilla action to a that of a major, if not fatal, obstacle.

NOTES

1. AC, Series C 11, Vol. 20, 1702.

2. AC, Ibid., April 10, 1702.

3. "During this same period, twenty-four *voyageurs* from Illinois came to La Mobile bringing peltries. While at the Gulf, they volunteered their sevices to Mr. de Bienville and Mr. de Chataugue against the Alibamons." *Relation de Pénicaut*, in Margry, *Etablissements et découvertes*, V. 435; Pénicaut's account was translated in its entirety with the unexplained exception of a few long passages—which include this one, trans. this author—by B.F. French as *Annals of Louisiana from 1698 to 1722*, in Historical Collections of Louisiana and Florida, New York, Sabin and Sons, 1869. Born in La Rochelle, Pénicaut had entered the King's service in 1698 at the age of fifteen, and was assigned to the frigate *Le Marin* in Iberville's initial expedition to the mouth of the Mississippi. He ended his career as Master-carpenter. Married in Louisiana with two children, he became blind at the end of his career and went to Paris to seek better treatment and a royal pension. The *Relation* was probably written under his dictation in 1721 as a document to support his request.

4. *Project d'un nouvel etablissmenet au détroit des lacs Eriés et Huron, Extrait du mémoire du Roi au sieur chevalier de Callières, Gouverneur, et au sieur de Champigny, Intendant de la Nouvelle France*, Versailles, 27 mai, 1699, in Margry, V, 135-37.

5. Ibid.,

6. Ibid.; a *fermier général* was an individual who had brought from the King the charge of collecting taxes for a particular field, such as salts' rights; he had to advance the amont of these taxes to the King's treasury.

7. *Deed From the Five Nations to the King of their Beaver Hunting Grounds, NYCD,,* IV, 908.

8. See the Speech of Miskouski, an Ottawa Chief, to the Marquis de Vaudreuil, Governor General of Canada, and reply, trans. by Colonel Charles Whittlesey of a French MS. brought by General Lewis Cass, in *Western Reserve Historical Society*, Cleveland, Ohio, December 1871, No. 8.

9. *ANC*, Series B, 29-58 ff.

10. Clarence Alvord, *The Illinois Country.*, 137.

11. In 1708, samples of copper and lead from Illinois were sent to France by Diron d'Artaguiete, then the *intendant* for Louisiana.

12. Father Marest was the first Jesuit priest to return, followed shortly after by a new arrival from France, Father Jean Marie de Ville.

13. Pénicaut., in Margry, V, 476-77.

14. Ibid., 488.

15. Ibid.,

16. In 1712, the Miami Indians, who were friendly towards the French, took over the control of the Upper Wabash.

17. Jean-Francois Dumont de Montigny, *Mémoires Historiques sur la Louisiane*, Paris, 1753, 2 vol.; this work by an officer who served in Louisiana from 1719 to 1738 was translated by Benjamin F. French as *Historical Memoirs of Louisiana*, New York, Lampert, 1853.

18. The complete English translation of this chapter can be found in French, *Louisiana Historical Collections*, III, 38-42.

19. See Jean-Baptiste Bérnard de la Harpe, *Journal Historique.*

20. Stanley Faye, *The Arkansas Post of Louisiana: French Domination*, The Louisiana History Quarterly, vol. 23, No. 3, July 1943.

21. See the correspondence of Ramezay to the Minister, November 3, 1715, published in *Wisconsin Historical Collections*, 16:325.

22. Philippe d'Orleans, born at St. Cloud on August 2, 1674, assumed the regency until 1723, when Louis XV became of age. He died in Versailles that same year.

23. John Law, 1671-1729, author of *Money and Trade Considered, With a Proposal for Supplying the Nation with Money*, published in 1705 and in 1720.

24. ANC B39:457.

25. The northern limits of Louisiana after the annexation of Illinois were never defined; see Alvord, *The Illinois Country*, 150-151, 169-170.

26. ANC, B43:103.

27. Natalia Belting's *Kaskaskia Under The French Regime* stands out among the historical works on Illinois as an examplary monograph. Much of the information used in this chapter has been first researched and published by Mrs. Belting.

28. Charles Claude Du Tisné, a Canadian-born officer who led fellow Canadians, including his wife, by land to Mobile in 1713, and joined the service of the *Company* in 1717.

29. Etienne Venyard, *Sieur de Bourgmont*, built Fort Orleans; see Houk, *History of Missouri*, 1, 255, and Stipes, *Missouri Historical Review*, 8:121 ff.

30. *Histoire et description générale de la Nouvelle France avec le Journal Historique d'un voyage fait par ordre du Roi dans l'Amérique Septentrionale*, par le P. De Charlevoix, Paris, 1744, ll, 393; trans. this author.

31. Charlevoix, *Histoire et description.*, ll, 393-94.

32. *Ordonnance de la Compagnie d'Occident qui fixe le prix des marchandises qui seraient reçues des habitants de la Louisiane, à Paris, le 25 Avril 1719* in La Harpe,

Journal Historique., 176.

33. The slow economic development of Louisiana is reflected by the slow growth of the slave population. Statistics show that for 1756, while the total slave population of Louisiana was only 4,700, the island of Martinique had a total of 65,900 for 1751 and Guadeloupe had 40,400 in 1753. Sugar cane, the main commodity produced by both islands, made the use of African slaves profitable; the lack of an identical large-scale plantation crop in Louisiana did not. On slave trade, see Philip D. Curtin, *The Atlantic Slave Trade*, Madison, Wisconsin, 1969.

34. Journal of Diron d'Artaguiete, April 19, 1723, trans. in Mereness, *Travels.*, 69-70.

35. Sieur Dubuisson, from the Canadian troops was the first officer to command Fort Ouatanon; NYCD, IX, 894.

36. Ibid., 83.

9

The Fox Wars

L arge-scale warfare occurred during the eighteenth century between the Indian nations and each of the three European powers in North America—France, England and Spain—for two essential reasons: instances when any one of the latter used Indian allies against one of the others; and occasions when Europeans interfered in Indian disputes. Confrontations between encroaching Europeans and Indians in North America had ceased by the end of the 1700s with the destruction of the last of the New England tribes at the hands of the Puritans. Such problems would not be seen again until the United States' western expansion following the Civil War. However, in the process of the "Invasion of America" [1] even the British could not do without some Indian support, as shown by their long-standing alliance with both the Five Nations of the Iroquois and the Cherokee Confederacies. [2]

The French penetration into North America was free neither from violence nor cruelty; but French expansion was violent and cruel as well during Louis XIV's 1689 campaign in the Rhineland.[3] The French did, however, resist the genocidal tendencies exhibited by British colonists who were bent on erasing all Indian presence from the fertile lands the colonists so coveted for their farms. Thus, the determined pursuit of the Fox by the French, until near total destruction, is unusually striking in the history of French North America, though the elements for a violent resolution clearly were present from the start.

The *Outagami* or *Mesquakie*,[4] commonly referred to by the French as *Renards* because they adopted the Fox as their emblem (not, as wrongly thought by many, as a connotation of their cleverness and devious nature), was a small but fiercely independent Indian tribe occupying an area south of *La Baye verte* (Green Bay, Wisconsin), along with several other tribes who also considered the general area home: the *Kickapoo*, the *Mascouten* (to whom the Foxes were related), the *Menominee*, the *Potawatomi*, the *Sac* or (Sauk), and the *Winnebago*.

The wars subsequently engulfing the Fox nation began with a chain reaction resulting from an actual French diplomatic success poorly exploited. In 1701, the Governor of New France, Callières, having

Detail showing the Upper Mississippi Valley. From Henry Popple, "A Map of the British Empire in North America," London, 1733. (The MacLean Collection) resolved to make peace with the Iroquois. While he invited delegations from the Five Nations to attend a parley in Montreal, and sent an emissary to all the French allies in the Great Lakes area asking them, in turn, to suspend all hostilities. Callières was indeed successful in getting all parties to agree to a treaty, however, once the alliances formed by war were gone, the Great Lakes Indian nations soon began quarrelling among themselves, mainly over the limited availability of French trade goods. Moreover, by bringing them into close contact with each other in *au Détroit*, Cadillac increased their rivalry. The French did succeed in suppressing potential major conflicts, such as those between the Miami and the Ottawa in 1706, but bitter memories simmered for years, while during the same period, the Fox began to style themselves as middlemen in all the transactions with the Sioux, a stand which would lead to worse confrontations later on. Meanwhile, in 1702, war with England had resumed (Queen Ann's War, mentioned in the preceding chapter). In 1711, Vaudreuil,[5] Callières' replacement, had reason to expect a large-scale landing of British troops at the mouth of the St. Lawrence River. Facing the eventuality of a British invasion supported by an Iroquois attack, he called on all the French allies from the west to assemble in Montreal. Following Cadillac's invitation, a large group of the Fox and their Mascouten cousins had moved the year before from Wisconsin to Detroit. While the British threat never materialized (a storm wrecked the invasion fleet and the Iroquois were never able to leave their villages), Vaudreuil seized the opportunity to harangue all the assembled tribes, exhorting them to put a stop to their quarrels; a speech particularly aimed at the Fox.

There can be little doubt their record was troublesome. Although small in number (no more than 500 warriors), they had made a habit of raiding the Sioux, who were trade partners of the French, as well as the French themselves:

> Fox war parties scoured the Mississippi, waylaying French merchants and confiscating their supplies of muskets and powder. Other Fox warriors ranged throughout Wisconsin intercepting French and Potawatomi voyageurs and exacting a growing tribute from the hapless traders. Since many of these merchants were unlicensed, at first French officials took no measures to stop the banditry. In turn the Foxes believed themselves immune from the French power and expanded their depredations into Illinois.[6]

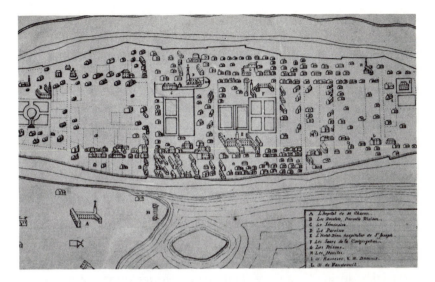

Anonymous manuscript map of Montreal in 1710. (The Newberry Library) (Original in the Archives Nationales, Paris)

In 1712, the Fox returned to Detroit in a hostile mood. Had they been approached by British agents or did they decide on their own to attack the fort? There had been a quarrel brewing with the Hurons and the Ottawa, but attacking the king's troops was another matter. It had been the intention of the British all along to try either to extend control of the waterway between Lake Erie and Lake Huron or at least to destroy the fort and the settlement of Detroit. The behavior of the Fox is better understood in this context, although it was also, no doubt, fueled by their own resentment. *Sieur* Jacques-Charles Dubuisson, who had replaced Cadillac as Commandant, would have been bound to intervene if violence erupted between the Indians, but now he was forewarned by the Potawatomi of the real intentions of the Fox. Dubuisson was told they planned to attack and destroy Detroit and then continue on moving east to join the Iroquois. Rather than sending out his small detachment (a garrison of twenty marines), Dubuisson regrouped all his meager forces, French and Indian, and burned down the outlying constructions. His messengers left to call for help as the siege began. The Fox's war talents were evident as they built a palisade around the fort, bringing them within range of the French defenses.

Illinois, vitally interested in the outcome, sent 600 French and Indian volunteers, the largest contingent to participate in the rescue expedition which included troops from Canadian garrisons, as well as warriors from the Huron, Ottawa, and Potawatomi nations. The battle took place in May 1712, and lasted twenty days. The besiegers became the besieged, when the Fox and Mascouten, short of water and other supplies, asked for a truce but were refused. A violent night thunderstorm gave them the opportunity to slip through the French lines, and expecting pursuit they laid a trap, but to little avail; they were soon overwhelmed by much larger forces. This hard-fought war cost the French and their allies sixty dead. Joseph Peyser, who has studied the Franco-Fox conflict extensively, gives the figures of 250 Fox killed in battle and 750 women and children massacred by Indian allies.[7] The remainder (estimated at one hundred warriors) made it safely to the lands of the Seneca Iroquois; able to return Wisconsin months later, they rejoined those who had not gone to Detroit. Diminished in number but not in resolve, the Fox resumed their hit-and-run tactics, during 1714 alone, their raiding parties killed seventy-seven Illinois Indians. They not only closed the Mackinac-Green Bay-Mississippi route, which used the Fox-Wisconsin portage originally taken by Joliet and Marquette,[8] but seriously endangered the Chicago portage, and communications between Illinois and Canada were threatened once more. The impact was felt as far as the banks of the St. Joseph River where the Potawatomi, finding their settlement unsafe, left to establish a new village in Detroit. This was the second time the Fox had driven them from their homes; they were understandably sanguine about resuming hostilities. Urged on by many, Vaudreuil decided on an all-out attack.

A military rendezvous of Indian allies was organized in Chicago for 1715, though gathering Indian allies was always a difficult task, and it was no less so this time. A French officer writing on August 28th from Chicago to the governor of Montreal, Mr. de Ramezay, betrayed his frustration, complaining that not only had the Miami contingent not yet arrived but the gunpowder earmarked for the campaign was still in Fort St. Joseph.[9] Another French officer writing from Prairie du Rocher,[10] described the difficulty in getting the Miami to rendezvous in Chicago. French volunteers were also actively sought; an officer, Le Marchand de Lignery, was sent to Mackinac Straits to recruit as many *voyageurs* and *coureurs des bois* as possible. To add to the problems, an epidemic of measles was raging along the Wabash, and British-inspired clandestine activities by Iroquois agents were discovered in the village of the Kaskaskia.[11] Eventually, 400 Illinois arrived in Chicago, joining a large Huron contingent from Detroit

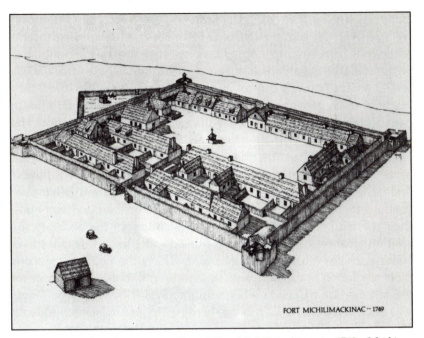

FORT MICHILIMACKINAC -- 1749

Artist's reconstruction of Fort Michilimackinac in 1749. (Mackinac Island State Park Commission)

and a considerable body of *voyageurs* and soldiers. They attacked the Fox and Mascouten warriors on the Fox River. The losses of the Fox were given as 150, but this appears to be an inflated body count. One must question either the arithmetic or the reports, when the total number of dead that the Fox were supposed to have suffered during the battle is larger than the estimated number of males of arm-bearing age that they could field at the time. At any rate, the Fox in this instance were again able to withdraw the bulk of their forces.

The following year Vaudreuil sent an experienced officer, Louis de la Porte, *sieur* de Louvigny, to take overall command of the Fox campaign, who arrived from Canada with 225 soldiers and 200 French volunteers from the general Mackinac area. The Straits of Mackinac were about to regain the commercial importance they had known in the late 1600s, a renaissance begun when the Fox wars made it opportune to build a new fort at Michilimackinac.[12] By the time Louvigny established contact with the Fox, he had been joined by 600 Indian allies,[13] promising to be a new major battle. The Fox were cornered in their fortified village of *Butte des morts* ("Hill of the dead") near Oshkosh, on Lake Winnebago, Wisconsin with 500 warriors and an estimated 3,000 women, all determined to fight to the end. Louvigny, opening a European-style siege of the compound with parallel lines, gabions and canons, and drums, believed that the Fox would accept France's control after such a demonstration of military might, and accepted an offer to negotiate. He agreed to settle for a fine in pelts and then allowed the Fox to withdraw, but peace did not last. The following year, in 1717, though Louvigny built a new fort near Green Bay, Fort St. Francois, it had little effect on the Fox who, having renounced the agreement the instant they reached safety, continued to harass Illinois and French alike. They began to receive occasional help from their former enemies, the Sioux, reacting just as European nations had, and tempering their old feuds with a pragmatic understanding of the necessity for shifting alliances. A direct result of this development was that travel became unsafe even between Kaskaskia and Cahokia. Louvigny's incomplete resolution of the campaign underscored Illinois' dependence on military help from Canada, while additionally, 1717 was the year Illinois was detached from New France to become Upper Louisiana; suddenly Vaudreuil's policy was forced to adjust to new circumstances.

Vaudreuil understandably had always opposed the separation of Illinois from Canada. From the initial foundation of the French colony by the Gulf, Illinois' fur business had found an alternate although illegal market in Louisiana; but when Illinois was made part of Louisiana, the fur trade for New France was even further reduced. The fur havest west and northwest of the Mississippi was now directed to warehouses in Mobile and Biloxi. This change happened just when the fur trade had found a new life: in 1714, when large quantities of furs were discovered in the royal warehouses badly stored and almost completely unusable, it had led to a marked increase in the cost of pelts, particularly beaver pelts. Overnight, glut in the market was replaced by scarcity, and for New France, it meant a new shot at economic prosperity. The favorable conjuncture included peace between Britain and France (since the 1713 Treaty of Utrecht) and full employment in the fur trade with cheaper trade goods, in turn, giving New France an advantage over British competition. In this context, Vaudreuil was ready to use whatever means it took to establish peace in the troublesome West, protecting access to the land of the Sioux for New France, an access the Fox wanted to control. Vaudreuil saw the solution in convincing the Fox that while Illinois traders were not his concern, New France *voyageurs* were not to be harmed:

Since it was the posts in the Illinois country that were suffering the most from this warfare and the attendant disruption of trade, and since these posts in 1717 had been placed under the authority of the governor of Louisiana, the governor general at Quebec, Rigaud de Vaudreuil, was accused of being less than anxious to take firm measures against the Fox. It appeared to the minister of marine that Vaudreuil and the Canadian fur traders regarded the Fox almost as allies in a struggle for control of the western trade.[14]

A delegation of Fox chiefs went to visit Governor Vaudreuil in 1719, they were accompanied by a Potawatomi chief; the Potawatomi were anxious to show their goodwill to both the French and the Fox.[15] Vaudreuil was concerned that his policy of "closing eyes and ears" to the Fox's attacks on the Illinois would be interpreted by them as a kind of implicit permission to harass the Potawatomi as well, but these nuances were too subtle to be understood by raiding parties criss-crossing prairie and forests. For this reason, answering a long-standing Potawatomi request, he ordered the building of a fort on the the St. Joseph River (Niles, Michigan). This was territory the Potawatomi had shared with the Miami since the Fox had forced them out of Wisconsin. Fort St. Joseph would also protect the route leading to the Kankakee portage (today crossing South Bend, Indiana), the only safe land communication between Canada and Louisiana.

The list of Fox attacks continued to grow, so that by 1722, they had practically closed traffic on the Illinois River, roaming at will around *Le rocher* (Starved Rock); they would eventually chase the Peoria Indians out of their home on the Peoria Lake all the way to Cahokia.[16] We have an eye-witness account from the Jesuit Father de Charlevoix of what it was like to travel from Canada to Illinois.[17] Pierre Francois-Xavier de Charlevoix taught at the Jesuit College of Quebec from 1705 to 1709, one of the reasons he had been chosen for a fact-finding mission ordered by the Regent. When Charlevoix began his journey, Louisiana was still the charge of the *Compagnie des Indes* which had barely survived John Law's crash. As the Company was not adverse to sacrificing the King's interests in order to salvage its investors, Charlevoix' mission was extremely important although, as in countless cases before and certainly since, his findings, written in a series of leters, had little effect on the course of events. Nevertheless, it is fortunate for history that they were published twenty years later. His twenty-sixth letter is dated from September 17, 1721, and starts with his departure from the *Fort de la Rivière S. Joseph*. His next letter, from October 5, in *Pimiteouy* (Peoria), describes the country he crossed:

> . . . At 50 leagues from its source, the river [Kankakee River] forms a little lake and then becomes larger. The country becomes beautiful; prairies as far as you can see, where the buffaloes travel by herds of two to three hundred, but one must be on his guard, not to get waylaid by the raiding parties of Sioux and Outagamis, that the country of the Illinois, their mortal enemy attracts and who give no quarter to the French that they meet on their way.[18]

On October 3rd, around noon, Charlevoix and his escort arrived at the entrance to Lake Peoria:

> Three leagues further down, there a second Illinois village on the right side, whose location is fifteen leagues from the village of *Le rocher*. . . . Nothing is more pleasant than its location. It has across [the river], as in one of these perspective pictures, a very beautiful forest which was then in full [Fall] colors and, behind, a prairie surrounded by woods. Lake and river are full of fish and their banks full of game. I met in the village four French Canadians who told me that we were in between four enemy raiding parties and that I was in danger regardless if I went ahead or retraced my steps. They added that on the way we came, there were thirty Outagamis waiting in ambush, that a same number was roaming around the village and that more, numbering eighty and divided into two groups were further downriver. This account reminded me of what happened the day before, when we stopped by an island to look for ducks shot by some of my men. We heard somebody cutting wood somewhere in the middle of the island and the proximity of Pimiteouy led us to believe that the noise was made by some Illinois. Apparently they were Outagami who had discovered us but had not dared attack as I had a dozen men, well-armed . . . but our lack of curiosity, no doubt, saved us, a curiosity that I would have had if I did not have an escort commanded by a man who did not believe in unnecessary stops [St. Ange de Bellerive]. The opinions of the four Frenchmen were reinforced to us by the fact that thirty Pimiteouy warriors and the Chief of the village had been out on reconnaissance since before our arrival; that a few days before they left a skirmish took place in the vicinity with each party capturing a prisoner.[19]

Now Charlevoix had to decide if he and his escort were going to spend Winter in Peoria (meaning a full year lost) or continue the journey and trust that his small group looked strong enough to discourage any Fox they might encounter on the way. Two of the Canadians offered to reinforce his escort as Charlevoix decided to go on. The next day, the 4th of October, heavy rain delayed the departure, allowing Charlevoix time to meet the Peoria chief, "A man of about forty, rather tall, thin, quiet and reasonable . . . the bravest soldier of his nation." The Chief urged him to reconsider on account of the danger, but as his guest insisted, he made a little speech that touched the heart of Charlevoix then, and moves the reader today, almost three centuries later:

> If then your decision is made, I believe that all the Frenchmen who are here join to strengthen your escort; I told them so as I have pointed out to them that their honor will be forever lost if they leave their Father in danger, without sharing it with him. I wished that I could accompany you myself with all my soldiers but you know that my village is about to be attacked any day and that I cannot leave in those circumstances. For the Frenchmen, nothing can retain them here but their business that they must sacrifice for your safety . . .

Charlevoix took only the two original volunteers, left the next morning, and on October 10th, they all arrived safely in Cahokia.

As more settlers arrived directly from France via Louisiana ports, they brought needed skills to the territory, but they also brought the burden of their inexperience in frontier life. For Boisbriant, the commandant, this element added to the immediate problem of protecting the villages—his tactics did not keep soldiers and militia behind stockades but instead aimed at seeking out the enemy in constant "search and destroy" raids. The newcomers from the gentler life of France were not yet accustomed to long treks and hours of paddling while still having to maintain enough strength to shoot their muskets accurately afterward.

Considering the imperatives posed by a large number of untried newcomers, Boisbriant reacted swiftly to what amounted to an invasion of Illinois by the Fox. Leaving only a few soldiers and one officer[20] behind to garrison Fort de Chartres, he went upriver first on the Mississippi, and then on the Illinois, with 100 men on an assortment of canoes and larger *bateaux*, while at the same time he directed the newly-selected captain of the militia, *sieur* Bourbon, to lead a combined force of 400 French and

Illinois to approach Peoria by land. The Fox were not at all interested in confronting regular troops in addition to a full contingent of Indian allies and French volunteers, and Boisbriant returned to Fort de Chartres without having been able to locate them. A few days later, Bourbon also returned with men exhausted by his badly planned incursion into the Illinois prairie; he was "more skillful at goading oxen in the ploughing than in leading a troop of warriors." [21] The year 1722 ended with the Fox contained--at least for the moment.

The following spring, the Fox renewed their harassment, and on May 31st, they attacked a canoe carrying an officer and his escort who were travelling from Cahokia to Fort de Chartres. The officer, Louis St. Ange de Bellerive, was carrying a pouch of dispatches and letters entrusted to him by his father, at the time in charge of the Post of Cahokia. Louis St. Ange survived the ambush and managed to reach the fort on foot with the news of an imminent attack on Cahokia by possibly as many as 300 warriors. Cahokia was then defended only by six regulars and a company of militia just formed the week before by Diron d'Artaguiette in the course of his inspection of Illinois. The news understandably brought great alarm, however d'Artaguiette, in a great show of calm, decided that before mobilizing all available men he should see the situation for himself, so he left with his secretary, St. Ange, a sergeant and sixteen men, arriving in Cahokia two days later, a post which he described as "A wretched fort of piles." [22] Having assembled all the Chiefs and Illinois warriors staying in Cahokia, he delivered the following message interpreted by Mr. Thaumeur de la Source, one of the missionary priests stationed there:

> That I come with my warriors both to aid them and to bring them provisions. That I thought that all the reports which they had sent to Fort de Chartres were false; that they should sent out parties to discover with certainty whether the enemy were coming, and, in case they should have sure news of it, that they, together with their wives and children, should retire to the fort of the French.. . . that I exhorted them to imitate the French and to defend themselves against the common enemy; that for this purpose I was going to give them a French flag; that they ought, as soon as they were attacked, to send their best runners to Fort de Chartres and that their father, De Boisbriant, would not fail to come with all the French warriors to aid them. [23]

As mentioned in the preceding chapter, Diron d'Artaguiette left shortly after, unconvinced that the magnitude of the Fox threat required further action, but the spring of 1723 brought no reduction of insecurity to Illinois, where blows were received and given with the randomness of chance. In June, near Cahokia, the Illinois captured three Fox warriors (whom they later burned, as was the custom of Indian warfare). In September of the same year two Canadian hunters were surprised and killed by the Fox just behind the walls of Fort de Chartres, giving some measure of the level of danger probably felt by civilians and military alike. Perhaps even more telling, in spite of the laconic nature of the document, is an excerpt from the Parish registers of Kaskaskia:

The same year [1722], on the 22nd of June, was celebrated in the parish church of Kaskaskia a solemn service for the repose of the soul of the lady Michelle Chauvin, wife of Jacques Nepven, merchant of Montreal, aged about forty-five years, and of Jeanne Michelle Nepven, aged twenty years, and Elizabeth Nepven, aged thirteen years and Suzanne Nepven, eight years, her children. They were slain by the savages 5 to 7 leagues from the Wabash. It is believed that Jacques Nepven was taken prisoner and carried away with one young boy, aged about nine years, named Prever, and one young slave girl, not baptized.[24]

They were killed within a few miles of their destination, while two daughters, Marie-Catherine and Theresa survived. Theresa married the *Sieur* Bourbon, Captain of the Militia, on November 9th of the same year.[25] For 1724, another entry underlining the audacity of the Fox:

The 12th of April were slain at day break by the Fox Indians four men, to-wit: Pierre Du Vaud, a married man about twenty-five years of age, Pierre Basceau, nicknamed Beau Soleil, also a married about twenty-eight or thirty years of age, and two others, of whom one was known by the name of *Le Bohemien* and the other by the name of *L'Etreneur* the three last dwelling and employed at Fort de Chartres. Their bodies having brought to Cascaskia the same day by the French were buried at sunset in the cemetery of the parish.[26]

It was obvious to the French in "Upper Louisiana" that the Fox were free from any military pressure from Canada, and thus concentrated with ease on Illinois targets, as it seemed that Vaudreuil's hands-off policy applied even when the Fox victimized Potawatomi, who still played an important role in New France's strategic defense.[27]

Boisbriant, acting governor of Louisiana since 1724, and Charles Du Tisné, who had replaced him as commandant in Illinois, joined together in protest, drawing support from clergy and the *habitans*, who sent a delegation directly to the king at Versailles to object to Vaudreuil's policy. The Jesuit Father de Beaubois along with an officer, Mr. de Bourgmont, had been chosen to lead the group which included four Illinois chiefs, one being Chicagou, of the Michigamea, after a long journey down the Mississippi to Mobile, then across the Atlantic, this colorful committee was received with great honors as well as curiosity. They were welcomed at the Court of Versailles, attended Mass in Notre Dame, were lionized by the elegant society, and finally written up in the prestigious newspaper of the times, *Le Mecure de France*, in the December 1725 issue.

Following this visit to Versailles, a new peace treaty, including Illinois, was concluded in 1726, between New France (represented by the commandant of Michilimackinac) and the Fox, as Vaudreuil had died the year before, a successor was on his way, and the tone was about to change radically.

Charles de La Boische, *marquis* de Beauharnois, was the new appointed governor general who arrived in Quebec in 1726. He carried with him a revised policy, resulting from a combination of the slow but inexorable supplanting of the Great Lakes region as fur country by the lands west of the Mississippi, as well as the Regent of France's personal interest in the discovery of a western passage to the Pacific Ocean. In the process "... it became imperative that the Fox barrier be breached."[28] The Fox were the greatest obstacle to a French policy that still emphasized the two same major objectives: insuring safe access to the Sioux trade, and preventing the infiltration beyond the Niagara of British merchants and their Iroquois stand-ins.

In June 1727, a first expedition was sent from Michilimackinac to the Sioux country, the French moving across today's northern Wisconsin, through the Fox lands, to reach the Mississippi where they built the post of *Lac Pépin* (near Lake City, Minnesota and Pepin, Wisconsin). The Fox, evidently and understandably concerned, sent an emissary to Fort St. Joseph with protests of submission. Possibly the Fox would have kept their word, however, Beauharnois, though new to the task, had received clear instructions from the Minister, had read all the reports, and had heard from his key officers. As *la raison d'Etat* now determined quick

"Canadian going to War on Snowshoe." In *Histoire de l'Amérique Septentrionale,* Paris, 1722.

(The Newberry Library)

elimination of the Fox obstacle to France's interests, humanitarian consid-erations for an Indian nation notorious for its many depredations proba-bly counted very little to Governor Beauharnois. The Fox record spoke loudly against them; if ever there was an instance of unanimous opinion among the French and the Indians, it was--destroy the Fox.

Information reached Quebec that the Iroquois had sent word to the Fox to unite in war on the French. By the terms of the Treaty of Utrecht, Britain was the recognized overlord of the Iroquois while they retained their autonomy, a set-up allowing Britain the advantage of denying respon-sibility for any Iroquois mischief. As the French suspected British machi-nations behind the Iroquois initiative anyway, the information added weight to Beauharnois' decision to open a swift campaign against the Fox.

An imposing column of 400 French soldiers and 1,000 Indian allies left Michilimackinac on August 10, 1728. Ferrying such numbers across even the narrow Mackinac Straits was not a sinecure, and the time it took was long enough for news of the French operation to reach the Fox in their fortified village near Lake Winnebago. Thus they had retreated to safety by the time the French force arrived, leaving only an empty village and abandoned fields, (including those of the nearby Winnebago) all promptly burned. This *promenade militaire*, however, impressed the Sioux across the Mississippi River, as well as the Kickapoo, the Mascouten and the Sauk, long time allies of the Fox from the days of easy pickings. Once more the Fox sued for peace, calling on Coulon de Villiers, the commandant of Fort St. Joseph,[29] but, while trying to bargain with governor Beauharnois, they were twice attacked by a coalition of Chippewa, Ottawa and even Winnebago (who had decided to change camps after the French burned their village). The situation was becoming increasingly murky.

Having asked and been refused help by the Sioux and the Iowa, the Fox, realizing their desperate situation, decided to seek refuge with the Iroquois. They started on their way south in May 1730, none too soon, as a second French expeditionary force of 600 was already on its way from Michilimackinac. Whether as a last show of bravado or as an expression of anger over their betrayal, on the way they ". . . struck at the Winnebago, their recent allies, who aided the Ottawa and the Chippewa in the attack of the Fox village." [30] This would be their last offensive action as they retreated through Wisconsin and then Illinois. We are indebted to Joseph Peyser, whose research was mentioned earlier, for having recently uncovered the details of the pursuit of the Fox.[31]

Through information passed on by Kickapoo and Mascouten to Jean-Baptiste Reaume, Villiers' interpreter, the French found out that the Fox planned to cross the Illinois River by *Le rocher*, and when an Illinois source confirmed this news, the chase was on. A full-length report written by one of the major participants, possibly Reaume himself, described the terrible and inescapable end:

> . . . upon which information Monsieur le Chevalier de Villiers notified Monsieur Deschaillons at Detroit, Monsieur de Noyelle at the Miami post and sieur Simon Reaume at the Ouyatanon post. In twenty-four hours Monsieur Deschaillons organized a party of 350 men composed of French-

men, some Hurons, some Ouyatanons and Potawatomis, commanded by
his two sons. Monsieur de Noyelle was at the head of several Frenchmen
and 140 Miamis. Sieur Reaume commanded 400 Ouyatanons and several
Frenchmen. They combined their forces and starting out for *Le rocher* they
learned that Monsieur de Villiers had come to a halt with 350 men, not
having been able to find the Foxes . . . [32]

The Fox had kept on moving all summer. When they reached a point
a few miles from *Le rocher* they established camp and began negotiating
with the Illinois. Travelling with their families, they did not have the
flexibility of a war party which could go undetected. During the negotiations an altercation took place which eventually led to the surprise killing
of seventeen Illinois by the Fox. From then on, the die was cast. Although
the Fox did succeed in forcing their way, Illinois war parties caught up
with them about 100 miles southeast of *Le rocher*. Now it was August. In
the endless prairie, the Fox retreated to the only wooded hill by a small
stream, known then by the Indians as the "Mabichi," a location tentatively
identified as the middle fork of the Vermilion River in Illinois. The Fox

. . . fortified themselves in the grove and the allies in the plain a half league
from each other. The Foxes fort was made of stakes crossed at the top one
foot apart. A ditch ran outside along the sides whith branches planted to
hide them, and they were communication paths from the the fort into the
ditches and others which went to the river. Their lodges were complete
with wallplates covered with *apavois*, comonly called straw mats, above
which there was two or three feet of earth. From lodge to lodge there were
paths which were covered in such a way that only a terrace to provide
shade in their fort could be seen.[33]

Several drawings of the fort built by the Fox would be executed later
by French military engineers from Quebec and New Orleans, the French
having considered the art of fortification demonstrated by the Fox seriously enough to warrant its study. Looking beyond the Fox War, the
French staff officers sought to develop tactics able to prove effective with
other Indian defense systems they might encounter in the course of
expansion of the French dominion.[34]

Villiers and Reaume were the first on the scene with their detachments.
Simon Reaume had with him twenty-eight French and 400 Ouyatanon,
Villiers about as many; Robert Croston de St. Ange, by then the comman-

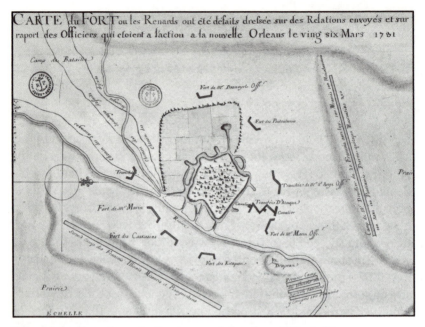

"Map of the Fort where the Foxes were defeated . . ." March 26, 1731. (Archives Nationales, Paris)

dant at Fort de Chartres, arrived with 300 Illinois and ninety Frenchmen; Nicolas-Joseph des Noyelles, with 150 Miami. By the time the ring of fire around the Fox was completed, the French had positioned 1,400 men.

The besiegers opened a trench with hatchets and knives. They built gun towers under the cover of gunfire. The siege lasted eighteen days during which time the besieged threw more than 300 children over their palisades in order to touch the hearts of the besiegers. . . . The Foxes seeing themselves without hope and absolutely dying of hunger, arrived at a decision, offering *Sieur* Baptiste Reaume to give themselved up to all the (Indian) nations, provided that their lives would be spared, but he was not a mind to grant this any more than his brother (Simon Reaume), foreseeing that they were capable of corrupting those with whom they would be living. It was decided by the commanders that no quarter would be given.

On the eighteenth night of the siege a violent storm broke out and, as in Detroit eight years before, the Fox were able to slip through the lines. To prevent his troops from shooting each other, Villiers, who as the senior-ranking officer had assumed command, held them back until daybreak of September 9th when the Fox, having gone only a few miles, with Villiers' men forming the rear guard, were overtaken and slaughtered wholesale. The report we have quoted above indicated 500 men, women and children killed, and 300 to 400 others captured and divided by the Indian allies among themselves.

The author of the report concluded with this paragraph:

> The routes to the Mississippi as well as to the Sioux country will now be open. The Green Bay country will be tranquil. and we will be able to build an attractive settlement there. The *habitants* of Lake Erie's Detroit will cultivate their gardens in complete safety. In short, this is a general peace whose authors well deserve to be remembered.

This was a peace the French and their Indian allies would continue to cement in blood. A few hundred Fox remained alive after September 1730; some had remained in Wisconsin and some had been released by their captors. The Illinois were the only ones who kept their captives, but those few hundred Fox were systematically hunted down during the following years as if Governor Beauharnois had made vengeance his personal commitment. In September 1733, Villiers, who had been appointed to the command of Green Bay, was ordered by Beauharnois to take the remaining Fox— now living with the Sauk near the post—back to Montreal. Villiers, who had with him two hundred Indian allies for this task, chose instead to meet the Sauk with only three other officers (his two sons and his son-in-law) and ten soldiers. When the Sauk chief resisted the demand, a scuffle erupted, and Villiers and one of his sons were killed. A short firefight immediately followed, in which more French soldiers were killed, including the officer commanding Michilimackinac. The Sauk and Fox were then pursued by the Indian allies and the remaining French officers; fugitives once more, they moved into Iowa. The news of this small disaster displeased Versailles, and the Minister of Marine ordered that Beauharnois not let the deed go unpunished. Subsequently, in 1735, a difficult campaign conducted in Iowa led to a precarious peace which was really a standoff in disguise. Finally, in 1738, the few remaining Fox were officially pardoned by Beauharnois and, as they had requested, a French officer was sent to live with them.

The impact of the Fox on the *Territoire des Illinois*, in addition to the obvious impact on the Green Bay area, had been considerable. Lasting for almost two decades their attacks, followig the Iroquois raids of the preceding century, pushed the decline of Illinois further and faster, but far jore serious, the Fox also prevented the French from buttressing the core of their establishment, the axis of Cahokia-Peoria-*Le rocher*-Chicago. On their account, the land north of this axis, between the Illinois River and Green Bay, remained inaccessible to all but a handful of hardy souls. While success led the Fox to believe themselves invincible, in fact they were only taking advantage of a quarrel between New France and Louisiana. Their mistake was not so much in the way they fought (killing and pillaging were within the norm of Indian warfare), but in their unbridled ambition. They were too strong to be overpowered by any single Indian nation living between the Mississippi River and Lake Michigan, but not for a coalition of these nations, and certainly not when this coalition was led and reinforced by the French. The Fox believed their aggressive stand would oblige the French to recognize their power and negotiate, while in fact it only strengthened the French resolve to destroy them. When the time for retribution came, had the French felt any inclination towards mercy (and they obviously did not), they could have done little to prevent their Indian allies from excercising what the Indians regarded as a legitimate right to revenge.

With the passage of time, the matter-of-fact attitude displayed by the governor of New France in deciding to eliminate the Fox is not difficult to understand. For the governor it was a discussion in council, an exchange of letters with the Minister, a signature on an order, a policy decision. A less clear issue involves the mentality of officers in the field, for whom policy is not an abstract but rather the reality of hundreds of people being slaughtered around them. It is even more difficult to understand because we might expect that the easy relationship between the French and their Indian allies (and often, relatives) would lead them to empathize with the cruel destiny of the Fox. But the key to understanding behavior that we find abhorrent almost three centuries later, may reside with this very proximity to Indian life. The last battle with the Fox was just another of those confrontations where mercy was neither expected nor granted, where all parties celebrated victories by burning prisoners on a slow fire with the willing help of the women and children of the camp. The French could only compensate for the ridiculously small number of their military forces, and the sparseness of their demography, by meshing with their cultural environment. The fact that some of their national traits facilitated this integration (to the great despair of the Jesuits) was also an important factor. In these Fox wars, the French behaved as just another tribe.

NOTES

1. The appropriate title of a book on this subject by Francis Jennings, *The Invasion of America, Indians, Colonialism, and the Cant of Conquest*, published by Norton and Co., 1976)

2. On both the subject of the treatment of the iroquois, see the book written by Francis Jennings, *The Ambiguous Iroquois Empire*, Norton and Co., New York, 1984.

3. The French army conducted a scorched earth policy in the War of 1688-1697 against the German emperor, ravaging the whole Palatinate region.

4. The Fox are only referred to as Mesquakie in the *Atlas of Great Lakes Indian History*, Helen Hornbeck Tanner ed., University of Oklahoma Press, 1987, 39.

5. Philippe de Rigaud de Vaudreuil, remained Governor-General until his death in 1725, at 82.

6. David Edmunds, *The Potawatomis, Keepers of the Fire*, University of Oklahoma Press, 1978, 27.

7. Joseph Peyser, "The Fate of the Fox Survivors: A Dark Chapter in the History of the French in the Upper Country, 1726-1737," *Wisconsin Magazine of History*, vol. 73, N. 2, Winter 1989-1990, 85.

8. The most complete research on the subject of the Fox fort has been the work of Joseph Peyser; the results of his painstaking study can be found in his article entitled: "The 1730 Siege of the Foxes: Two Maps by Canadian Participants Provide Additional information on the Fort and its Location", *Illinois Historical Journal* (formerly: *Journal of the Illinois State Historical Society*), vol. LXXX, No. 3, Autumn 1967, 147-154. The footnotes of this article give a complete listing of references and past literature. In a later paper, "In search of the 1730 Fox Fort: An analysis of the Topographical Evidence" Peyser painstakingly demonstrates the location of the fort on the Vermillion River, in Illinois.

9. AC, Series C11, 35, August 28, 1715.

10. Prairie du Rocher is located three miles from Fort de Chartres.

11. Ibid.

12. "The earlier settlement, known as the DeLignery's fort was a small compound which dates from 1715 to sometime in the 1730s . . ., The second settlement resulted in a total rebuilding of the fort, and was the largest expansion in its history. . . . This rebuilding occurred sometime in the 1730s. . . . with another slight expansion taking place in 1744. . . . The third and final rebuilding of Michilimackinac may be attributed to the British. . . . Evidence suggests that the 1730s and the minor 1744 French expansions comprised the fort when the French surrendered it to the British in 1761. . . . The earliest known map of Michilimackinac is

that by Lotbiniere in 1749. . . . which illustrates the fort after the second rebuilding and expansion of 1744. . . . The structures included within the fort at this time
were a powder magazine, forty-five houses, a church, the house of the Jesuits,
with an adjoining court and garden, and a forge. A parade ground was located
in the center of the fort, and on an enclosed outwork to the west of the fort stood
an icehouse, bake oven and a "post of the meridian." Additionally, outside of the
fort and to the south were located a stable and two bake ovens." Judith Ann
Hauser, "Jesuit Rings from Fort Michilimackinac and Other European Contact
Sites," *Archaeological Completion Report Series*, Number 5, Mackinac Island State
Park Commission, Mackinac Island, Michigan, 1982, 19-21.

13. Louis de la Porte, *Sieur* de Louvigny, 1652-1725, commanded Mackinac
from 1690 to 1694; Fort Frontenac (Kingston, Ontario), in 1699 and was put in
charge of the 1716 campaign against the Fox. Adept at negotiating with the
Indians but also, as many frontier officers, prone to indulge in shabby dealings,
he had been implicated in some illegal activities in 1703.

14. William Eccles, *The Canadian Frontier, 1534-1760*, revised edition, University of Mexico Press, 1983, 148.

15. See Vaudreuil to the Council of Marine, October 28, 1719, in *Wisconsin
Historical Collections*, XVI, 380-81, also quoted in D. Edmunds, *The Potawatomis*, 32.

16. Kellog, "The Fox Indians During the French Regime, " *Wisconsin Historical
Society Proceedings*, 1907, 142, ff.

17. *Histoire et Description Générale de la Nouvelle France avec le journal historique
d'un voyage fait par ordre du Roi dans l'Amerique Septentrionale*, par le P. De
Charlevoix, Paris, 1744, 2 vol.

18. Ibid, vol. II, 379-80; trans. this author.

19. Ibid.

20. Lieutenant Mellicq was left in charge of Fort de Chartres.

21. *Journal of Diron d'Artaguiette, 1722-1723*, trans. Newton D. Mereness, in
Travels in the American Colonies, New York, 1916, 33.

22. *Journal of Diron d'Artaguiette*, in Mereness, 80-81.

23. Ibid.24. "Kaskaskia and its Parish records," E.G. Mason *Magazine of American History*, March 1881, vol. VI, No. 3, 12.

25. Natalia Maree Belting, *Kaskaskia Under the French Régime*, 43.

26. Ibid., 13.

27. Alphonse de Tonty, then commandant of Fort St. Joseph, would not take
any action against the Fox in spite of pleas from the Potawatomi.

28. Eccles, *The Canadian Frontier..*, 148.

29. Nicolas-Antoine Coulon, *chevalier* de Villiers, had the rank of Lieutenant
in the King's Marine infantry.

30. *The Potawatomis.*, 35.

31. Joseph L. Peyser, "The Fate of the Fox Survivors: A Dark Chapter in the
History of the French in the Upper Country, 1726-1737," *Wisconsin Magazine of
History*, vol. 73, No. 2, Winter, 1989-1990, 83-111; Professor Joseph Peyser has written a very detailed article on the subject of the Fox War, an article that I have used
extensively in the writing of this chapter. Professor Peyser concentrated on the

concluding years of the conflict and judged severely French policy in this instance and its tragic outcome. Although I would agree with my friend and colleague that Governor General Beauharnois went to extremes of brutality in stamping out the problem that the Fox represented for the French, I disagree on two points: first, that the Fox were no longer a danger by the time Beauharnois made the decision to destroy them and, second, on the wisdom of a moral judgment which—in spite of denigrations—does betray a twentieth-century standard applied to an eightheenth-century context.

32. *Lettre de M. d'Auteuil de Monceaux datté de Québec le 7 Novembre 1730 au sujet de la destruction des Renards*, trans. Joseph Peyser, in "The Fate of the Fox Survivors.,"

33. The most complete research on the subject of the Fox fort has been the work of Joseph Peyser; the results of his painstaking study can be found in his article entitled: "The 1730 Siege of the Foxes: Two Maps by Canadian Participants Provide Additional information on the Fort and its Location", *Illinois Historical Journal* (formerly: *Journal of the Illinois State Historical Society*), vol. LXXX, No. 3, Autumn 1967, 147-154. The footnotes of this article give a complete listing of references and past literature. In a later paper, "In search of the 1730 Fox Fort: An analysis of the Topographical Evidence" Peyser painstakingly demonstrate the location of the fort on the Vermilion River, in Illinois.

34. These drawings are found in the *Archives Nationales, Section Outre-mer*, see Peyser, "The siege of the Foxes . . ."

10

The Chickasaw Wars

I n 1724, Boisbriant took temporary command of Louisiana, replacing
Governor Bienville who had fallen into disfavor. Before leaving for the
Gulf of Mexico, he entrusted Illinois to the care of the next senior officer,
Captain Charles Du Tisné, who, however, was shortly after reassigned to
Natchez; this vital post on the northern edge of Lower Louisiana justify-
ing the choice of an experienced officer. Du Tisné, in turn, was automatically replaced by the senior officer of the garrison of Fort de Chartres,
Captain de Pradel, of whom not much is known except that he had been
on Bourgemont's staff at the Fort d'Orleans on the Missouri. His tenure
as interim commandant of Illinois was short, as whether unlucky or un-
skillful, he managed in a few short months to provoke the ire of most of
the Illinois inhabitants, and several violent incidents led the *Compagnie
d'Occident* to order his arrest and transfer to New Orleans. As of September 1725, Pierre de Liette, a familiar face in Illinois, was again placed in
command of the territory he knew so well, where he would remain until
his death, in 1729.[1]

Unfortunately, once again, Louisiana was going through an economic
crisis, and the Company, because it was losing money, demanded from
Boisbriant a considerable reduction in expenses. Garrisons were to be cut
in size; shipments of supplies from the Gulf to the north limited; and the
settlers living upriver pressured to come and buy their goods in New
Orleans. In addition, credit to semi-independent entrepreneurs such as
Philippe Renault was cut, a regrettable decision particularly in this case
as success was beginning to compensate work and investment. Although
in February 1725, Renault owed the sizable sum of 140,000 *livres* to the
Company, his mines were already producing a ton and a half of lead a day.
Renault, the first to have built an efficient furnace and to study the
geology of both the banks of the Mississippi and Illinois Rivers, was a rare
example of civilian leadership in a milieu commanded by officers and led
by clergy.

Recalcitrant in all of these measures, Boisbriant was replaced in the fall
of 1727.[2] His recall was a sad demonstration of the power wielded under
the new reign by short-sighted private interests over sound colonial

policies. The Company expected to find in his replacement, Mr. Etienne de Périer, a more pliant administrator. Budgetary cuts were already greatly affecting Illinois in the usual terms of supplies and manpower, and they affected the political climate as well: some Illinois Indians, in spite of more than fifty years' association and countless inter-marriages with the French, began to become susceptible to the approaches of British agents. In fact, French traders were already selling pelts to the British more or less openly as the price for beaver in France was maintained at too low a level, while French trade goods received from France were too high. In the huge expanse of land between the Ohio and the Mississippi Rivers, Iroquois or British infiltrators from the East had little trouble carrying out contraband trade from the Illinois country to the warehouses of Albany and other English towns. Along with conducting business clandestinely, the British and their Iroquois agents spread suggestions of revolt, and several among the French allies were starting to listen to them. During the 1720's, there had seemed to be no end in sight to the war against the Fox, and a few disgruntled elements among the Illinois had begun to have second thoughts about their allegiance to the French. It was precisely during this delicate period that Pierre de Liette died. His death was another painful loss for French Illinois as he was a man who had inherited from his uncle, Tonty, the art of controlling an explosive situation single-handedly. Captain Charles Du Tisné was then ordered to transfer back from Natchez to Illinois. As fate would have it, he was hit by a gunshot in the cheek during a skirmish with the Fox. Badly treated, the wound caused his death, which probably occurred in 1730.[3] For the second time in a row, the French of Illinois had lost a most capable leader. A temporary successor was found in the person of Robert Groston, *sieur* de St. Ange de Bellerive, who was serving in Illinois along with two sons, a situation not uncommon during that period when soldiering was a family business. By all counts, St. Ange was a character high in color. He was also the "old hand" par excellence, having arrived in Canada probably as a young child in the late 1680's to serve as a cadet.[4] St. Ange, who knew the territory perfectly (he had also served on the Missouri at Fort d'Orleans), owned a house in the village near Fort de Chartres. For both new appointees, this posting could not have been more fortunate; for the governor, it was an immediate relief.

More than the rapid change of personnel, it was the change in 1717, from Canadian to Louisiana's government, which would further the direction taken by the human and economic evolution of *Le Pays des*

Illinois. This added to the conjuncture of factors pushing Illinois' center of gravity away from the valley of the Illinois River, the heartland, towards the Mississippi River.

The change began at the turn of the century when the Kaskaskia, Illinois Indians' largest nation, left Fort St. Louis at the Peoria Lake, in circumstances we have already examined (see chapter VII, *Illinois Enters Modern History*). The abandonment of the interior was furthered with the necessity of bypassing the Chicago portage; the Fox' perennial incursions had rendered use of this portage dangerous to all but the largest parties, as it was no longer under the protection of the fort erected in the preceding century. Communications, therefore, between Louisiana and Canada were maintained almost exclusively through the Ohio-Wabash corridor; even when traveling from the Mississippi to Michilmackinac and back, it was safer, although longer, to use the route marked by the posts staggered between the Wabash River and Lake Michigan. Finally, French administrators in Louisiana were influenced by their environment; the whole colony was then, in actuality, little more than the banks of the Mississippi River. They naturally looked to Illinois with the same set of references (one might say, blinded by these references), when building Fort de Chartres, a major endeavor, right on the Mississippi, with no concern given to dangers of flood and erosion. Paradoxically, while nothing was done to maintain and nurture a presence in the center of Illinois, the structure of several developments was slowly put into place on the southeastern flank of the territory along the St. Joseph-Wabash-Ohio.

The idea of reinforcing the connection between Canada and the lands west of the Great Lakes using the Ohio Valley was not new. La Salle, who had never liked the Chicago portage (too long and arduous) founded the first *Fort des Miamis* in 1679 (abandoned, however, three years later); in 1691, Augustin Le Gardeur de la Courtemanche opened *Le Poste à la Rivière St. Joseph*. In 1702, a trading post, Fort St. Vincent, had been set on the Wabash River but closed two years later.

The renewed impetus came from Vaudreuil whose command then still included Illinois, as we have seen, his concern was to guarantee a Canadian monopoly over the furs harvested west of Illinois, rather than maintaining communications with Louisiana. He had been governor for only three years when he assigned Jean-Baptiste Bissot, *Sieur* de Vincennes, a Canadian-born officer, to represent the king's authority with the Miami; Vincennes immediately proceeded to build a post on a location which is today near the city of Fort Wayne. In 1715, Vincennes built a new

Fort St. Joseph; in 1716, he was sent from the Miami post to what was then simply known as *Le Poste au Ouabache;* he died there in 1719. Vincennes lived but a few years in the area, but he displayed such seemingly tireless energy in carrying out his mission that while most of the French who planted the seeds of the modern Midwest have been forgotten, the name of his family has remained associated with the beginnings of the future State of Indiana.

Vincennes' death did not bring about a halt in activity; the same year— 1719—M. de Buisson created Fort Ouatanon, near the present West Lafayette, Indiana, (the dividing line between Canada and Louisiana passed through Terre Haute). But we have to wait until Vaudreuil's own death, in 1725, to see the hiatus in cordiality between New France and Lousiana, inspired by him, replaced by closer links. The *marquis* de Beauharnois, Vaudreuil' successor,[5] steered policy away from past parochialism. Animated with identical spirit, or at least, with a new understanding of the reality of the day, the Company argued in the same direction ". . . that all the other officers placed among the savage nations of the government of Canada who live at the mouth of the Wabash River may protect as much as they can the post, which the company is establishing there, and shall join together with the commandant there to drive away the English, who may penetrate as far as the river."[6]

Following news that the British had established houses and stores on an affluent of the Wabash River, the Company wrote to Perier, Louisiana's governor, that:

> Since the first of these rivers [Wabash] is the means of communication between Louisiana and Canada, and since this communication will be entirely broken if the English form a settlement at the confluence of one of these three other rivers, which would expose, at the same time, the country of Illinois and place in danger all the upper country of the colony, the company has ordered the establishment of a post on the Wabash River and has begged the governor of Canada to order the Sr. de Vincennes who is in command among the Ouyatanon-Miamis settled near the source of the Wabash, to get into communication with the commandant of the new post.[7]

The Vincennes referred to in the letter was Francois-Marie Bissot de Vincennes, the son of Jean-Baptiste, promoted second ensign the same year, and commandant of Ouatenon. Following an agreement between Louisiana and Canada, Vincennes was sent to take over his father's old

Poste au Ouabache with the mission of building a fort and organizing a settlement.[8] On April 4, 1730, Vincennes was confirmed as a half-pay lieutenant and officially attached to the government of Louisiana.

To have any chance of success, the containment of the British demanded a concerted effort between both colonies. The obvious need for such policy had been facilitiated by the important administrative change in 1731: the return of Louisiana to direct royal control following the revolt of the Natchez Indians.

This change took place at a time when the importance of Illinois as the bread-basket of the rest of Louisiana was increasing. A direct royal rule could only be an improvement, giving priority to order and security over consideration of expenses. A case in point for Illinois, was the handling of a minor disturbance fomented in 1735 by the Cahokia, suppressed before it started with the prompt arrival of a contingent of Kaskaskia Indians and of two companies of Marine infantry led personally by the new commandant of "the military district of Illinois," Pierre d'Artaguiette. While Illinois suffered its share of problems, however, the whole of Louisiana was deep in the midst of a struggle which threatened its very survival.

For several years, the Natchez, an Indian nation settled on the lower part of the Mississippi, and another nation further to the East, the Chickasaw, had had difficult relations with the French. Along with the Cherokees and the Iroquois, the Chickasaw were considered by the British as major allies. The Natchez, on the other hand, were torn between the reality of profitable daily dealings with the French, and a hostility to their presence, fanned by gifts and trading favors trickling down from the Carolinas. There can be no doubt that resistance to the French by the Natchez and the Chickasaw was orchestrated ("organized" would be too strong a word: Indian nations could be manipulated, but never regimented) from the offices of the governors of Carolina, Virginia and New York. The British routinely bought the captives that the Natchez and Chickasaw brought to them to be used as slaves on their plantations. They naturally provided weapons and ammunition, feeding inter-tribal warfare and leading to the capture of more slaves; that vicious circle of destruction later to be seen in full development in Africa. The major victims of the Natchez and Chickasaw were their neighbors the Choctaw, who naturally became allies of the French. In the case of the Natchez, however, it would be erroneous to attribute all the problems the French experienced solely to British intrigue. A spirit of fierce independence

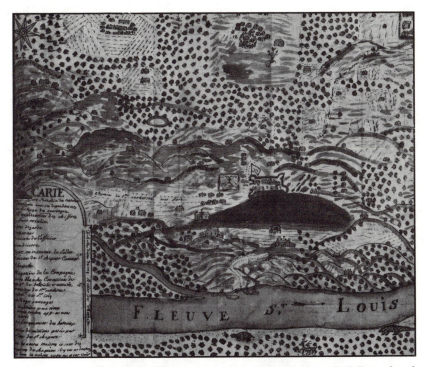

Map of Fort Rosalie at Natchez as it appeared in 1747. Reproduced from Dumont de Montigny. (The Newberry Library)

animated the Indian nations of the lower Mississippi. Especially with the Natchez, this spirit was reinforced by strong religious beliefs based on sun worship—quite similar, incidentally, to those of the Aztec, in Mexico, while conflict between Catholic missionary zeal and the Natchez religious structure could but only add to the other problems.

In 1716, the French had established a fort near the Natchez lands, Fort Rosalie (named for the wife of the Duke of Pontchartrain, Minister of the Navy), which became the foundation of today's small town of Natchez, Mississippi. By 1729, the settlement had grown considerably, even including craftsmen representing the essential mechanical trades of the time. Fort Rosalie was built in the proximity of the Natchez town; it fostered the usual close relationships between French and Indians, but was not free from problems. The planned acquisition of additional Natchez land by the commandant, *a sieur* de Chopart, who combined incompetence with greed, brought to a head a brewing conflict, leading to a surprise attack on the settlement and garrison, on November 28, 1729. By four o'clock on the same day, except for a few women and black slaves, all French civilians and soldiers were dead. News of the slaughter brought panic to New Orleans, but French reaction was swift and hard: the Natchez had little time to celebrate before they were in turn cut down en masse, the remaining warriors fleeing on a trail we know today as the Natchez Trace to the refuge provided by the Chickasaw in northeastern Mississippi.[9]

Over the next few years, the Chickasaw remained a source of irritation to the French, not only because they stubbornly refused to return the Natchez fugitives, but also due to their own harassment, both of the Choctaw and of French shipping on the Mississippi. In 1732, the Post of Arkansas received a much needed garrison of an ensign and twelve men. This post was a vital halt between Natchez and Illinois; however, it had fallen into semi-abandonment under the rule of the Company, always looking for ways of cutting costs.[10] The Arkansas Post, whose foundation dated back to the days of La Salle and Tonty, stood on the grounds of the Quapaw, a nation friendly to the French. In part due to the efforts of the Post's new commandant Ensign De Coulanges, the 300 Quapaw warriors began to confront raiding Chickasaw in a much more aggressive manner. The Chickasaw, in fact, were raiding in every direction, including far north. On March 21, 1733, Vincennes wrote to the Ministry that the preceding Fall the Chicakasaw had killed six Frenchmen and a Miami, along with his wife, near the fort. Therefore, a military solution was urgently in order if the French did not want to get involved all over again in the type of protracted affair they had known with the Fox.

By that time, displeased with Périer's stewardship of Louisiana, the minister of the Navy, Phelypeaux de Maurepas, in 1732, had reappointed Jean-Baptiste Le Moyne de Bienville Governor.[11] Four years later, Bienville was ready to engage in an all-out war against the Chickasaw, and a new, serious crisis lay at the doorstep of Illinois.

In plotting the conduct of the campaign, Bienville assigned a major role to the troops garrisoned in Illinois, the Illinois militia, and also the Indian allies. The plan was to encircle the Chickasaw between two pincers: the contingent from Louisiana, led personally by Governor Bienville starting from La Mobile, and the contingent from Illinois, led by Pierre d'Artaguiette, the newly appointed Commandant of the District. D'Artaguiette was instructed to wait: ". . . at the Prudhomme Bluffs

Canadian soldier. Taken
from *Narrative and Critical
History of America,* Vol 4,
Justin Winsor, ed., 1884.
(The Newberry Library)

(Memphis, Tennessee), estimated to be some 120 miles from the Chickasaw villages (near today's Tupelo, Mississippi), until he had word of
Bienville's arrival in the Chickasaw country. After this contact, the two
armies were to join and attack the Chickasaw together."[12]

The two were to rendezvous between March 10th and 15th, 1736.
D'Artaguiette had assembled a force of 400, including 130 French Marine
infantry and militia, the Cahokia Indian volunteers under them, and
Piankashaw[13] volunteers reinforced by forty Christian Iroquois led by
Vincennes. D'Artaguiette and his column left in February and arrived on
time, but Bienville was not at the rendezvous---the Governor had been

delayed. Worse yet, D'Artaguiette had not received the message meant to inform him of this contretemps, and he was not in a position to wait many days, as his provisions would not last longer than the previously expected duration of the campaign. With the growing impatience of his Indian allies, he had only two choices: attacking the cluster of Chickasaw villages alone, or abandoning the plan and returning to Illinois. To his scouts, the villages looked unprepared for war; therefore, on March 25th, he led the attack. He fell into the classic ambush.

Unbeknown to him, a large party of British traders staying in the Chickasaw villages had received information about the imminent attack, and accordingly had organized their defenses. When the French and their allies were already well inside the perimeter of the villages, they were suddenly confronted by the concenrated fire and attack of a force of five hundred men, and though the Iroquois responded well, the contingent of Illinois volunteers panicked and fled, and D'Artaguiette, in order not to be outflanked, had to order a retreat. Although it was conducted in good order, with the officers covering the rear of their troops, losses mounted rapidly, and in a short time the column was overwhelmed by the sheer number of the Chickasaw. D'Artaguiette, along with the majority of the officers, among them Francois de Vincennes; Louis Du Tisne, son of the past commandant Charles Du Tisne; Pierre Groston de St. Ange; De Coulanges, the chaplain; the Jesuit Antoine Senat; and sixteen soldiers; were all captured, and scores of others were killed.[14] The chaplain could have escaped but decided to stay behind with the prisoners. As mentioned before, capture by the enemy in Indian warfare meant death by fire; with the exception of two prisoners that the Chickasaw kept to exchange against their own captured, all the French were burned alive. From testimony obtained later, the French displayed a remarkable fortitude throughout their ordeal. [15] Total disaster was avoided thanks to the courage of a sixteen-year old trooper named Voisin, who, taking over the command of his comrades, had them execute an orderly retreat carrying the wounded, despite the constant fire of their pursuers from the first twenty-five miles.

Reading the letters found on the French officers, the British traders were able to warn the Chickasaw that other French troops were on their way from the south. As a result of this information, by the time Bienville was finally ready to begin his operations at the end of May, the Chickasaw, well retrenched in their complex of villages, were able to present such a well-organized resistance that he was forced to retreat. Interestingly, a unit of freed African slaves with their own black officers had been part of Bienville's expedition, inaugurating what would become a long tradition of African troops serving in the French Army.[16] Illinois had lost a large number of men and a complete cadre of administrators. And last, but certainly not least, the successful inroads made by the British traders threatened to become a permanent enclave, cutting communications on the Mississippi River. If successful, the British would sever Louisiana from its "upper" part, Illinois, as well as from New France, thereby threatening the whole structure of French North America.

Bienville now concentrated on repairing the damage; he organized the annual convoy of barges, the *bateaux* to Illinois, giving its command to an able officer, Captain de Benac. Forty-three soldiers, selected to make up for the losses of the garrison of Fort de Chartres, and two hundred men including *voyageurs*, Indians, and Black slaves, manned boats and canoes upstream against the currents of the Mississippi. Orders were sent to Louis St. Ange de Bellerive (Louis' brother) to the Missouri fort, directing him to take over the Post on the Wabash. This post, Vincennes' last command, known briefly after Bellerive's arrival as "Poste St. Ange", would receive a succession of names over the years until its last, Vincennes, finally remained in use.[17] The Piankashaw families who lived around the fort were fearful of raiding by the Chickasaw, and St. Ange had to report that all but a dozen "have gone higher up on the Wabash to another village."[18]

Most important of all the necessary measures, however, Bienville had to replace D'Artaguiette. He selected a veteran of sixteen years' service in Louisiana, forty-five year old captain Alphonse de la Buissonniere, who was already acting commander in Illinois.[19] La Buissonniere got along well with Indians and *habitans*, perhaps in part because of the romantic circumstances of his marriage. As a lieutenant he met and fell in love with the daughter of an Illinois settler of very limited means. The projected union was considered not acceptable for an officer in the King's troops by both civil and religious authorities in Louisiana, but un-daunted, the couple eloped and got married in the Spanish city of Pensacola. The intense social pressure they felt on their return eventually relented and was replaced by grudging acceptance. La Buissonniere's high quality of service received more attention than the circumstances of his marriage; to a governor, an officer like Bienville, service was more important than social perception.

From 1736 to 1739, the Chickasaw raided the Illinois, and the Illinois raided the Chickasaw, these sporadic actions having more to do with sport than war; but this status quo was interrupted in September 1739, when Governor Bienville made a new attempt to destroy the Chickasaw military power. The destruction of their stronghold had become a burning issue, far exceeding the dimensions of a local affair the numbers involved would have otherwise indicated. French military engineers studied the problem and a series of elaborate plans of attack were drawn in Rochefort, France; but it was the resolve of Maurepas, the minister, who sent additional troops and material and had the governors of New France and Louisiana coordinate his troop movements, that brought about a new face-off.

As in 1736, Bienville followed the same two-front attack strategy with troops coming from Louisiana and troops coming from New France. From the latter, a thousand French and Indian allies included contingents from Michilimackinac, Fort St. Joseph and Montreal: additionally, there were regular troops recently arrived from France, and even a company of young Canadian cadets, all led by capable officers such as Charles Le Moyne de Longueuil, (Bienville's nephew) and Pierre-Joseph Céloron de Blainville. La Buissonniere arrived from Illinois with forty soldiers and about an equal number of Illinois Indians, mostly Kaskaskia. On this occasion everyone was on time for the rendezvous called in September, but heavy rains made movements very difficult and what was supposed to be a fast, swift operation bogged down in months of waiting and inaction. This inaction was brought about in great part due to a complication in the chain of command. The King had appointed a naval officer, Captain Noailles d'Aime, to head all the troops from New France and Louisiana, both metropolitan and colonial. Noailles, however, remained under the direction of Bienville. Each had their own views on how to pursue the war. "For a time it looked as if the Chickasaw, by merely awaiting an attack, could obtain an even greater triumph than in 1736; but when the French forces began to move, the Indians offered to make peace." [20]

The main battle took place on February 22, 1740, and lasted from 9:00 a.m. to noon, with the French trying to take fortified cabins while being fired upon "from superior position." Far from decisive, it still had the desired effect of bringing the Chickasaw to the point of signing a peace treaty, which they promptly did, often afterward failing to observe the it, but their efficiency as a cohesive force was no longer a threat. The Indian allies gradually perceived the change and began to wear down a foe they no longer considered formidable. In the end, this sort of counter-guerrilla warfare achieved what the planning for parallel trenches, batteries, and crossfire plans could not seem to effect.

The Chickasaw campaign of 1739-40 recalls similar preparations—although not as detailed—that the French made during their campaigns against the Fox, in which European warfare style preparations had met with mixed success, contributing little to the final outcomes. The campaign against the Chickasaw demonstrated certain facts to the French; without passable roads, there could not be any meaningful artillery and without artillery, sieges of fortified Indian positions were not feasible. [21]

Bienville knew that his career was at an end, and he chose to request retirement, which was promptly granted. He had not achieved the crushing defeat over France's adversaries he had promised to deliver; instead, Captain Blainville had saved the day and received the coveted Cross of the Military Order of Saint Louis for his troubles.

Among Bienville's last decisions before leaving for France was the selection of a new commandant for Illinois, following the sudden and much regretted death of La Buissonniere on December 11, 1740. [22] He chose another experienced, mature officer, forty-three year old Captain de Bertet, who happened to be in France at the time and would not be able to take effective command until August 1742.

Leaving Louisiana, Bienville did not have the satisfaction of handing over a relatively peaceful colony to the next governor: the very same year, the convoy of boats for Illinois, although relatively formidable in appearance, was still attacked and a brigade of twenty-six voyageurs on their way from Illinois to the Miami was set upon, losing nineteen men.

The next governor, the Marquis de Vaudreuil, would take over amidst a certain indifference at the Court of Versailles. France's foreign policy had always concentrated on European affairs, and it was no different in the 1740's. We must not lose sight of the fact that the continuous problems the French had in North America with Indians supported by the British colonies did not reflect a continuous state of war between Britain and France. France, in fact, was at peace with Britain under the ministry of the venerable Cardinal Fleury, seventy-three years old when he acceded to office in 1726, an office he retained until his death in 1743. [23] During that period French foreign policy focused on the problems of the Polish Succession and Austrian Succession; and at home, on the rebuilding of the French economy after the detrimental effects of Law's system and of the War of Spanish Succession. Fleury was helped by the presence at the helm in Britain of Robert Walpole, another moderate man with whom he worked closely.[24] Short of open war, the governors of the British colonies were given to following their own expansion policies. They operated with a latitude conforming to the character of British colonization. The French, on the other hand, as we have amply seen by now, operated in a structured administration staffed by officers and responding directly to a ministry in France. Their limited resources obliged them to call continuously for supplies and reinforcements whose financing, in turn, had to be extracted from a Council and a King who, most of the time, were not particularly interested.

NOTES

1. De Liette intervened on behalf of Pradel who was subsequently cleared and reinstated in his rank.

2. Boisbriant died in Canada in 1740.

3. AN, Series C. 13 A, 12:178, 293.

4. See Douglas, "The Sieurs de St. Ange," in the *Transaction* of the Illinois State Historical Society, 1909, 135.

5. Charles de la Boische, *marquis* de Beauharnois, a patronym later spelled "Beauharnais." He was Imperatrice Josephine's grandfather.

6. Letter to M. de Boisbriant, December 22, 1725, trans. in Pierre-Geoges Roy, "Sieur de Vincennes Identified," *Indiana Historical Society Publications*, vol. 7, No. 1, 1905.

7. September 30, 1726, trans. in "Sieur de Vincennes . . .,"

8. The Vincennes family has long excercised a particular fascination for the afficionados of regional history, not least in Indiana. The family originated from Pont-Audemer, in Normandy, where it had acquired both respect and fortune. Francois Bissot received the Canadian *fief* (feudal property) of Vincennes on November 3, 1672. As often was the case in eighteenth century French usage, the son, Jean-Baptiste, officer with the Marine infantry, became known by the name of the newly acquired land, acquiring the flavor of nobility; (Robert Cavelier became known as "de La Salle," a land owned in Normandy, well before he received letter patentes of nobility from the king.) Francois-Marie Bissot de Vincennes, born on June 17, 1700, also officer in the troops of Marine, commanded at the Wabash Post until his death in 1736, during the battle against the Chicachas. He had married a girl from Kaskaskia, the daughter of a Philippe Lane, in 1733, from whom he had two daughters; in "Sieur de Vincennes.,"

9. The numbers of French dead given months later by a priest, Father Philibert, were: 144 men, 35 women and 56 children.

10. In 1727 the Post of Arkansas counted thirty white residents, one Jesuit, Father Paul du Poisson, but no soldiers. See Stanley Faye, "The Arkansas Post or

Louisiana: French Dominion," *The Louisiana Historical Quarterly*, July 1943, 633-47.

11. Bienville was the brother of Pierre Le Moyne d'Iberville, who led the settlement of Louisiana at the end of the preceding century.

12. Joseph Peyser, "The Chickasaw Wars of 1736 and 1740: French Military Drawings and Plans Document the Struggle for the Lower Mississippi." *The Journal of Mississippi History*, Feb. 1982, 1-25.

13. Piankashaw and Wea are groups related to the Miami; see Helen Hornbeck Tanner, *Atlas of Great Lakes Indian History*, University of Oklahoma Press, 1986.

14. Jean-Francois Liveron de Montchevaux apparently survived the battle as we find him in 1744, listed as lieutenant, commanding the Arkansas Post, and, in 1748, captain, commanding at Kaskaskia.

15. Seven officers of Marine infantry and four of the militia died in this affair; details of the battle from various correspondence, private and official, were reproduced in "Sieur de Vincennes," *Indiana Historical*, 99-105.

16. See Roland C. McConnell, *Negro Troops of Antebellum Louisiana. A History of the Battalion of Free Men of Colour*, Louisiana University Press, 1968.

17. We owe to Joseph Peyser, who studied in-depth the Chickasaw campaign (see "The Chickasaw Wars of 1736 and 1740: French Military Drawings and Plans Document the Struggle for the Lower Mississippi." *The Journal of Mississippi History*, February 1982, 1-25), many of the details mentioned here. The tale of the 1739-40 campaign is the tale of plans which never had the opportunity to be put into action: the elaborate plans that Captain Dupin de Belugard drew in Rochefort, *Plans des forts et des Attaques du village des Chicachas*. His son, also an artillary captain, travelled to Louisiana and served on Bienville's staff. But the hero of the hour happened to be a young cadet, Drouet de Richeville, who first escaped death and then escaped the Chickasaw (he lost three brothers in the battle) and was able to bring to the French commanders essential information on the details of the Chickasaw position.

18. Bienville to the Minister, June 21, 1737, quoted in several published studies such as "the Sieur de Vincennes.,"

19. AN C, series C 13A, 25:86.

20. Clarence Walworth Alvord, *The Centennial History of Illinois, The Illinois Country, 1675-1818*, 183.

21. Au Ouabache, Au Poste, Poste des Pianguichats, Poste Vincent, Poste St. Vincent, Poste Vincennes; the British also called it: Fort St. Anne, an anglicized version of St. Ange, Little Ouyatanon, abbreviated as "L. Wiaut." See Jacob Dunn, "Mission to the Ouabache," *Indiana Historical Society*, vol. IV, 1902, 256.

22. Letter from the commandant of La Mobile to the minister, April 25, 1741; AN, C Series, 13A 26:27.

23. André Hercule de Fleury, born on June 22, 1653, was made cardinal when he became minister of state; he died in Paris on January 29, 1743.

24. Robert Walpole, lst Earl of Orford, was in power from 1721 to 1742.

11

"Les habitans"

P ierre Francois de Rigaud, baron de Cavagnal, *marquis* de Vaudreuil, was the third son of Philippe de Vaudreuil, the governor of New France who had strongly opposed the withdrawal of Illinois from his administration (see Chapter IX, "The Fox Wars"). A product of the French aristocracy, the new governor was cut from different cloth than Bienville. Vaudreuil fought the Fox in 1728, but otherwise had seen little military action. His experience as an administrator was limited as well; his only post had been as commandant of the small Canadian town of Trois-Rivières when appointed to Louisiana's highest office. Neither experience nor achievement having prepared him for his new responsibilities, trying times were ahead for Louisiana and New France.

With barely 8,000 settlers, the mere ability to survive in a new land, rather than concern for its development, had been the major question for French North America since its very birth. Much more than the well-publicized quest for religious freedom, Britain's harsh living conditions, contrasted with the relative prosperity of France's countryside, in a twisted kind of fortune sent a steady flux of British immigrants to the thirteen colonies, so that by the mid-1700's the difference in figures was staggering, with less than fifty thousand French versus more than a million English settled in North America. To add to their woes, a large proportion of the French who emigrated to New France, possibly more than 30 percent, found conditions there so harsh that they chose to return home. While British indentured workers crowded the piers to leave for North America, guaranteed only free passage and the first seven years of work at no pay (and fifty acres if they survived that long), the French *engagé* served only thirty-six months and received a minimum salary of sixty livres a year.[1] The situation might have improved somewhat had the French authorities allowed the protestants (the Huguenots) to emigrate to New France rather than forcing them into exile in places like Berlin, the Dutch colonies of southern Africa, and even the Carolinas. It was only a prolific nature, accompanied by a unique low mortality rate among the young, that gave the French population some strength in numbers: from 1700 to 1765 it increased fivefold, from 13,000 to 60,000.[2] The

Marquis de Montcalm, arriving in Quebec in 1755 to take command of the regular troops, noted in his diary that one soldier of the regiment of *Carignan-Salières* who settled in Canada 100 years earlier, had 220 descendants.[3] Even illegitimate children who would have been much neglected in France were treated as precious additions: for instance, of 390 children born out of wedlock in 1736 (128 in Quebec, 11 in Trois-Rivières, and 251 in Montreal) only 12 deaths were registered.[4] Such spectacular fertility, uniquely free from the ravages of death among postpartum women and infants common in those days, would not restore a demographic balance between French and British North America. Pressure on the French was growing all the time. Like rivulets escaping through an earthen dam—here, the Alleghenies—parties of English traders were constantly appearing in lands thought to be under French control.

But what the French population lacked in numbers, it made up in resiliency, and even today, Quebec enjoys the lowest level of infant deaths in the world.[5] Interestingly, environment and genetics may have played equally important roles in forming the strength of the French-Canadian character. Although many provinces, as well as Paris, were represented among the French who made New France, a majority came from Brittany, the Atlantic coast, and Normandy. The land of Brittany, a windswept rocky peninsula battered by fierce seas, was a perfect "basic training" ground for anyone settling in seventeenth century Canada. Slightly more hospitable, the Atlantic coast was home to a breed of individuals who would take to the rugged life like fish to water; while from fertile, green, rich Normandy came a large number of individuals of mixed Celtic and Viking stock.

The crucible for all of these people was a country where neither nature nor natives gave them much of a second chance. Professor Eccles put it quite well:

> In contrast to the English colonies where the frontier became ever more remote from the settled areas along the seaboard, Canada was part and parcel of an all-pervasive frontier, for all the houses in the colony had the river at their doorsteps and along it came the men of the wilderness, French and Indian alike, bringing the values and customs of the wilderness into the homes.[6]

Most of the *voyageurs* and *coureurs des bois* of the generation of Louis Jolliet were, as he was, born in New France. They were men who: "were an entirely different breed from the frontiersmen of the English colonies. They made no attempt to destroy the wilderness, because their way of life required its preservation."[7] Along with a few soldiers of marine infantry, these were the same men who comprised the French population of Illinois during the first years of Tonty's command.

We can hardly illustrate the beginning of the French population of Illinois with only silhouettes of marines and *voyageurs*, when even before French women arrived from Montreal, Trois-Rivières, and other locations, there were the Indian women—the first mothers of the next generation of French Illinois.

We have already alluded to the fact that, from the inception of their North American presence, the French quickly developed personal relationships with Indian women of the Huron and the Ottawa nations, and with the Indians roaming Illinois from Lake Michigan to the Mississippi River as well. "The French" in this context generally excludes governors, *intendants* and their staffs, and most officers commanding posts (however, at least one, Etienne Véniard de Bourgmont, married a Missouri Indian woman), rather they were comprised of the traders, the military, and civilian rank and file, free from the restraints of command and social standing. Their behavior horrified the missionaries who viewed their own compatriots as the greatest obstacle to the Indians' conversion to Christianity. The missionaries periodically asked for, and obtained from the royal authorities, publication of futile edicts forbidding unsanctioned consorting. Add the laissez faire attitude of most of the commandants to the determination of the traders who frequented their posts, and the results were countless sexual unions, often on a seasonal basis. At year's end the novices, the *mangeurs de lard* (pork eaters), were given the loads of collected furs to convoy from lake warehouses to Montreal. Eighteen months later the veterans, those who spent winters in Indian country— the *hivernants*—returned, happy and loud; they quickly invested or squandered wages and profits, only to start the cycle all over again, and, for many, resume the relationships established with their Indian consorts.

Winter ice and the hunting season restricted navigation to a May-December period during which long and arduous voyages, about ten weeks in each direction, meant not only hours of paddling on lakes and rivers but back-breaking portages as well. Each portage—a French word for "carrying"—obliged unloading the four to five hundred pounds of trade goods or furs and transporting them back-pack style from one body of water to the next. Distances to be covered on foot by the heavily-laden

Voyageurs at Dawn. Painting by Francis A. Hopkins. (National Archives of Canada)

men varied: they could be very short or very long, as the St. Joseph-Kankakee portage, [8] or very hard, as the bypass of the Niagara Falls. While crossing open stretches of water on loaded birch-bark canoes was no sinecure along with the reality of almost continuous danger of one sort or another, it was matched by a feeling of freedom that these open woods imparted to the men of the fur trade; not unlike, a century and a half later, the effect that the open plains of the West would have on cowboys.

The fur traders—be they *voyageurs*, trading with a license, or the illegal *coureurs des bois*—were masters of their skills; maneuvering their fragile crafts and repairing them when needed, surviving when provisions ran out. Undoubtedly they were a cocky bunch. Physically, by today's standards, they were on the average quite short, barely over five feet, but incredibly strong. Pushing their canoes against the water from dawn to dusk, they sang melodies; some forgotten today, like "My Birch-bark Canoe," or "La belle Lisette," and a few still familiar, like "*A la Claire Fontaine.*" They knew dozens of songs, working rhymes analogous to sailors' chanteys. They dressed in deerskin leggings and moccasins, a linen shirt, a bright sash around the waist, and a woolen cap with a tassle hanging to one side or a colorful kerchief circling the head. During the cold weather they added a hooded blue coat, the *capote*. Picture them at camp with their long-stemmed white clay pipes, tireless raconteurs, and you will have conjured an image of the heroic past of North America.[9] Once back in Montreal, the *hivernants* did somewhat more than let off a little steam. In his memoirs Baron de La Hontan, who had been an officer in New France and a bit of an adventurer himself, wrote this eyewitness report:

> I saw twenty-five or thirty of these canoes return with heavy cargoes; each canoe was managed by two or three men, and carry hundred weight, i.e., forty packs of Beaver skins, which are worth a hundred Crowns a piece. These canoes had been a year and eighteen months out. You would be amazed if you saw how lewd these traders are when they return; how they feast and game, and how prodigal they are not only in their clothes but upon women . . . Eat, drink, and play all day as long as the goods hold out; and when these are gone, they even sell their embroidery, their lace, and their clothes. This done, they are forced to go upon a New Voyage for subsistence.[10]

A small, but growing, number of them who found life less confining in the West interrupted this cycle, contracting more formal alliances with Indian women, "in the fashion of the country," thereby gaining not only more stability in their lives but also the political advantage of a blood alliance with an Indian nation. Those living at or near trading posts were more susceptible to the remonstrances of the missionaries, and generally ended up marrying the Indian women they wanted or took for their mates.

The best known example of a trader who followed the pattern of legitimacy, marrying an Illinois Indian girl, was Michel Accault, one of La Salle's companions in 1680. Years later he could be found at *Fort St. Louis de Pimitoui,* where he worked closely with Tonty and La Forest. Coveting the seventeen-year-old daughter of Rouensa, Chief of the Kaskaskia, Accault had no difficulty obtaining the Chief's prompt approval, however the deal had not taken into account the obstinate refusal of Marie Rouensa to join Accault, "famous in all the Illinois country for his debaucheries." It was only when Father Gravier, the Jesuit missionary, was able to convince Marie to accept a proper marriage, that the union took place. Father Gravier could write later, in 1694, that "Accault is now quite changed, and has admitted to me that he no longer recognizes himself, and can attribute his conversion solely to his wife's prayers and exhortations. . . ." [11]

Marie, with two sons by Michel Accault, but widowed young, remarried; this time to the captain of the militia in Kaskaskia, with whom she had six more children. Through her descendants alone, many ancient French families of Illinois could claim the heritage of the Illinois Indians. Many others married Indian women, like Louis Delaunais, born in Canada in 1650, who wedded Marie Catherine Resecanga on July 25, 1692, and we know that they had at least two sons; as well as Jean Colon La Violette, who married Catherine Ewipakinsca, and had three sons: the youngest, Henri, bastized in 1698 (see chapter VI, "The Lonely Command"), had Tonty for a godfather. Pierre Chabot married Symphorosa Merstapscsc; Nicolas Migneret married Suzanne Kerami; and others, like Pierre Boisjoly Fafart "are all names which appear in the parish registers of the twenty years of the village's (Kaskaskia) existence. Most of them had Indian wives or children by Indian women who were baptized in the time of the Mission of the Immaculate Conception." [12]

Even more revealing as regards the nature of these original race relations in Illinois is the fact that Indian parentage was no obstacle in marriages among the higher class of administrators and officers. Examples can be found in Kaskaskia and St. Anne de Fort de Chartres' parish registers: Marie-Rose Tessier, who married Pierre Groston de St. Ange; Marie Philippe, who married Francois Bissot de Vincennes; Elizabeth de Celle Duclos, who married Frederic d'Arensbourg. The first two had Kaskaskia Indian mothers; the last was Marie Rouensa's granddaughter, [13] Marie-Rose, who lost her husband during the Chickasaw War, and remarried in 1741. When in turn she died six years later, her second husband married a woman also of mixed parentage. [14]

Unfortunately for these unions, the authorities' view of mixed marriages changed in 1735; they argued the *métis* (mixed blood) children growing to adult age were for most part maladjusted, torn between their mothers' Indian heritage and this extension of France in America that they were committed to further. This fallacious argument ignored the reality of a second and third generation of French population already quite successfully integrated, having been raised in households where French influence was dominant, albeit rustic. Evidently for the officials back in New Orleans, a far more elegant crowd, the standards of French Illinois would have to be raised. While there were instances of lawlessness displayed by some of the *metis* and Indians, much of this could be attributed to the behavior of unruly French traders, who were often their close blood relatives. To be objective, it must be noted that the *voyageurs* and, of course, the *coureurs des bois* were continuously castigated and made the object of repeated—and useless—repressive legislation. With all the records of marriages and baptisms to contradict overwhelmingly the opinions of the authorities, here and there instances of cultural conflict do appear. One is provided by Marie Rouensa-Philippe, who, before her death on June 25, 1725, disinherited her second son by Michel Accault, also named Michel, ". . . unless he should come back to live among the French." [15] The Jesuits protested vehemently but to no avail; an order was issued in October 1735 which "prohibited the priests in the future from solemnizing such marriages without the consent of their commandant. The policy was not acceptable to the Jesuits; a memoir of 1738 emanating from them pointed out the evils that would result." [16]

The Jesuits, better acquainted than anybody else with the behavior and attitudes of both communities, were right. The new policy did not prevent the French from looking for mates among Indians, not only the Illinois, but across the Mississippi River from the Pawnee as well. [17] The scarcity of available French women no doubt played a role in the obstinant nature of the French and if the commandant rarely consented, he also did little to interfere and consequently, [18] "the number of illegitimate children in the villages was always relatively large."

The language of records, once deciphered, can help greatly to reconstruct the realities of the time. Records tell the story of Marie-Josephe Deguire Larose, one of two children born of an Indian slave, redeemed and recognized in 1747, by the father, Jean-Baptiste, a tailor in Kaskaskia; she married three times, each time to solid citizens from Kaskaskia and Ste. Genevieve, and saw her own daughters enter matrimony by the time of her death, in 1788. Records show that Marguerite Vallé, the daughter of an Indian woman and a wealthy citizen from Ste. Genevieve during the same period, "married a respectable French Creole, Louis Caron." [19] Records recount the tale of murder and abduction in Ste. Genevieve in 1774, then the capital of the Spanish-controlled portion of French Illinois, involving the *métis* hunter Celodon, and Marianne, the Indian slave he freed, and the friends who trusted and protected them. Ekberg, Ste. Genevieve's historian *par excellence*, called them: ". . . a gallant couple caught between two cultures." [20]

The founding of Kaskaskia, in 1703, had signaled a switch from nomadic existence to village life in Illinois. The fur traders were still essential to the economy and the French were still originating from

Canada; but cultivated fields, grazing cattle, mills, and soon, mines, began to add a more stable layer to the settlement. As we have seen, in this environment French-Indian unions remained predominant until the 1730's, when Indian villages were ordered removed a certain distance from French communities. The same period coincided with a marked increase of women arriving from Canada through the *voyageurs'* route. [21] These were women already married, however, joining their husbands or traveling with them. Single women did not have to make the perilous journey from Canada to Illinois to find mates as the chronic shortage of French women in New France guaranteed that any new arrival of *les filles du roi* ("the King's daughters")—the nickname given respectable poor and orphan girls sponsored by the royal authorities—would be besieged by eager bachelors (under the watchful eyes of civil and religious authorities) and married off within days. As their numbers were too few—1,189 from 1634 to 1673—to provide wives for all, their arrival made only a dent in a colony where the ratio in the 1660's was twelve males for every available female.[22] Understandably, in Illinois widows and young girls who reached puberty did not languish long.

> It was common for an inventory of the late husband's goods and a marriage contract between the widow and another habitant to be drawn up on the same day. . . . sometimes one or two of the bans were dispensed with by the priest; marriages did take place occasionally immediately after the reading of the first ban. Even the Lenten prohibitions were frequently lifted to allow for the ceremony.[23]

Matchmaking, in not a few instances, might have been arranged while the body of the dead spouse was still warm, if not before. For all the feelings of insensitivity, or even cold calculation, that this picture evokes, we must understand the overall concern for stability. The Church—which in Illinois was embodied by the ever-pragmatic Jesuits—sharing this concern, stood always ready to cover an occasional bout of lust with the mantle of respectability. In a sort of instinctive and collective folk psychology, death was not given the opportunity to discourage a small community which daily faced adversity, distance, danger, isolation, and more. There was a certain wisdom in letting *charivari* noises quickly drown requiem sounds; it reflected French-Canadian endurance, which by the early 1700's had already acquired a solid reputation.

This French-Canadian character of Illinois was about to change, how-

The Illinois Country in 1744. From Charlevoix, *Histoire et description générale de la Nouvelle France*, Paris, 1744. (The Newberry Library)

ever. The profile of arrivals in Illinois began to be altered after the territory was made part of Louisiana in 1717, and the following year, when Louisiana was handed over to the *Compagnie d'Occident*.

Only twenty-four individuals settled in the short and narrow band of fertile land stretching from Kaskaskia to Cahokia during the period from 1699 to 1718. All of them were Canadian men, who were fur traders averaging thirty-six years of age, and almost all were married to Indian women.[24]

Starting with the summer of 1718, these circumstances would change radically, with the arrival of one hundred soldiers of marine infantry, dozens of *engagés*, and a complete set of civil and military administrators. The buildup of Illinois financed by the Company had begun.

More soldiers directed to the new Fort de Chartres, more skilled workers, and a brigade of miners continued the buildup, increasing the population of Kaskaskia and led to new communities. But by 1721, the quick profits which had been proclaimed from Paris housetops had not yet materialized; the Company curtailed investments and slashed expenses. The change to austerity brought little loss of population (except for the temporary reduction of the garrisons). Still, even taking into account the normal birth rate, statistics show a decade with no demographic growth: from 334 people in 1723, to 321 in 1726, and 321 in 1732. Census information for 1732 also shows a majority of the male population no longer solely occupied with the fur trade: there were now 108 settlers versus approximately fifty *voyageurs*. We see more than a coincidence in the fact that these figures almost precisely match a count of only forty Canadians of the total 144 men living in Illinois in 1726. The reduced number of Canadian arrivals reflected the impact that the Fox and Chickasaw Wars had on Illinois for almost a half-century. Twenty years later, there was a marked revival of Canadian immigration, but it came too late. In 1752, the effect of stunted growth was evident: the same area, including the new village of Ste. Genevieve across the Mississippi, supported only 768 whites, 445 black and 157 Indian slaves. Illinois was also home to 385 soldiers making up the various garrisons; an impressive figure but one which cannot be included in the total count, as it fluctuated in response to the whims of needs and budgets. While some soldiers married local women and settled, their numbers would remain small. When their tour of duty overseas was completed, the majority of soldiers of marine infantry were happy to return home; as we have observed before, the French did not easily take to expatriation.

Although initially an extension of New France, from its beginnings, Illinois developed along different settlement patterns. The people were similar, but the conditions were not. Whereas in New France, the objective was to achieve the maximum effective occupation of large tracts of land with a small number of colonists, planners, given what was for the time an incredibly free rein, broke from the traditional French (and

European) setup of villages grouped around a castle and a church.

In Illinois, however, village development was approached differently. To understand how similar to the traditional French model the Illinois villages remained, we need to look in contrast at the unique and progressive concept that the administrators had developed for New France.

New France began as a serious possibility only after the *Compagnie des Cent-Associés* (also known as *Compagnie de la Nouvelle-France*), was appointed in 1626 by Cardinal Richelieu to administer the colony. Six years later Samuel de Champlain, "the Father of New France," again made governor, returned to Quebec with a fleet of three ships. These were humble beginnings but the plans for colonization had been carefully thought out and would be implemented from the start.

The *Acte pour l'établissement de la Compagnie des Cents-Associés pour le commerce du Canada* embodied the principles governing the distribution of land concessions, and the social ranking assigned to the recipients. The Company divided the land into *seigneuries*, subdivided in turn among *censitaires*. All this may sound terribly feudalistic, but the terms in this case covered "a method of apportioning land, bringing it into production, and obviating the evils of speculation."[25] It was an inexpensive way to populate the colony, making the *seigneurs* responsible for bringing new settlers at their own expense; settlers who would clear the land, the *défricheurs*, and enter the cycle of productivity. The settlers on seigneurial lands would pay very low dues, about ten percent of their revenue, and owe practically nothing else. "The seigneurs were little more than land settlement agents and their financial rewards were not great. What they did gain, and what made men eager to become seigneurs, was the greatly enhanced social status, made manifest in a variety of ways."[26]

Facing both a need to support the fur trade, as well as develop agriculture in a country virtually paralyzed during the winter months, the Company actively promoted the granting of *seigneuries*, all fronting the St. Lawrence River. The River from the start was French North America's *Main Street*: "The River being defined as the main resource, the maximum number of parcels had to border the water... the individual exploitation surface had to be sufficiently large and accessible to attract settlers and allow rentability."[27]

The properties granted by the Company became a series of vast rectangles aligned along both sides of the St. Lawrence River. In thirty years, from 1633 to 1663, seventy-four seigneuries were granted. With everybody wanting to have access to the river, urbanized French Canada remained limited to three towns: Quebec, Trois Rivières, and Montreal.

In Illinois, with the exception of the *seigneurie* granted originally to La Salle, and then transferred to Tonty and La Forest—a seigneurie which had uniquely huge dimensions, from Lake Michigan to the Mississippi—this system was not applied. Original land assignment to settlers evolved from simple squatter's rights to the distribution of concessions by Tonty, La Forest, and later by the Company and the King.

The reasons behind this difference were multiple. First, for Versailles, French establishment in North America essentially meant the banks of the St. Lawrence River, with agricultural development as the main resource along with logging and fishing. The planning and colonization of New France originally did not take into consideration the impact of a fur trade centered around posts pushed farther and farther west. Although prone to Iroquois raids, mainly on the southern bank of the St. Lawrence, the relative concentration of settlers, and the proximity of strong garrisons, made the large tracts of fertile Canadian lands still very attractive to French peasants who had never owned anything before. In the west, Indian dwellings and traders' cabins stayed close to posts and missions. There, until the 1700's, agriculture was somewhat present, but only in the form of corn and squash fields and as a side activity. From the start, security remained a primary concern for the commandants of Illinois. Iroquois had laid siege to Illinois strongholds and devastated large Illinois Indian villages; the Fox, later, did much of the same for as many years. By the time serious danger had subsided, Illinois had adopted the system of grouping dwellings: Kaskaskia would be the prime example of the French village in the west, with houses and gardens neatly laid out in close quarters, branching out from both sides of the *Grande rue,* leading to the Illinois River. One major aspect of Canadian organization, however, was retained: the system of big common fields divided into *champs en long,* or longlots.

"Common field" did not mean land held communally by the *habitans:* to the contrary, the fields were divided into long strips of land, each individually owned. Lots were measured in arpents (an arpent corresponded to about one-and-a-half acres). In Kaskaskia the common fields were located south and west of the town. In his monograph on Ste. Genevieve, Carl Ekberg presents a clear description of the French system:

> The common fence is the source of the expression "Big Field Commons,"
> for the strips of arable land themselves were not held in common but were

freehold possessions of individual *habitants*. Most adult male citizens
owned, in addition to their respective residential lot [*un terrain*] or [*emplacement*] in the village, a strip of land [*une terre*] within the Big Field Commons.
For the pasturing of domestic stock there was a true commons, land held
in common . . . The strips of arable land, privately owned, were usually one,
two, or three arpents wide . . . The parcels of plowland had no fences between them and no habitations on them, and thus constituted a system of
open field agriculture, which was traditional in much of Europe. The
peculiar [to modern American eyes] strips of plowland had their origins in
a number of factors—historical, geographical, and technical. That was the
manner in which Frenchmen and French Canadians had customarily laid
out their farm lands in the Illinois Country, in Canada, and in parts of
northern France.[28]

Although the system of longlots had originated in Europe it was
particularly adaptable to new France, where in each instance it was an-
chored on a waterway. Similar common fields could be found in St.
Philippe, Prairie du Rocher, Cahokia or Vincennes, and later in Ste.
Genevieve. In Vincennes, the commons were a 5,000-acre tract.[29] It is
interesting to note that the influence of the French longlots did not
disappear with French domination. A map of the village of Vincennes
drawn in the late 1820's displays their regular pattern starting from the
Wabash River. Even more telling are aerial photographs and satellite
images; in Cahokia and in Vincennes, the French-designed longlots for
the most part remain intact to this day,[30] a silent but living monument to
the French period.

While many French *habitans* worked on their own land some hired
journaliers (day laborers), or rented out their properties, and starting with
the early 1700's, increasingly used slave labor. The introduction of slave
labor coincided with the changeover of jurisdiction from New France to
Louisiana, and the accompanying introduction of new enterprises sponsored by the Company. Slave labor in Illinois grew gradually from the beginning of the eighteenth century, and by 1746, the total census for Louisiana indicated that 300 whites lived in Illinois, along with 600 black
slaves. Except for the Jesuit mission and the mines which owned large
numbers, families had only one, two, or three Indian or black slaves at
most, a setup conducive to more familiar, humane relations.

These slave owners were not distant, plantation-style aristocrats (although their Illinois was not exactly the original territory born out of the

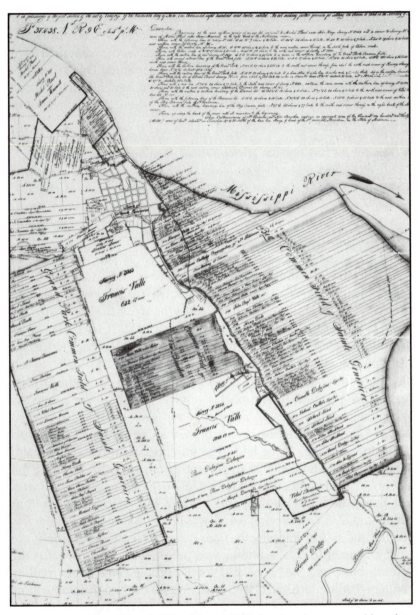

General Land Office Map of 1815 showing the system of long-lots and fields around the town of Ste. Genevieve on the Mississippi River. The town can be seen near the top center of the map. The Mississippi River defines the eastern border. (National Archives, Washington)

ambitions of Canadian freeholders). They were French common folk who had "no stomach" for the sort of intensive exploitation seen during the same period in the West Indies. Many were not very far removed from ancestors who had toiled in somewhat similar servitude. On the negative side, this more casual behavior extended to the agricultural methods used. The French methods seemed primitive, even then, in the eyes of foreign travellers:

> None of the new methods of crop rotation, with intermixing of legumes, that Dutch and English farmers were using had penetrated to the remote Illinois Country. The alluvial soil of the Big Field was of course extremely fertile and was from time to time rejuvenated by the floodwaters of the Mississippi, just as the land in Egypt had been kept productive for millenia by the annual spring flooding of the Nile.[31]

Fertilization was unknown or simply not practiced, and even the best soils could become exhausted. Perhaps that was the case in Kaskaskia and the reason for several families to begin looking across the Mississippi for new lands, eventually leading to the founding of Ste. Genevieve. Tools and plows were, for the most part, identical to those that the French had used since medieval times, but despite this (save for the floods, which along uncontrolled rivers could be as devastating as droughts), crops were more plentiful than probably anywhere else on the continent. Wheat, corn, barley, tobacco and even cotton, grew quite well in Vincennes, and only grapes, so important for the making of wine for Mass, had difficulty adapting. Wine had to be imported from France or Spain. Wheat, by far Illinois' most important commodity (bread being the essential French food), needed to be ground, a step accomplished with less than efficient horse mills (there was a functioning water mill in Cahokia in 1735, however). When all was finally said and done, there was still the question of shipping the flour down to New Orleans safely.

The state of Illinois' economy was reflected in the houses that the *habitans* built, and the household goods and the items of luxury they contained. Manufactured objects from overseas, although commanding hefty prices, were still found commonly at least in the homes of the officers and leading families. Illinois may have been at the western tip of the civilized world for more than a century but it definitely belonged to that world.

The classical French house in Illinois was made of vertical posts sunk

The Bolduc House, in Ste. Genevieve, was built by Louis Bolduc in 1770-71, moved to its' present site and enlarged in 1785; restored in 1956, it is owned and operated by the National Society of Colonial Dames of America and the State of Missouri. (Photograph by Mike Coles)

in the ground known today among Illinois historians and frequent visitors to Vincennes, Cahokia, Fort de Chartres or Ste. Genevieve, as the *maison de poteaux en terre*, or post-in-ground homes. Oak, walnut, and mulberry provided the materials for the logs, but a much better—and more expensive wood—was the rot-resisting cedar. Interstices were patched with *bouzillage*, essentially clay and hay mixed to form a sort of waterproof putty when dry; or *pierrotage*, a mixture of clay and small stones. Houses were also built more safely and sturdily (and more expensively) with the logs sunk in stones or in scantings, a system called *poteaux sur sole* and *colombage sur sole* (the Amoureaux House, on St. Mary's Road in Ste. Genevieve, is a good example of a *poteaux en terre* building). Houses were whitewashed in and out, and the plots they stood on were always surrounded by picket fences to keep animals away from the orchards and herb gardens. A continuous line of fences would also serve as a defensive wall. Here and there a few houses were built of stone;

French Colonial home in the Mississippi Valley. From Victor
Collot, *Voyage dans l'Amérique du Nord*, Paris, 1826.
(The Newberry Library)

the first of their kind in 1723, by Philippe Renault, near Fort de Chartres.

As in Canadian houses, all had chimneys for their fireplaces; they
differed from Canadian houses, however, by the fact that posts in ground
were retained as a construction mode even when the floors ceased to be
at dirt level. Another distinguishing feature was the *galerie*. Galleries
were open porches running sometimes on three sides, and sometimes all
around, giving a Caribbean flavor to the houses. Galleries were not an
original feature of the houses in Illinois, "although there is at least one
reference to a gallerie in French Illinois in the 1720's."[32] Similarly, the
double pitched-roof houses, which along with the galleries today symbol-
ize the surviving French houses in Illinois, originated in the later part of
the French period. If you look at the finished detail of the Norman-style
hand-hewn oak trusses of the roofs, you will agree that the quality of
construction of these surviving houses is testimony to the excellent
craftsmanship of the early French carpenters.

The same type of functional country furniture used in France during
this period, with little embellishment could also be found in Illinois.

Chests, tables, and chairs were generally left unpainted. *Armoires* (wardrobes), on the other hands, where generations of linens were stored, were massive affairs, built as elaborately as those in France and sometimes barely fitting into the small rooms. We must remember that the houses in relation to the size of families, not even counting slaves, were small. In Ste. Genevieve,[33] "The wealthy Jean Morel had a family of nine pesons living in a residence of less than 1,100 square feet..." The most important piece of furniture of every household, however, was the bed:[34] "Frequently it was the only dowry of the Illinois bride, and the marriage contract carefully assured its ownership to the survivor of the union." A bed always included the big feather comforter and "inevitably ... its '*traversin'*, the long sausage-like pillow that often perplexes American tourists on their first trip to Europe."[35]

The inventories of dozens of estates have provided insight into the most cherished and the most common possessions of the inhabitants of French Illinois. We borrow here from the numerous examples cited by Natalia Belting in her book on Kaskaskia.[36] First, the example of a wealthy settler, Jacques Bourdon, the captain of militia we last encountered floundering under the responsibilities of his command during the Fox Wars. Bourdon had married in 1722 and died a year later. The furniture he left included one walnut *armoire,* eight walnut chairs and one armchair, one dresser with a buffet, copper candlesticks, three trunks full of clothes, and one chest containing ten shirts, capotes, hats, waistcoats, stockings, and more. He had fourteen plates, two pewter dishes and twenty pewter spoons, three plates and two spoons of Spanish silver, and twelve glass bottles. He also had fourteen guns and one musket, ten Flemish knives, and hundreds of gun flints, all this representing only a portion of his estate. His widow, Theresa, would marry three times more.[37]

Marie Catherine Baron, a lady whose financial status was not as exhalted, after her death in 1748, left two chests, one cot, one small cupboard, one armchair, one square table with drawers, one (old) *armoire,* and one bed, but also, a rare object: one large framed mirror. Items never mentioned were the spinning wheel and the loom: cloth had to be bought from the royal warehouse or from merchants. Dresses were expensive; a widow, Marie Francoise Rivard, spent the enormous sum of 800 livres (not in cash but in peltries), to acquire "a complete outfit of a rose-colored taffeta dress, pair of silk stockings, anklets, slippers and mitts."[38] Everyday dress was obviously simpler and identical to what women wore in

"Festivities of the Early French in Illinois." From Henry Howe,
Historical Collections of the Great West, Cincinnati, 1851.
(The Newberry Library)

Canada: brightly colored bodice, with or without sleeves, skirts, and
moccasins.

The poorest inventories were often those of the belongings of deceased
military, including officers. The defeat at the hands of the Chickasaw of
1736, left practically all the officers of the Illinois contingent dead. Among
them was Antoine de Tonty, whose belongings were inventoried at Fort
de Chartres on June 23, 1737: a beaver hat embroidered with silver, three
dress coats, a regulation outfit, and a few more things like stockings, all
amounting to a value of a couple hundred livres.

Inventories also included kitchen utensils: cauldrons, salting tubs for
meat, ladles, pie dishes, iron frying pans, crockery salad dishes, pots and
bowls, pans, forks, funnels, and measures.

By and large, people in Illinois ate well. Each household made its own
bread in outdoor ovens, similar to the one you can see today reconstructed
at Fort de Chartres. No doubt bread provided the essential food; but in
Illinois vegetables were abundant, meat and fish easily available. The
French prepared the traditional well-spiced *boudin*, or blood sausage.
Butter was rare, but bear grease abundant and used commonly. In
addition, there were fruit jams, honey, and pies and crepes. They drank

herb teas sweetened with maple syrup, imported wines, and rum from the Islands.

Natalia Belting wrote a paragraph on social life and customs which can hardly be improved:

> The Illinois habitant was a gay soul; he seemed shockingly carefree to later, self-righteous puritans from the American colonies. He danced on Sunday after Mass, was passionately attached to faro and half a dozen other card games, and played billiards at all hours. He gossiped long over a friendly pipe and a congenial mug of brandy in the half-dusk of his porch or in the noisy tavern. And every conceivable occasion he celebrated with religious rituals and pagan ceremonies.[39]

There were a total of twenty-seven official holidays, each an occasion to parade one's fineries, to enjoy whatever quality of life the times provided. This was a population which did not attack the soil day in and day out with the relentless fervor of the Anglo-Saxon farmer. The *habitans' joie de vivre* filled the river banks and burst across the centuries. Escaping rigid obedience of any kind, they listened to the Church only to a point, sometimes a very small point. They were reverent to the King but without affectation; happy to share in the bounties of the world, but not demanding them all. In a way the French from Illinois, not unlike their cousins from Canada, announced the French revolutionaries, not of 1792, but of 1789.

A verse of *La Guignolée*, the song that young men serenaded each house with on New Year's Eve, while collecting for the poor, says it all: *Nous vous demandons pas grande chose*—"We do not ask you for very much."

NOTES

1. An exhaustive study of French emigration by Peter N. Moogk, "Reluctant Exiles: Emigrants from France to Canada before 1760," in *The William and Mary Quarterly*, 3rd series, Vol. XLVI (July 1989).

2. Much has been written on the subject of population immigration and growth in Canada versus the British colonies. We would like to suggest here only two books, both offering basic information on the subject. In French, *Le Canada Français*, by Raoul Blanchard, published in Montreal in 1960. In English, the more erudite work of Professor William Eccles, *The Canadian Frontier, 1534-1760*, the

revised edition published in 1984; see particularly pages 68-70.

3. *Journal du marquis de Montcalm*, 8 mai 1756; the regiment of Carignan Salières counted one thousand officers and men, many remaining in New France following their discharge.

4. *Arch. col.* Canada, *correspondence generale*, 65, 1736, fol. 248.

5. While the Canadian average of deaths per 1,000 births in 1988-89 was 7.6, in Quebec it was only 5.2. Figures published in *Quebec Update*, vol. 91, no. 15, August 15, 1991, Quebec Government Office, Chicago, IL.

6. Eccles, *The Canadian Frontier*, 9.

7. William E. Foley, *A History of Missouri*, Vol. 1, 4.

8. The longest, appropriately called *Le grand portage*, was a nine-mile trail between Lake Superior and Pigeon River; the site, restored, is in Minnesota, along the Canadian border, on an Indian reservation.

9. The work and living conditions of the fur traders was examined in a paper presented to the French Colonial Historical Society by Claiborne Skinner, "Wages, Tips, and Other Compensations: *Voyageurs* Hiring Contracts for the Illinois Country, 1684-1694." See also Grace Lee Nute, *The Voyageur*.

10. Louis-Armand de Lom d'Arce, baron de La Hontan, 1664-1716, participated in the 1683 and 1684 campaigns against the Iroquois. He left New France in 1692; his memoirs, *Nouveaux Voyages dans l'Amerique Septentrionale*, not always reliable, were published in 1793.

11. Thwaites, *Jesuit Relations*, LXIV, 193-215.

12. Natalia Belting, *Kaskaskia Under the French Regime*, 15-16.

13. Marthe Faribault-Beauregard, *La population des forts français d'Amerique*, XVIIIeme siecle, Vol. 11.

14. Belting, *Kaskaskia Under the French Regime*, 87.

15. Ibid., 14.

16. Clarence W. Alvord, *The Centennial History of Illinois, The Illinois Country, 1673-1818*, 220.

17. "Pawnee" or *Panis*, more often than not was a geneal term for all Indians west of the Mississippi brought in as slaves. See the *Atlas of Great Lakes Indian History*, 4.

18. Alvord, *The Centennial History*.

19. Carl J. Ekberg, *Colonial Ste. Genevieve, An adventure on the Mississippi Frontier*, 115.

20. Ibid, 112.

21. See E.G. Mason, "Kaskaskia and its Parish Records," *Magazine of American History*, March 1881, Vol. VI, No. 3.

22. On the subject of female emigration to New France, see Gustave Lanctot, *Filles de joie ou filles du Roi*, Ottawa, 1966, and Peter N. Moogk, "Reluctant Exiles," 483-4.

23. Belting, *Kaskaskia Under.*, 74.

24. Ronald Leonard, Jacques Mathieu and Lina Couger, "Peuplement colonisateur au pays des Illinois," *Proceedings of the Twelfth Meeting of the French Colonial Historical Society*, 1986.

25. Eccles, *The Canadian Frontier*, 67.

26. Ibid., 68.

27. Serge Courville analyzed Quebec settlement patterns in depth in a paper for the French Colonial Historical Society, *L'origine du rang au Quebec: la politique territoriale de la France dans la premiere moitie du 17eme siecle.* (1991).

28. Ekberg, *Colonial Ste. Genevieve*, 44, 129.

29. Ronald L. Baker, *French Folklife in Old Vincennes.*

30. David Buisseret, *Historic Illinois From the Air*, 34-42.

31. Ekberg, *Colonial Ste. Genevieve*, 132.

32. Melburn D. Thurman, *Building A House 18th Century Ste. Genevieve*, 25; the title refers to the Bequette-Ribault house, in Ste. Genevieve, Missouri.

33. Ekberg, *Colonial Ste. Genevieve*, 296.

34. Belting, *Kaskaskia Under the French*, 42.

35. Ekberg, *Colonial Ste. Genevieve*, 296.

36. Belting, *Kaskaskia Under the French*, 43-51.

37. Theresa Nepven, who we have already met in the chapter "The Fox Wars," had children by Jean-Baptiste Girardeau, and Louis du Tisne; her last husband was Pierre Rene Harpain de la Gaurais, a lieutenant, whom she married on June 5, 1741, before moving to New Orleans.

38. Belting, *Kaskaskia Under the French*, 49.

39. Ibid., 68.

12

Serving God and Country

I n similar fashion to the earliest times in New France, the missionaries who accompanied the explorers and *voyageurs* west of Lake Michigan assumed a role of importance beyond their religious responsibilities. The majority of these were priests of the Society of Jesus--the Jesuits--exercising their relentless ministry regardless of weather vagaries, illness, or the threat of ever-present violent death. Stories of their struggles captivated the imaginations even of those nineteenth-century Americans who were not especially nostalgic about the French. In contrast, history has all but forgotten both the Recollects who accompanied La Salle, and the priests of the Seminary of Foreign Missions who arrived in 1699.[1] It is true that Illinois began as "Jesuit country" and that no other order would have been able to compete with the hallowed image of Father Marquette; in addition, the Recollects' stay was too brief, and the area assigned to the Missionary priests too small, to give either order an opportunity to gain full partnership in the evangelization process. Yet this evangelization had begun in North America with the four Recollect priests who landed below Quebec in 1615. Ten years later, with little to show for their efforts, they welcomed reinforcement from the Jesuits who succeeded so well in their conversion endeavors that in 1632, Cardinal Richelieu granted exclusivity to their Order. Sixty-six years later the Jesuits, believing they had already secured the spiritual monopoly of New France, objected strenuously when the Mississippi Valley was awarded to the priests of the Society of Foreign Missions in Paris---Missionary priests---who had been invited originally by the Bishop of Quebec, François Laval de Monmorency, to run his seminary. But the Missionary priests were not satisfied operating a school for long , especially while the self-styled "shock troops" of the Church, the Jesuits, were enjoying the glory (and occasionally, martyrdom) of their achievements. Finally, in 1698, Bishop Laval answered their pleas by allocating the Mississippi Valley to the Missionary priests, a decision which unleashed a quarrel of astonishing dimensions.

Three priests, Francois Jolliet de Montigny, Antoine Davion, and Jean-Francois Buisson de Saint-Cosme, were selected to found the first mission in Illinois, and carrying their *Lettres patentes* signed by the new Bishop of Quebec, Saint-Vallier (who had replaced retiring Laval), they made their way to the Mississippi. Escorted by Tonty, they traveled the old route: Michilimackinac, down Lake Michigan, stopping at the Jesuit mission in Chicago, at Fort St. Louis at Peoria, and the village of the Tamaroa and Cahokia (their journey is detailed in the chapter "The Lonely Command"). Descending the Mississippi River, the priests built missions at the Arkansas and Natchez Posts, but it was their return to Cahokia, in April 1699, that unleashed the Jesuits' fighting spirit.

The arrival of the Missionary priests in Illinois coincided with the naval expedition that Iberville led to the mouth of the Mississippi in 1699. Some Jesuits were automatically included in Iberville's expedition, and their superior could not understand the logic of permitting another religious group to take the responsibility for the spiritual welfare of Illinois, a land locked between Louisiana and Canada: "They complained to the King of France of the intrusion into their mission district of missionaries who belonged to another body." [2] Reluctant to get involved in the dispute, the King referred the problem to a committee of bishops who sided against the Jesuits in favor of the Missionary priests, ensuring that their Church of Cahokia would be safe. Their mission, however, never completely prospered because Kaskaskia, and later Fort de Chartres, were both stronger magnets to the French and Indians alike than Cahokia was. It felt safer to live in either of these two communities, with soldiers, riverboat hands, miners, and authorities easily acessible. In contrast Cahokia, although only a short distance away, labored under the constant threat of Sioux or Fox attacks, in part explaining why its respectable total of forty-seven French families, in 1715, did not become leaven for future growth.

In addition to the middle Mississippi Valley, the Missionary priests also opened a mission at La Mobile, on the Gulf of Mexico—testimony to ambitious plans far beyond their means, considering that their ranks were constantly diminished by sickness and death, and that they were unable to maintain properly what they had already established. No longer able to sustain themselves at La Mobile after 1724,[3] it appeared that they might give up altogether, but they managed to cling stubbornly to their Cahokia enclave until 1765, the very last year of the French presence there.

One of the Missionary priests who labored in Illinois was destined to acquire notoriety in his time: Dominique Marie Varlet arrived in Cahokia from France in 1712, with a reputation for piety and theological knowledge, and remained there about five years. What makes his appointment particularly interesting is that following his return to France he rose to the rank of bishop, and then, not only made public his Jansenist tendencies, but defied ecclesiastic disciplinary action and three excommunications. He finally fled to Holland where, then as now, an open-door policy existed for political and religious dissidents. (The doctrine of Jansenism takes its name from Cornelius Jansen, a bishop famous for his treatise exalting the theology of St. Augustine and emphasizing the state of grace and moral austerity).[4]

Unfortunately, we know little of Varlet's ministry and can only speculate on the sort of relations he maintained with the many earthy characters living in Illinois in the early 1700's. If a pastoral letter that Bishop Saint Vallier sent in 1718 is any guide, Father Varlet had among his parishioners individuals who had complete

> . . . disregard of religion and purity, in which the French recently arrived from France, of every kind of condition, live in the vast country which they have come to inhabit along that great river. . . we order those who under our authority have the conduct of souls, to declare to them that is our intention to regard as giving public scandal all who in contempt of divine and human laws go so far as to commit scandalous impiety by their words, or by their actions, or by public concubinage, persons who in disregard of all prohibitions intimated to them, persist in frequenting and dwelling together . . .[5]

How did Varlet relate to the common people of Illinois whom St. Vallier so roundly stigmatized---as well as to the Jesuits and the commandant? Jansenists held the Jesuits in horror---they considered their political flexibility an exercise of immorality---and were critical of the absolute powers of the Monarchy. We can only surmise that during his stay Father Varlet either ignored the situation or realized the intrinsic weakness of his position, as he left no paper trail to give us any inkling of his reactions or of any involvement in the jurisdictional disputes perennially arising between Jesuits and Missionary priests. Some of these disputes bordered on the ludicrous---well-illustrated by the quarrel revolving around the Church of Ste. Anne.

Ste. Anne was a sanctuary built in 1718, simultaneously with the first Fort de Chartres, but first, the Jesuits informed the parishioners that no priest would be assigned there. Upon learning, however, that the Missionary priests filled the position, they reversed their decision. When a Jesuit arrived to claim the church, he found a Missionary priest in place who refused to turn it over. This dispute lasted for ten years. Finally, the Jesuits' claim was recognized as valid, but by then habits had been formed and *Ste. Anne de Fort de Chartres* kept its Missionary priest until the last days of the French garrison.[6]

Nonetheless, we must balance this acrimony between orders—which fills volumes of church archives—with the personal and day-to-day relationships of individuals who were laboring in identical situations for identical causes. From this viewpoint, Recollects and Missionary priests (and Capuchins in Louisiana after 1721) got along with the Jesuits, and although the dispute over religious jurisdiction was raging in ecclesiastic chanceries, the Jesuit Father Pinet, attending the Indians, and the Missionary priest Reverend Berger, attending the French, maintained close relations with each other. The Jesuit Superior could write to Rome that: "Although we are in contention with the Gentlemen of the Seminary of Foreign Missions over a village of Illinois savages which they wish to take from us, we have nevertheless dealt with one another amicably and the affair has been handled in such manner that both parties live together in peace."[7]

This closeness was in great part due to the fact that the demands made on all missionaries were equally severe; the very nature of their work made them continually vulnerable to hardships and death. Pierre de Leitte observed that:

> I must say to their glory that they must be saints indeed to take as much trouble as they do for these people [Indians]. Every day as soon as the sun rises they go about among the cabins to find out if anyone is sick; they give them medicines, and if necessary bleed them, and sometimes they even make broth for them. After which they have it cried through the village that they are about to say mass. Then they teach the catechism or they preach sermons. In the afternoon after having applied themselves to the language, they return to the village to teach catechism, which always takes two hours. The pieces of wood, husks of Indian corn, and even the stones which are thrown at them do not dismay them. . . . No weather prevents them from going through with the same exercises.[8]

Whatever opinion one may have regarding the arrogance of their faith, the narrowness of their views of society, or the unrealistic loftiness of their moral stands, the courage of the missionaries was never in question. They made no concession to difficult material conditions, routinely ignoring frequent bouts of poor health; they worked alone among Indian groups led by hostile medicine men (whom the French called *jongleurs*, or jugglers), and their cassocks were just as often targets as talismans.

In 1702, three years after they arrived, the Missionary priests lost Father Nicolas Foucault, who was killed en route from the Arkansas post to Mobile.[9] Then, in 1706, Father Jean-Francois Buisson de St. Cosme and his small party were massacred while on the way from Natchez to Mobile. The following year, Father Marc Bergier became sick while travelling on the Mississippi on his way to Cahokia, where he died soon after. A hiatus in their series of misfortunes ended in 1730, when Father Gaston, newly ordained in Quebec, was killed in Cahokia within months of his arrival. In 1735, his colleague, Father Courrier, after ten years of exhausting ministry was sent to New Orleans for a respite, but died soon after he arrived. A shortened life and career also befell Father Antoine Thaumur de la Source: a young man when assigned to Cahokia in 1718, he would return to Canada a decade later to die following three years of poor health. Father Laurens, a priest who came directly from France in 1738, fell sick almost immediately and died the following year, reportedly of bad nutrition. These were all trained men, some with invaluable acquired experience, that the Order was losing. Few seemed able to serve more than ten years, although flying in the face of this high attrition rate stood the isolated case of Father Mercier, whose physical endurance matched his fortitude of spirit. In writing about him, an officer of the garrison of Fort de Chartres notes: "He passed forty-six years in cultivating the Lord's vineyard of these distant countries. The savage nations always respected him. A man of this character would not live too long for the welfare of these people."[10] Father Mercier served Cahokia from 1718 until he died, in 1753.

Sickness and violence exacted their toll on the Jesuits as well; Father Julien Bineteau died in Peoria on Christmas Day of 1699, after only three years in Illinois; in Kaskaskia, Father Pierre-Gabriel Marest fell to an epidemic in 1714. During the 1729 revolt of the Natchez and their allies, the Yazoo, two Jesuits were ambushed and killed, Father du Poisson and Father Souel; and we have seen how during the Chickasaw Wars, Father Antoine Sénat chose to remain with the captured officers and troops from the Illinois contingent and share their death.

The list of fallen Jesuits, however, is relatively short considering their number was much larger (counting Jacques Marquette, thirty-two Jesuits worked among the Illinois Indians from 1673 to 1764). This small number may be attributed to a more demanding novitiate and better discipline; young men attracted by the Society of Jesus knew that it was organized along military lines, demanding rigorous intellectual preparation and strenuous physical activity. Jesuits, once in the field, were expected to adapt to any local conditions while retaining an unbending strength of character. The Jesuits also approached native Americans with more patience, certainly a great deal more than they displayed toward French behavior. Even when their rate of success over "barbarism," "savagery," and "immoral practices," was less than spectacular, they maintained their high spirits. In fact, not above a little statistical manipulation regarding the number of conversions when pickings were slim, they claimed victory no matter what the circumstances, and then forged ahead. In similar situations, their Missionary priest colleagues were more likely to give in to discouragement. Typical of the Jesuits' ingenuity is the example of Christian Priber, a Jesuit missionary who, in the 1740's, lived among the Cherokee under the nom de guerre "Pierre Albert," totally adapting himself to their social environment—including dress and customs—and becoming their "guru" in the process. Here was a Jesuit (incidentally, German-born) who doubled as a very effective political agent of the French Crown.[11]

As the French colonial presence in Illinois and in Louisiana approached a degree of maturity, both colonies began to shed some of their frontier characteristics. Houses sprung up among cabins; powdered wigs and silk stockings appeared here and there during Sunday Mass. Gentility was moving in from Quebec and New Orleans—moving slowly, but moving—and reaching the Mississippi wilderness. But this was a gentility carried almost exclusively by the canoes and bateaux bringing the royal officers who set the new administrative structures. In the French colonial empire institutions shaped the society, in contrast to the English colonies where the reverse was true. The building of Fort de Chartres, in 1718, therefore must be viewed not as an ordinary event but as the beginning of a completely new era (this was also the date of the beginning of the construction of New Orleans). We will look at the administration and administrators later in this chapter, but first we need to see how the Church adjusted to the changes.

For fifty years, Illinois had been a land of missions, a label that projected an image many—including ecclesiastics—found no longer

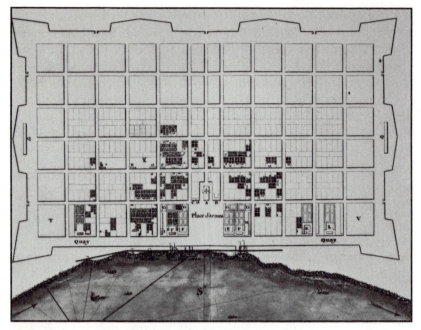

New Orleans in 1722. Reproduced from the *Cartes Marines*.
(The Newberry Library)

compatible with the more formal administrative structures being installed. It was an opportune time to redefine jurisdictions and roles, as
1718 was also the year that Louisiana was entrusted to the *Compagnie
d'Occident*. Like the preceding chartered companies, the Company assumed among its other obligations the building of churches and the financial support of its priests. The fifty-third clause of the charter specified
that "the said Company shall be obliged to build at its expenses churches
at the places where it forms settlements; as also to maintain there the necessary number of approved ecclesiastics; either with the rank of parish
priests or such others as shall be suitable . . ." [12]

   The 1718 charter gave the Bishop of Quebec authority over Louisiana,
making him the only French official with a jurisdiction combining the
whole of French North America,[13] a decision which had the advantage of
avoiding the complications of fixing boundaries for a new diocese. In
1722, Louisiana was subdivided into three ecclesiastical sections, a measure forestalling potential disputes between the aggressive Jesuits and,
this time, the Capuchins, who had been given the lower portion of the

colony. However, this did not work entirely as planned: the Jesuits insisted that their zone of exclusive influence be extended south to Natchez, and that they receive the right to open missions anywhere in Louisiana as long as they operated under the authority of the Superior of the Capuchins. What subsequently happened was not unlike the experience of the Missionary priests before: the Capuchins "... had more zeal than ability to furnish men."[14] The *Compagnie d'Occident* felt it necessary to limit their ministry to the French, inviting the Jesuits to extend their own missionary work with the Indians of Lower Louisiana. The arrival of the Capuchins on the scene had been a bit of a fluke: in 1714, the Bishop of Quebec, Saint Vallier, wisely realizing that travel time to and from Louisiana made communications difficult, appointed a co-adjutant he expected would take office on his behalf in Mobile. The person selected for this position accepted the honor and the title but never actually left his residence in Meudon, a village near Paris.[15] In the meantime, the Compagnie, dutifully fulfilling the terms of the charter, asked the co-adjutant to recruit priests for Louisiana: he, naturally, opened the new province to his own Order, the Capuchins.[16]

But the Capuchins were unable to supply the manpower, while the Jesuits had no difficulty in filling the ranks. Their arrival greatly alarmed the Capuchins. Alarm became open conflict in 1726, when the superior of the Jesuits, Nicholas Ignace de Beaubois (previously from Illinois), having extracted the title of Grand Vicar from the Bishop of Quebec, began to claim complete authority over all religious establishments. The crisis was resolved when the Company, facing a threat from the Capuchins to withdraw totally from Louisiana in protest, dismissed and expelled Beaubois. The whole experience left ill feelings that time did not heal. In referring to this affair, a French officer who served in Louisiana twenty-five years later, wrote: "These cunning politicians [the Jesuits] have found means to get the richest settlements in the whole colony which they have obtained through their intrigues."[17]

Nowhere do official instructions show the change from "missions" to "parishes", but the latter term begins to appear here and there beginning with the 1720's.[18] For instance, when Beaubois was still in Kaskaskia, he titled the register of baptisms on July 9, 1720, *Registre des Baptêmes faits dans l'église Paroissiale de la Conception de Notre Dame des Cascaskias*, and wrote under his signature the mention of *curé de cette Paroisse*, "curate of this parish." The change from the word mission to parish was important as the latter involved the setting of a lay administration. The lay administration of a parish in Illinois was naturally identical to the century-old system in France. Church wardens, known as *marguillers*, were elected to run the material side of the parish; appointing the sacristan and the beadle, collecting tithes, renting pews, distributing alms, overseeing the properties, and maintaining the buildings. Together, the wardens made up a *conseil de fabrique*, or vestry.[19]

Although the word "elections" projects a sense of democratic participation, it would be erroneous to conclude that the change from missions to parishes resulted in the type of freedom that leads to self-rule. Again, we must keep in mind the different mentalities of the British populations east of the Appalachian Mountains and the French concept of freedom, an exercise of exacerbated individualistic behavior. And, when disagreement occurred, one could always count on the Commandant to infuse a sense of appropriate military order to the situation, as in Ste. Genevieve, in 1777. Although by then French Illinois had officially disappeared, with the East bank of the Mississippi under British rule and the West bank nominally Spanish, a dispute between wardens accusing the parish priest of all sorts of malfeasance ended when royal authorities intervened, siding with the former.[20]

As sound as the economy of Illinois could be, relative to Louisiana and even Canada, it could only support the development of a modest infrastructure. It was costly to the chartered companies to maintain churches and garrisons in Illinois with money included in a budget that revenues were never able to cover. While priests were paid—more regularly than were the officers—credits for church construction were far more spartan and tended to be channeled toward the budding urban development of Louisiana. In the case of the Missionary priests, their Order from the start laid out considerable sums of money. They founded the missions on the Mississippi with 10,000 *livres*, but almost a half-century later, in 1739, the unfortunate Abbé Laurens arrived from France carrying 25,000 *livres* allocated only for his expenses and improvements to the parish. This example gives a clearer idea of the rise in prices over the years, particularly in Illinois where enormous transportation costs had to be added, when compared to the salary received by the resident priest and the curate of Mobile in 1704, respectively 1,000 and 600 *livres* a year.

The cost of building in Illinois led to modest churches, with the exception of Kaskaskia. Nevertheless, while not Canada—where to paraphrase Mark Twain, one could not throw a stone in any direction without hitting a church window—Illinois had a respectable number of sanctuaries, some of which survived for many years.

The original *Notre Dame de Kaskaskia* was replaced in 1753 by a building measuring 104 feet long and 44 feet wide. We have a description of the building, before the Mississippi River's changing course led to the slow destruction of the village. The church was

> . . . a huge old pile, extremely awkward and ungainly, with its projecting eaves, its walls of hewn timber perpendicularly planted, and the interstices stuffed wih mortar, with its quaint old fashioned spire, and its dark, storm-beaten casements. The interior of the edifice is somewhat imposing, notwithstanding the sombre hue of its walls; these are rudely plastered with lime, and decorated with a few dingy paintings. The floor is loose, rough boards, and the ceiling arched with oaken panels. The altar and the lamp suspended above are very antique.[21]

This traveler's description, barely disguising contempt, shows an essentially functional building, large and solid. The founding Jesuit fathers were known for the simplicity, the sobriety of their churches. As rustic as Notre Dame de Kaskaskia may appear from this description, it was a cathedral in comparison to the other churches. A description of St. Anne's, at the Fort de Chartres, in an inventory from 1732, described the building as being "... thirty feet long and twenty feet wide made of stakes driven into earth and covered with straw, in which there are an altar, a tabernacle, and an altar plaform, and a little cupboard in which are included the ornaments."[22]

At Prairie du Rocher, a village built on land granted to Dugué de Boisbriant, a Church was also built, although the community was only four miles from St. Anne. The church of Prairie du Rocher was named for St. Joseph; both the names of the village and the church have survived to our time. Across the Mississippi in 1752, the village of Ste. Genevieve, growing rapidly after the development initiated by Kaskaskia inhabitants, also acquired a parish church, where Father Phillbert Watrin at first would travel across the Mississippi from Kaskaskia to celebrate Mass and "administer the sacraments at least to the sick."[23] That same year, the Commandant of Illinois, Major Macarty, made

> land grants in St. Genevieve, contingent upon the grantees furnishing logs for the new church. These logs were probably set upright in the ground, creating a vertical-log church that would have looked much like the

The French church at Cahokia as it appears today. (Photograph by Charles Balesi)

residences surrounding it, although larger and without galleries. The parish church was the focal point of community life in Old Town, and in front of the church door most public business, including auction sales was conducted.[24]

The same applied to Cahokia, to the Holy Family Parish, an ancient establishment: the Missionary priests had inaugurated their first sanctuary, a log chapel, on May 14, 1699. A quarter of a century later, in 1724, the priests asked the *Compagnie* for a land grant of four square leagues (twelve square miles) for both the church and an agricultural enterprise large enough to support the whole establishment. Following the transfer of Illinois to Britain, British troops were quartered in the Church, while ten years later, it was the American soldiers' turn to use the Church as billets. Badly damaged by fire in 1783, the church was razed and replaced by a new building used for the first time on September 24, 1799. This church, which we can visit today in Cahokia, is the closest example of the style of buildings utilized not only as places of worship but also as centers of social activities for the French in Illinois. The new church, although erected more than thirty years after the end of French rule, retained the old style, *poteaux en terre* and *bouzillage*. The church was constructed by the collective effort of the community, led by its priest. Though about to enter the nineteenth century, the French of Cahokia, now part of the United States, still lived by the drumbeat of the past. [25]

On the other side of the *Pays des Illinois*, on the *Ouabache*, the first mention of a missionary appeared on the Company's documents in 1728, when the Jesuit father Etienne d'Outreleau was expected to arrive at the post (later called Post Vincennes) to assume his duties. However, a letter witten in 1733 by Bissot de Vincennes, from the post, listed only the fort, the stockade and two houses, but no church. It was years later that the parish of St. Francois Xavier would be founded.

The Church in Illinois, as everywhere in France and its possessions, would experience a major upheaval when the Society of Jesus was expelled. Inspired by the decision of the *Parlement* of Paris (in spite of the similarity of names, French *parlements* were not legislative bodies but civil courts) which banned the Jesuits in 1762, on June 8, 1763, the Superior Council of Louisiana decreed the Society ". . . dangerous to the royal authority, to the rights of bishops, to the public peace and safety, and they consequently declared the vows taken in the order to be null and void." [25]

The Society of Jesus was banished from France on a technicality: as a means of supporting his mission, a Jesuit stationed in Martinique had engaged in commerce (another example of the flexibility in method mentioned earlier). Unfortunately, his ships were captured by British privateers and he found himself unable to pay his creditors, who thereupon pursued not only him, but the whole Order, reasoning that such strategy would better insure the return of their investments. Having lost in the first instance, the Jesuits appealed to the *Parlement* of Paris which proved a fatal move, as the French jurists leaped at the opportunity to expel them all. As with the Templars before, this was another example of success leading to downfall, although this time it was mere exile rather than a trip to the scaffold.

The *Parlement* of Paris had used the opportunity of a minor case of unpaid debt in the West Indies to settle a decades-old account that the French had against the Jesuits. Several segments of French society comprised the undermining forces: those who wanted a Gallican church and chafed under Rome; the King's administrators experimenting with the idea of a French nation; the liberals feeding off the riches of the Enlightenment; and others, composing a vast spectrum of views. The King of Portugal had begun this anti-Jesuit "crusade;" now France, and soon Spain, would follow. In 1773, Pope Clement XIV, in considering the European political climate, put an end to the drama by abolishing the Society. It was not a courageous decision but it disarmed some of the Church's adversaries. (The order was re-established in 1814, after the fall of Napoleon.)

The departure of the Jesuits from Louisiana had serious repercussions for Illinois. When the news reached Illinois on September 24, 1763, the royal authorities went to the house that the Society had built in Kaskaskia in happier times, read the decree of expulsion, and confiscated all properties. They were all to leave: the Superior, Father Warin, who had lived in Illinois thirty-one years; Father Jean-Baptiste Aubert, *curé* of Kaskaskia; his colleagues, Jean-Baptiste de Salleneuve and Sébastien Neurin, who had worked with the Kaskaskia nation for twenty-two years. Also notified were Jean-Baptiste de La Morinie, from Ste. Genevieve; and Julien Devernal, *curé* of St. Xavier in Vincennes. All were to leave without waiting for any other ecclesiastic to take over their spiritual duties. On November 6th, the Jesuits said their last mass in Kaskaskia and then left for New Orleans. Within minutes, the royal bailiff, Jean-Louis Robinet, started the auction of their properties and possessions on the threshold of the church.

It is not difficult to imagine the poignancy of this scene in the cool fall afternoon: the wide river, the cliffs, the boats and their motley crew of *voyageurs* waiting to take the Jesuits downriver, the last goodbyes to tearful French and Indian well-wishers standing on the muddy banks. How many *habitans* had chosen instead to stay at the Church to pick up some bargains? We know at least three whose bids won them the best of the Jesuit holdings: Jean Baptiste Beauvais, Raphaël Beauvais, and Captain Philippe de Rocheblave (an officer on half-pay whom we shall meet again later).

What happened later to some of the estates that the Jesuits had built over the years, could have been written in a bad play where evil and virtue are opposed: Beauvais rented the chapel as a storehouse, and the cemetery as a garden to the British garrison, no less, as in the meantime, in 1763, the French had lost the war and signed the Treaty of Paris. The British, arriving after the sale, found it quite extraordinary that the French authorities could confiscate and dispose of property in a territory no longer *de jure* under their control. But the British could do little else except acknowledge what they labeled as another flagrant example of classic

French underhanded behavior.

In these confusing circumstances, generosity was personified by sixty-one year old Father Meurin who convinced the French authorities in New Orleans to allow him to resume religious work under the nominal responsibility of the Capuchins. Meurin and Gibault, the lone remaining Missionary priest, had to answer the needs of the French and Christian Indians on the west side of Illinois; no small task, this required constant traveling on both sides of the Mississippi, as "...for five years, 1768-1773, the citizens of Ste. Genevieve had no pastor of their own."[27]

There can be little doubt that the removal of the Jesuits from Illinois, in 1763, took away a much-needed stabilizing factor in a period of transition; in hindsight it might be said that it precipitated the demise of French influence in the Upper Mississippi Valley. There is a certain irony in the almost simultaneous disappearance from Illinois of the Society of Jesus and the officers of the King of France. These officers had maintained the King in often very difficult circumstances, but neither dedication nor heroism would have an impact on the destiny of the *Terre des Illinois*. Although it had been a part of the government of Louisiana since 1717, Illinois would be tossed in with Canada as the price the French crown was ready to pay for peace with Britain.

Had Illinois remained the western outpost of New France it was originally, it may have acquired a different face—more robust, more open. There certainly was a great difference in the management styles between the colonial governments of Canada and Louisiana. Both, to a large degree, operated on precarious budgets and fragile economies, and both embodied an element of venality. But in Quebec, venality was an exercise of individual entrepreneurship, almost disarming in its refreshing effrontery. Governors like Frontenac or Vaudreuil hired frontmen to run their peltry business and made secret deals with chosen merchants; officers in the splendid isolation of their posts, more often than not, doubled as "super traders." On the other hand in Louisiana, the venality was institutionalized, part and parcel of the philosophy of a government overseen by chartered companies[28] for whom profit was the only *raison d'être*. One may argue that the difference between the character of administrators who went overseas to do the King's bidding, and administrators who were appointed to operate in the name of a syndicate of investors, exists only in the perception of historians. There was a difference, however, and it colored all aspects of colonial policy. By the seventeenth century the notion of France, the real estate of the Bourbons, was rapidly

being transformed into the notion of France, the State, and what was that
State if not the public good guaranteed by the King's rule?

In the 1700's chartered companies were an expression of an anachro-
nistic system of colonization. The failure of Louisiana to develop into a
bedrock of French influence, as did Canada, can be traced to the overrid-
ing intents of mercantilism dictating policy to administrators. It was only
when mercantilism reached extremes that administrators refused to go
along with and implement instructions which could only lead to disaster.

Such was the instance when Governor Périer refused to carry out the
Company's decision of October, 1727, to remove all properties from Illinois, and to leave only two officers and six men behind to guard Fort de
Chartres.[29] Had Périer obeyed these orders, the consequences for the
French establishment in North America would have been dire. How long
would have it taken for the British to punch a hole in the already fragile
chain of forts linking Quebec to New Orleans? The Fox at that time were
still active and dangerous, but it was the terrible lesson inflicted by the
Natchez' revolt of 1729, that would demonstrate beyond doubt the fool-
ishness of the Company's views, and in the aftermath, would bring down
the system.

On July 1, 1731, Louisiana, including Illinois, reverted to direct King's
rule. The administrative structures remained the same, however. At the
colony level, in Mobile and later in New Orleans, the governor was
flanked by a *commissaire-ordonnateur* who, like his counterpart in Canada,
the *intendant*, handled affairs of finance and justice in total independence,
a balance of power leading to many a dispute between the two officials.
In theory, a Superior Council assisted them both. The system was reproduced on a smaller scale in *Le Pays des Illinois*.

French Illinois was both a military district and a "commandery,"
whose boundaries are worth listing again as we tend to forget how much
more encompassing they were: on the north, an imaginary line running
from Chicago straight west; on the east, the Wabash River, including
Vincennes, and the Ohio Valley; also included were the Arkansas post
and the Arkansas River; on the west, the boundary was less clear but it
included the left bank of the Mississippi and the Missouri. While Canada
was subdivided into three major administrative districts (Quebec, Trois-
Rivières and Montreal), Louisiana was carved into nine military districts
and three major administrative centers: La Mobile, the first capital, New
Orleans, the new capital, and Illinois. The commandant of Illinois was an
officer in the troops of marine infantry, given the rank of major, who had

Some members of *Les Compagnies Franches de la Marine* (including Marv Hilligoss in officer's uniform) during one of the annual Rendez-vous at Fort de Chartres, organized by the State of Illinois during the first weekend of June. (Photograph by Charles Balesi.)

direct authority over all troops and militia of the territory. The garrison of Fort de Chartres, the largest—the numbers varied, 135 men and 13 officers in 1747, 300 men in 1751—was commanded by a captain, while lieutenants and ensigns were detached to smaller posts: when Diron d'Artaguiette inspected Illinois, in 1723, St. Ange Senior commanded at Cahokia with his son as an assistant, and six soldiers. The availability of troops in Illinois was relatively good considering that the total number of *troupes de marine* in Louisiana hovered under a thousand (24 companies in 1744) and that, in 1749, the whole of Canada was defended by 28 companies mustering a grand total of 812 men! Given such figures, any loss had an adverse effect. Conditions among the troops of Marine infantry did not improve over the years, leading to a sizable number of desertions. In Illinois alone, in 1742, sixteen soldiers deserted, in all probability joining the ranks of the *coureurs des bois*. Men who completed their service and did not re-enlist, were given land near posts and forts, following a practice begun with the Roman legions. Along with regular troops, commandants could call on the militia but considering the reality of the demographic conditions in French North America, calling on all physically able-bodied men meant little. During the same years Louisiana, including Illinois, could count on only 8,000 men, and Canada, on 12,000.

The commandant's administrative tasks were made easier by a *garde-magasin*, a title which can be loosely translated as "keeper of the royal stores," by an *écrivain principal*, a *notaire royal*, and by an *huissier*, or bailiff. The function of the *garde-magasin* was much more than the title might lead one to believe. The royal stores meant practically the entire economic life of the territory, as all the supplies purchased from the Crown, and all the commodities acquired in turn by the Crown, went through their shelves or at least through the accounting books kept by the *garde-magasin* and his clerk. The first *garde-magasin* for Illinois, Nicolas Michel Chassin, arrived in 1718, in the same convoy with the commandant and the troops, received a land grant, married, and did so well that he aroused the suspicion of the Company and was recalled to New Orleans in 1729, where he apparently died without returning to Illinois. His successor, Joseph Buchet, was paid 600 livres a year in 1733, a modest compensation for officials with access to easy riches.

The function of *écrivain principal*, best translated as "chief clerk," combining legal and financial responsibilities, was introduced in Illinois during the same period. The *écrivain* was an appointee of the *Ordonateur*, acting as his *subdélégué*. The French royal notary had nothing to do with the "public notary" that we know in the United States, working from behind the teller of a currency exchange. Like his successor in today's France, he was responsible for many tasks we learn to associate with attorneys, as without ". . . his signature affixed to the bills of sale, the marriage contracts, the leases, the inventories, and the agreements of partnerships, the documents were invalid." [30]

The *huissier* served summons, insured the presence of litigants in court, made public announcements. While the notary was paid by the fees he collected, the bailiff was paid by the King. It is worth noting that very often in Illinois, many of the functions were assumed by men not trained in the task at hand but who were the best the commandant could find. For instance, the notary from 1737 to 1757, Jean-Baptiste Bertior, was ". . . the best educated and certainly the best trained in the notarial art . . . Leonard Billeron, a *habitan* who was notary at Kaskaskia . . . also wrote quite legibly, but his spelling was entirely by ear." [31]

While at least in theory, *ordonateur* and governor shared responsibilities for Louisiana—just as governor and *intendant* shared responsibilities for Canada—there was never any question that in Illinois the commandant was the man in complete command. All the officials we have listed, in addition to the engineer and the junior officers in the garrison at Fort de Chartres, made up the council, again mirroring the *Conseil Supérieur* sitting in New Orleans. Like the superior council, the smaller council in Illinois chiefly acted as a court of law for cases which neither the commandant nor the parish priest were able to settle on the spot. Law in pre-revolutionary France was embodied in sixty different *coutumes*, regional "traditions" which preceded written law. Over the centuries, the centrifugal effect of Kings and Court gave the *coutume de Paris* a definitive ascendant over the others. [32] From the perspective of the twentieth-century reader, justice in French Illinois may seem to have been extremely arbitrary: the French legal system had no jury, and lawyers were not permitted to practice in French colonies. Addressing this very point, the Minister of the Navy—who had the overall responsibility of all French colonies—would state peremptorily in 1732, in a letter to Bienville, that: "Experience has shown only too clearly how dangerous people of this sort are to the colonies, where chicanery is even more unfortunate because of the obstacles which it brings upon commerce and the cultivation of the land." [33] Yet the simplicity of the approach, the directness of the proceedings, and their quick resolve, served the French well in the sense that it prevented investment of time and resouces in any but justified litigations.

The military officers who administered Illinois for the King of France from 1717 on were by and large competent, some even outstanding, like Boisbriant, D'Artaguiette, De Liette. Other officers come to mind, such as Vincennes, and the St. Anges, father and sons, also dedicated servants of the King. But if it is relatively easy to judge the professional capacity of the French in positions of power, it is much more difficult to assess the threshold of their honesty within the context of the times. For some, there could be no question: D'Artaguiette was incorruptible and the men who worked in Illinois in his administration, like Louis Auguste de la Loëre Flancour, who arrived in 1734, to exercise the functions of delegate for the *ordonateur*, had a great sense of probity.

But these were the seventeenth and the eighteenth centuries. French

The *Bateaux.* Reproduced from *Centennial History of Illinois,*
Clarence Alvord, ed., Chicago, 1917. (The Newberry Library)

officers often received their pay with incredible delays, sometimes, as was
the case for Tonty and La Forest, measured in years. We have seen how
in Canada, from Governor down, French officials were directly or indirectly involved in the fur trade; most undoubtedly with dreams of
personal fortune, but for more than a few, simply to ensure some sort of
revenue for themselves and at times for the establishments entrusted to
their care. Since Louisiana had been developed because it embodied the
speculating hopes of half of France, the main protaganists of this development could hardly be expected to operate on their behalf without an
attempt to share in the profits.

In 1721, Boisbriant, then Commandant of Illinois, was granted land—
one square league—that in theory, as an employee of the Company, he
was not supposed to receive. Boisbriant transferred this land to his
nephew, Jean St. Thérèse Langlois, an officer of the garrison of Fort de
Chartres. That land would soon become the village of Prairie du Rocher.
Such a transaction, which would lead to indictment today, was not
unusual. All settlers received grants; the fact that with positions of
responsibility went sizable land cessions did not raise eyebrows then.
Annual salaries for the important officials were high by the mid-1700's:
20,000 *livres* for the governor of Canada and 16,000 *livres* for his *intendant*,
12,000 for the governor of Louisiana and 8,000 for his *ordonateur*. The
commandant of Illinois for the same period was paid 3,000 *livres* plus a
gratification, or bonus, of 1,000 *livres* and he had complete control of the fur
trade.

In addition to the fur trade, supplies, trade goods, and presents to

Indian allies, were commodities lending themselves naturally to misappropriation. An opportune time for embezzlement was the three-month period that it took for the yearly convoy of *bateaux, canots* , and *pirogues*, to travel from New Orleans to Illinois. The convoy left under heavy escort during the summer, with all the miseries of heat and low waters added to the already difficult task of rowing and pulling against the current of the largest river of North America. Crafts capsized, went aground on sand bars, sank after hitting submerged trees, and losses could be exaggerated: "Great expenses and abuses . . . existed in the practice of sending up the Illinois convoy each year . . . The abuses in connection with the convoy were sometimes so flagrant as to cause investigation, even in Louisiana."[34] A case in point was the convoy of August 1749, under the command of Lieutenant de Montchervaux, making excessively slow progress. Montchervaux, among other outrageous actions in the course of his command which eventually led to disciplining, " . . . submitted a bill of 1,200 *livres* for a hunter who furnished game for his table!" [35]

When the convoy reached Illinois in 1750, barely more than a decade of French rule remained, yet it was to be an important period, a period which saw the reconstruction of Fort de Chartres from a log affair into a powerful stone-built defense position; the development of Ste. Genevieve, just across the Mississippi; an increase of agricultural production; and a growing role in military campaigns against the British. The officers who carried out the responsibilities for Illinois during the 1750's, and until the change from French to British rule, were able men. However, they could do little to affect questionable policies formulated in Versailles, and questionable leadership in Quebec—all of which would eventually bear responsibility to France for the loss of Canada, the Great Lakes region, and, of course, Illinois.

NOTES

1. The Recollects were an off branch of the Order of St. Francis, whose complete name was *Frères mineurs de l'étroite observance de St. Francois* or *Recollets*, meaning those who engage in meditation or contemplation; their order was introduced in France in 1592. The *Séminaire des missions étrangères* was founded in Paris in 1663, by a discalsed carmelite, Dom Bernard de Sainte-Thérèse, bishop *in partibus*, for the purpose of diffusing Christian faith overseas.

2. In John G. Shea, *The Catholic Church in Colonial Days*, 543.

3. The last recorded manifestation of a Seminary priest at La Mobile is an entry

from Father Alexandre Huve, of January 13, 1721.

4. Dutch-born Otto Cornelius Jansen, 1585-1638, bishop of Ypres, wrote the treatise *Augustinus*, published after his death.

5. Shea, *The Catholic Church.*, 560-61.

6. The last missionary priest sent to Illinois was Francois Forget who arrived in Cahokia in 1754.

7. October 5, 1700, General Archives of the *Société de Jésus*, trans. Borgia-Palm, *Jesuit Missions of Illinois*, 34.

8. De Gannes *Mémoires concernant le pays des Illinois*, trans. in Borgia-Palm, *Jesuit Missions*, 25.

9. Shea, *The Catholic Church*, 545.

10. Jean-Baptiste Bossu, *Nouveaux voyages dans l'Amérique septentrionale*, 138; the translation used here is from Clarence Alvord, *The Centennial History of Illinois, the Illinois Country,1673-1818*, 200.

11. See the *Journal* of Antoine Bonnefoy, 1741-1742, translated by Newton D. Mereness in *Travels in the American Colonies*, 239-251.

12. Charter of the *Company d'Occident*, trans. in Shea, *The Catholic Church*, 562.

13. Ibid., 563.

14. Jacob Platt Dun, "The Mission to the Ouabache" *Indiana Historical Society Publications*, III:IV, 255-82.

15. Louis Francois Duplessis de Mornay, Superior of the Capuchins of Meudon; he was consecrated "Bishop of Eumenia" in Paris, on April 22, 1714, when appointed coadjutant of the Bishop of Quebec.

16. *Ordo Fratrum Minorum Capuccinorum* or O.F.M., a branch of the Franciscans (therefore spiritually related to the recollects) which became a separate order in 1619; austerity, simplicity, poverty, were an essential part of their rule.

17. Bossu, *Nouveaux Voyages aux Indes Occidentales*, Paris, 1768; trans. as *Travels through that part of North America formerly called Louisiana*, 1771, London, 25.

18. "It is impossible to determine the date of the establishment of parishes in the Illinois country; the archives of Quebec contain no records of it." *The Centennial History*, 197-98.

19. Vestry is a term used in English by the Church of England and the Episcopalian Church to describe the same system of lay administration.

20. Carl Ekbeg, *Colonial Ste. Genevieve*, 391-93.

21. Flagg, *The Far West*, in Thwaites, *Early Western Travels*, 62, and in Alvord Carter, *Illinois, The Critical Period*, 77.

22. ANC, Series C13 A, 14:28-29., trans. in Borgia, *Jesuit Missions*, 57.

23. Ekberg, *Colonial Ste. Genevieve*, 45-46.

24. Ibid.

25. Cahokia Parish Archives.

26. Shea, *The Catholic Church.*, 587.

27. Ekberg, *Colonial Ste. Genevieve.*, 386.

28. Limited resources, generally already earmarked for other enterprises, lack of interest from populations happier at home, led to the King's granting charters to companies, thirty-two from 1600 to 1664 alone, the period most propitious to their development. All charters were identical in character; the charter granted to

the *Compagnie des Indes occidentales,* officially born from an act of the *Parlement de Paris* on July 14, 1664, gave the directors the choice of appointment of the governor and lesser officers, appointments routinely endorsed by the King's commissions. Canada was fortunate to escape the system later reintroduced in America with the foundation of Louisiana. See on the subject a published thesis, *Les compagnies à charte et la politique coloniale sous le ministère Colbert,* presented in 1906 by L. Cordier, a French army officer.

29. Company to Périer, October 27, 1727, ANC, C13 A 11:89-92; also in Alvord, *The Centennial History,* 160.

30. Natalia Maree Belting, *Kaskaskia Under the French Regime,* 20.

31. Ibid.

32. The *Coutume de la prévoté et vicomté de Paris avec le procès-verbal,* was first published in Paris in 1512; France under the monarchy was divided into 60 *coutumes générales* and 300 *coutumes locales.* The *coutumes* (a word which originated in the Latin *consuedineum*) were compilations of ancient and general practices based on traditional law in each region. Each *coutume* reflected elements of the type of practices brought to France by the different Germanic tribes which invaded after the collapse of the Roman empire, of older Gallic ways and Roman law. *Droit coutumier* was much stronger in northern than in southern France where Roman Law had developed better roots. Along the course of the centuries, the *coutume de Paris,* no doubt thanks to King and Court, exercised a centrifugal effect on all others. Interestingly, many elements of the *coutumes* of Paris and Tours were integrated in Code civil written under Napoleon's direction.

33. ANC., B, 57:797; also quoted in *Centennial History.,* 195.

34. Norman Ward Caldwell, "The French in the Mississippi Valley, 1740-1750," *Illinois Studies in the Social Studies,* Vol. XXVI, 27, 1941, The University of Illinois, Urbana.

35. Ibid., 28.

13

The Indians and the French

S ymbolic of the French approach to colonization was a penetration of North America spearheaded by missionaries. From the vantage point of contemporary thought it is easy and even fashionable, to deride their efforts to convert Native Americans to Catholicism as merely a spiritual dimension of imperialism, an avenue for which the French were better suited than their Dutch or British rivals. But in the minds and hearts of the *Recollects*, the priests of the *Missions étrangères*, and the Jesuits who ventured by themselves thousands of miles from the safety of Quebec in incredibly harsh conditions,[1] theirs was a genuine quest for the souls of the *sauvages*.

Much has been made of the word *sauvages* used by the French to designate Indians. Its literal translation into English, "savage," in present-day language carries a connotation of bestiality. Francis Jennings, one of the leading specialists of Native American history, and who most certainly is free of pro-colonial bias, has painstakingly examined how the French used the word *sauvage* to describe Indians, concluding "that throughout the eighteenth century French colonials seem to have used the term as a mere synonym for Indians, and their meanings vacillated with their attitudes."[2] Abundant French literature starting in the sixteenth century (and the equally abundant modern outflow) studied and commented on the values of American native societies. The Gallic fascination with the notion of the *noble sauvage,* living freely in harmony with nature, acquired mythical proportions in France thanks to philosophers and writers like Montaigne, Rousseau, and Chateaubriand, perhaps in contrast to the pre-revolution "inequalities and inequities of French society."[3]

But those who debated passionately on the individualism of Native Americans, and their free exercise of will in untamed Nature, lived in France and expounded their opinions in the coziness of literary salons and cafés. Although those opinions were interesting and revealing for the comprehension of seventeenth-and eighteenth-century French intellectual preoccupations, we must examine the testimony of the men and women who were engaged in daily contact with the Indians to form a more valid opinion of French attitudes. As written in a thoroughly researched monograph on Indians of the Great Lakes: "What Rousseau thought about Indians matters, but to understand the *pays d'en haut* (Upper Country) it does not matter as much as what the habitants of Vincennes or Kaskaskia thought, or what the governor at Quebec, thought."[4]

The Age of Enlightenment accelerated French infatuation for the myth:

> Because the French were literate, knowledge of Indians was diffused far from the site of actual contact. Such knowledge, unchallenged by actual experience with Indians, survived as a potent cultural relict. Long after it ceased to govern the actions of those who actually lived among Indians, the idea of Indians as literally *sauvages*, or wild men embodying either natural virtue or ferocity, persisted among intellectuals and statesmen in France...in the *pays d'en haut* actual Indians and whites of widely different social class and status had, for a variety of reasons, to rely on each other in order to achieve quite specific ends. It was these Frenchmen [for French women would not appear until much later] and Algonquin men and women who created a common ground—the middle ground—on which to proceed.[5]

From the early days of exploration, this "middle ground" was anywhere French officers, missionaries, men seeking furs, and a rich diversity of Indian nations met, discussed, bartered and generally groped towards some kind of accommodation to correspond with the wishes of the man in Quebec the Indians called "Onontio," the governor.[6]

The original goal of the missionaries was to convince the Indians to give up what was perceived as an uncontrolled way of life—uncontrolled passions, capricious wanderings, limited industry—and persuade them instead to adopt the "three essential qualities: Order, Industry, and Manners."[7] But the Jesuits rapidly discovered the error of such an approach. They found that what seemed like anarchy in Native American's behavior was deceptive: in fact, it covered complex political, religious, and social systems.

The *sauvages Illinois* saw a Black Robe for the first time in the person of Father Claude Dablon at *La Pointe du Saint-Esprit* (Bayfield, Wisconsin) on Lake Superior. This occurred sometime between 1665, the year the mission was built, and 1670, when Father Dablon reported in his *Relation*, "[We] have given [them] the name Illinois because the first who came to La Pointe de Saint Esprit for commerce, called themselves Illinois; [they

A Kaskaskia Indian. Repro-
duced From Victor Collot,
*Voyage dans l'Amérique du
Nord*, Paris, 1826.
(The Newberry Library)

are] very numerous and dwell toward the south." [8] The origins of the
word Illinois lie in the distant past of the nations who, from the Atlantic
to the Mississippi, spoke some form of the Algonquin language. The first
transliterations of their name by the Jesuits were diverse: Illimoueck, Illin-
ewek, Alliniwek, Liniwek—until Father Jolliet, having spent a longer
period of time in their company, determined that the correct word was
"Illinois" (phonetically in English: "EE-LEE-NWA"). Like the Iroquois,
they were not a single group, but a confederacy of subgroups, in their case
numbering five: the Cahokia, the Kaskaskia, the Peoria, the Tamaroa, and
an adopted band, the Metchigami. The Metchigami were refugees from
the West who crossed the Mississippi in search of protection at a time
when the Illinois were at the apogee of their power.

For several centuries, the Illinois had roamed far and wide, sending
war parties against Iroquois towns, raiding the southern tribes along the
Mississippi, crossing the river regularly to capture slaves—the

"Pawnee"—making their presence felt in the north where they had almost totally destroyed the Winnebago nation. They were still powerful in 1655, when they pursued a large band of Iroquois returning home after having failed to destroy the villages of Indian refugees clustered around Green Bay. By the time the French arrived in the Great Lakes area, however, the situation had begun to change; no longer feared by their neighbors, the Illinois saw their portion of territory decrease in size until it had become a narrow band along the Illinois River. The pressure exercised by their enemies at the end of the seventeenth century had even obliged the Illinois several times to temporarily abandon the sites of their encampments along the Illinois River, including their largest town. There were no clear boundaries, of course; indeed, by the time the French arrived, the whole Indian world between the Great Lakes and the Mississippi River was in a state of chaos. Weakened in numbers owing to the widespread reach of a variety of bronchial diseases coming from the east, they had long been victims of seasonal Iroquois raiding. In a sort of tragic game of musical chairs, Indian nations found themselves continual refugees:

> In these fragments of contact and change are glimpses of both a world in disorder and the attempts of people to reorder it through an amalgam of old and new logics. The very nature of the Iroquois assault shaped the Algonquin response. . . . As refugees moved west to avoid the Iroquois hammer, they encountered an anvil formed by the Sioux, a people that the Jesuits called the Iroquois of the West. . . . The clustering of diverse people had its own social and environmental consequences. It disrupted older notions of territory; geographical boundaries remained, but now villages of different groups bordered on each other, or previously separate groups mingled in a single village.[9]

When La Salle arrived, just seven years after the visit of Jolliet and Marquette, the Illinois were being threatened with total destruction. Squeezed between attacks by Dakota Sioux [10] from the Northwest, and by Sauk, Fox, Mascouten and Kickapoo from the north (all of whom the Illinois badly mistreated when they had the upper hand), as well as raids from the Iroquois, naturally the Illinois looked to the French as saviors. As we have seen in preceding chapters, the French developed particularly strong links with the Illinois, mainly through intermarriage. But despite these close ties, and despite the French presence, two major calamities occurred: first, the Iroquois attacks of the 1680's (which would qualify as genocide if applied the yardstick of contemporary political morality); [11] then, the Fox Wars raging from the early to mid-1700's. The demographic results were catastrophic: a survey taken by the French of Illinois males available for war in 1736, indicated only one hundred Kaskaskia, two hundred Cahokia and Tamaroa, fifty Peoria (including those dwelling by *Le rocher*), and two hundred and fifty Metchigami living at Fort de Chartres.

Somewhere between the Illinois and Wabash Rivers began the land of the Miami, a nation related to the Illinois and who spoke an analogous language. Theirs was also a confederacy, but composed of only four groups, Miami, Eel-Rivers, Wea, and Piankeshaw. Like the Illinois, the Miami moved far and wide. Although for centuries their center had been in present-day Ohio, we find them in 1670, in the multi-ethnic village located at the confluence of the Fox and the Wisconsin River near Portage, and also, in 1689, among the thousands of Indians who lived at the foot of *Fort Saint Louis des Illinois*. The Wea maintained their own large village in Chicago for fifty years, until 1718, when threatened by the Chippewa and Potawotami, they moved to Kekionga (the future Fort-Wayne), the portage between the St. Joseph and Miami Rivers. The Piankeshaw, who dwelled at Fort Saint Louis in La Salle and Tonty's time, later moved back east to sites on the Vermillion and Wabash Rivers. The Eels (translated from the French *l'anguille*) had their biggest town six miles north of present-day Logansport (Indiana). Like the Illinois, the Miami intermarried extensively with the French but, unlike the Illinois, they remained a strong nation able to push the limits of their territory far east, and to confront and often defeat the Iroquois at their own game.

At the time of the French, the land lying between Lake Michigan and the Mississippi River was home not only to the Illinois and the Miami, but also to the Kickapoo, the Winnebago, the Menominee (the French called them *folles-avoines*, because of the wild oats growing around their settlement), the Mascouten, the Sauk, the Fox, the Potawatomi, and even, for a shorter period, the Delaware and the Shawnee, to name the most prominent protagonists in the ongoing struggle for survival. The Delaware and the Shawnee, also driven from their homes (present-day, Pennsylvania) by the Iroquois, had moved to the Great Town of the Illinois, at Fort Saint Louis. The Shawnee later settled in Tennessee, then in Florida and in Maryland, and finally ended their wanderings back in this region in early 1730's, when they established their town on the Ohio River. The Kickapoo and their Mascouten cousins also covered long distances. They met the French for the first time in 1612, while settled on Lake Huron near Saginaw Bay. They also settled, in 1670, at the village by the Fox-Wisconsin portage, where they remained until pressure from the Sioux pushed them south towards the Wabash, a movement which put them into direct conflict with the Piankeshaw and the Illinois. The Kickapoo reached the Wabash River, carving lands for themselves eventually to be ceded to the United States in the two successive treaties of 1809 and 1819.[12] As with the other Indian nations, great numbers of dispersed settlements existed; there were Kickapoo villages in Illinois, near Charleston by the Kaskaskia River, and near Hudsonville, as well as in Indiana, near Logansport and Lafayette.

The Kickapoo nation, from the start, was not receptive to Christianity and rebuffed all Jesuit efforts at conversion. There are no records of inter-marriages nor liaisons between Kickapoo women and Frenchmen. Being natural allies of the Fox and the Sauks they were just as naturally enemies of the Illinois and the Miami nations, and consequently, in the beginning at least, involved in numerous hostile acts against the French. With the years, however, Kickapoo and French came to an accommodation with each other. By the time the British made their first attempt to occupy Illinois after the Treaty of Paris of 1763, they found the Kickapoo firmly opposed to their incursions; and, three decades later, when American settlers were filtering west of the Ohio River, igniting Indian guerilla warfare in the process, only the French were safe in the woods and the prairies.

If we draw a line starting in Green Bay, Wisconsin through Portage, crossing Chicago, and ending in Vincennes, Indiana, we will have traced an axis for the area that for a century and a half was a melting pot of Indian cultures and languages, nearly all Algonquin in character and origin. The Winnebago, who had come from the west in the early 1600's, and who were Dakota Sioux in origin and language, were the exception. Referred to by the French as *Puants,* "stinkers," a literal translation of the nickname the Algonquin speakers gave them, meaning "those who came from the fetid [or stinking] water," or, simply, the ocean, they had been driven out of Illinois after a failed attempt to penetrate, finally settling around the Wisconsin lake which now bears their name, Lake Winnebago. The Winnebago were prudent allies of the Kickapoo, the Mascouten, and the Mesquakie or "Red Earth." The Mesquakie, better known by the other Indians as *Outagami,* meaning "Fox," because of their totem, were conse-

quently called *Renards* by the French. They, too, were part of the
Algonquin linguistic family as were their companions, the Sauks, or
"Sacs," an English corruption of O-sa-wah Ha-kee, or Yellow Earth. The
Sauk shared a village at Green Bay with the Fox, by the time the war with
the French was about to drive both nations west of the Mississippi. They
had been long-time wanderers, leaving behind place names such as
Saginaw Bay, in the present-day state of Michigan. After the French drove
them west of the Mississippi, both Fox and Sauks managed to rebuild
their strength in numbers as one nation. They became powerful enough
by the end of the eighteenth century to wrest control of Iowa from the
Osages, establish towns on the Rock River and Rock Island, and even to
return to their ancient Wisconsin home. During the War of 1812, having
been turned down by the government of the United States, they sent a
band to serve the British who promptly commissioned their Chief, Black
Hawk, as general in his Majesty's Service. The same Black Hawk would
be heard of again in 1832.

Latecomers to the heart of the Illinois country were the Potawatomi,
"the people of the place of the fire." [13] Their oral history indicates that:

> Ottawas, Chippewas, and Potawatomis originally were one tribe, part of
> the great wave of Algonquin-speaking peoples who entered the Great
> Lakes region from the north and the east. Chippewa legends suggest that
> the three tribes separated at the Straits of Mackinack no later than the
> sixteenth century, the Ottawas remaining at the straits, the Chippewas
> migrating to the north and the west, and the Potawatomis moving down
> the eastern shore of Lake Michigan.[14]

The life of the Potawatomi nation also had been greatly affected by the
massive Iroquois raids. During the seventeenth century, Green Bay had
become home to hundreds of refugees from different nations whose
villages lived side by side within earshot of the Jesuit Mission of Saint
François Xavier. There, the Potawatomi built a fortified settlement which
became the largest in the area; they also occupied the chain of islands
north of the Straits of Mackinac. By 1721, the Potawatomi also had
villages in St. Joseph and Detroit, both French posts, as well as along the
Illinois and Kankakee Rivers. They were among the strongest allies of the
French and remained faithful to their cause to the bitter end, and even beyond.

This chapter began with an examination of the attitudes of the French vis-à-vis the Indians, rather to say, of the Ancien régime French intelligentsia attitude back in France. What of the French primary actors on the scene? We can form certain judgments, through the writings of some, a minority made up principally of officials representing Church and government, and further assessments through the behavior of many more, whose only written records were registrations of births, marriages and deaths, and sometimes, last will and testaments. As a representation of the collective behavior of the common French folk living between Lake Michigan and the Mississippi, nothing rang louder than the countless sexual unions, with or without benefit of clergy, contracted between themselves and the Illinois, the Potawatomi, the Miami, and other Indians. In terms of writings, the first and foremost observers of Indian behavior, customs, and mores, were the Jesuits whose *Relations* often have the uncanny flavor of modern anthropological treatises.

But the Jesuits, as well as other members of the clergy, judged Indians relative to their attitudes towards Christianity and Christian morality. The "good news" was that race was not taken into account; but the "bad news" was that Indian customs and ways of life were seen negatively, when not corresponding to the models of European industry and order. However, we should look long and hard before dismissing "Christian morality" brought to the New World as an oppressive tool resulting in the destruction of native cultures.

In the atmosphere of the 1992 commemoration of the five hundredth anniversary of the arrival of Christopher Columbus, revisionism may lead to a flagrant disregard of the context of the times. A case in point is the Indian conception of warfare. Although European nations might wage war with ferocity—the Wars of Religion in France, the Thirty Years' War in Germany, and on this continent, King Philip's War—none, and certainly not by the end of the seventeenth century, would compare with the ardor of the Iroquois in burning, mutilating, roasting, and eating prisoners of both sexes and all ages. The Jesuits, who maintained missions with both French and Indian allies as well as with their Iroquois enemies (a demonstration of their independence from temporal power) wrote for their *Relations* descriptions of the worst kinds of inhumanity they witnessed and tried to abate, most of the time without success.[15] What is also remarkable in their letters is how careful they were to blame instigators or drunken warriors for these atrocities, while never indicting the nation as a whole, and to the contrary, were quick to marvel at the slightest expressions of kindness. Even from the vantage point of three hundred years of intellectual progress, there is hardly ground to castigate their attempts at converting the Iroquois away from their cultural interpretation of warfare.

Half a century after, Father Charlevoix, a Jesuit traveling across French North America, devoted several pages of his *Journal Historique d'un voyage en Amérique* to Indian lifestyles, including vivid descriptions of Miami, Potawatomi, and Illinois social behavior. Here again, opinions are mixed: like all his fellow men of the cloth, he deplored (and described detailed instances of) the terribly destructive effects of alcohol, the endemic thievery, and the pervasive promiscuity of the Indians among whom he spent many months during 1721. But Charlevoix was no casual visitor: he had a mission of information to carry out (his book, a collection of letters, was published twenty years later). His observations are impressive for their overall sense of objectivity, and contain fewer judgmental statements than we might expect from a man whose primary call in life was to foster the tenets of Christian morality as interpreted by the Catholic Church. Charlevoix admired the Indians' physical condition, a condition that he attributed to "... this liberty and the [physical] exercises that the children enjoy very young; the mothers nurse them for a long time and we see sometimes some six or seven year-olds who still suck on their mother's breast."[16] Beyond recounting and praising the virtues of Indian motherhood, Charlevoix was addressing and lecturing the French mothers of the nobility and the bourgeoisie classes, for whom it was then fashionable to entrust their newborn children to the care of country wet-nurses, a practice reputed to have caused the death of half of these infants.

Focusing on Indian life, Charlevoix explained that this long nursing time was "an usage preventing them from living with their husbands," a gentle euphemism meaning that they would abstain from sexual intercourse as long as they nursed, one of the major reasons, he correctly observed, for the low Indian population. The taboo which forbade Indian men from having relations with their nursing wives strikes one as a societally induced form of birth control, matching demographic growth to limited supplies for, aside from a few plots of corn, hunting, gathering, and fishing provided the only sources of food. The wives' unavailability as sexual partners (they did continue, however, to perform all the heavy work) probably played a role in the excessive taste for *lubricité* (lewdness), stigmatized by Charlevoix, and may explain the sexual freedom of unmarried girls, and the existence of homosexual transvestites. Father Marquette had noticed this practice, writing in his journal that there were some Illinois boys who "while yet young, assume the female dress, and keep it all their life. There is some mystery about it, for they never marry, and glory in debasing themselves to do all that is done by women." [17] He asserted, however, that this "corruption of morals," came from the southern nations, adding that "The Iroquois, particularly were quite a chaste people until they had contact with the Illinois and other neighboring nations from Louisiana." [18] But even as Charlevoix castigated the Illinois' morals, he admired their *"perfection de leurs sens"* which enabled them to find their way as if by magic, and to enjoy a photographic memory, a superior sense of smell, and incredible eyesight. Above all, he admired most:

> The beauty of their imagination [which] equals its vivacity. . . . and their speeches are filled with luminous bursts which would have been applauded in the public assemblies of Rome and Athens. . . . It would be surprising if with such a beautiful imagination they would not have an excellent memory. . . . Their narration is clear and precise, and although they use many allegories and other figures of speech, it remains lively. . . .. Their judgement is straight and strong, they go right to the point, without pause, without deviation, and without accepting substitution.[19]

Two other eyewitness accounts come to mind in terms of the perception of Indians during French control: The *Relation* dictated by Pénicaut, a soldier from Rouen, who served in Illinois in 1711, and the journal kept by Diron d'Artaguiette during his inspection of Illinois, in 1723. [20]

Pénicault called the Illinois Indians *laborieux et adroits dans la culture des terres* (hard-working and skillful farmers). They were in such remarkable physical condition that they could run down the buffaloes they had wounded with their arrows. In war: "They are very brave. . . . They are not unhuman towards their prisoners like the other savages. If they capture young children, they raise them in their village, taking pains to have them instructed in the Catholic religion by the Jesuit Fathers." [21]

Pénicault also admired the ability of the women who made yarn out of buffalo hair, and wove it into pieces of "cloth they dye in three colors, black, yellow and dark red. They make dresses which looked a little like those of the women from Brittany." [22]

The Illinois were Catholic and attended Mass; in church, one could hear verses alternately sung in Illinois language by the Indians and in Latin by the French. Marriages, either between Illinois themselves or

between Frenchmen and Illinois women (the later mentioned in a way
that suggested routine occurrence) took place within an orderly system,
from engagement rituals to publication of banns, solemn weddings,
banquets, and all-night dancing. For Pénicault, the *Sauvages catholiques*
compared advantageously to the French when it came to care and
concern. If this idyllic picture seems almost too good to have been true,
we must remember that this was the Illinois before the Fox and Chickasaw
Wars. A decade later, under intense pressure from Sioux and Fox raids,
the picture we get from Artaguiette is quite different. Here are his most
striking observations:

> The Illinois are in general the handsomest and the best built savages that
> I have seen. Proud and arrogant at home, they are the most cowardly of
> men when they are out of sight of their own village. . . . The Jesuit fathers
> who have for more than thirty years been among them, have up to the
> present failed in their attempts to make them understand that God made
> himself man and died for us. . . . The men concern themselves only with
> hunting and with making war, employing the remainder of the time in
> eating. . . . Their manner of making war is as barbarous as their persons. If
> they go to war and have the good fortune to capture any children, women
> or men, they kill them and remove their scalps, which they carry home in
> triumph. . . . The husband has full power and authority over his wives,
> whom he looks upon as his slaves, and with whom he does not eat.
> However, they separate one from the other, upon the consent of both
> parties. The married women indulge very little in gallantry [although they
> are all naturally inclined towards love] because of their fear of punishment
> from their husbands, who are more jealous than the Spaniards, who might
> scalp them upon the least proof of their infidelity. As or the young girls,
> they are the mistresses of their own bodies [to use their own expression].
> The good Jesuit fathers are endeavoring as much as possible to instill virtue
> in them, but they have not as yet succeeded. [23]

A large number of Illinois did refuse Christianity—principally because it would have meant relinquishing polygamy: however, just as
large a body of the Illinois confederacy did embrace the new faith. But
whose accounts are the most reliable? Pénicaut, Artaguiette, or Charlevoix? All three are truthful, all three reflect a specific view. Of the three,
Artaguiette was probably the most removed from the Illinois Indians. A
layer of officers and administrators separated him, an inspector from

Louisiana, from the rest of the troops, the budding French community, and the Indians. Ironically, it is these very close ties between French and Illinois that some historians view as among the principal factors in the demise of the Illinois as a nation. Yet, the Miami and the Potawatomi followed the same course and maintained their strength and cohesion down to the turn of the nineteenth century. The particularly unhappy destiny of the Illinois as a people is captured eloquently by Helen Tanner:

> The tragedy of the French Era in the western Great Lakes was the population loss of the Illinois. In this period of migration and trade expansion, western tribes—including the Mesquakie [Fox] after the end of hostilities—increased in population. But the Illinois, the people most closely attached to the French through intermarriage, Christianization, and commerce, declined dramatically. Between 1700 and 1763, the number of Illinois dropped from about 6,000 to 2,000 persons. Although disease, alcohol, and factionalization all contributed to this decrease, the most important factor was the constant raiding and warfare upon the Illinois by their anti-French tribal enemies . . . [24]

A moving statement, although it was the Potawatomi and not the Iroquois who destroyed the Illinois almost to a man, well after France no longer held power in the region.[25] The remaining Illinois who found refuge in Kaskaskia and Ste. Genevieve, the Miami who tried to hold on to their ancestral lands, and in short order all of the other Indian nations of the region (along with the few thousand French, many of whom were relatives), would soon be overwhelmed by the nineteenth-century onslaught of land hungry American farmers swarming across the vast expanse of land.

Within the context of the times, when all is measured there is ample evidence that from the beginning the French were little concerned with race. Too few in number to build their empire in North America alone, they sought to establish it along with the Native populations they encountered. Once Gallicized, and Christianized, the Indians were to become French; a fact already determined legally under Louis XIV. Legislation is a reflection of mentality. A century and a half ago, Francis Parkman, one of the first and few American historians to write extensively on the French period in North America,[26] became an ardent apologist for his subject. Since then, scholars using new methods of analysis, and examining new sources, have challenged among Parkman's ideas his very favorable view of French colonial behavior in North America. The French, they claim, were not this paragon of prejudice-free people that Parkman would lead us to believe, and they take issue with his well-known pronouncement,[27] "Spanish civilization crushed the Indian; English civilization scorned and neglected him; French civilization embraced and cherished him."[28]

Relations between French and Indians in North America were certainly more complex than Parkman's pithy observation would lead us to believe. There were great differences between the Indian nations from Canada and those of Louisiana; the dynamics created by economic survival and choice of alliances differed from one area to the next and within the same, and moreover, were not free from conflict. But overall, the French maintained a set of attitudes that allowed them a freedom to interact with the Indians, less inhibited by prejudice than their European contemporaries. Had they felt and behaved differently, they never would have been able to claim for France an uninterrupted empire stretching from Quebec to the Gulf of Mexico, much less defend it for over a century with so few resources available.

NOTES

1. At the time of this writing, the environment of the French missionaries and *voyageurs* in the early days of New France has been depicted with a rare eye for authenticity in the motion picture *Black Robe*; Brian Moore, who wrote the book— *Black Robe*, Fawcett Crest, New York, 1985—a fictionalized account primarily based on Jesuit Relations, benefitted from no less an eminent scholar of French North America than William Eccles.

2. Francis Jennings, *The Invasion of America, Indians, Colonialism, and the Cant of Conquest*, New York, 1976, 73-75.

3. Cornelius J. Jaenen, *Friend and Foe, Aspects of French-Amerindian Cultural Contact in the Sixteenth and Seventeenth Centuries*, Toronto, 1976, 30.

4. Richard White, *The Middle Ground, Indians, Empires, and Republics in the Great Lakes Region, 1650-1815*, Cambridge University Press, 1991, XIV.

5. Ibid., 51.

6. The Indians of New France have called the French governors "Onontio," since during a parley between the Iroquois and Charles Jacques de Huault de Montmagny, Lieutenant-general for the King in New France from 1636 to 1648; the Iroquois, on finding that the meaning of the governor's last name, Montmagny, was "large mountain," translated and adopted it. See William Eccles, *The Canadian Frontier, 1534-1760*, 1969, 201, FN 15. On the interesting career of the first

"Onontio," see Jean-Claude Dubé, "La carrière mouvementée de Charles Huault de Montmagny, 1601-1657," *Proceedings of the Fifteenth Meeting of the French Colonial Historical Society*, Martinique and Guadeloupe, May 1989, 61-70.

7. James Axtell, *The European and The Indian, Essays in the Ethnohistory of Colonial North America*, Oxford University Press, New York, 1981, 46.

8. *Jesuit Relation* for 1670-71, trans. Hiram W. Beckwith, *The Illinois and Indiana Indians*, Chicago, 1884, 100.

9. In *The Middle Ground*, Richard White devotes a most informative chapter entitled: "Refugees: a world made of fragments," 1-49, to the complicated diaspora of the Algonquin speaking nations.

10. "Sioux" is a simplification of the nickname "Nadous-sioux," meaning "enemies" and applied by all western nations to the Dakota.

11. The Iroquois confederacy grouped five nations: the Seneca, Cayuga, Onondaga, Oneida, and Mohawk.

12. Treaty of Vincennes, December 9, 1809, and Treaty of Edwardsville, July 30, 1819.

13. David Edmunds, *The Potawatomis*.

14. Ibid., 3.

15. See the letters of Father Jean de Lamberville, 1682, translated in Reuben Thwaites, ed. *The Jesuit Relations and Allied Documents*, 1610-1791, Cleveland, Burrows Brothers, vol. LXII, 54-106.

16. Charlevoix, Vol. III, 303.

17. Translation of Father Marquette's text was by John Gilmory Shea, *Discovery and Explanation of the Mississippi Valley*, 34; Redfield, NY, 1852.

18. Charlevoix, Vol. III, 303.

19. Ibid., 305.

20. Pénicaut, *Relations*, and Artaguiette, *Journal*, see chapter 8, notes 3, 34.

21. Pénicaut, *Relations*, in Margry, *Etablissements et decouvertes*, see chapter 2, note 1 V, 490-493.

22. Ibid.

23. Artaguiette, *Journal*, (see chapter 8, note 34, 71-74).

24. Tanner, *Atlas of Great Lakes Indian History*, (see chapter 8, note 4); 42.

25. The Potawatomi siege of the Illinois atop the *rocher*, Fort St. Louis, is the origin of its renaming as "Starved Rock;" Francis Jennings, in *The Ambiguous Iroquois Empire*, Norton, New York, 1984, 175, argued against the myth of the Iroquois destruction of the Illinois.

26. Francis Parkman, 1823-1893, wrote seven books on the subject of France in North America, applying his considerable writing skills to the presentation of his research.

27. Francis Parkman, *The Jesuits in North America in the Seventeenth Century*, Toronto, 1899, 1, 131.

28. This quote from the first lines of the introduction in Jaenen, *Friend and Foe*, written to dispute the claim; 7.

14

The Blacks

B lacks first arrived in *le pays des Illinois* as a direct consequence of the 1717 transfer of its government jurisdiction from Canada to Louisiana. As mentioned before,[1] in its transformation to Upper Louisiana, the Illinois Country was marked for intensive economic development by John Law's *Compagnie de l'Occident.* Intensive exploitation meant that slavery, prevalent in the West Indies, was now to be introduced in North America. Consequently, the first shipment of slaves was unloaded in Louisiana in June of 1719; they were, however, only distributed among the plantations along the Mississippi from the Gulf to Natchez. Africans did not make their appearance in the Illinois Country before 1720, when they were brought by Philippe Renault who had bought them in the French island colony of Saint Domingue (now, Haiti). Renault employed them in order to build his settlement, St. Philippe, near Fort de Chartres, and also to exploit his mines.

How many slaves were brought remains unclear. It was originally thought to be 500, an astronomical figure considering that the needs of labor-poor Lower Louisiana had priority, and considering the financial output it would have signified for even as well-heeled an entrepreneur as Renault; the initial number of slaves arriving in Illinois more likely numbered fewer than one hundred. A year later, in 1721, out of three ships bringing another 925 slaves from St. Domingue, only a very small percentage ended up in Illinois: "Forty of these Negroes are reserved to row the boats that will ascend to the Illinois Country." [2] The 1732 census for the Mississippi Valley, from Kaskaskia to Cahokia, showed a total population of 471, including French, Blacks, and Indians, the Blacks numbering 168; in the census of 1737, the Blacks numbered 314; and in 1752, there were 768 French and 445 Black slaves,[3] a high percentage but far from the typical ratio of a "plantation" country, like St. Domingue, where whites represented ten percent of the total population. Across the Mississippi, the newly prosperous Ste. Genevieve would see the slave population grow along parallel lines: two slaves in 1752, but an increase to 276, out of a total of 676, under the Spanish regime in 1773.[4]

St. Domingue was France's main slave distribution point (Jamaica assumed an identical role for the British colonies), and as such received Africans from all areas. By the seventeenth century, however, the ethnic origins of slaves played an important part in their distribution, as each colony developed definite preferences. For many planters, African origins were tied to behavior, some nationalities being considered less pliant than others. It is doubtful that the first shipment of slaves which reached Louisiana was from Guinea, as originally advanced,[5] as slaves fom Guinea and Senegambia generally ended up in Martinique, while those from Central Africa went to St. Domingue. Because African-born slaves were registered in shipment lists, sales lists, lists prepared by notaries, and census and baptismal registers, we have a reasonably clear indication of their origins with, however, a serious caveat:

> Two tendencies were at work. One was the European habit of identifying nationalities customarily shipped from a particular African port by the name of the port, as in the case of "Senegalese." The second was to pick one ethnic or linguistic term to identify a much larger group as in the case of "Bambara." These tendencies make for confusion and overlapping terminology.[6]

A case in point was the term "Poulard" which appears on French lists, meaning the West African Pular language, a language which could have been spoken by people from Senegal as well as from Futa Jallon. Interestingly, there are today Afro-American families by the name of "Pullen" originating from the Prairie du Rocher area. Possibly Africans identified as Bambaras from Senegal were among the first arrivals; Senegalese were appreciated in Lower Louisiana for their leadership qualities, and rapidly given responsibilities not usually associated with the idea of slavery, including a primary military role in the defense of the colony.[7] Determining the geographical and ethnological origins of Africans brought to the Illinois Country, although a formidable enterprise, may not be insurmountable.

Few in Upper Louisiana—with the exception of the Jesuits' establishments—could afford the price of a male laborer fixed at 660 *livres* and, consequently, French households rarely counted more than one or two slaves, if they could afford them at all. Slaves in the Upper Country were treated very differently than in the West Indies for the reasons of environment and attitudes previously discussed. In 1724, the treatment of Black slaves living in Louisiana became regulated by application of what is commonly known as the *Code Noir* or "Black Code."[8] Fifty-five articles covered all aspects of daily life, from trade to discipline and justice, a recycling of the decree originally promulgated in 1685.[9] Although an enlightened piece of legislation for the times, we should make no mistake: the purpose of the *Code Noir* was to regulate slavery, and to bring a sense of organization and order, a very typical French concern, to a system of colonial exploitation. Colonial trade was part and parcel of the prosperity of the French Atlantic Coast harbors (Nantes, La Rochelle, and Bordeaux), with slave trade representing by no means a negligible percentage of the total picture.

Against the mercantilist realities, reformers philosophically opposed to slavery could only hope to improve its nature, as there was yet no possibility of abolishing it. The Spanish Dominican priest Bartholome de Las Casas had been the first to denounce the cruelty of slavery in the New World, in this case applied to Indians. His campaign culminated in a book widely read at the time, and led Spain, as early as 1542, to eliminate many of the excesses indulged in by rapacious conquistadores through enactment of the *Nuevas Leyes* (New Laws);[10] which also, in an ironic twist, resulted in the introduction of African slavery as a replacement for Indian slavery. An analysis of the *Code Noir* shows the impact of Las Casas' thought on a number of rules. Article II stated that "All slaves . . . shall be educated in the Apostolic Roman Catholic religion, and be baptised. . . . We charge the directors-general of said company, and all our officers, to enforce this strictly," followed by Article IV stipulating that "No overseers shall set over the Negroes to prevent their professing of the Apostolic Roman Catholic Religion under pain of forfeiture of such slaves . . . " Article V prohibits masters from making their slaves work on Sundays and holidays. Concubinage with slaves is forbidden to whites, naturally, but also to "blacks affranchised, or born free," in Article VI, indirectly acknowledging their existence. Marriages between slaves, when consented to by the master, must take place observing all "solemnities," but such marriages are forbidden if they are against the slave's "inclination," (Article VIII). The overall importance of motherhood is recognized, as the children of a free mother and a slave father are to "be free like herself," (Article X). Slaves not fed, clad, or maintained properly can lodge complaints to the courts (Article XX), and when sick or incapacitated by old age must be supported (Article XXI). Although the Code includes all the expected regulations with regard to right of assembly, punishments in cases of physical violence against their masters, or running away,

Article XXXVIII forbids: "all our subjects in said country, or every rank and condition, from putting their slaves, or causing them to be put by their authority, to the torture or rack, under any pretense whatsoever, or from inflicting or causing to be inflicted any mutilation of the limbs. . . . "

While clearly considering the slaves as "movable property," the Code also forbids the sale of husband and wife separately, "and their chidlren under age" (meaning under fourteen years old), (Article XLIII). Article L authorizes manumission, but requires that masters must first request permission, and Article LII stipulates that the slaves freed by act of manumission "enjoy the privileges of the native born subjects of our kingdom, lands and countries within our sovereignty. . . . " Article LIV reinforces the concept of equality. It is worth quoting in extenso:

> We grant to persons affranchised the same rights, privileges, and immunities, enjoyed by those born free: decreeing that the blessings of liberty thus purchased, shall effect for them, as well with respect to their persons as their property, the same objects that result from the advantage of natural freedom to our other subjects: and all this, notwithstanding the exceptions specified in article fifty-second of the presents.

Slavery in French North America, governed by a body of laws emanating from a central royal power, was markedly different from slavery in the North American British colonies, where a large degree of self-government allowed the white populations in the Carolinas or in Virginia to create and maintain systems exclusively to their advantage. The Catholic clergy's determination to include slaves in the Church needs also to be contrasted with the indifferent attitudes of the Protestant clergy in the British colonies (with the exception of the Quakers). In attempting to recreate a picture of Blacks in Illinois, we must not forget the effects of living in close physical contact, which led to some degree of miscegenation, in turn leading to the manumission of offspring and the creation of a class of free mulattoes. Sexual contacts between Blacks and Whites were not as prevalent in Illinois, where the French had remedied the original paucity of available women by a tradition of intermarriage with Indians (in Lower Louisiana, particularly in New Orleans, where contact with Indians was limited, the Free Mulattoes became an important class until the United States' purchase of Louisiana).

The application of the *Code Noir* in Illinois tended to be in step with the general laissez-faire attitude animating the enforcement of all other laws and regulations, and certainly was more relaxed than in Lower Louisiana, where some large plantations had developed a duplication of those conditions already in existence in the West Indies. No one was shackled or locked in at night on Illinois plantations; in fact, "plantation," in the context of the Illinois Territory, where large land grants amounted to less than 200 acres, is rather a misuse of the term. Moreover, when these properties were sold, auctioned off or simply inherited, chances were that the transactions took place within the same small community, and consequently did not translate into drastic uprootings of slave families. In 1750, the Jesuit Father Vivier wrote from Kaskaskia in one of his *Relations*: "We have here Whites, Negroes and Indians, to say nothing of the cross-breeds . . ." This was an environment where one could not hide in comfortable anonymity.

In 1751, Governor Vaudreuil issued new legislation concerning slavery in Louisiana. This new *Règlement* was to complement the original *Code Noir*, as the evolution of French society brought more freedom to the Black slaves than originally expected:[11] Vaudreuil clearly felt that Louisiana colonists were losing their grip on their slaves, and his "reglement" represented an effort to clamp down on such nefarious activities as consumption of alcohol, nocturnal roaming, frequenting of disreputable establishments (operated by freed Negroes), and reckless horse racing.

The individual lives of some of the Afro-Americans in Illinois have been examined by Carl Ekberg, for the town of Ste. Genevieve, as closely as they can be. The picture which evolves from several individual cases is one of compromise between the difficult juxtaposition of the unnatural structures imposed by the institution of slavery, and the natural body of human reactions brought on after two or three generations of close cohabitation. As mentioned above, some miscegenation took place; at times discreet, and at times less so, when whites would encounter serious mischief with the law for being more open than they should with their black mistresses and their mulatto children. Records show that in the 1770's, Jean-François La Buche lived with a black companion, Elizabeth, with whom he had four children; that Antoine Aubuchon had ten children from Elizabeth, a freed black woman, by the time he died, in 1798. We also see Antoine Janis, scion of a prominent family, taking up a relationship with Marie-Louise, a mulatto woman, a slave belonging to his brother-in-law; three children were born of this union, in 1792, 1795, and in 1802, as Antoine, overcoming all obstacles, in the meantime succeeded in buying Marie-Louise's freedom. And there was Pierre

Viriat, a miner who came from Lorraine, who bought a mulatto woman in 1800, Rodde Christi, then freed and married her.

These intimate relationships alone cannot begin to give the total picture of the situation of the Blacks, but they are a sort of litmus test by which everything else can be measured. The records for Ste. Genevieve show that Blacks and mulattoes, freed or slaves, by and large exercised many professions vital to the economy of the community, earned money, obtained redress from the courts, bore arms, and, generally speaking, moved freely. By the time Ste. Genevieve had grown to respectability, Western French Illinois was under the rule of Spain, but almost all "Spanish" officials were still the same French individuals, now simply enforcing Spanish law. This Spanish law, in the matter of slavery, was more lenient than French law; the vast Spanish Empire, like the Roman Empire, could not have functioned without the contributions made by slaves.

On the eve of the 1800's, the situation of the Blacks in Western Illinois that was Spanish *de jure*, but French *de facto*, was improving, slowly moving away from slavery, as the integration into that small, rural French society continued. The Louisiana Purchase would put a halt to this trend. Slavery for the Americans was neither paternalistic nor lax, and racial lines were not to be trifled with. When Virginia, in a military action independent of Congress, directed George Rogers Clark and his Kentucky militia to Kaskaskia in 1778, bringing Americans for the first time inside the former French territory, it would take but a short period before new attitudes towards slavery would supplant the French laissez-faire: the same year, Clark enacted a decree denying slaves the freedom to walk the streets after sundown or to assemble for night dances; both these offenses were punishable by flogging. When Virginia, however---whether cajoled or coerced, depending on the interpretation--turned over to Congress on March 1, 1784, the entire Northwest Territories heretofore claimed as her own, the legality of slavery developed into a controversy. Virginia's deed of cession included language which the few remaining slave owners, among the minority of French inhabitants who had not crossed the Mississippi, gladly interpreted in their own favor, but Congress, as will be seen later, thought otherwise, and in 1787 legislated accordingly. In any event, in the year 1800, the number of black slaves as indicated in the census for the whole Indiana territory (including present-day Wisconsin, Illinois, Indiana, the western half of Michigan, and portions of Minnesota) had dwindled to a population of only 133. When, following the Purchase, the newly appointed American governor of Louisiana, William

Claiborne, discovered the existence of a colored militia—a unit which traced its history back to 1736, when the French first mustered a company of "free men of color" officered by Blacks—anxiety would all but overcome him, [12] as armed blacks were absolute anathema to the Southern states.

There is no better known French Black in Chicago than Jean-Baptiste Point du Sable (or Pointe de Sable), who is credited with being the first non-Indian settler in the location later to become that city. If such credit is debatable—Chicago earlier had been home to Jesuit missionaries and a French garrison—what is not debatable is the strength of his spirit. Du Sable probably was born around 1745, of a French father and a Black woman from St. Domingue. Was his father originally a Canadian? A "small piece of land jutting out into Lake Erie, south of what is now Windsor, Ontario, Canada, marked *Pointe de Sable*," [13] where his roots may have been located, and may explain why he became one of the last among the breed of fiercely independent entrepreneurs who started their careers as *voyageurs*. We find him in Peoria, in 1771, where he married a Potawatomi woman and exploited a thirty-acre farm; and, in "Eschikagou" in 1772, where he built a successful trading post. He sold this post to Jean Lalime in September 1800, but it would later be remembered as "his," linking his name with the founding of Chicago. In 1792, his daughter Suzanne would marry a Frenchman, Jean-Baptiste Pelletier, also in Chicago. Before returning to Peoria, Du Sable claimed and received four hundred acres of land, given by an Act of Congress of March 3rd, 1791, to all individuals who were heads of families and could prove American citizenship prior to 1783. He died in 1818, in a part of the former *Pays des Illinois* which had become Missouri; as with all the "French," be they Indians, Blacks, mixed-bloods, or European, the time of their adventure was fast disappearing into history. But I like to think that the genes of Point Du Sable's granddaughter, Eulalia Pelletier—part French, part African, and part Indian, married to Michel De Roi in 1813—are alive today somewhere among us.

NOTES

1. Chapter VIII, *The Growing Years*.

2. Governor Bienville to the Company, April 25, 1721, quoted in *Colonial Ste. Genevieve*, 200.

3. See the well-researched chapter "Black Slavery French Style," in *Colonial Ste. Genevieve*, 196-239.

4. Ibid.

5. Norman Dwight Harris, *The History of Negro Servitude in Illinois and of the Slavery Agitation in that State, 1719-1864*, McClurg, Chicago, 1904; 1.

6. Philip D. Curtin, *The Atlantic Slave Trade, A Census*, The University of Wisconsin Press, Madison, 1969, 184.

7. Roland C. McConnell, *Negro Troops of Antebellum Louisiana, A History of the Battalion of Free Men of Color*, Louisiana State University Press, Baton Rouge, 1968.

8. *Edicts du Roy Servant de Règlement pour le gouvernement et l'Administration de la justice, Police, discipline et le commerce des esclaves Nègres dans la Province et Colonie de la Louisiane donné à Versailles au mois de mars 1724* .

9. *Edict du roi concernant la discipline de l'Eglise et l'état et la qualité des nègres esclaves aux Iles d'Amérique*, promulgated in March 1685, prepared by Colbert just before his death.

10. Bartholome de Las Casas, 1474-1566, the "Apostle of the Indies;" went to the island of Hispaniola (Santa Domingo) in 1502 to help Christianize the Indians. He was ordained priest in 1512 and became a Dominican in 1523. By 1515, he had begun an intense campaign against Indian slavery, writing extensively on the subject of colonization.

11. *Colonial Ste. Genevieve*, 207.

12. *Negro Troops of Antebellum*, 33-38.

13. Shirley Graham, *Jean Baptiste Pointe De Sable, Founder of Chicago*, Julian Messer, New York, 1953, 176.

15

The Last Years under the Fleur-de-lis

T he 1740's were to be the first of two crucial decades for the French in America. As in the past, the history of the French Colonial Empire would be determined by the course of events in Europe. Would there be growth or ruin? War between France and Britain was once again in the air; neither power could accept the possibility of the other achieving supremacy. On both sides of the English Channel, Fleury and Walpole, the moderates who had been at the helms of their respective kingdoms had both died, and the War of the Austrian Succession was increasing in tempo. The spring of 1743, saw the Royal Navy harassing French shipping in the Atlantic, an action facilitated by the inferior level of its adversary's preparation. Meanwhile, after long circling each other in the northern European countryside like two wary pugilists, the two armies—one French, the other British—saw battle in Germany, near Frankfurt-am-Main;[1] a year later, in March 1744, Louis XV, the King of France, finally made it official by declaring war on Great Britain.

For a time in North America it appeared as though this war would be ignored. "King George's War," as it was nicknamed, did not generate strong enthusiasm among the merchants of New York who were enjoying profitable commerce with the French West Indies and Canada, and were loath to disrupt it. Even the turbulent British allies, and the Iroquois were happy with peace. Only the New Englanders were anxious to join the fray. [2] Their target was Louisbourg, this "Gibraltar" of New France,[3] a massive fortress on the island of Cape Breton (Nova Scotia), serving ". . . as a haven for the French navy and privateers who were causing havoc on the New England fishing and trading fleets." Garrisoned by near mutinous French marines and short of supplies, Louisbourg was captured by a 4,000-strong New England militia in June 1745, after a month-and-a-half siege. Louisbourg would be returned to France with the general peace treaty of Aix-la-Chapelle of 1748,[4] but not before the echoes of the battle for its possession reverberated from one end of colonial America to the other.

The loss of Louisbourg was a rude awakening for the French; forts were repaired, militia rolls re-checked, supplies assembled, and word sent to all Indian allies. But it also gave the French a new sense of resolve. In the business of raiding and coup de main, the French were masters: it did not take long for them to bring death and destruction to the New York and New England communities in brutal retaliation. Governor Beauharnois planned a two-prong counteroffensive in Ohio and in the Hudson Bay area. "The English Colonies had to fend for themselves, and in this type of warfare their militia was no match for the Canadians." [5] In November, 1745, 600 French and Indians attacked and burned Saratoga, in New York, capturing 100 prisoners. Rigaud de Vaudreuil led 400 Canadian militia and 300 Indian volunteers to Brookfield, Massachusetts, destroyed the town, and brought back thirty prisoners. The British called upon their allies, the Mohawk, to retaliate against the French, but after some initial success the Mohawk raiders were almost all annihilated or captured. The momentum, however, seemed to be on the side of the British colonies.

Firstly, the British fleet's quasi-mastery of the ocean between Mother Country and New France led to a serious drop in the availability of supplies, including goods essential to the fur trade. True enough, the French merchants, the Post commandants, and the voyageurs, might have overcome this drying up of supplies from France—in any case, very overpriced—but the interruption of overland trade between Montreal and New York was another matter. For years, the French had bought English-made goods (officially contraband) for trade with the Indians; these were transactions advantageous to Montreal, and good business for Albany, but the war brought a halt to this traffic. Prices on the French side went up 150 percent; and as the French could no longer trade, could no longer make their customary gifts, many Indians began looking to the British as willing customers.

And willing they were. More and more British traders began to infiltrate the ever-fluid Ohio and Wabash frontier. Over a period of two years, by mixing business and politics, the British were able to foment a large conspiracy among disaffected Indian allies, with the goal of eliminating the French all the way from Detroit to Illinois. The Commandant of Detroit, Mr. de Longueuil, reported to Quebec that English traders would venture near the post, trade with Indians, and tell them that the French were on the way out. All sorts of reports from loyal Indians would reach the French. More often than not these proved to be wild rumors; nevertheless, they still added to their apprehension. But to see such an ambitious plan converted to a successful end required a degree of military

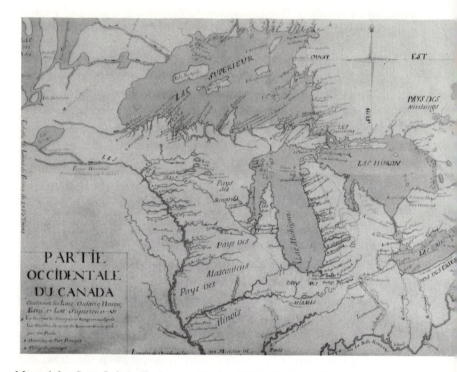

Map of the Great Lakes. By Jacques-Nicolas Bellin, *Partie Occiden-
tale du Canada,* 1750. (The MacLean Collection)

sophistication and discipline the Indians who entered the conspiracy did
not have.

Although the rebellion had been planned for the Pentecost of 1747,
outbreaks began to take place throughout early spring. It was a far cry,
however, from the thought to the deed. There were a series of nasty
episodes: five *voyageurs* were killed at Sandusky and their canoe stolen;
rebels also killed three Frenchmen near Michilimackinac, and eight more
near La Baye Verte (Green Bay), in both cases traveling in isolated canoes.
The Miami Fort was also attacked and partially destroyed by the Miami
Chief, La Demoiselle, won over by the British. More isolated men were
attacked here and there, but this was definitely not the Sicilian Vespers.
News of the oncoming insurrection had spread throughout the West,
including Illinois, however, the commandants were not only ready, but
actively trying to de-fuse the situation through endless talks with the
Indian nations. The conspirators had remained a minority and by the time

the peace treaty was signed, the French had the situation well in hand. A 150-man reinforcement for Detroit, coinciding with the return of the voyageur brigades from the Northwest, had the desired effect with the Huron, the Ottawa, and the Potawatomi of the area who hastened to send deputations to profess their allegiance to the French alliance. Instigators were brought to the posts and surrendered to the French.

After receiving the reinforcements, Longueuil sent detachments to posts in need, small units led by able officers such as Marie François Picoté de Bellestre, taking twelve men to St. Joseph, and Charles François de la Perade, marching to Ouiatanon with a handful of soldiers. Larger contingents were sent to Michilimackinac, La Baye Verte, and Fort de Chartres, and the "... show of force ... the arrival of considerable goods for the trade had a salutory effect."[6] Further helping to reestablish the situation was the arrival of a new governor in Quebec, the Count de la Galissonière, an intelligent man who rapidly developed remarkable insight into the situation of New France, both its potential as well as its foibles. Professor Eccles, "the grand old man" of French colonial history in North America, analyzed Galissonière's assessment of *la Terre des Illinois,* in his *mémoire* dated September 1748:

> [Galissonière] declared categorically that the Illinois country was of very little economic value to France, that for a long time posts and settlements there would merely be a source of expense to the crown and that the French settlers in the region would certainly not become very prosperous. Yet, he declared, the crown must maintain them, regardless of the expense, to protect the investment already made, but more significantly, because they served as a barrier to English expansion, enabling the French to dominate the Indian nations of the lower Mississippi and retain their trade and allegiance. . . . But were the Anglo-Americans ever to seize the Illinois country —and they had easy access to it—Canada's trade with the interior would be destroyed. Louisiana would quickly be lost, and the Spanish colonies, even Mexico, would then be in grave danger. [7]

To seize the land lying between Lake Michigan and the Mississippi, the Anglo-Americans (a better term to define the population of the British colonies of the mid-1700's) first had to capture the Ohio Valley. Their scheme was simple: detach the Indians from their alliance to France, send them to attack and capture the chain of forts and posts, ensuring the security of communications between Canada and the West: Fort Frontenac (present-day Kingston, Ontario), Fort Niagara, Sandusky, and Detroit. Then, taking advantage of the enormous surplus of population they enjoyed along the Atlantic seaboard, push a large migration of settlers over the Alleghenies. After first obtaining title to the land from Virginia to the Ohio River from the allied Iroquois in 1747, three colonies—Maryland, Pennsylvania, and Virginia—backed the forming of the Ohio Company, specifically chartered to bring settlers to the area. The fact that this land was claimed by France, at least on paper, was of course irrelevant to them; in any event, these were war times. Once the Ohio Valley was occupied, it would then be only a matter of time for all the land between Lake Michigan and the Mississippi River to fall under British control.

With the Western fur trade in British hands, Canada would have lost its economic base and *raison d'être*. The pragmatic French of Versailles would probably come to an understanding if offered a concession of the sort the British were always ready to make on the backs of their allies on continental Europe, and the whole of North America would come under British control. Then, it would be time to look south, and move against Lower Louisiana and the Spanish colonies.

On the eastern fringes of *Le Pays des Illinois,* the renegade Miami Chief La Demoiselle had a pivotal role to play in the grand scheme. At the start of the unrest, the British had won him over with the help of generous gifts of merchandise. Leaving the Miami post with his followers, he built a new town on the Great Miami River, at the mouth of Laramie's Creek, Pickawillany (near present-day Piquo, Ohio); another defector, Chief Nicolas, came to join him with his Huron village of Sandusky (these Hurons were Catholics, but the origin of their disaffection was their jealousy for the Catholic Iroquois and the heathen Ottawa, who they felt were better treated by the French than they were). Pickawillany quickly became a stronghold for British agents. Major de Bertet (who had commanded in Illinois since 1742) informed the governor in August, 1747, of the clandestine arrival of Indians from the East, bringing an invitation for the Illinois to join their pro-English coalition—or perish with the French. During that very period, the whole territory was without news from either Canada or Louisiana due to a combination of lack of trade and large militia calls up and down the St. Lawrence and the Lower Mississippi Rivers, and the Illinois felt very vulnerable to all sorts of rumored attacks. A large expedition (almost 2,000 men), mounted jointly in 1739, by Canada and Louisiana with militia and regular troops (including a sizable Illinois contingent) after assembling at the Chickasaw Bluffs (Arkansas) to "... finally crush the Chickasaw power," [8] could not even locate the enemy and ended in an abysmal failure.

The commandant of Illinois, La Buissonière, had led forty soldiers of Marine infantry and 150 Illinois, who like all the other participants in this affair were dismayed and disgusted by Bienville's (then governor of Louisiana) indecisiveness. Concerned by the military impotence of the French, half the Choctaw nation then defected; this turn of events led to a considerable cooling of feelings toward the French from many of the 150 Illinois warriors. They had received large quantities of powder and musket balls to continue to wage war on the Chickasaw, but after the 1739 fiasco, chose to remain on the sidelines. All sorts of reports now reached Bertet about these disaffected veterans plotting their revolt, giving him a vision of renegade Illinois joining with Sioux, Missouri, and Osage from the western bank of the Mississippi, Chickasaw from the south, and revolted Indians from the East, all overrunning the territory. Looking at Fort de Chartres in a serious state of disrepair, the storehouse empty of ammunition, and concluding that it was indefensible, moreover haunted with visions of a new Natchez massacre, Bertet ordered evacuation. He regrouped in Kaskaskia the 135 officers and men of the garrison, all the civilian population, and the loyal Indians of the valley. In hindsight, he had clearly overreacted, as the danger always had been more apparent than real. The crisis over, his prudence was appreciated by the governor of New France but sharply criticized by the governor of Louisiana, the latter, after interrogating the Illinois chiefs suspected of treason, concluding that the danger had been overblown. In spite of criticism, Bertet was maintained in his command until his death during the first days of January 1749. [9] He was replaced at the helm of Illinois by Jean-Baptiste Benoist, *sieur* de St. Claire, the officer who had preceded him.

Peace could not have been more welcome to the French who, chastised by their experience, hurried to take measures to strengthen the two colonies before the inevitable next war with Britain. Military considerations took priority; thought was even given to reverting Illinois to Canada in order to help centralize command. While Illinois did remain an administrative part of Louisiana, Canada took a much more preponderant role in its affairs having to do with trade and the military. Generally, the trend during the last years of French administration was toward a much closer cooperation in military matters between Canada and Louisiana, answering an ever-present British threat oblivious of administrative boundaries.

In the meantime, the last rumors of the Indian revolt continued to be felt here and there. On May 10, 1749, a few of the turncoat Choctaw joined a large band of Chickasaw and three Englishmen in a surprise attack on the Post of Arkansas. Their target was the fort and the Quapaw, most loyal Indian allies of the French in the region. The garrison, twelve men and an ensign, plus a handful of settlers, gave a good account of itself obliging the assailants to give up the siege.[10] The same year, a 230-man strong expedition was sent to Ohio to "show the flag." Led by a Canadian-born veteran of many skirmishes, Pierre-Joseph Céloron de Blainville, it went smoothly, until their arrival in Pickawillany, where days of lengthy discussion with Chief La Demoiselle ended with his vague promise of returning to Fort Miami by the next spring, a promise that would not be kept. Arriving in Fort Miami, Blainville found the establishment in wretched condition, manned by a twenty-two-man detachment in miserable health. The total picture confirmed the fact that the Ohio frontier remained the Achilles heel of the French.

At the precise moment when Canada would have benefited from continuity, La Galissonière's lucid policy was replaced by the venal and inefficient actions of a new governor, Pierre-Jacques de Tafanel, Marquis de La Jonquière, and his *intendant* François Bigot; (under their administration, the post of *La Baye Verte* alone was reputed to represent an annual illicit profit of 150,000 *livres*). This climate of corruption would trickle down from Quebec to the most isolated posts, and Illinois, naturally, was not immune.

In the fall of 1751, one of the most colorful characters among the Commandants of Illinois, Major de Macarty-Mactique, was proceeding up the Mississippi to reach his new post. Born in 1705, to an Irish family who found refuge in France during the Cromwell years, Macarty began his military career as *Mousquetaire*, then appears in 1732 in the records of New Orleans as *adjudant-major*, and, in 1735, as Captain. He was appointed Commandant of the Illinois Territory, on June 11, 1750, and, the same year, made *Chevalier de St. Louis* (Knight in the Order of St. Louis), then France's highest decoration.

Macarty left New Orleans in August 1751, leading the customary imposing convoy of *bateaux* (six this time) and canoes, slowly making its way against the current of the Mississippi. On these *bateaux* were four companies of troops of marines. Their arrival could not have been more timely, just a few days before, a band of thirty-three Miami Piankashaw had come to Fort de Chartres to ask for supplies and ammunition, claiming that they were on their way to raid the Cherokee, one Indian nation allied to the British. The Piankashaw then continued on to Kaskaskia where they behaved in ways that St. Claire, the acting commandant, found suspect; having learned of their true hostile intentions (they were Illinois who were involved in the plot but did not keep it secret), he prepared to face the danger. One of Macarty's officers who made the voyage upriver ahead of the main convoy to prepare quarters for the new arrivals, Jean-Baptiste Homère Bossu, then a thirty-year old lieutenant, recounted the details in one of the two books he wrote about his experiences. The story as told by Bossu is exact in all points except regarding his presence during the event: "... loving a dramatic story, Bossu places the event on December 25th and pictures himself not only as a spectator but even as the inventor of the ruse by which the intention of the Indians was discovered." [11] The following is part of an English translation of his second book, published in London, in 1771:

After these adventures [his boat hit a submerged tree and sank], I am at last arrived at Fort Chartres. I had not been long here, when I was witness to an event which might have had very unhappy consequences. The Pehenguichias and the Ouwatawons had agreed upon the total ruin of five French villages among the Illinois. M.de Macarty had sent me beforehand to prepare quarters for some troops that came in a convoy. The Indians had meditated their enterprise, and intended to come before the convoy. I was then at the Kaskaskia, where M. de Montchevaux commanded, who could not justly know the whole extent of the plot of those barbarians; by their caresses, their affectation, and calling to mind the massacre of the Natchez, we suspected their design.

On such occasions as these, an officer feels all the weight of the command. M. de Montchevaux was not discouraged; he was seconded by M. de Gruise, an intelligent, brave officer. He held a council with the oldest and most considerable people of the place, and did me the honor to consult me in this circumstance. . . . My opinion was that in order to penetrate the design of these Indians, we should keep on the defensive, without showing the least suspicion; that we should send out some armed inhabitants on horseback, as if they went ahunting; recommending to them, that, after they had gone the rounds, they should return into the village full gallop, as if something had happened to them: this was to give a false alarm. There remained nothing further to be done in that case, but to examine the countenances of the Indians who would certainly betray themselves.

This advice followed, the Indians believed that the French had discovered the plot they intended to execute on Christmas-day, when the people came from the great mass; they had exactly inquired after that day, asking in their way, when that day came on which the Son of the great Spirit came into the world.

As soon as they believed they were discovered, they thought only of making their escape; we fired upon them and killed twenty-two on the spot. A sergeant called La Jeunesse, a Creole, and a good hunter, killed four in my presence. M. de Gre, on his side, attacked those who were in the Jesuit house, he wounded several of them and took five alive, among whom there was one Illinois; they were put in irons.

M. de Macarty hastened to dispatch messengers to New Orleans to the Marquis de Vaudreuil to give him an account of this expedition; the governor sent back orders to deliver the prisoners to their countrymen, who came crying, the calumet at hand and disavowed the plot, saying that the English had taken their senses from them. They received peace very thankfully, and all is quiet at present. However, for precaution's sake, the inhabitants have received orders to carry their muskets when they go to mass, and the officer of the guard to place two sentinels at the church door during divine services.[12]

As if this violent experience would not be enough to test the fortitude of the French *habitans* of Illinois, another major and quite dangerous event took place during the month of June 1752. It began when a hunting party of Cahokia coming by chance upon a few Fox Indians, decided to capture and burn them in spite of the existing peace treaty. But, as one of the Fox managed to escape; the Cahokia, knowing they were in for a revenge raid, moved to the village of the Michigami, near Fort de Chartres. The Fox in the meantime called on the Sauk, the Sioux, and the Kickapoo. A thousand warriors came down the Mississippi. Let us leave the description once again to an eyewitness, Captain Bossu:

They embarked in one hundred and eighty canoes made of birch tree bark, on the river Ouisconsing which falls into the Missisipi. . . . They passed in good order by the Fort of Kaokias where the Chevalier de Voisei, an officer of my detachment, commanded . . . The Foxes had fixed upon Corpus Christi day for fighting the Illinois. They knew that the latter would come to Fort Chartres to see the ceremony which is performed by the French on that solemn day. The fort was only a league from the Indian village. . . . Everything being in readiness for the attack, the general of the Foxes ordered ten or twelve of the best runners to throw away their bodies. These young men immediately fell upon the enemy's village and killed all they met as they came in, crying the cry of death, and having discharged their arms, they fled with as much quickness as they came. . . . The Illinois took up their arms and pursued them, but the army of the Foxes, lying on the ground, in the high grass, discharged all their arms and killed twenty-eight Illinois at the same time they fell upon the village, and killed men, women and children, set fire to the village, and bound and led away the rest as captives. The Foxes lost but four men . . . I was a spectator of this slaughter, which happened on the sixth of June 1752. . . . This account will inform you that nothing can be more dangerous than being taken unawares by these nations. None but those who were gone out of curiosity to see the procession at the French fort of Chartres escaped the revenge of the Foxes, who contented with their victory, re-embarked in their boats, and put the prisoners well bound in the van, and passing by the French fort of Koakias, they gave a general salute with their guns. The Chief, or admiral of the Foxes, had hoisted the French colours on his canoe, and was as proud of his victory, as if he had subdued a great empire. M. de Macarty, our governor, has written to those in the posts of Canada to treat with the Foxes concerning the ransom of the Illinois whom they have taken prisoners. These cunning Indians had conducted their undertaking so well, that we knew nothing of it till it was executed; they hid the knowledge of it from us, justly fearing that we would interpose our mediation between them and the Illinois, as being friends and allies of both.[13]

The commandant of the fort at Peoria, Mr. Adamville, was particularly helpful to Macarty during the difficult negotiations meant to restore peace among the Indian nations. Peoria, abandoned as a military post for several years, had been re-established, probably with the outbreak of the war with Britain, and would be maintained until the end of the French regime. The Fox raid, although not directed towards the French, happening on the heels of the attempt on Kaskaskia, could not but render the construction of major defense work an urgent matter. In 1753, Vaudreuil, then still governor of Louisiana, had already written to the Minister that a new fort should be built next to Kaskaskia, the largest settlement, while the old site could be used for a small detachment. When Vaudreuil left Louisiana to become Governor of Canada, his successor, Louis Billouert de Kerlerec, a navy captain, followed through on this matter, directing a military engineer, Jean-Baptiste Saucier to draw up plans. Once in Illinois, Saucier met with Macarty and the officers of the garrison organized in a consulting committee; and together, they began looking for a new site. The result of their deliberations was to reconstruct Fort de Chartres on the old site. Kerlerec went along with the decision and, in 1754, wrote to the Minister, supporting the choice.[14]

The cost of the fort was estimated at 450,000 *livres*, an enormous sum for the time. Kerlerec gave the authorization to begin construction after reducing the budget allocation to 250,000. Work on the foundations began in 1753, but ten years later when the British took possession the fort was still not completely finished. This was the third fort. The first, built in 1719, was a wooden construction;[15] the second, built sometime in the 1720's, was also a wooden construction. The last, built entirely of stone quarried nearby in the bluffs overlooking Prairie du Rocher, would last almost intact until the beginning of the nineteenth century, when neighborhood farmers began to use the stone for themselves. (Today, Fort de Chartres is well reconstructed on its foundations, with the powder magazine being the only original building.) The new Fort was later described by Captain Pittman, a British engineer, as a polygon built of stones, four hundred and ninety feet wide, with walls two feet two inches thick, but only good enough "as a defense against Indians," which could house a garrison of four hundred men.[16] The true final cost of the fort added up to millions of *livres*, and Governor Kerlerec was in all probability deeply involved in the financial scandal of the construction.

La Jonquiere died in 1752, and a new governor general of New France was appointed: Ange de Menneville, marquis de Duquesne, who carried orders from the Minister to drive the British out of Ohio. The determination of the British colonies to expand west, either through trade or settlement, was bound to lead to a direct head-on collision with the French, who were just as determined to maintain their claim to the land. Both colonial empires were slowly drifting towards war, almost independently from the policies of their respective mother countries.

Before Duquesne had time to draw his plans, an expedition of impatient French traders and Ottawa Indians from Michilimackinac led by Charles Langlade drew the first blood, raiding and destroying Pickawillany. La Demoiselle was killed, and for good measure, butchered and eaten—this was not going to be a campaign for the faint-hearted. The British traders who were found in town were imprisoned but otherwise

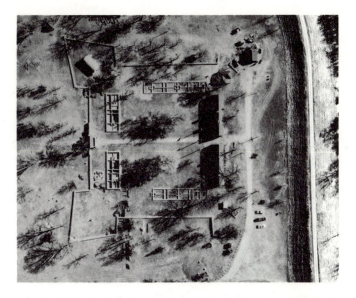

Fort de Chartres today. (Illinois Department of Transportation)

unmolested. In the spring of the following year, Governor Duquesne was ready and, considering his limited resources (the total number of men on the Canadian militia rolls for 1750 was 11,687), committed the heart and soul of New France to the integrity of the Ohio frontier: 300 regulars from the companies of the troops of marines, 1700 militiamen, and 200 Indians, entrusted to Captain Pierre-Paul de la Maigue, *sieur* de Marin, "...a tough veteran of the west born...with a tomahawk in his hand."[17] In February 1754, another expeditionary corps of 800 men walked from Montreal to the junction of the Monongahela and Ohio Rivers through the winter snows, and built Fort Duquesne (better known today as Pittsburgh). Illinois was involved in all of these actions underlining the newly acquired spirit of cooperation between Canada and Louisiana, although primarily in a supporting role, sending flour and meat to the forts of Ouiatenon, Miami, and Detroit.

In 1753, orders came to Macarty to prepare for a massive supplying of the expedition bound for the location of the future Fort Duquesne. The British made few attempts to stop the French from reclaiming the Ohio Valley. One of them, however, would prove to have tragic consequences and remain a blemish on the career of the future United States' greatest hero: Lieutenant-Colonel George Washington was leading a sizable detachment sent to challenge the French claims when it came into contact with "a small party of thirty-three men led by Ensign Joseph Coulon de Villiers de Jumonville [sent] to meet them and deliver a summons requiring to retire or suffer the consequences."[18] Washington had the French plenipotentiary encampment surrounded and then ordered fire; ten Frenchmen died, including Ensign de Jumonville. On that date, May 28, 1754, Washington had fired the first volleys of a war yet to be declared. Retreating to a poorly chosen site where he was soon besieged by a superior French force, Washington was forced to surrender and accept a return to Virginia with his disarmed troops after having signed a document acknowledging responsibility for *l'assassinat* (the murder) of Jumonville. Coincidentally, Captain Coulon de Villiers had left Illinois escorting a convoy of 120 tons of flour and 40 tons of salted pork meat for the troops at Fort Duquesne. Once at the Fort, Villiers asked for the honor to avenge his young brother and led a successful raid against Fort Granville, in the Allegheny Mountains (near present-day Altoona, Pennsylvania). The prisoners, including three women and seven children, were protected from the fury of the Indian allies and brought back to Fort de Chartres where they were held for ransom.

The 1750's, years of the crisis that would prove fatal to the French establishment of North America, in a perverse way were good years for the Illinois Territory. Illinois, long known as the breadbasket of Lower Louisiana, was now also the major source of food supplies for the Canadian troops in Ohio. New lands needed to be opened to cultivation, and many residents of Kaskaskia, Fort de Chartres, and Cahokia had fields across the Mississippi; a few began to look to the possibility of permanent settlement. Prominent among the satellite communities grafted onto the original geography of dispersed lead-miners, salt-workers, hunters, and occasional traders' *habitations*, was the new town of Ste. Geneviève. Its beginnings were slow: the 1752 Louisiana census gives a total population of twenty-three, including nine landowners, their families, and a few slaves.[19] However, the outcome of the conflict would dramatically increase the population of the Illinois left bank.

The Illinois territory, for once, would not provide a stage for battle. But, as the old French song goes, *Le roi a fait battre tambour*, "the king had ordered to beat the drums," and the call was answered. Illinois faced an uncertain future.

NOTES

1. Battle of Dettingen, June 16, 1743.

2. William Eccles, *The Canadian Frontier, 1534-1760* (revised edition), University of New Mexico Press, 1983, 150.

3. Ibid., 131.

4. The peace parley began at Aix-la-Chapelle on April 24, and the Treaty signed on October 18, 1748.

5. Eccles, *The Canadian Frontier.*, 151.

6. Caldwell, *The French in the Mississippi.*, 89; it took forty-five days for the convoy to Michilimackinac to reach its destination. It carried 9,600 pounds of flour, 489 containers of brandy and 160 of wine; ANC, Series C11A.

7. Eccles, *The Canadian Frontier.*, 151; the dispatch analyzed is from Galissonière to the Minister, September 1, 1748, ANC, Series C11A, vol. 91, 116-123.

8. Norman Ward Caldwell,*The French in the Mississippi Valley, 1740-1750*, The University of Illinois Press, Urbana, 1941, 83.

9. Mr. de Bertet died on January 7, 1749.

10. See Morris S. Arnold, *Colonial Arkansas, 1686-1804*, The University of Arkansas Press, 1991.

11. Alvord, *The Centennial History of the Illinois Country*, 235, FN 27.

12. On the life and career of Jean-Baptiste Bossu, born on September 29, 1720, the son of a surgeon, see Bourée de Poney, *Notice sur la vie et les relations de voyage du Capitaine Jean-Baptiste Homère Bossu*, Châtillon-sur-Seine, 1852; the books by Bossu are: *Nouveaux Voyages aux Indes Occidentales*, 2 vol., Le Jay, Paris, MDCCLXVIII, and *Nouveaux Voyages dans l'Amerique septentrionale*, M. Bossu, ancien Capitaine d'une Compagnie de la Marine, Paris chez A.M. Douin, MDCCLXXVII. The English translation is entitled: *Travels through that part of North America formerly called Louisiana*, by M. Bossu, translated by John Foster, London, 1771.

13. *Travels through that part.*, 131-135.

14. Kerlerec to the Minister, July 14, 1754, ANC, C13A, 38:17; quoted in *The Centennial History.*, 237.

15. The site of the first fort has been the object of intense research, the results of which were published by Edward B. Jelks, Carl J. Ekberg, and Terrance J. Martin, *Excavation at the Laurens Site, Probable Location of Fort de Chartes I*, Illinois Historic Preservation Agency, Springfield, April 1989.

16. Pittman, *Present State of the European Settlements*, 88.

17. Eccles, *The Canadian Frontier.*, 160.

18. Ibid., 164.

19. Ekberg, *Colonial Ste. Genevieve.*, 26-38.

16

British East, Spanish West

T he hostilities in North America began before a formal declaration of war. In the games all nations play, both eighteenth-century Britain and France had already refined the art of diplomatic double-talk to a very modern high level. It was as if both countries had two separate personalities, one European and one Colonial, each government integrating the policies of their two aspects only sporadically.

In Europe, Great Britain and Austria had traditionally allied themselves against French ambitions, and France had supported Prussia, just as traditionally, against the former two. However, this cozily balanced arrangement was about to be radically overturned. Prussia, under Frederick the Great, had been growing more powerful and influential by leaps and bounds, with an ultimate goal of replacing the Austrian dynasty on the throne of the German empire (German emperors being chosen by German electors). Prussia had already gobbled up the rich province of Silesia at the expense of the Austrian Empire, which immediately began seeking a means to retrieve this lost land. Simultaneously, Austria's ally, Britain, was highly motivated to protect the German state of Hanover, now united to her in the person of the King.

To follow the thread of this script—complicated even when simplified in the extreme—we must remember that the King of England, George II, was a German by birth, and had inherited Hanover and Brunswick from his father, George I; these German states made him the most powerful of the German prince electors. Britain, lacking trust in Austria's ability, entered into a secret agreement with Prussia in January, 1756, a secret promptly uncovered by all interested parties. Austrian intrigues vied with those of France, whose King conducted a personal foreign policy quite separate from that of his ministers', all of which led to what is known as the Reversal of Alliance, effectively taking place in May 1756, when France and Austria signed a first treaty at Versailles. Adding their own elements to this tangled imbroglio were Swedish, Polish, Portuguese, Spanish, and Turkish fears and interests, while the main actors were the troops of Britain-Hanover, Prussia, Austria, Russia, and France. Thus was born the Seven Years' War.

But even prior to that declaration of war, and before the appointment of William Pitt as War Minister[1] (the man who would make Britain's struggle a personal anti-French crusade), the British were on the move. The Colonies and the home colonial establishment were clearly determining their own policy.

On land, Major General Edward Braddock had arrived in Virginia the year before, and crossed into the Ohio Valley on July 3, 1755, with 1,459 British regulars and 700 Colonial militia (including Lieutenant-Colonel George Washington). Five days later, only eight miles from Fort Duquesne (present-day Pittsburgh), while crossing a ravine, he and his army were intercepted by a sacrificial small French force of 250 regulars, and Canadian militia accompanied by 600 Indian allies, led by a passionate commander, Captain Daniel de Beaujeu. Braddock's army was almost totally destroyed; a handful of men fled, but the majority were either killed or captured. Braddock himself was mortally wounded.[2] The prisoners were subsequently massacred by the Indian auxiliaries, whom the French officers proved unable to control (Beaujeu was one of the three French officers killed). Engaging in a looting frenzy, the Indians, deaf to command, returned to Fort Duquesne pushing cattle and horses loaded with British baggage in front of them, to the great dismay of the Commandant of Ohio, Claude-Pierre Pecaudy de Contrecoeur, a man whose orders were not usually ignored. This was, unfortunately, not the only instance during the French-Indian War in which prisoners were massacred. It also occurred with Indian allies of the French at Fort William Henry in 1757, and again, with the Iroquois allied to the British in 1758, at Fort Frontenac, as well as at Fort Niagara.

On the high seas, the British were noticeably more successful: one of their naval squadrons had already struck in June 1755, and like a rerun of the preceding war, a French convoy was attacked off the coast of Newfoundland. The French were fortunate to lose only two ships in this action, but elsewhere the British were able to capture, by surprise, 300 merchant vessels and their crews, 8,000 sailors in total. These losses underlined the idea that victory in North America required France to keep the lines of communication open across the Atlantic. The French convoy had carried a reinforcement of 4,000 regular troops, and seventy-one companies out of seventy-eight landed safely in Louisbourg and Quebec.[3] Had the French been able to throw into the conflict a portion of the troops they were using in Europe, conditions would have been favorable to their success. But, reality determining otherwise, they needed to rely on better maneuvering abilities to compensate for their lack of manpower.

Appointed in January 1756, Major General Marquis Louis Joseph de Montcalm-Gozon landed in Quebec on May 13th, charged with the command of the regular troops arriving from France, while the Colonial troops, militia, and Indian contingents remained under the command of the governor.[4] Such an arrangement would have created seeds of conflict in the best of situations; as it was, Montcalm and Vaudreuil, the Governor (who, until 1753, exercised the same function in Louisiana) developed a deep personal dislike for each other. With Montcalm, "hot-tempered, supercilious, continually fuming over petty slights, real or imagined," and Vaudreuil, "resentful, vain, unsure of himself," it was amazing that, at least initially, such a conflict of personalities between the two men responsible for the survival of the colony did not translate into military disaster. In fact, although their plans were sound and well-prepared, for the better part of the first years of the war, the British were constantly out-maneuvered.

In the meantime, the war was coming closer to Illinois. Lieutenant Bossu was about to leave Fort de Chartres, to return to France on medical leave, when a courier arrived in July 1756, from: "*Fort du Quene* to our Commandant, through whom we learned that the English are making big preparations to come to attack this post. Mr. de Macarty has prepared a convoy of food to supply the fort. The *chevalier* de Villiers will command instead of me."[5]

Bossu commanded the downstream convoy to New Orleans; it had arrived from New Orleans with an officer who was a welcome addition to Fort de Chartres, Charles Philippe Aubry. Aubry was later sent to build a new fort on the Ohio River, Fort Ascension, in order to provide an additional lock on the only practical avenue of penetration to the interior. This fort, later known as Fort Massac (across from present-day Paducah, Kentucky) was in operation starting with June 1757. By 1758, British pressure in the West had much intensified. The French had received a re-inforcement of 3,500 regular troops the previous summer, but they were needed to guard the approaches to Quebec. Calls for combattants were sent to the farthest limits of the colony, and post commandants like Hertel de Beaubassin at La Pointe, on Madeline Island, Lake Superior (across from present-day Bayfield, Wisconsin) marched out with his militia and his Chippewa contingent. Aubry left again, this time back to Fort Duquesne, with seventeen *bateaux* carrying troops and supplies. Seven thousand regular and colonial British troops were advancing now on Fort

Duquesne buffeted by several successful delaying actions but not stopped by them. One of the French actions, on September 14th, was conducted by Aubry and the Illinois contingent; they routed the British vanguard, capturing its commander, Major Grant. The handwriting was on the wall, nevertheless; in November of the same year, the French had little choice but to burn Fort Duquesne and withdraw to Fort Machault, on the Allegheny River (near present-day Franklin, Pennsylvania).

Aubry and his detachment returned to Illinois and rested until spring of 1759, when a new corps was organized. This time, Aubry left with 400 men, still by boat and canoe, up the Ohio, then the Wabash River, his mission to establish a liaison with Fort Presqu'ile (Erie, Pennsylvania) and Fort Niagara. The first was found abandoned; near the second he was attacked by General William Johnson. Aubry's fortunes turned and, defeated, he was captured. The contingent from Illinois lost six officers, thirty-two soldiers, fifty-four militiamen, and several Illinois warriors. Among those who managed to elude the trap laid by the British and Iroquois, and return to Illinois, was Philippe Francois de Rastel, *chevalier* de Rocheblave. He had learned his trade under the command of the well-known Charles-Michel Langlade and had "developed a knack for dealing with Indians and a skill in the guerrilla style warfare of the American frontier."[6]

Although by 1759, the British enjoyed overwhelming numerical superiority, the situation was not hopeless, not as long as the British were unable to capture Quebec or draw out its garrison. A naval force brought a new army commanded by Major General James Wolfe to achieve just that end. To provoke the French, General Wolfe unleashed the American Rangers in a campaign of systematic destruction of the countryside and the killing of its inhabitants. The French responded with a call to arms of all boys from the age of fifteen on, a true *levée en masse*, a general uprising of the Canadian people for the defense of their homes. The Battle of the *Plaines d'Abraham*, under the walls of Quebec on September 14, 1759, sealed the fate of Canada. The *chevalier* de Levis, who took command of the French army after the battlefield death of Montcalm, continued a gallant fight; but on September 7, 1760, in Montreal, Levis had only 200 men left, and Major General Jeffrey Amherst had 17,000. Denied the honors of war, Levis wanted to fight on, but was overruled by Vaudreuil. During the night Levis burned his flags and the British entered the town the next day.[7]

By the Fall of 1761, only the Illinois Territory was not under the British flag. Macarty, who had been made a colonel as reward for his services, had left for New Orleans in 1760, summoned to serve as an aide to the Governor. His replacement was Captain Pierre Joseph Neyon de Villiers (brother-in-law of Governor Kerlerec, but who shared little in character with him otherwise). Captain Saucier, the military engineer who had built Fort de Chartres, but who at the time commanded Cahokia, resigned his commission, remained in the town, and took up residence. His house can still be seen today, one of the region's most outstanding examples of the colonial-style architecture favored during the French period.[8]

Illinois was put on war footing. Fort Massac was totally repaired; this was where the British would first appear if they mounted an expedition by boat. On May 22, 1760, Rocheblave was sent with fifty soldiers of marine to reinforce the garrison. Indian runners had already signaled the British at St. Joseph, at Miami, at Ouiatenon; the enemy was coming. Luckily, unexpected help arrived from the North: apprised of the imminent surrender of New France by Vaudreuil, the commandant of Michilimackinac, *sieur* de Beaujeu-Villemonde, had left with 132 soldiers and, after a difficult trek, arrived at Fort de Chartres during the spring of 1761.

Meanwhile, overseas the French army, successful during the beginning of the war, was equally the victim of bad leadership. By 1760, Prussian and Anglo-Hanoverian armies were victorious all over Germany, and the French colonial empire had suffered grievously from the whole experience. Senegal, France's first African colony, had been lost to the British, as were the colonies in India and the West Indies. It was time for able professionals to replace ineffectual courtiers. On December 3, 1758, the Count of Stainville, a highly recommended diplomat, was recalled from his embassy in Vienna, made Duke of Choiseul and Secretary of State for Foreign Affairs.

The initial peace negotiations between France and Britain began in March 1761; they were to be long and arduous, complicated for the French by the need to protect the interests of their Spanish allies, with whom they were to sign the same year a *pacte de famille*, or family compact, linking the interests of all reigning Bourbons. Negotiations were momentarily interrupted in the fall, and Britain declared war on Spain on January 2, 1762. While Spain moved into Portugal, Britain's long-standing ally, in quick succession she lost Cuba and the Philippines. Neither of the major parties wanted nor could afford to continue on a course certain to bleed its economy. William Pitt was no longer present in the British govern-

Re-enactment of British soldiers from the French & Indian War period during one of the annual Rendez-vous at Fort de Chartres, organized by the State of Illinois during the first weekend of June. (Photograph by Charles Balesi.)

ment to argue in favor of a "hard line" position; he had been forced to resign in October, 1761, and King Geoge III, who came to the throne the year before, was anxious to obtain a speedy peace. France and Spain resumed peace negotiations; both could expect some loss of territory. Not a small part of the business community in England considered the French island of Guadeloupe, with its sugar and molasses, a better spoils of war than Canada, plagued by long winter months and a hostile population. When it became obvious, however, that France was finally ready to cede Canada, and Britain ready to accept it, the question of boundaries arose, and along with it, the fate of Illinois. During the sensitive negotiations that ensued, the French attempted to assert the idea that Canada included neither Ohio nor Illinois. Nivernois, the French ambassador to the Court of St. James, had as part of his instructions "to endeavor to secure a neutral Indian buffer state in the region near the Mississippi." [9] All these diplomatic efforts came to naught, and Section VII of the Treaty of Paris, ratified by King Louis XV in 1763, included all the lands of the Illinois up to the Mississippi. By the terms of the Treaty, Spain recovered Cuba and the Philippines, but had to cede Florida to Britain. France suffered the biggest losses: Grenada, St. Vincent, Dominica, and Tobago joined the British West Indies; the other islands were saved because French troops still occupied portions of Prussia. The French departure from the North American continent was complete when, by the secret treaty signed in Fontainebleau on February 10, 1762, Louis XV gave Louisiana (the western bank of the Mississippi) to his cousin Carlos III, King of Spain, as compensation for the loss of Florida. The new Governor of Louisiana—his title having been changed to Director-General—Jean-Jacques d'Abbadie, had just arrived in Louisiana (during June 1763) and was not informed until 1764 of this momentous news.

With the ratification of the Treaty of Paris, Illinois became nominally part of the British colonial empire; nominally only, until such time as British troops would relieve the French garrisons. In the meantime, the population continued life much as before, dreading the day the white ensign with the fleurs-de-lis would be struck down and replaced by the Union Jack, and hoping it might never arrive. As soon as he learned of the signing of the peace treaty, the Commandant of Illinois, Villiers, decided to regroup his forces. Toulon, the officer commanding at Peoria, was recalled to Fort de Chartres, and the garrison at Fort Massac reduced to fifteen men and one officer, its cannons sent to Ste. Genevieve. Villiers was then in the rare position of ruling a territory over which France had relinquished jurisdiction, and unfortunately, in so doing, forced to incur expenses to the Crown.

While under the provisions of the Treaty of Paris the French metropolitan regiments returned to Europe, and most of the Canadians returned to homes often devastated by the war; most, but not all, as the majority of those holding regular officer's commissions chose to leave with their families. But if the French-Canadians, seething in a bitterness compounded by the sense of their King's betrayal, experienced only powerlessness in the face of the invasion, the Indians, although just as angry and bitter, believed they could rise to the challenge and throw the English back to the sea. A leader was needed to bring them together; and he was found in the person of Pontiac, an Ottawa Chief, [10] well-regarded by the Marquis de Montcalm.

Pontiac's diplomatic ability was remarkable; his emissaries left in all directions and even attracted to his conspiracy Indians, until then friendly to the British, who had discovered that with the war over they were no longer deferred to as a powerful force, but regarded as undesirable barbarians. For the first time, Indian nations from the Mississippi to the Atlantic seaboard began to realize their shared common culture; in the exhilarating atmosphere of their new-found consciousness, many among them saw a future free from the Western world, its values, and even its technologies. Pontiac, who operated at a high level of sophistication, knew better and based his plans on the return to the scene of the French. This line of thought may seem foolish from our vantage point, aware of the hard facts behind Choiseul's decision to sue for peace; but, from the perspective of New France, while the last war had been lost, there was always the next. The French civilians wanted to believe that their abandonment was nothing but a temporary tactical move, and so naturally supported Pontiac.

The Ottawa Chief began the general uprising with an attack of Detroit on Monday, May 9, 1763.[11] But the British garrison had been forewarned, and Pontiac and his warriors could not penetrate the fort. A few days later he sent a deputation of five Frenchmen to Illinois with a letter asking the Commandant to send back "... a French officer skilled in the white man's art of siege warfare."[12] But if the British garrison (supported by the cannon of small crafts sailing the lake) kept Pontiac at bay, other Indian contingents were more successful. Fort Sandusky was captured on May 16th, and Fort St. Joseph on the 25th. Fort Miami fell to the French emissaries and their escort on their way to Illinois on the 27th; and still on the same day, two *bateaux* going to Michilimackinac were taken on the Ste. Claire River. On the 28th a detachment of Queen's Rangers, who had put to shore for the night at Pointe Pelée, was almost completely destroyed. June 1st, the same emissaries who took Fort Miami seized the British garrison of Fort Ouiatenon, carrying it off with them to Fort de Chartres. On June 2nd, it was the turn of Fort Michilimackinac to fall to the surprise attack of the Chippewa. Twenty British soldiers out of a 35-man garrison were killed outright.

Other actions followed. Fort Pitt was besieged for one entire month; on June 16th, Fort Venango (Franklin, Pennsylvania) was destroyed, the garrison massacred; Fort Le Boeuf (Waterford, Pennsylvania) was attacked the next day (the garrison escaped), Fort Presqu'ile (Erie, Pennsylvania) was taken on the 20th. In spite of these successes, Pontiac was doomed to face the eventual reaction of the British command. By the beginning of fall, British reinforcements were in Detroit, and British columns were fanning across the land to retake the lost forts. On the night of October 23, the Cadet Dequindre, from the French garrison of Fort de Chartres, arrived in Detroit, carrying letters written in response to Pontiac's appeals. They were letters for Pontiac, for the French settlers, and for the British commandant, Major Henry Gladwin. The tidings were not good: "Pontiac's dream was broken off. There would be no help from the French, no army coming up the St. Lawrence or up the Mississippi. The French were through fighting the English, and the English were masters of the French forts and dominions. He, Pontiac, was fighting a hopeless war. There could be no victory if the French opposed him too."[13]

All that Pontiac could do was to sign a peace treaty with Gladwin and accept the French invitation to move across the Mississippi with his followers (an invitation extended also to the French settlers), escaping possible reprisals once the British would have reestablished their position. Furious to see Pontiac escape, the British nevertheless had little recourse. General Gage, writing to Minister Halifax, read beyond the words and offers of good offices in the letter that Villiers addressed to Major Gladwin: "Your lordship will observe that Monsieur de Neyon in the letter to the Indians, gives them a hint of sending them supplies from the Mississippi, and acquainting them [that] the French are to possess this side of the River opposite to the English."[14]

For General Gage, Villiers' letter to Pontiac was a not too subtle attempt to redirect the fur trade away from Montreal towards New Orleans. These fears were not unwarranted, as a party of 150 Detroit Indians was already in New Orleans to sell pelts. A direct consequence of Pontiac's action was a reinforcement of British resolve to limit the settlers' western expansion to the Alleghenies—and protect the fur trade—a major cause of unhappiness for the Anglo-Americans.

Pontiac slowly made his way west, accompanied by many Ottawa families and French settlers. In early spring 1764, he stopped at Fort Miami, Fort Ouiatenon, and Fort Vincennes, the last being where more than one hundred French families lived and where Captain Louis St. Ange de Bellerive was in command. On April 12th, Pontiac arrived at Fort de Chartres where he was received with respect by the officers, and with awe by the Illinois Indian chiefs. Pontiac had not given up and tirelessly embarked upon a campaign to federate the Indians west of Lake Michigan in armed resistance to the British. Meeting three days later in council, he had not been able to convince Villiers, of course, but had hoped that his words would reach the Governor and reach the King: "My father, we pray the king to have pity on us.... All thy children, my father, even when beat and conquered by the English love better to die than to fail the French in anything."[15]

On June 13, 1764, Neyon de Villiers passed his command to Ste. Ange de Bellerive, who would retain forty men; a few were assigned to Ste. Genevieve, but most of them left for New Orleans with Villiers. Bellerive was ordered to wait at Fort de Chartres until the arrival of the British troops. In August of the same year Pontiac, with his ally and friend Charlot Kaské, the metis Chief of the Shawnee (his father was German), came back to Fort de Chartres seeking help from St. Ange who could only turn them down. They did find aid from the French settlers who gave them enough supplies to continue their travels. Pontiac went on criss-crossing Illinois and made bold trips back to Detroit, looking for ways to rekindle a general uprising. In November, Kaské left Illinois to directly appeal to the Governor in New Orleans where he was soon joined by the Illinois Chief, Levacher. D'Abbadie was moved but could not give them any comfort. After his death in February, the determined ambassadors pleaded just as vainly to his successor, Charles Philippe Aubry, the veteran of the War for New France, now the new—and the last—Director General of Louisiana.

Back in England controversy immediately arose over which of the two, the Crown or the American Colonies, was to assume control of the western territories, including Illinois. Lord Egremont, Secretary of State, proposed in a communication to the Lords of Trade to place these Illinois territories under the control of Canada.[16] The text of the proposal, referring only to "Indian country" and "fugitives from justice," established for the French in Illinois the possibly dangerous precedent of a legal vacuum. While Lord Shelburne, President of the Board of Trade, expressed concern about the enormous expense in troops the proposal would incur, "No hint appears in the correspondence that the Minister had any idea of the existence of the several thousand French inhabitants of the West."[17]

Those who were partisans for direct rule of Illinois by Canada's military government won out, with control of the Indian trade the major factor in the Crown's decision. To turn the West over to the colonial governments would open the land to settlers who would have encroached upon the Indians and destroyed the fur trade; a trade which, now that the French had been pushed out of the picture, was expected to bring untold riches to the mother country and help pay for the war costs. It was not until December, 1764, that at last, the presence of French people in Illinois was acknowledged by the British. On the 30th, General Thomas Gage, "Major-General of the King's Armies, Colonel of the 22nd Regiment, General Commander-in-Chief of all the forces of His Majesty in North America," issued a proclamation from his headquarters in New York City which read as follows:

> Whereas, by the peace concluded in Paris on the 10th of February, 1763, the country of Illinois has been ceded to His Britannic Majesty, and the taking possession of the said country of the Illinois by the troops of His Majesty though delayed, has been determined upon, we have found it good to make known to the inhabitants: That His Majesty grants to the inhabitants of the Illinois the liberty of the Catholic religion, as it has already been granted to His subjects in Canada. . . . That His Majesty, moreover, agrees that the French inhabitants, or others who have been subject of the Most Christian King, may retire, in full safety and freedom, whereas they please, even to New Orleans, or any part of Louisiana, although it should happen that the Spaniards take possession of it in the name of His Catholic Majesty, and transport their effects, as well as their person, without restraint upon their emigration. . . . That those who choose to retain their lands and become subjects of His Majesty, shall enjoy the same rights and privileges, the same security for their person and effects and liberty of trade, as the old subjects of the King: They are commanded by these presents, to take the oath of fidelity and obedience to his Majesty, in presence of Sieur Sterling, Captain of the Highland Regiment, the bearer hereof, and furnished with our full powers for this purpose.[18]

It was a sensible declaration and meant to reassure. It remained, however, for Captain Stirling to be able to communicate its contents to the French themselves. Bringing about effective British control over the western territories would be long and difficult. The first officers sent to reconnoiter Illinois failed to complete their mission and were fortunate to escape with their lives on a journey in the midst of open Indian hostility. It was somehow ironic that now the Indians, alone, were continuing the

Thomas Hutchins, *A Plan of Several Villages in the Illinois Country*, London, 1778. (The Newberry Library) resistance as the time of the French in the West was slowly but surely coming to an end. The people who lived along the Mississippi had only to watch the troops and the administration packing, and leaving behind only a skeleton crew to man Fort de Chartres, to understand the inevitable. The best military building complex west of Quebec was now essentially a warehouse and an office for a newly arrived entrepreneur whose fortunes would have great impact on the future of the West.

Pierre Laclède, who headed the firm of Maxent, Laclède and Dée, had been granted exclusive Indian trade rights for the Upper Mississippi by Governor D'Abbadie, on the look-out for ways to spur Louisiana's economy. Within weeks of receiving his grant, Laclède had left, along with his fifteen-year old assistant, Auguste Chouteau, to seek an appropriate site for a trading post north of Ste. Genevieve. The location he selected was south of the junction of the Missouri and Mississippi Rivers, almost across from Cahokia. On Feruary 15, 1764, the young Chouteau and a team of thirty laborers felled the first trees on the tract which would become the city of St. Louis. To the French of the Misssisippi Valley, Laclède and Chouteau symbolized the future. With the shrewd entrepreneurial acumen that seems to span nationalities, Laclède, while building on the west bank, was busily contemplating the commercial possibilities the British were opening, with grand plans to make the most out of the settlers' bad dreams:

> . . . all in his power to hinder the French from going down . . . telling them that the English government was not so terrible as they wished to make them believe; that for his part, he had a much more favorable opinion of it. However, if, in consequence of false prejudice, they did not wish to remain under the British government, he would recommend them to go up to his new settlement, and he would facilitate for them the means of getting there with their effects. . . . several famlies accepted these offers.[19]

Between those who left with Neyon de Villiers for the glitter of New Orleans, and those who went across to Laclède's settlement, their impact on the eastern bank was consequent: Nouvelle Chartres, the village adjacent to the Fort, where forty families had lived at the close of the war, was now deserted. In leaving, the French removed all that could be taken—not even the door frames remained. The British would enter a ghost town. In Prairie du Rocher, twenty-five famlies remained; in Cahokia, sixty. Kaskaskia, the largest community, with 600 whites and

500 blacks, was less immediately affected, although Ste. Genevieve, across the river, already numbered seventy famlies, most of them newly arrived.[20]

The correspondence between General Gage and the Minister, the Earl of Halifax, contains savory details of British difficulties in taking effective possession of Illinois.[21] It includes countless litanies against French and Indians, the first invariably treacherous, and the second, unredeemingly barbarian; still smarting from Pontiac's war, Gage reminded Colonel Bradstreet that if the Indians started new hostilities, ". . . the colonel will use every means in his Power to destroy them . . . "[22] The French? "make the French inhabitants sensible that they are now British subjects..." Having failed to establish British control by means of individual officers with light escort, such as Captain Thomas Morris of the 17th Regiment of Foot—in early fall, 1764, he was prevented for the second time from going any farther than Fort Miami by a coalition of Senecas, Delaware, and Shawnee—Gage resorted to sending large detachments. Taking over Illinois was becoming an urgent matter; all together there were a series of nine failed attempts. Finally, on October 9, 1765, Captain Stirling and 100 men of the 42nd Regiment of Foot—the Black Watch Regiment—reached Fort de Chartres. The next day, Bellerive officially handed over the fort, bringing to an end the last remnant of French political control over the east bank of the Mississippi River. On the 23rd, he walked under the gate of the Fort for the last time, embarked with his troops in *bateaux*, and sailed fifteen miles upstream to the future St. Louis, where he immediately assumed his new position.

From the very first day of his command over Illinois, Captain Stirling was confronted with a bevy of problems, ranging from a shortage of food supplies, to the continuous emigration south and west of the French communities. Aside from the article in the Treaty of Paris concerning the cessation of Illinois to the English and the guarantees granted to the Canadian population, Stirling's only general guideline, serving as well as his sole source of political instructions, was the text of General Gage's "Proclamation." When Stirling went to Kaskaskia a week after his arrival, he quickly learned that this was insufficient to deal with immediate demands of a political nature. In Kaskaskia the French presented him with a petition protesting the eighteen months given them to decide whether they would take the oath to the British Crown or leave. They argued that the date of Gage's petition (December 1764) meant that they would have to make up their minds on the spot. Stirling's initial reaction was to refuse, since his mission was to carry out measures, not to take them; nevertheless, he quickly realized that unless some kind of compromise was immediately devised, the French population would leave en masse within a few days. He offered the possibility of taking a temporary oath, with a final decision no later than March 1766, which they accepted. He then sat down and wrote his report to General Gage. Months later, Gage read it and approved.[23]

What was then inaugurated in British Illinois was a policy of makeshift legal and administrative decisions, promulgated and implemented by British line officers.

Returning to Fort de Chartres, Stirling hoped that after this compromise, few people would cross the river, but, as he wrote shortly later:

> I have found since that, that was only a blind, for many of them drove off their cattle in the night and carried off their Effects and grain, which I did everthing to prevent but I was not in condition to end partys to the two ferrys of Cahokia and Caskaskias, considering the disposition of the Indians, a good deal of cattle and some grain has been carried off, and if the gentlest methods are not used with those that stay, who are the best, we shall lose them too.[24]

Stirling had the additional problem of trying to establish some type of local administration. After talking to various members of the community, he appointed a judge, Mr. Lagrange, "to decide all disputes according to the law and Customs of the country,"[25] meaning the *Coutume de Paris* , and with the right for the plaintiff to appeal to the Commandant. The flag had changed, the language of the troops had changed, but the system remained the same.

Captain Stirling's functions ended with the arrival of Major Farmar, who arrived from Mobile overland with a detachment of the 34th Regiment of Foot, after an incredible eight-month march. It was none too soon, for Stirling's hundred men were hard put to carry out normal duties much less to prevent the French traders from New Orleans carrying on business as usual with the Indians. The state of supplies, however, was made worse with the arrival of additional soldiers, the French sending food clandestinely across the river rather than selling to the British. Major Farmar complained that: "The soil of this country is in general very good and fertile. . . . but the present inhabitants are and always have been too indolent and lazy to bestow any pains upon cultivating their lands." [26]

Major Farmar made several attempts to create some business trust, signing five-livre coupons for the soldiers to use as payment, for instance, but also made his share of psychological mistakes, such as renaming Fort de Chartres "Fort Cavendish." Farmar's poor opinion of the new subjects of His Majesty's were more than shared by an officer of his staff, Lieutenant Fraser who wrote: "The Illinois Indians are about 600 able to bear arms; nothing can equal their passion for drunkenness but that of the French inhabitants, who are for the greatest part drunk every day. While they can get drink to buy in the colony, they import more of this article from New Orleans than they do of any other and never fail to meet a speedy and good market of it." [27]

To this description, Fraser added that they, the French, were all transported convicts whose essential traits were cruelty and dishonesty. They were, however, extravagant in their display of friendship which meant only to be deceiving, hardly more than six months had passed since the arrival of the British troops and the pattern of mutual distrust had now solidified into well-rounded attitudes. The French expected the worst from the British troops and with the other side of the Mississippi as a constant reminder of what they once had had—even though it was now under the government of Spain—they would not accept the *fait accompli* of the British annexation. The British officers, engrossed in their multiple and conflicting responsibilities toward their soldiers and the King's new subjects, lacking a good system of intelligence, with communication problems because of language (Stirling had to ask New York, where the Military headquarters was, for more interpreters), reverted to the cliché of the drunken, unambitious Frenchmen and their Indian accomplices as the source of their troubles. Yet, this same area had been Louisiana's granary and the same individuals, once across the Mississippi, were able to build anew.

The French, in addition to their inherent hostility, had some legitimate concerns regarding the protection of their traditional rights. The disappearance of the French administrative apparatus had left a vacuum the British government was not filling. This lack of government was in fact also the concern of the English civilians who wanted to trade in Illinois, as is clearly reflected in the Articles of Agreement of the Illinois Company, drawn up in March, 1766, between John Baynton, the Philadelphia merchant, and the Commissioner of Indian Affairs in North America. It reads, in part: "Whereas it is expected that a Civil Government will be established by His Majesty with Illinois country at or near Fort de

Chartres and that sufficient quantity of land for the settlement of an English colony there will in a short time be purchased of the parties for that purpose. . . . "[28]

Such a settlement would have been in complete contradiction with the terms of the Royal Proclamation concerning the newly-acquired territories issued on October 7, 1763, which clearly stipulated: "And we do strictly forbid . . . all our loving subjects from making any purchases or settlements whatever, or taking possession of any of the lands above reserved."[29]

In the meantime, while there was still no provision contemplated for the formation of a civilian government, suggestions were made for the closing of the forts and the removal of the garrisons because of the cost and also the difficulty of communication.[30] General Gage disagreed. There was a large commercial traffic on the Mississippi River, he argued, which was open to both French and Spanish nationals, as well as to the English, and the only way to control illicit trade from Illinois to New Orleans was to maintain a military presence in the French settlements.

While the discussion on what to do with the garrisons continued, a new commandant for Illinois, Lieutenant-Colonel John Reed, had been appointed, and under him the situation in Illinois deteriorated even further. While this senior officer was accused of all sorts of petty tyrannies by the French inhabitants and his subordinates as well, the French traders from Louisiana continued to enjoy the run of the country. The British traders, on the other hand, unwelcome by the Illinois Indians, were forced to remain in the settlements, or very close to them. In fact, the Indians there, even after the failure of Pontiac's uprising, were still a threatening force to the British. When Reed, through his excesses, was finally recalled and temporarily replaced by an officer who seemed to have excelled in the art of "mending fences," Captain Forbes, the rumblings of an imminent insurrection lapped the walls of Fort de Chartres with a few killings, rather daring, of English civilians. Captain Forbes ordered all male English civilians to form a militia (they numbered about sixty) and instructed the French militia captains to call out their men. The latter bluntly refused; they had no quarrel with the Indians. Forbes insisted and the French threatened to cross the river. Forbes remained polite but firm, and the French militia was finally called out.

On September 5, 1768, Illiois received its most controversial commandant—Lieutenant-Colonel Wilkins. With none of the tact that Forbes was able to display, Wilkins took all sorts of unpopular measures including granting lands to English merchants, in particular to the Baynton, Wharton, and Morgan Company. Not surprisingly, when a conflict between the Missouri and Illinois Indians erupted, the French flatly refused to be called out for military service. Gage was informed, though not given the underlying reasons.

The only aspect of Colonel Wilkins' tenure not a source of complication was his relations with the Catholic church; this was due to a great extent to the majority of Irish Catholics among the soldiers of the garrison. Further, since the French crown had expelled the Jesuits from Louisiana in 1764, there was no one to service Illinois until the bishop of Quebec was able to appoint an older priest in 1768, and after his death in that year, another somewhat controversial figure, Father Pierre Gibault.

On October 23, 1768, Johnstone wrote to Hillsborough back in London that: "It had been expected that the Illinois villages would be the center of trade for the English side of the Upper Mississippi Valley, just as it had been one of the centers during the French regime."[31] But the villages no longer were such centers. The business they used to carry on was now done on the other side of the river, at Laclède's settlement at Ste. Genevieve. This was a great disappointment to the Crown. The traffic of peltries had been the main reason for French and British quarrels in North America for the past hundred years. It was then expected that the traffic would continue exclusively along trade routes leading to the East, and instead most, if not all, of it was floating down the Mississippi. Looking at the customs receipts for the 1763-1775 period shows that since the capture of French holdings east of the Mississippi, the British fur trade had in fact declined. The loss of revenue was even more injurious to the British treasury because the maintenance of British garrisons in the West was so costly.

The failure of the British to divert the trade to themselves can be traced directly to the attitudes of their traders towards both the Indians and the French. British methods were often a combination of cheap whiskey, double talk, and arrogance. While the British traders could barely leave the settlements, French traders were still roaming the rivers of Ohio and Illinois years after the cession of Canada and the Western Territories. It would have been to the advantage of the British Crown to entrust her new subjects with complete responsibility for the fur trade and to have kept her own traders out of it, and while some companies did realize after a time that hiring French agents was profitable, the enmity between the two peoples was too deep for such an arrangement to be adopted throughout.

On August 24, 1770, the French inhabitants assembled in Kaskaskia and resolved to send a delegation to see General Gage in New York to ask for a civil government. The two Frenchmen sent by the five villages reached New York one year later with an outline of a local constitution but it was rejected by Gage, who instead proposed a plan to combine a few representative voices of the community with a larger number of appointed officers of the Crown.[32]

Colonel Wilkins, against whom serious charges regarding the finances of the regiment had been sworn by junior officers, was dismissed from the service during September, 1772. Major Hamilton took over temporarily the responsibilities of command and turned them over to Captain Hugh Lord before returning to New York. That year, Captain Lord had to abandon Fort de Chartres after a disastrous flood ruined the western wall, and he then moved to the fort above Kaskaskia, renamed "Fort Gage."

During the next two years, Captain Lord, with a greatly reduced garrison, was able to gain the confidence of the French subjects through a consistent good-will policy. The French seemed to have given up on the matter of a civil government and concerned themselves with day-to-day subsistence. Lord reported to Gage in 1773 that "The little money that circulates now comes first from the troops."[33] The area would have been ripe for colonization by British settlers, the French having lost much of their spirit. Ironically, the integrity of the French character of the area was being maintained by the British Crown. In 1774, General Gage annulled all the grants and purchases of land which had been made in Illinois in contravention of the Proclamation of 1763, a decision adversely affecting the two major trading companies of the area.

On May 7, 1774, the Earl of Darmouth introduced a bill in the House of Lords to propose persuading the conquered French Canada to accept the surrounding British empire with a better heart. This bill became the Quebec Act, which took effect on June 14th of that year. By the terms of this piece of legislation, French law applied to all civil and property litigations; indeed, along with the integrity of the Catholic religion, one of the main concerns of the Canadians. But for Illinois, the Quebec Act was of major importance for it brought to an end the administrative limbo that had been its lot for the past decade, and reaffirmed its link with Canada. As Clarence Carter wrote: "The Quebec Act did more. The Illinois country was still under military administration. Since most of the white people living there were French, it was decided to incorporate that part of Great Britain's possession into the Province of Quebec."[34]

The American colonies had expected to extend their claim all the way to the Mississippi and were very bitter that the Crown would favor French Catholics and savages over them. Although not generally mentioned as a cause of the American Revolution, the Quebec Act did, in fact, have an effect on the decision for independence.[35]

In the spring of 1776, Captain Lord left Illinois and with him went all the troops. Troubles in the West were increasing and the commander-in-chief of the British forces in North America had made the decision to regroup the isolated garrisons of the west.

Before his departure, Captain Lord appointed as his successor and the sole representative of the British government in Illinois, the *Chevalier* de Rocheblave. What an extraordinary turn of events! Rocheblave, who had fought the British, was now the embodiment of their rule. His career was certainly interestingly varied. We found him captain on half-pay in New Orleans in 1763; the same year he was back in Illinois and married to the daughter of a bourgeois from Kaskaskia, and an officer in the militia. Then he was the commanding officer of Ste. Genevieve in 1765, a position he occupied under the Spanish regime, whom he rallied against without hesitation. Falling from grace with the Spanish government, he left the Mississippi in 1770, leaving a few debts behind. It is easy to imagine that as an authentic gentleman, he must have been welcomed in the British officers' circle, leading to the eventual appointment as His Majesty's representative.

Rocheblave may, or may not, have been a man who "cherished no flag and was willing to serve any sovereign that suited his interest."[36] But certainly he was one of those extraordinary characters that only the combination of vast lands and wars can conjure.

Rocheblave, who was granted an annual stipend of 200 pounds a year, remained the acting Lieutenant-Governor until his capture by George Rogers Clark and his American Rangers on July 4, 1778, a raid that terminated British rule in Illinois. Rocheblave had kept up an active correspondence with his British superiors, and to all appearances, he seems to have been an effective official although totally without means. His tenure, however, does not qualify as a continuation of British military presence. That ended with Captain Lord.

In April 1764, Pierre Laclède left Fort de Chartres and crossed the Mississippi to inspect the progress made on the post by his young assistant. As news of the cession of Louisiana to Spain had not reached western

Detail showing Cahokia and St. Louis in 1796. From Victor Collot, "A Map of the Country of the Illinois" in *Voyage dans l'Amérique du Nord*, Paris, 1826. (The Newberry Library)

Illinois, Laclède named the post St. Louis, honoring the King of France, Louis XV. The prospect of starting a new life would not prevent disgruntled settlers with movable property—to wit, slaves, tools, and cattle, plus the means to ferry them across the Mississippi—from tempting fortune in the new settlement, and thereby, increasing its population. It mattered little to them that St. Louis was nicknamed *Pain court*, or "bread shortage," because as all energies were turned to the fur trade and none to the plow, the flour had to come from Ste. Genevieve. Nicknames can be deceiving; after all, didn't the few Spanish soldiers sent upriver nickname Ste. Genevieve "Miseria?"

Laclède's action symbolized the future. If both the highest authorities, Bellerive and Rocheblave, were now acting on behalf of the King of Spain, nothing else changed during these crucial first years. When Spain's first governor, Don Antonio de Ulloa, arrived in New Orleans in 1766, accompanied by a token force, he had little choice but to work with the French administrative structures still intact under Aubry. Aware of the commercial importance of the Upper Mississippi in 1767, Ulloa sent a small contingent under a captain, Don Francisco Rui, with orders to establish two posts on the Missouri, near its confluence with the Mississippi. In short order, Rui managed to alienate all the personnel working under him during construction of the new fort, Fort Don Carlos, as well as the inhabitants of St. Louis, who were infuriated by the captain's new restriction on their trade. Wisely, Rui was recalled and replaced by a much more amiable administrator, Don Pedro Piernas, who made his first voyage to St. Louis in 1768, but had to return to New Orleans where the French had just expelled Ulloa in a bloodless coup. Ulloa's successor, Alexander O'Reilly, an Irishman serving Spain, would prove to be a brutal overseer; landing with a large contingent of troops, he quickly crushed the French, and had several high-ranking officers shot. If Illinois was not affected by the repression which fell on the capital, it was due in great part to Bellerive, the commandant of the territory, and Rocheblave, commandant of Ste. Genevieve.

These two individuals, whether due to their wisdom or a shrewd evaluation of their interests, were not about to join some new heroic, but doomed, adventure. To support their policy of adaptation, they were able to count on the influence exercised by the Vallés, who were the richest family of Ste. Genevieve. Francois Vallé senior (to distinguish him from his son, similarly named Francois) was also Captain of the Militia in Ste. Genevieve, a function that had retained all of its original importance. When Piernas returned to Illinois in 1770 as Lieutenant-Governor, a new position created by O'Reilly to insure effective control, he carried with his instructions the reconfirmation of Francois Vallé's rank, effectively establishing him as "a one-man court." [36] Rocheblave, whose actions were increasingly being criticized, was replaced on June 15, 1770, by Lieutenant Louis Dubreuil Villars, a French officer in the Spanish service, who later, by wedding one of Francois Vallé's daughters, certainly proved that harmony had returned to the seat of power. Ste. Genevieve, a growing community (census for 1772 indicated at 691 people, black and white) with half the population involved in the fur trade, was threatened only by cyclical flooding of the Mississippi. Eventually, in the mid-1780s, after a particularly devastating incursion of the Mississippi, the inhabitants began to resettle the village from its original location, near the bank, to the position it now occupies, approximately a mile up a rise from the water.

While Ste. Genevieve was well on its way to becoming the center of activities that Kaskaskia had been, a successful demographic growth of Western Illinois was of constant concern to Spain, well aware of the continuous attempts by British traders to cross the Mississippi in search of furs.

The British were reacting to the persistent drain in fur trade in their new western territory. The most successful British expeditions across the river were ones to recruit French *voyageurs*, but transacting business under two different flags, neither one their own, was threatening to force the French into fratricidal competition. In 1772, Jean-Marie Ducharme and a party of *voyageurs* from Montreal went up the Missouri with two boatloads of trade goods, passing Fort Don Carlos undetected under the cover of night. For four months they traded in the Osage country before interception by an expedition led by Pierre Laclède. Ducharme himself as well as several of his men escaped, but the furs he collected were confiscated and the remaining voyageurs brought to St. Louis where they were questioned by the Lieutenant-Governor. Even if, on balance, there were more Canadians clandestinely travelling down the Mississippi to sell their goods in New Orleans, the Spanish authorities knew that eventually, enough British traders would succeed in crossing the Mississippi and bringing serious disruption to the colony they had just begun, to incorporate them into their empire. A project was advanced to give incentive to the Illinois settlers living under British rule to cross and resettle under the flag of Spain. The obvious difficulties encountered by the British military administration recounted earlier in this chapter made the Spanish project feasible. French Illinois under the British was slowly disintegrating and this unrest had been communicated to the Indian population. Pontiac's assassination in Cahokia in 1769, by a Peoria Illinois at the instigation of English merchants (his body had been brought back to St. Louis and buried with full military honors by Bellerive) had led to a full-scale civil war among Indians, making the country even less safe.

Communications between the two artificially separated communities remained strong; the Mississippi was no "Berlin Wall," even if British launches patrolled its waters checking the contraband. There was only one serious obstacle to bringing the remaining households over to the western bank: financial guarantees to subsidize the impoverished farmers. By the time the Spanish Crown authorized the governor to provide such assistance in 1778, the British were no longer present to enforce their government's authority as the American Revolution in the East had necessitated their withdrawal from the area. Uncertainty paralyzed Illinois; Indians, suddenly deprived of support from supplies they had depended on for a century, first from the French, then from the British, were flocking to St. Louis and Ste. Genevieve for relief, creating new problems for the new Lieutenant-Governor, Don Francisco Cruzat. Last, but not least, rumor was rife that the American revolutionaries were on their way to the Mississippi.

NOTES

1. William Pitt, 1st Earl of Chatham, 1708-1778, English Statesman, whose name is associated with the British policy aiming at diminishing the role of France on the Continent and overseas.

2. General Edward Braddock had left from Cumberland, Maryland, the preceding spring; his soliders cut the first road west crossing the Alleghenies; he is buried in Great Meadows, Pennsylvania.

3. Their commander was Baron Jean-Armand de Kieskau; he would be captured during the battle for Fort William Henry, at Lake George.

4. Montcalm, born near Nimes in 1712, a soldier since age twelve; he died in Quebec, on September 12, 1759, of wounds received during the battle of the *Plaines d'Abraham.*

5. Jean-Baptiste Homere Bossu, *Nouveaux voyages dans l'Amerique Septentrionale*, M. Bossu ancien Capitaine d'une compagnie de la Marine, Paris, A.M. Douin, 1772, 205.

6. Carl Ekberg, *Colonial Ste. Genevieve.*, 336.

7. The conduct of the Seven-Year War, or so-called "French-Indian War," was the object of an unprecedented in-depth study prepared by the *Ministère de la Défense, Etat-Major de l'Armée de Terre, Service Historique,* Château de Vincennes, 1978, for the *Commission Française d'Histoire Militaire,* participating in the international Colloquium of Military History, in Ottawa, August 19-27, 1978. This study, which would have deserved translation into English, included four parts: I, Colonel Jean Delmas, *Conflits des sociétés au Canada français pendant la Guerre de Sept Ans et leur influence sur les operations;* II, Jean Bérenger and Philippe Roy, *Les relations des troupes réglées (troupes de terre et de la marine) avec les canadiens;* III, Colonel Roger Michalon, *Vaudreuil et Montcalm, les hommes, leurs relations, influence de ces relations sur la conduite de la guerre 1756-1759;* and, IV, Chef d'escadron André Cousine and Patrice Romet, *La politique indigène de la France au Canada de 1750 à 1760.*

8. John Francis Snyder, *Captain John Baptiste Saucier at Fort Chartres in the Illinois, 1751-1763,* Peoria, Illinois, 1901.

9. Instructions of September 2, 1762, quoted in Theodore Calvin Pease, *Anglo-French Boundary Disputes in the West, 1749-1763*, collection of the Illinois Historical Library.

10. Pontiac's tribal origins have been given many versions; he probably was born around 1718.

11. See Howard H. Peckman, *Pontiac and the Indian Uprising*, The University of Chicago Press, 1947, and Milo Milton Quaife, *The Siege of Detroit in 1763*, The Lakeside Press, Chicago, 1958.

12. Ibid., 147.

13. Peckman, *Pontiac.*, 236-37.

14. Letter from General Gage to George Montague Dunk, Lord Halifax, appointed Secretary of State for the Southern Department, New York, December 23rd, 1763.

15. Minutes of the Council held at Fort de Chartres, April 15, 1764, in Peckman, *Pontiac.*, 246-50.

16. Lords of Trade to the King, July 14, 1763, *Canadian Constitutional Documents, 1759-1801*, 10-11.

17. Clarence Edwin Carter, *Great Britain and the Illinois Country, 1763-1774*, The American Historical Association, Washington, 1910, 17.

18. New York, December 30, 1764, in *American State Papers*, 11, 200, and in John B. Dillon, *History of Indiana*, Bingham and Doughty, Indianapolis, 1839, 80-81.

19. John Francis McDermott, *The Early History of St. Louis*, Historical Documents Foundations, St. Louis, 1952, 53-54.

20. Natalia Belting, *Kaskaskia Under the French Regime*, 39.

21. The correspondence of General Gage, a collection of 6,000 documents, is kept at the Public Records Office, in London. A partial transcript can be found at the Library of Congress, the missing copies, *Collection of Viscount Gage*, are kept at the Library of the University of Michigan. The documents were published by Clarence Edwin Carter, *The Correspondence of General Thomas Gage with the Secretary of State, 1763-1775*, 2 vol., Yale University Press, New Haven, 1931.

22. Ibid., May 12, 1764, vol. 1, 28.

23. Stirling to Gage, October 18, 1766, Public Records Office, American and West Indian Series, vol. 122.

24. Stirling to Gage, December 15, 1765, Public Records Office, Colonial Office, 5-84, folio 223.

25. Stirling to Gage, December 16, 1765, ibid.

26. Major Farmar to General Gage, March 19, 1766, Public Records Office, Colonial Office, 5-84, folio 421-C.

27. Lieutenant Fraser to General Haldimand, May 5, 1766, British Museum, man. 21686, folio 34, L. 8.

28. Historical Society of Pennsylvania Document, in Alvord and Carter, *The New Regime*, 203.

29. *Canadian Constitutional Documents*, 119.

30. William Wildman, Viscount Barrington's *Plan for the West*, May 10, 1766, Landsdowne Manuscripts, 30:95.

31. Johnston to Hillsborough, New York Collection of Documents, VIII, 105-

6.

32. Kaskaskia Papers, seat of the Circuit Court, Chester, Randolph County.

33. Lord to Gage, September 3, 1773, Canadian Archives, Series B, vol. 31, 7.

34. *Constitutional History of Canada*, 1906, 401-5.

35. The Continental Congress on October 21, 1774, drafted an address to the English Canadians, protesting the Quebec Act: "that we think the legislature of Great Britain is not authorized by the Constitution to establish a religion fraught with sanguinary and impious tenets," meaning the protection of the Catholic Church of the French.

36. Carl Ekberg, *Colonial Ste. Genevieve.*, 340.

17

The Americans Arrive

T he first vessels carrying immigrants from the British Isles carried the seeds of the American Revolution in their hulls as well. Whether they sought freedom of worship, were escaping starvation in England, or oppressed conditions in Ireland or Scotland, most of the subjects of the United Kingdom harbored resentment rather than tender feelings toward their mother country. In contrast, the French, some born and bred in North America, others in France, did remain one nation in their hearts and souls until the Treaty of Paris made it otherwise.

In the preceding chapters we have seen countless examples of the cultural chasm evident between the French and the British colonists; for the French in America, cutting ties with the mother country was a tragedy. It would require all the energy of the Catholic Church to recreate a nation, the French-Canadian nation, out of the despair of a community which had lost its soul when cast adrift by the King. In contrast, the energy of the entire British military could not prevent the Anglo-Americans from shedding their roots as just so much excess baggage. Even within their dominion, the Americans had long transferred their true attachment from the whole to the microcosm of their own colony; early in their histories, New England, Pennsylvania, Virginia, and Carolina, to mention only the major entities, found more divergences between them than common points of interest. The war against the French had temporarily brought the colonies together and temporarily closer to the Crown, but the Americans had fought for immediate rewards while the Crown fought for imperial mastery. This is not the place to retrace, even in the most general fashion, the chain of events which resulted in the break between the American Colonies and their mother country. It must, however, be underlined that the final disposition of the territories acquired from the French had a major impact on American public opinion, and moreover, on the decisions of the Continental Congress.

We have mentioned in the preceding chapter how Britain grew increasingly concerned over the integrity of the Western lands in terms of the fur trade. Placing the Western Territories, including Illinois, under the Military Government residing in Quebec seemed to give some guarantee these lands would not fall under the jurisdiction of the colonies. The Quebec Act, passed by the British Parliament on June 22, 1774, enraged the Americans because, among other aspects, it formalized the rights of the King's new French subjects to exercise the Catholic religion and still continue to enjoy the protection of French civil law. The French inhabitants from Ohio to the Mississippi River, and indirectly, the Indians as well, benefited from the same Act. It is with some irony that one reads today the virulent texts of American pamphleteers and gazeteers, who on the one hand argued eloquently for colonial liberties, and on the other attacked the Quebec Act with equal vehemence when it granted certain similar rights to the French (1774 was also the year of the Boston Tea Party). But the luxury of juxtaposing blatantly contradictory texts with the ability to compare them was not an option for the French living west of the Lake Erie-Mississippi line, the boundary determined by the Quebec Act. Scattered rumors only reached them at the whim of merchants, boatmen, and other assorted travelers. Settlers were beginning to filter illegally through the boundary; Pittsburgh, outside the Western Territory, was crowded with English-speaking people of all kinds, anxious to settle in the West. From that jumping-off point, *bateaux* and flaboats took many of them on the down current of the Ohio River. Most landed on the southern bank of Ohio, from where they spread through the woods of the new Kentucky County.

In Illinois, Rocheblave was but only a few months into his new capacity as commandant on behalf of England when, on July 4, 1776, the Second Continental Congress (after having determined two days earlier that "These United Colonies are, and right ought to be, free and independent states") approved the Declaration of Independence. In spite of all the odds against the success of his command, Rocheblave worked diligently to counter the influence of the men who had rallied behind the American cause, such as George Morgan, British-appointed Commissioner for Indian Affairs, who kept correspondence with agents in Kaskaskia. Ironically, if Rocheblave was able to count on prominent Frenchmen (particularly on three: Gabriel Cerré, Louis Viviat, and Nicolas Lachance), he could not count on the support of the few English civilians living in the area whose sympathies lay with the Revolution. Among them, Thomas Bentley who had settled in Kaskaskia and married Marguerite Beauvais, the daughter of a relatively well-to-do family (Rocheblave had him arrested during a trip that he made to Michilimackinac).[1] Rocheblave was further frustrated in his efforts by intrigues being fomented on the other side of the Mississippi by his former colleagues. Rocheblave tried sending several dispatches to Detroit, now the headquarters of the British command in the West, vainly requesting some military presence; one of these was particularly striking, as it preceded by only a short period the arrival of the Americans, stating that: "We are upon the eve of seeing here a numerous band of brigands who will establish a chain of communication which will not be easy to break, once formed." [2]

Bentley, as Rocheblave had correctly surmised, provided intelligence to the American Revolutionaries; before his arrest, he signaled the complete lack of defense of the French communities along the Mississippi. Thus, with an American force on the Mississippi, the British garrison of Vincennes could be threatened, leading to the eventual fall of Detroit. The man to act upon this suggestion and convince the Governor of Virginia, Patrick Henry, of its feasibility, was George Rogers Clark, who had already made a name for himself as a promoter of the colonization of the West.   His accomplishment in newly-organized Kentucky County had resulted in his appointment as major of its militia.   On January 2, 1778, Virginia voted its approval of a military expedition, officially limited to protecting Kentucky County against Indian attacks, but whose true assignment was to occupy Illinois. Clark, now commissioned by Virginia as Lieutenant-Colonel, set to work recruiting volunteers.

In February of the same year, France declared war on Britain, a welcome piece of news for the Americans. France until then had clandestinely supported the American Revolution, but their joining the war gave rise to American hopes that the French living under British rule in America might also be rallied to the cause. For Clark, who learned of France's decision only after he had begun his march towards the Mississippi, the news had particular importance; he had succeeded only in mustering a very small force, and had been warned that the French in the Mississsippi were opposed to the Americans. He hoped that, with France on the side of the United States, he might persuade them not to oppose his mission. These concerns were unfounded; his main problems after he landed near the deserted Fort Massac would be only poor guides (he lost his way), and a dire shortage of food.

Rocheblave had assembled the militia, and sent runners to Vincennes for reinforcement; but, contrary to the reports reaching Clark, the French settlers remained indifferent. Had they known the true sentiments of the Americans—virulently anti-Catholic—and their intentions—acquisition of land—as well as the Canadians did, they might have reacted differently. The Canadians, much closer to the political centers of Philadelphia and New York (and who enjoyed a larger, more sophisticated and educated class) were all too aware of the American intentions, which were to absorb the former New France, and then open it to mass settlement. The French-Canadians knew that their most determined enemies of fifteen years ago had been the Anglo-Americans, the same now again at their door, and by a curious reversal of alliances, the integrity of their community was now dependent on the British military. Their reasoning was amply illustrated during the American invasion of Canada in 1775, when ironically, only the British merchants of Montreal welcomed the troops of General Arnold; it would be the French-Canadians who defeated the Americans under the walls of Quebec, on December 31st of that year.

At dusk on July 4, 1778, Clark and his 175 men crept from under the trees on the bluff along the Illinois River and spied the Kaskaskia inhabitants retiring for the night. Waiting until dark had fallen, the "Long Knives," a surname the Indians had given the Americans, made their way across the river, then separated into three columns and took the town with much noise and yelling. Rocheblave was seized in his bed and sent under escort to Virginia, where he would be subsequently offered the opportunity to return to Illinois if he cared to govern in the name of Virginia, an offer he could not accept. He would be found back in Canada, in 1782, making plans for the reconquest of Illinois. The next morning, apprehension ran high among the people of Kaskaskia who looked upon this contingent of *Bostonnais* (to the French, all Anglo-Americans were "Bostonians") with great suspicion. Clark went out of his way to reassure them, as well as their priest, Father Pierre Gibault—who now had become the de facto leader of the French inhabitants, an ironic return to the conditions during the early days of the town when it was run by the Jesuits. Continuing to act with speed, Clark sent one of his officers, Captain Joseph Bowman, with thirty men along with some Frenchmen to formally take over Prairie du Rocher, St. Philippe, and Cahokia. Fort de Chartres by then had lost all military importance, the British troops having dismantled the essence of its defenses before regrouping in Kaskaskia. A canoe with three soldiers and two Frenchmen was sent to Peoria. Among the soldiers was one Nicholas Smith, whose son, Joseph, would later become one of the original American settlers in Peoria; through him we have a rare description of the town as it appeared in the 1770s: "... a large town, built along the beach of the lake, with narrow, unpaved streets, and houses constructed of wood."[3]

Detail from "A Plan of Cascaskies." From Captain Philip Pittman,
The Present State of the European Settlements on the Mississippi,
London, 1770. (The Newberry Library)

Vincennes also rallied the American cause responding to Father Gibault's persuasion who, soon after the arrival of Clark, had traveled from Kaskaskia along with one lone American, Captain Leonard Helm. Canadian-born Father Gibault was not only the parish priest of the Parish of the Immaculate Conception of Kaskaskia, but also the Vicar General of the Bishop of Quebec, and as such carried an important prestige throughout the old *Pays des Illinois*. After Kaskaskia, Vincennes had been the largest French town west of Detroit. In 1778, it still counted 621 inhabitants, and for them emigrating away from the Anglo-Saxon world was not the simple task of crossing a river, as it was for their compatriots of the Mississippi Valley. Isolation helped retain their population at a high level. Father Gibault returned to Kaskaskia, leaving Helm behind to administer the town.

Having now occupied the country and reassured its inhabitants, Clark began to reorganize its administrative structure along the lines of the laws of Virginia; he established courts in Kaskaskia, Cahokia, and Vincennes, empowered to handle both civil and criminal matters, with judges selected through elections. The first one ever held in American Illinois took place in Cahokia, in October 1778, where seven judges were selected. Far more significant, however, than this apparent great step forward for democracy, was the fact that the records were in English; conscious or not, the process of the elimination of French language and culture from the landscape was underway. The Governor of Virginia, writing to Clark on December 12, 1778, pointed to the Bill of Rights of his state as the proper instrument "to guide the French people." [4] Beyond its arrogance, the statement had an ominous air.

Yet, at the time Governor Henry wrote his letter, the American establishment in Illinois was far from secure. Although on the map the land acquired by Clark's raid looked like an impressive parcel of real estate, reality proved otherwise: Clark was very much alone with less than 200 men, in the midst of a French population whose political commitment remained volatile at best. Directly north, in Michilimackinac, Langlade,[5] the hero of the War against Britain, like the Canadians had understood early that the integrity of the French communities had much to fear from American imperialism, and thus had organized a force of French and Indians to fight alongside British troops. Langlade's early assessment was perhaps facilitated by his own mixed French and Indian origins (his mother, Domitilde, was the sister of an Ottawa Chief at L'Arbre Croché, a few miles away from the fort). The Indians were the first to suffer the brunt of the American frontiersmen's depredations. On the banks of the Ohio, the Kentuckians had simply ignored treaties guaranteeing the integrity of Indian lands, and the Indians had reacted violently. In a matter of a couple of years, changing interests had caused the British military to inherit the former French mantle and the Indians flocked to them with their requests for arms and ammunitions. A typical frontier war followed in its usual merciless style.

The British military was quick to assess the overall situation and promptly sent a small military force to occupy Vincennes. Henry Hamilton, the Lieutenant Governor seated in Detroit, organized a 250-men expedition which reoccupied Vincennes. This action, in turn, led to Clark's counter-measure, a remarkable military feat. To prepare for this expedition, Clark was forced to appeal to French merchants, who raised $11,102 between December 20, 1778, and February 5, 1779, at which time Clark marched out of Kaskaskia with 172 men, among whom were several Frenchmen.[6] The expedition crossed waist-deep flooded rivers and suffered enormously from cold and hunger, but succeeded in surprising Hamilton. Intrenched in the fort, Hamilton realized the desperate situation of his position and surrendered on February 25th with his garrison of seventy-nine men. Clark had acted before Hamilton was able to receive reinforcements. At the time of Hamilton's surrender, Langlade's party, en route to Vincennes, was already at the site of present-day Milwaukee.

Clark's victory in Vincennes and his subsequent return to Illinois paradoxically coincided with a resurgence of hostile feelings from the French population. Clark was dependent on the French for most of the supplies for his men, and had only the much devalued paper money issued by the Continental Congress to pay for them, along with drafts which many French settlers later refused as worthless. To Clark's credit, it must be said that he had little other recourse, as the financial support promised to him by Virginia never materialized, despite the bill passed on December 9, 1778, by both houses organizing the "County of Illinois."[7] But the real source of friction was the arrogant attitude of the "Kentuckian" troopers deeply resented by the French. In a lengthy *memoire* sent on May 24, 1779 to John Todd, the newly appointed County Lieutenant, the Kaskaskia Court complained that:

> The soldiers of Fort Clark go into the commons of this place to hunt the animals of the undersigned petitioners and without giving any heed to the brandings or to whom they may belong they have enclosed them in the fort

and killed them without giving notice to anyone. Such acts have never been seen in this country before. It is contrary to all law and particularly contrary to the usages and customs of an independent country like this one, which has been announced to be free. . . . three soldiers have killed dray-oxen, milch cows, and other animals of people who can not subsist without them. . . . If such abuses continue, which tend to the ruin of the colony, what will become of the colonists? [8]

Todd was sympathetic to the plight of the French, but could do little to rein in the soldiers or prevent the constant influx of adventurers and speculators whose heads were filled with land schemes. It seemed no one was immune from the temptation of profit; even Father Gibault, whose action for the American cause in Vincennes had earned him the nickname of "the patriot priest," was involved. He secretly and without authorization sold the twelve-thousand-acre property of the Missionary Priests, in Cahokia, to a middle man acting on behalf of Clark. In a wise action, the United States Government later annulled the sale. The French were bewildered by the Americans' behavior; their disregard for the law and lack of respect for authority was a different kind of roughness, never displayed by even the most unruly *voyageurs*. But for the Americans, the French were just a temporary nuisance.

For them the Catholics were enemies, as they had been on many a battle field of the Old World. The French lived in good terms with the Indians, the pioneer knew no good Indian save a dead one. With unremitting and relentless watchfulness they waged that war of extermination until the Indian was driven from the coveted prairies.[9]

Todd's responsibilities also included the militia, an institution long a source of power for the leading families. He wisely made few changes, appointing only one American, but otherwise reconfirmed the existing officers. The roster lists Pierre de Girardot for the settlement of St. Philippe, and Jean-Baptiste Maillet for Peoria, an indication that these two communities, though having lost many inhabitants through emigration, still remained more than a collection of abandoned dwellings. The condition of the militia was of crucial importance in 1779, as Clark was planning an expedition against Detroit. In spite of the fact that Clark had entrusted the expedition to a Frenchman, Godefroy de Linctot, preparations did not go well; the contingent needed was far below the expected strength, and as usual, supplies were lacking. News of these preparations had reached the British, however, who proceeded to plan attacks of their own in order to defend the Northwest Territories.

From Michilimackinac, a force composed of a small detachment of regular British troops, sixty French militiamen, and three times as many Indians, arrived in Fort St. Joseph in the middle of summer, 1779. Their task was to intercept Linctot's column before it could reach Detroit. More than ever, war was a game of gathering intelligence and spreading false rumors. A victim of that game was Jean-Baptiste Point Du Sable, the trader we met earlier, who, suspected of spying for the Americans, was arrested and taken back to Michilimackinac by a party from St. Joseph's British garrison. The situation was now complicated by Spain's entrance into the war on the American and French side against the British. Captain Richad Lernoult, the officer temporarily in command at Detroit (replacing Hamilton) built a new fort, as he correctly expected to be the object of Clark's direct attack. At the territory's other extremity Major Patrick Sinclair, the new commandant of Michilimackinac, made the decision to move the fort from the left bank of Lake Michigan to the Island of Mackinac, to increase his security. With their base consolidated, the British went on the attack. Aside from the attempt to reoccupy the Mississippi Valley, one of their major objectives was to interrupt trade between the Spanish and the Americans.[10] Once again, the success of the mission fell to the indomitable Charles Langlade, who left Mackinac in 1780 to assemble a force of 700 French and Indians at Prairie du Chien. His targets were St. Louis, in Spanish Illinois, and Cahokia. In yet another instance, French were going to fight French under foreign flags.

Don Fernando de Leyba, the Lieutenant Governor of Spanish Illinois, appointed in 1778, had only learned of Spain's declaration of war against Britain in 1780. Certain of an attack, he ordered immediate erection of fortifications to protect St. Louis, by then already a town of 700. On May 9, 1780, De Leyba, apprised that a hostile force was fast approaching, ordered a detachment of sixty men then garrisoned in Ste. Genevieve, to move without delay to St. Louis. The expected attack took place on May 23rd with about 1,000 Menominee and Winnebago Indians in assault, but the waves of attackers were repelled by well-concentrated fire from behind the stockade. The small number of defenders, a mere total of 300 men (among whom were three sons of François Vallé, Ste. Genevieve's leading citizen) had been considerably helped by five cannons manned by disciplined crews. The same day, across the river at Cahokia, another

British-led force had also attacked but was equally unsuccessful; Clark, forewarned, arrived in time to reinforce the militia.

Meanwhile, a third attack was launched on Peoria, also by an Indian contingent mustered in Michilimackinac and led by a French officer, Charles-Gauthier Verville. The town was sacked and burned, later to be temporarily abandoned. In St. Louis, where De Leyba had died shortly after the attack, the Governor of Louisiana returned Francisco Cruzat to the post. Cruzat immediately proceeded to surround the town with a new wooden stockade nine feet high. With the whole region in an extraordinary state of flux, this added precaution was justified. (Kaskaskia was attacked on July 17th, by a large Indian force.) A combined force of French militia and Spanish and American soldiers marched against the Indian allies of the British, gathered at Prairie du Chien, without much effect. Then Clark turned south and engaged his American contingent in a raid against the Shawnee. But in this instance, Clark did not succeed; the French in Vincennes had communicated information to the Shawnee, their long-time friends, on the American movements.

In December, further muddling an already complicated situation, sixteen Cahokia men, angered by the attack on their homes, embarked on a raid of British-controlled St. Joseph. Initially successful—they were able to capture several raiders and seize a considerable number of trade goods—the raid ended as a disaster when the garrison, out when the Cahokians erupted in the fort, caught up with them. Tragically, the garrison was made up not only of British soldiers and Potawatomi Indians but French as well, and was commanded by a French officer, Lieutenant Dagneau de Quindre and, ". . . as the raiders were retreating down the shore of Lake Michigan, they were overtaken near the present site of Michigan City, Indiana. . . . Four were killed, two were wounded, seven surrendered, and three escaped in the woods." [11]

The disaster which befell the little band of Cahokians, rather than leading to discouragement, energized a new larger, better organized expedition, this time from St. Louis. Cruzat sent sixty-five men from both St. Louis and Cahokia, for the most part French, with a handful of Spaniards and an equal number of Indians, under the command of Eugene Poure, who was Captain of the Militia of St. Louis, back to Fort St. Joseph. They left on January 2, 1781 and arrived at Fort St. Joseph on February 12, 1781, having made very good time on a journey executed in the dead of winter, when partially frozen waters made canoe travel difficult (they took the Kankakee-St. Joseph River portage, first used by La

Salle). Adding to the unsavory element of a French "civil war," was the presence of Louison Chevalier among the raiders; his father, Louis Chevalier, was a trader in St. Joseph and allied, at least officially, to the British cause (he, along with the other forty French inhabitants of Fort St. Joseph, was removed to Michilimackinac on orders of the British Lieutenant-Governor). The raid was short: the occupation of St. Joseph lasted exactly a day, and the party returned to Cahokia and St. Louis making off with the goods they could carry on their canoes. De Quindre, again, was not in the fort and returned too late to organize a serious pursuit of the "Spanish" raiders. Historians have long speculated on the real motivation behind this sort of senseless expedition. Was it purely an exercise of revenge, or a calculated demonstration ordered by a Spanish government desirous of establishing foundations for future claims? Careful perusal of the Spanish archives seems to indicate the former as the probable reason. Nevertheless, the "victorious party" returned to a triumphal welcome in St. Louis, on March 6th.

As though the state of affairs existing in the whole area was not already confused enough, consider the strange mission of a French nobleman, Colonel Mottin de La Balme, sent by Mr. de La Luzerne, the French Plenipotentiary Minister in Philadelphia, to help stir the pro-American sentiment among French inhabitants. La Balme first surfaced during the spring of 1780, in Pittsburgh; then later in Vincennes, in Kaskaskia, and Cahokia, delivering speeches to the French population along the way. His objective was the capture of Deroit, but the best that he was able to achieve was the recruitment of a mere eighty men. La Balme's failure was directly linked to the increased disillusionment the French were experiencing towards the Americans. Writing on November 3, 1781, to Major Sinclair in Michilimackinac, Antoine Girardin, one of Cahokia's leading citizens, openly declared that if British soldiers were sent to Illinois they would be welcome, and he offered his assistance in achieving this end.[12] Cahokia's feelings were particularly inflamed by the behavior of Captain Richard McCarty, who commanded the small American garrison there and proceeded to arbitrary requisitions. Perhaps it was La Balme's sense of honor, or perhaps foolish optimism, which sent him on a march against Fort Miami, where he and most of his men lost their lives at the hands of Miami warriors led by Chief Little Turtle.

Clark's Americans were finally pulled out of Illinois, with the exception of a small detachment left in Kaskaskia, who departed in turn before the end of 1781. In the meantime, a clique of profiteers including the aforementioned Thomas Bentley (who had been released from British imprisonment), the Captain of the American troops, Captain John Rogers, and the Virginia-appointed Indian Agent, John Dodge, were busily buying for a pittance the claims and properties of the French, who were in a state of ruin after five years of military occupation. The great disarray of the French population, tired and confused, was pathetically—and naively—expressed in their many *memoires* sent indiscriminately to the Governor of Virginia and to the French Minister, in Philadelphia, stating that they had decided "not to receive any more troops in their villages except those that should be sent by the King of France." [13] But, unbeknownst to all the protagonists roaming the land from Lake Michigan to the Mississippi, the War of American Independence was coming to an end. On October 19, 1781, Major-General Charles Cornwallis surrendered his forces to a combined French and American army commanded by Washington, Rochambeau, and Lafayette.

By 1782, after a last bloody exchange between Clark's soldiers and the Miami Indians, military operations were winding down; on January 18, 1783, the Illinois battalion was dissolved. The same year, negotiations opened in Paris between the warring parties were brought to a reasonably quick end, in great part due to the strong personal relations existing between Lord Shelburne, Britain's Prime Minister, and Benjamin Franklin, combined with mediation by the French. Spain, concerned by the presence of a powerful United States on the Mississippi, had initially supported a British Northwest; Shelburne, however, was convinced by Franklin that hard-to-control American populations constantly flowing westward would bring unending problems to Britain, and consequently to the relations between the two nations—relations that both countries greatly desired be founded on a natural closeness engendered by language and culture. The Treaty of Paris, bringing an official end to the war, was signed on September 3, 1783.

While transcontinental order was restored in the rational and courteous atmosphere permeating the high-ceilinged suites of the royal palaces of Paris and Versailles, in contrast, anarchy reigned in Illinois.

More than one hundred settlers, ignoring Virginia's prohibition, had brought their families to a site a few miles south of Cahokia, called Bellefontaine (near present-day Waterloo), and rapidly set out to establish their own court system, but remained: ". . . never satisfied with this subordination to the French, whom they held in contempt and regarded as aliens settled on American soil." [14] Attracted by the prospect of easy land acquisition, a myriad of ambitious English-speakers progressively changed the ethnic face of the Valley—among them John Edgar, an Irishman who had served as an officer in the British Navy, and who arrived in 1784. There were some ambitious French-speakers arriving as well: "... among the new arrivals were men with money and business acumen who recognized the potential for Illinois." [15] Certainly Pierre Menard, who opened a store in Kaskaskia in 1791, qualified for the distinction, and also Jean-Baptiste Du Sable, whose commercial successes in Peoria and Chicago were recounted earlier. But, in the days that followed the end of the war, the man of the hour, unfortunately, was John Dodge, the former Indian agent. A character of few scruples and great greed, Dodge was able in a short time to build a power base (partially with the help of the settlers from Bellefontaine) sufficient to challenge the authority of the County Lieutenant, Canadian-born Jacques Timotheé Boucher, (*sieur*) de Monbrun. Monbrun had served as a lieutenant in the Militia of Vincennes and also in Clark's Illinois battalion, but his experience proved to be insufficient for him to handle the factions which were at work tearing apart the fabric of the Kaskaskia community. Although trying to temporize, he instead ended up as a sort of frontman for Dodge, who was able to take over the fort on the bluff above Kaskaskia; from there, until 1786, he ran the affairs of the town with complete impunity, in a manner akin to nineteenth-century Turkey. His only serious opposition was centered around Huet de la Valiniere, a French maverick priest who was the new Vicar General for Illinois, appointed by the Bishop of Baltimore. Father Gibault, who had left for the safety of Ste. Genevieve, described the situation best in a letter sent on June 6, 1786, to his bishop:

> In Canada all is civilized, here all is barbarous. . . . Everybody is in poverty, which engenders theft and rapine. Wantonness and drunkenness pass here as elegance and amusements quite in style. Breaking of limbs, murder by means of a dagger, sabre, or sword are common, and pistols and guns are but toys in these regions. . . . No commandant, no troops, no prison, no hangman...I could name a great number of persons assassinated in all the villages of the region . . . In spiritual matters everything is the same or even worse.[16]

Prairie du Rocher and Cahokia, in spite of their proximity, fared much better. In fact, Cahokia in 1787 counted 240 males, and in 1790, could muster three companies of militia versus Kaskaskia which could only painfully provide enough men for one. Much of the calm and prosperity of Cahokia was due to its energetic Militia Commandant, Francois Trottier, illustrating the powerful political role of the militia, a role much overlooked when considering existing institutions during the time of the French. Cahokia remained outwardly French, perhaps helped by the vicinity of St. Louis. At any rate, even the few Anglo-American merchants in town—among them perhaps the first Jew, Isaac Levy—were quickly gallicized, even marrying local French girls. The bulk of the Americans, who emigrated later to Cahokia, resided in their own settlement called Grand Ruisseau; although they had their own magistrates and militia, they remained under the jurisdiction of the French town until the organization of the territory. But the prairies and forests between Lake Michigan and the Mississippi continued to be a battleground of untold skirmishes. Jumping into the fray, George Rogers Clark appointed himself to lead a contingent of Kentucky militia to war against the Shawnee, Potawatomi, and Miami Indians. The town of Vincennes, Clark's center of operations, once again had to endure the undesirable military rule of his volunteers. As usual and as expected, Clark, being short of supplies, sent one of his aides, John Rice Jones, to the Mississippi Valley, this seemingly inexhaustible land of plenty. Jones was refused any succor by Dodge—a grievous error, as Clark's deputy returned a second time, on this occasion with a sufficient body of troops, and: "... entered in the above said fort on the hill occupied by John Dodge; he threatened him to cast him out from it if he continued to be contrary to America, as he was before. He stood there some days with his troops, during which time the wheat had been delivered peaceably and no body had been hurted." [17]

Dodge considered the moment had come to make a timely trip to the Spanish side. But the wounds he left behind (temporarily, as he was to return again and attempt to resume his activities) led to the separation of Bellefontaine from the Kaskaskia district, and moreover to the election of judges who could not communicate with the French magistrates. An agreement was, however, signed between the two parties; this achievement due in part to negotiations organized by John Edgar, whose conciliatory attitudes would lead to further political prominence in the years to come (and further wealth, as he would be Illinois' largest landowner by the time of his death in 1830). In the meantime, to the north, in the future states of Wisconsin and Michigan, despite the terms of the treaty specifying that Britain surrender the Northwest to the United States, the status quo was maintained through the stubborn inertia of the fur syndicates which operated from Montreal, and to whose advantage it was to retain the western post. Britain was to remain in Mackinac Island, in Niagara, In Detroit, in Oswego, and other points, for another thirteen years, until 1796.

The anarchy in Illinois was brought to an end—at least officially—with the organization of the "Territory of the United States northwest of the river Ohio," on July 13, 1787. Article Six of the Bill of Rights was attached to the ordinance, and had been included to satisfy New England. It specified that, "There shall be neither slaves nor unvoluntary servitude in the said territory," posing an immediate problem for those among the French who owned slaves; several among them crossed over to Ste. Genevieve and St. Louis, and some to New Madrid, a settlement founded in 1788 by George Morgan, an astute entrepreneur who had come to Illinois in the wake of the British garrison (he is credited with introducing the cultivation of potatoes in Illinois). When Morgan failed to establish himself in Illinois, he moved to Mississippi, easily obtaining the consent of the Spanish authorities to found a new settlement there, as the Spanish were always anxious to shore up their fragile line of occupation along the river. The blows Kaskaskia had suffered during the preceding years proved fatal to the French presence. The statistics are clear: when Clark arrived, there were 194 French heads of households, but by 1790, the number was down to forty-four.[18] Carl Ekberg, Ste. Genevieve historian *par excellence*, has carefully tracked down the well-to-do Kaskaskia families who crossed the river with their slaves. In one year, from 1788 to 1789, 135 persons left Kaskaskia. Emigration was encouraged, even organized, by the Spanish officials, a particularly agreeable task for those among whom many were themselves French.

> When in March 1788 Commandant [Henri] Peyroux informed Governor [Esteban] Miro about the substantial immigration from the east side of the Mississippi, Miro was delighted. He replied to Peyroux that "the new French families from the American side moving to our side pleases me. I have given Monsieur Perez [Lieutenant Governor in St. Louis] orders to admit American families as well.[19]

There was a danger inherent, however, in the admittance of Americans, even if all efforts would be made to convert them to Catholicism: American immigration had a momentum of its own and could prove to be difficult to control. One could foresee a West Illinois, Spanish in name,

French in structure, and American in character, a possibility not un-thought-of by the more prescient souls on both sides of the Mississippi. Meanwhile, the growth of Ste. Genevieve, slowly shifting position from its original location in the Mississippi flood plain to its new site, up a rise, was helped by a different category of immigrants: French who were fleeing the French Revolution.

News of the events taking place in Paris and Versailles during the turbulent month of July, 1789—the Bastille fell on July 14, 1789—puzzled the French living in the heart of North America, sometimes separated by generations from the social and economic problems afflicting their moth-erland. The realities of Revolution, which generously abolished heredi-tary privileges, while at the same time undertaking to burn castles, desecrate churches, and lynch the opposition—not only in France, but in the French West Indian colonies as well—troubled many. Consequently, the "flotsam" of French aristocracy, who voyaged in search of a new life, found sympathy and precious asylum in Spanish Louisiana. In New Orleans and the surrounding parishes, these French families and their slaves would reinforce the Creole element, black and white, but in Spanish Illinois, the demographic impact was less evident. Nevertheless, it did lead to the foundation of an interesting new community, of which little is known today; *Nouvelle Bourbon*, a few miles south of Ste. Genevieve, was perched on bluffs overooking the site of the Old Town and the even more ancient Indian Mound. No traces remain in New Bour-bon of its aristocratic roots, but for a few houses displaying the unmistak-able mark of French Mississippian architecture.

Appointed by President Washington, the new Governor of the North-west Territory was Scottish-born Arthur St. Clair (a veteran of General Wolfe's army, a man who was at the *Plaines d'Abraham* and had also served as President of Congress. He arrived in Kaskaskia on March 5, 1790, and visited Cahokia a month later. Before returning to the more urgent task of facing the swell of unrest among the Miami Indians, St. Clair created the first county in Illinois and named it after himself. He then left behind him "eyes and ears" in the person of his cousin, William St. Clair, as the court clerk. It was important that he return to the town of Marietta on the Ohio River, where he had established the seat of the territory's government.

St. Clair had negotiated patiently, and he believed successfully, with the Indian nations living in the eastern part of the territory (Ohio and Indiana). His successes, however, were constantly pre-empted by the actions of the pioneers, who having branded the Indians as an inherent aspect of the wilderness, had set out to tame them, if not stamp them out entirely. Naturally, the Indians stood their ground, in their customary fashion of hit and run warfare. In 1790, in answer to the hue and cry of the settlers, an army was sent from Fort Washington (Cincinnati). The army was unable to establish contact, except for one of its columns which was annihilated, losing 183 soldiers in a well-prepared ambush. In 1791, St. Clair himself led a 3,000-man army into another disaster: he was attacked at night while camping along the Miami River. He lost nearly a thousand men in the course of a few hours, while the rest fled in disorder. This time President Washington appointed a proven officer, Anthony Wayne, who, ignoring the clamor for immediate action, took the time instead to prepare methodically. In October 1793, finally ready, he began his march west. On June 30 and July 1, 1794, Chief Little Turtle and 2,000 Miami (including a certain number of "British" who, in reality, were French militiamen) attempted vainly to stop Wayne's advance near Fort Recovery (Ohio). On August 20, 1794, the final battle took place twelve miles south of the present-day city of Toledo, on a spot called Fallen Timbers(a tornado had felled the trees). The Miami suffered greatly in contrast to the Americans' insignificant losses (thirty-three dead). The back of the Indian resistance had been broken; nothing now stood between massive American emigration and the lands to which, until this point, French communities and Indian nations had managed to cling.

NOTES

1. See the *Michigan Pioneer and History Collections*, XIX, 321.
2. In Alvord, *The Centennial History*, 323.
3. David McCulloch, *History of Peoria County*, 22-23.
4. Alvord, *Collections of the Illinois State Historical Library*, IXII, introduction.
5. On the fascinating personality of Charles Langlade, see the article written by Keith R. Wildder, "The Persistence of French-Canadian Ways at Mackinac after 1760," in the *Proceedings of the Sixteenth Meeting of the French Colonial Historical Society, Mackinac Island, May 1990*, 44-56.
6. Alvord, *Collections*, XIVI, FN 1.
7. For details on the early days of the American regime in Illinois, see Clarence Alvord, *Collections*, introduction.
8. *Kaskaskia Manuscripts*, quoted in Alvord, (Collections), XVII.
9. Alvord, *Collections*, XV.
10. Much more detailed information on the role of men and locations in

present-day Michigan can be found in Willis Dunbar, *Michigan, A History of the Wolverine State*, Eerdmans, Grand Rapids, 1965.

11. Willis Dunbar, *Michigan*, 98.

12. Alvord, *Cahokia Records*, 559.

13. Alvord, *Collections*, 351.

14. Alvord, *The Illinois Country*, 360.

15. Robert P. Howard, *Illinois, A History of the Prairie State*, 68.

16. Gibault to Bishop Briand, June 6, 1786, Alvord, ed., *Kaskaskia Records*, 542-44.

17. Father Pierre Huet de la Valiniere, in *Papers of Old Congress*, quoted in Alvord, *Collections*, CXXXIV.

18. Alvord, *Collections*, CXLIV.

19. Carl Ekberg, *Colonial Ste. Genevieve*, 433.

18

The Time of the French Fades into History

D uring the ten years spanning 1789 to 1799, while Europe was being battered by forces unleashed by the French Revolution, the micro world of the ancient *Terre des Illinois* was undergoing a transformation of its own; and though not so violent, it was equally upsetting in nature. On the eve of the nineteenth century, the landscape west of the original thirteen colonies was essentially the same in appearance as it had been in the late 1700s, but the similarity was in appearance only. Before the arrival of the Americans, each French town, whether on shore or inland—whether it be Detroit, Kaskaskia, or Mackinac—remained a small hub of colorful activity, more resembling a stage set for a rustic play than what they all truly were: stakes worthy of intensive conflict between world powers. A passage describing the populated stretch of the Mississippi left by the British Captain Philip Pittman might have applied to any of them

> The village of Notre Dame de Cascasquias. . . . stands on the side of a small river, which is about eighty yards across. . . . the principal buildings are the church and jesuits house, which has a small chapel adjoining to it; these, as well as some other houses in the village, are built of stone, and, considering this part of the world, make a very good appearance. "La Prairie de Roches" is . . . a small village, consisting of twelve dwelling-houses . . . two miles from Fort Chartres, it takes its name from its situation, being built under a rock that runs parallel with the river Mississippi . . . Saint Philippe. . . . five miles from Fort Chartres, in the road to Kaoquias, (has) about fifteen houses and a small church standing. . . . The village of Sainte Famille de Kaoquias . . . stands near the side of the Mississippi, and is masked from the river by an island of two leagues long . . . it contains forty-five dwelling-houses, and a church near its center . . .[1]

Within a few years, this situation would alter radically, and the witnesses to this alteration would be the various travellers in this world in flux, roaming the countryside in search of opportunities. Whether for themselves or on behalf of some syndicate of hopeful investors, or at other times directly commissioned to gather intelligence for some unclearly defined chancery, these individuals moreover managed to circulate not only unscathed, but sometimes rather in style.

Two travellers of notable importance during this interesting period, which marked the twilight of the French in North America, were Constantin François de Chasseboeuf, Count de Volney, and Nicolas de Finiels. Volney, a typical product of the Enlightenment, was a rationalist who had already travelled and published extensively by the time he arrived in North America. As deputy to the Constituent Assembly, and a member of the Girondist faction, he had been thrown in prison in 1793, during the Terror. Whether to distance himself from this particularly unpleasant experience, or perhaps, as later suspected, acting on behalf of the French government, he arrived in Philadelphia on October 12, 1795. As a friend of Benjamin Franklin, he was received by George Washington, and was also a guest of Thomas Jefferson for three weeks in Monticello.[2] Afterwards, he left for the former French territories on a sort of fact-finding tour, carrying diverse letters of recommendation given to him by Jefferson, a true illustration of the founding father's eclectic interests: among them was one to Jean-Baptiste DuCoigne, an Illinois Chief living in Kaskaskia, another to Henri Peyroux de la Coudrenière, who commanded Ste. Genevieve under Spain. Volney first ventured to Gallipolis Ohio, where he found a hapless settlement founded in 1790 by five hundred French people, most of whom would today be termed middle class, who had fled the turbulence of the Revolution. Volney met unhappy French settlers, abused by unscrupulous promoters and experiencing extreme difficulties; people who, having been "raised in the ease of Paris' lifestyle, were obliged to sow, weed, cut wheat, bind into sheaves, carrying them home, cultivate corn, oats, tobacco, watermelons in temperatures from 24 to 28 degrees [celsius]."[3] Continuing his travels, Volney and a small escort arrived on horseback on August 2, 1796:

> at the Louisiana village called *Poste Vincennes*, on the Wabash River. . . . corn, tobacco, wheat, barley, watermelon, and even cotton fields surround the village made of about fifty houses whose bright white walls is a pleasant sight after the monotony of the woods. These houses are lined up on the left bank of the Wabash. . . . each . . . as per the Canadian custom, separated from the other, in the center of a yard, and orchard and fenced in by a palisade. . . . Contiguous to village and river, there is an enclosure made of stakes six feet high, surrounded by a ditch eight feet wide, this they call a fort . . .[4]

Detail showing Kaskaskia and Ste. Genevieve in 1796.   From
Victor Collot, "A Map of the Country of the Illinois" in *Voyage dans
l'Amérique du Nord*, Paris, 1826.   (The Newberry Library)

In comparing the newly arrived Americans with the long-established
French people, Volney was immediately struck by the differences in their
appearance, outlook, and attitudes.   As he symbolized some sort of
authority from the mother country, the French complained bitterly to him
of their abandonment.   Volney clearly understood their disillusionment
and recorded with some dismay that the 400 acres granted by Congress
meant little to the French: not really farmers at heart, they only wished to
regain their former lifestyle based on the fur trade, longing for the easy
commerce with the Indians—their friends and, often, their relatives as
well.   They did not speak English, few were literate: they lived on what
they could hunt, fish, or the fruit from their orchards, and seemed unable

to overcome their anger and bitterness. For Volney, who spoke at great length as well to the Americans, their future facing "... the sedentary, active, patient life of the Anglo-American farmers ..."⁵ seemed irrevocably doomed.

After a journey of forty-three hours, Volney and his party next arrived at Kaskaskia, where he found similar conditions, with a country so "... spoiled that only twelve Canadian families remained."⁶ In Prairie du Rocher, there were ten families, in Cahokia, forty instead of the eighty formerly living there in 1790. Volney, always the rationalist, sought clues in the *habitudes nationales*, those national traits whose existence no one seriously denies, but whose reality and significance equally can never be pinpointed with any certain accuracy. Volney's lengthy analysis of both the Anglo-American and French character is a well-written, carefully measured comparison. From his eyewitness observations, we have another demonstration—if indeed it was needed—that the very traits enabling the French to be so successful in acquiring title to an empire, would in turn doom their survival as a community.

The second traveler of note, Nicolas de Finiels, was in all probability a French officer who had emigrated at the time of the Revolution (though he may have come from the West Indies). His marked antipathy for the new French régime would lead him first to find refuge in the United States, and later to serve Spain whose King nonetheless was a Bourbon. Finiels, too, visited Philadelphia where he came to know the Minister of Spain who would eventually appoint him to survey the fortifications of St. Louis; this on recommendation from, of all people, General Collot, who in turn had been sent to Philadelphia by the French revolutionary government, underlining the complex nature of the world of politics in existence throughout the community of emigres at that time.

Finiels' account differs notably from that of Volney, for he surveyed an area whose French community under Spanish rule was able to remain intact—unquestionably, the absence of any massive arrival of Spanish colonists, compared with the radically different situation on the other side of the Mississippi, had much to do with this stability. The future of Spanish Illinois, though facing the danger of possible invasion by French revolutionaries, or perhaps the threat of an unstoppable wave of American settlers, appeared reasonably hopeful upon the arrival of Finiels and his family in Ste. Genevieve, in 1797. Finiels remarked that the Shawnee Indians, having crossed the Mississippi to resettle at Cape Girardeau with their Chief, Louis Lorimier, were back to normal life. Lorimier was another example of a Frenchman born from an Indian mother who easily bridged two worlds. Among those who had understood early the danger that American expansion represented, he had led the Shawnee to the British side during the American War of Independence.[7] Further in his account, Finiels spoke of Nouvelle Bourbon and Ste. Genevieve as comfortable communities, whose common fields (when not washed out by intemperate floods), mills, and large holdings of cattle, were sources of prosperity. There were revenues from salt exploitation at the nearby Saline Creek, as well as lead mines from both *Mine à Breton* and the banks of the Meramec stream. The Fur trade—Finiels terms it the "Indian trade"—remained however "an issue of great urgency and competition among the inhabitants of (Spanish) Illinois."[8] A revealing remark, when for all the towns on both banks of the Mississippi, as well as the rest of the Northwest, the main engine pulling the economy continued to be the fur trade; but if traders were to ply the rivers and toil under their loads on ancient portages for several more decades, reckless and wanton harvesting would certainly exhaust that precious commodity.

In the space of two or three generations at most, hundreds of men from Montreal and other French Canadian localities would disappear from the waterways, and along with them, a prodigiously rich culture. At the turn of the nineteenth century, however, the fur trade continued to remain an important piece on the economic chessboard of the region. The problem now was that there were three players: Spain, Britain, and the "new kid on the block," the United States. It was, of course, neither Spain's nor Britain's intention to stand by idly; therefore, to this end, Spain's Baron Francisco Luis Hector de Carondelet, Louisiana's governor since 1792, approved the construction of a fort at the main Osage village, situated on the Osage River(present-day Vernon County, Missouri).Built by Auguste Chouteau, it was meant to accomplish two important tasks: first to instill a sense of awe in the Osage who were becoming increasingly rebellious (in part, a result of the clandestine trade they were maintaining with Montreal traders); and secondly, to corner the fur market of the far western regions. A year later, the newly appointed Lieutenant-Governor, Zenon Trudéau (as was true of most of the "Spanish" officials, a French officer who had remained in Louisiana) gathered the traders in St. Louis for what corresponded to an early version of a brain-storming session. Out of that meeting a decision was made to organize more large-scale expeditions west as a remedy for the poor results in trade.

In spite of their efforts, very little was accomplished. Nineteenth-century economics pointed away from these adventurous investments; in the past they had earned up to 200 to 300 percent for their stockholders, but now the profits were down to barely twenty-five percent, hardly a viable return in consideration of the real risks involved. Spain was confronted by the reality of a fur trade by and large British-controlled; but, the irony, of course, was that on both sides the trade was almost exclusively carried out by Frenchmen. What about the Americans? With very few French *voyageurs* in their employ, they fared the worse by far until after the War of 1812, when British influence was completely eliminated south of the Canadian border. Following the Act of Congress of 1816, conveniently excluding foreigners from operating any fur trade in the United States, German-born John Astor [9] bought out the shares in his company owned by the Montreal syndicate as well as their own holdings. The Act was carefully worded so as not to forbid the hiring of foreign employees, meaning the French-Canadian *voyageurs* (second or third generation British subjects by now), whose expertise and rapport with the Indians were deemed essential to any successful endeavor. By 1817, from Green Bay to the Wabash River, the American Fur Company was rapidly becoming the biggest enterprise in the west; Mackinac Island, the site chosen by Astor for maintaining his warehouses, and as a gathering place for his *voyageurs*, underwent a quick transition from slumbering community to turbulent beehive. There, during the annual weeks of *rendez-vous*, one might see up to 3,000 *voyageurs* and an equal number of Indians, trading, drinking, and gambling until exhaustion. South of Mackinac, the communities of Prairie du Chien, St. Louis, and Chicago, were also becoming major trading posts. A pattern was created and survived in Canada all the way to the 1960s: top management spoke English, while their agents (and of course the crews) on the waterways bore French names, like St. Jean, Jean-Baptiste Charbonnais, Antoine Deschamps, or Jean-Baptiste Beaubien.

But the crucial new element, and the one that would lead to the irreversible change in the picture of the Northwest, was the continuous immigration of English-speaking settlers from the east. By the time it became a state, in 1802, Ohio already numbered 43,365 people. The wave of new settlers would take some time to reach further west, but only because the single important penetration route in that direction was the Ohio River; to the north, the British presence prevented access to the Great Lakes region. The settlement of new immigrants in Illinois was greatly facilitated by the law that Congress had passed in 1785, simplifying land

survey to "the neat and orderly system of rectangle . . ." [10] This was the
system used to create townships (six-mile-side-squares), subdivided into
thirty-six sections of 640 acres each, an innovation partly due to Thomas
Hutchins, the officer assigned by the British army to draw up the maps of
the former French territories.

By 1804, land offices were open in Detroit, in Vincennes, and in
Kaskaskia. During their first years, they would not yet handle large
volumes of transactions but rather would essentially process French land
claims. These French claims were to keep the fledgling Illinois courts busy
during the next two decades. Speculators enticed the French to sell their
claims, whose value increased as they were changing hands. Determining authenticity was a difficult problem, as not only did the property titles
possessed by the French antecede American jurisdiction, but more often
than not, the French were unable to produce the kind of precise records
required by the American system. Additionally, French family heads
living in Illinois up to 1783, had received 400 acres from Congress as
compensation for hardships experienced during the Revolutionary War,
and such grants were also objects of speculation. Along the Mississippi,
only 244 had filed and received the grants, a number which, incidentally,
reflected the continuous demographic erosion in that area. Already tem-
peramentally ill-prepared for legal quibbling, the French were even less
able to follow the intricacies of land transactions in English, a language
few could understand. Moreover, their lands needed to be surveyed,
another complication, as well as an expense far too great for many who
would be among the first to fall easy prey to speculators.

However scorned, ridiculed, and taken advantage of as the French
might be, their treatment did not begin to compare with what was
accorded the Indians. There never existed a doubt in the minds of the men
who established the budding infrastructure for the American system of
government in the new territories that the Indians would be continuously
removed to lands farther and farther west; the arrival of new settlers in
Illinois would be inversely proportional to the rhythm of this removal.
Following the means, by now proven successful, and able to assuage the
pangs of conscience for the few humanitarians, a "treaty" was employed
to cover the whole operation with a semblance of legality. In 1803, in
Vincennes, the Kaskaskia, having been reduced to a shadow of the nation
they once were, finally gave up all their land between the Mississippi and
the Wabash. The treaty extracted from them exemplified a trend begun
in 1795, at Greenville. [11] Continuing the unhappy process, the whole of the

Illinois confederacy, the Potawatomi and the Kickapoo, jointly abandoned the lands they held from Vincennes to the Vermilion River in 1809. The final blow to the Indian presence between Lake Michigan and the Mississippi would be struck on September 25, 1818, when ". . . all the remnants of the Illinois tribes met Governor Edwards and Auguste Chouteau, United States commissioners at Edwardsville and agreed to a treaty." [12]

Meanwhile, thousands of miles across the Atlantic Ocean, the future of French Louisiana was under the deliberation of one man: Napoleon Bonaparte.

Under attack from every direction, revolutionary France of the terrible years, 1792 and 1793, raised a guillotine in every large city's central square, and called to arms a one-million-man army. In a feat of unprecedented military passion, the massed columns in the French Republic, roaring revolutionary marching songs, bayonneted their way, battle after battle, throwing back the disciplined phalanxes of kings and emperors. In the momentum of their victories, the French soldiers, inventing the concept of ideological war, "liberated" most of the monarchies of western Europe, big and small, within their reach. Following a difficult military campaign, Spain chose accommodation rather than defeat. The Franco-Spanish peace treaty signed in Basel on July 22, 1795, forced Spain to hand over Santo Domingo, her half of the island of Hispaniola (the other was French Saint Domingue, later Haiti) to France, and join her in an alliance. Following the seizure of power of the French republic by a thirty year-old general, Napoleon Bonaparte, on November 9-10, 1799, [13] it was not long before this forced alliance led to further concessions by Spain, as Bonaparte began to redesign foreign policy to bring it in line with his vision of a Europe completely dominated by France. Assuredly no match for the powerful French war machine, on October 1, 1800, King Charles IV agreed to restore Louisiana to France. [14]

In obtaining the return of Louisiana, Bonaparte was simply transforming French revolutionary thought into action. The men who rose to high position during the French Revolution were blunt practitioners of a policy of hegemony hammered out by the armies of the Republic. These men were not encumbered by the same protocol of eighteenth century ministers and diplomats as was the French minister to the United States (until 1789, Eleonoré François Moustier) who indeed had suggested the possibility of a retrocession of Louisiana in a long memoire written to the King. [15] But it would have been too ill-mannered for the ancient regime to break a solemn agreement between the two blood-tied reigning families of France and Spain. No such scruples were to interfere with French interests henceforth. Even before the assumption of power by Bonaparte, French agents from their base in Philadelphia, then capital of the United States, had been busily plotting a change of direction for Louisiana. There were as many as 25,000 French refugees in the United States (most of them living around New York and Philadelphia), representing all shades of the French political spectrum, from royalists to moderates to extremists. Past and future famous names crossed paths; there was Moreau de Saint-Mery (as Vice-President of the Paris municipality he had been at the attack on the Bastille, and now ran a print-shop); Talleyrand (Napoleon's foreign minister), or the Duke of Noailles, (Lafayette's father-in-law). In this milieu, teeming with individuals who haunted cafés and private circles while haboring thwarted ambitions and fledgling hopes, it was not difficult for any minister representing the French Republic to recruit auxiliaries for practically any scheme. Edmond C. Genet, who assumed the post from 1793 to 1795, employed many of them to concoct some incredible invasion plan of Louisiana which even involved George Rogers Clark. In 1796, under a different minister, citizen Pierre Auguste Adet (but with the same mission), sent General George-Victor Collot to gather information in Louisiana, where he would be arrested by the Spanish authorities and accused of spying; he was, however, eventually released.

The prospect of the return of French rule over Louisiana was viewed with elation by a few hundred die-hard republicans, mostly in New Orleans and in St. Louis, but it grieved just as many still staunchly attached to the monarchy, and moreover, horrified by the excesses of the French Revolution. Concerned over the possibility of an invasion by French Republican volunteers banded with American supporters, the Spanish Governor ordered new fortifications for Upper Louisiana, and Nicolas de Finiels was asked to draw the blueprints. Finiels eventually moved to New Orleans, where he worked directly for the Spanish governors and later, after the retrocession, for the French appointed *préfet*, Pierre-Clement de Laussat, who arrived in March 1803. For Laussat, Finiels wrote a carefully studied report on Louisiana's conditions, adding a detailed map he had originally prepared for the Spanish authorities.

Unbeknownst to Laussat, however, by the time he landed in New Orleans, Napoleon had already decided to sell Louisiana to the United States.

News of the retrocession of Louisiana greatly alarmed the United

States. Thomas Jefferson, newly elected President in 1801, was deeply troubled, and in dispatches to Robert Livingston, American minister in Paris, and in letters to Volney and to Dupont de Nemours, he darkly hinted of rapprochement with Britain and a possible declaration of war on France. In the opposition, the Federalist Party was making loud demands for the occupation of Louisiana before the arrival of French troops. In 1801, the French had sent an army of 25,000 men to St. Domingue to put down the rebellion of Toussaint Louverture. It would have been a short cruise, once this task was achieved, from the island to New Orleans, but an outbreak of yellow fever decimated the French troops (it killed Charles Leclerc, who was the commanding General, as well as Napoleon's brother-in-law), and changed the course of history. Napoleon began to reconsider the worth of a French empire in North America when funds were greatly needed for his war plans in Europe. Upon consultation, Volney and Talleyrand, both with the advantage of having lived in America, strongly recommended selling rather than fighting. In Paris, on May 2, 1803, James Monroe and Robert Livingston signed the Treaty of Cession, giving the United States three-fourths of its future continental territory for the sum of fifteen million dollars, probably the greatest bargain in history.

The actual American take-over of Louisiana embodied a touch of comedy, as it appeared that Spain actually "...had never transferred Louisiana to French officials."[16] A quick double official transfer of jurisdiction within a three-week interval—Spain to France and France to the United States—was obligingly arranged in New Orleans; and in St. Louis, on March 9 and 10, the newly appointed interim American governor, Captain Amos Stoddard, ended up representing both the United States *and* France during the series of ceremonies. True to form, all the way to the end of what had proved to be a most peculiar arrangement throughout, Spain was represented by French-born Lieutenant-Governor, Charles De Hault Delassus. Two months later, on direct orders of President Jefferson, U.S. Army Captains Meriwhether Lewis and William Clark left St. Louis for a journey that was destined to open the West. Occupying a prominent role in the expedition were George Drouillard, Toussaint Charbonneau, and his wife, Sacagawea.

The year 1804 saw a new structure rise in Illinois. Fort Dearborn was built at the mouth of the Chicago River on Lake Michigan, on a location used for trade by the Miami Indians, and also originally the site of both a Jesuit Mission and a French fort. This was a strategic location par excellence, as it controlled access from the Lake to the Illinois River, the most direct route from the East to the West despite the long and difficult portage linking the Chicago and Des Plaines Rivers. Across from the fort, on the other side of the river, stood the house that Jean-Baptiste Point du Sable had built and sold to John Kinzie, an American trader. With the Louisiana purchase, it was now even more important for the United States to maintain better communication between the developed East and the wide open West, and so Fort Dearborn was needed to guard the long communication lines. Although small, a military presence was welcomed by American settlers, as "The militia, from its inception and for several years thereafter, existed in little more than name only."[17] It must be said, however, that the militia was essentially made up of French volunteers, a group not entirely reliable if called upon to intervene against hostile Indian activities.

It is not easy to believe that, despite the continuous and sizable waves of settlers—with the succession of defeats at the hands of troops, others at the hands of negotiators and government agents—with any French support totally eliminated, there might still be Indians who would refuse to surrender their dignity and what little lands remained, and moreover, be ready to pick up where Pontiac and Little Turtle had left off. Tecumseh, a Shawnee (Creek by his mother) was such a man. Along with his brother, "the Prophet," he attempted to galvanize young warriors from all the nations against the sell-out of their traditional chiefs. Like Pontiac, Tecumseh visualized a pan-Indian movement, but time was running out. Millions of acres of land previously held by Indians had already been turned over to the United States government just in the last ten years. It was on November 7, 1811, that Tecumseh's followers attacked the American troops led by William Henry Harrison, the Governor of the new Indiana Territory, near their town of Tippecanoe in the Wabash Valley, and met with defeat but not discouragement; a year later they were fighting again, this time alongside the British, once more at war with the Americans.

The War of 1812 began in early spring. From Fort Mackinac in the north, to Fort Massac at the southern tip of Illinois, the news of the war spread hope among the Indians, anxiety to the American settlers, and uncertainty among the remaining French. The British had not surrendered the line of forts along the Great Lakes, and were embarking on war in the Northwest from an obvious position of strength. In order to defend the Illinois Territory, Governor Ninian Edwards not only raised, but personally subsidized, mounted ranger companies; aside from this force of questionable military value, however, nothing other than Fort Dearborn stood in the path of a possible British and Indian attack from Mackinac. Eventually, the Potawatomi attacked and killed most of the garrison of Fort Dearborn, on August 15, 1812, and the Great Lakes were left undefended and vulnerable. The expected invasion did not occur, but fear among the American settlers who regarded all Indians as potential attackers, and the French as their accomplices, created a volatile atmosphere. Into this uncertain situation a detachment of American rangers led by Captain Thomas Craig, arrived in Peoria on November 5th. The town of Peoria had been moved in 1778 from its original site to a contiguous new location called "Ville à Maillet" (named after Jean-Baptiste Maillet, responsible for the relocation), and was a reasonably prosperous community.

Captain Craig went to Peoria because it was suspected the town not only had become an assembly point for hostile Indians, but that the French were supplying them with stolen cattle, weapons, and ammunition as well. What occurred following the arrival of the Americans remains unclear; we have only the versions left by chroniclers, memorialists, and antiquarians, whose writings are permeated by a notably anti-French bias. The Americans claimed they were told by the French that the Indians had left town when:

> sentinels on the boats had seen Indians passing through the town with candles and heard their canoes crossing the river all through the night. On the following night, one of their boats dragged its anchor and drifted ashore and so, the report continues, in the morning the boat was fired on, as the Captain thought, by ten or more Indians. He then gave battle, but the Indians at once took to their heels and escaped. This convinced Captain Craig that the French were in league with the Indians and guilty of treason and he took all of them prisoners after having located them all in one house. How many there were he does not state in his report. He then finished his work by setting fire to the buildings and practically destroying the town.[18]

The French civilians were then loaded onto boats and forced to travel down river with scant protection against the elements, until they reached an Indian encampment near present-day Alton on the Mississippi River, where they were given shelter and comfort. The following year, Benjamin Howard, the retiring Governor of the Louisiana Territory and now a

Brigadier General, organized an 800-man army composed of Missouri and Illinois American militiamen and also some regular troops. Howard's army had been assembled during the first days of August on the eastern bank of the Mississippi near Quincy, and promptly began to make its way across the prairie. The column burned a couple of Kickapoo villages near present-day Springfield, then ascended the Illinois River by both boat and horseback for forty-five miles. Testifying to the inexperience of the improvised staff, the troops on the water arrived in Peoria on Sunday, August 29th, days ahead of the cavalry, who were supposed to have reconnoitered the terrain. A party of about "...150 to 200 warriors then in their town attacked them with great resolution and not until after an hour's hard fight and using several pieces of small cannon, could the boats effect a landing at Peoria." [19] From an eyewitness trooper's account conjuring up a memory of his youth some forty years later, we have this vivid view of a pre-industrial age Peoria:

> As the army approached Peoria from the northwest and got a first view of its situation from the high-land prairies, two or three miles from the lake, looking easterly and southerly, beheld the smooth prairie gradually descending to the town, the lake stretching miles far to the northeast, the gunboats lying quietly at anchor upon the water, the towering forest across the water, and the lovely prairies bounded only by the horizon, there was an unvoluntary halt—the men all gazed in silence for a moment, and then of a sudden, as if moved by one impulse, expressed universal admiration of the beauty and grandeur of the prospect spread out before them.[20]

Though the American troops built a new fort in Peoria, Fort Clark, it was soon abandoned and afterward burned by a passing party of Indians, in 1818. The French never returned to their town, aside from a handful of isolated individuals. After 1819, American settlers from Virginia and Kentucky began to rebuild the comunity. The French land claims, however, were to take several decades of litigation before they were finally settled. [21]

The War of 1812 precipitated the Americanization of the territory; the French were no longer a matter of any consequence, and the Indians were headed for either complete removal, or worse, destruction, sanctioned by the authorities as shown by the decisions of the legislature which, in 1814, "... ten days after the war officially ended, established a system of bounties for the killing of hostile braves. The state obligated itself to pay

The Pierre Ménard House, across the river from Kaskaskia. (Photograph by Charles Balesi)

fifty dollars for the death of an Indian who entered a settlement with mur-derous intent."[22] Dispossession of Indian lands accelerated. When, in 1816, they abandoned the Military Tract, more than three million acres between the Illinois and Mississippi Rivers, the land was then distributed to veterans of the war in parcels of 160-acres each.

On December 3, 1818, President Monroe signed a resolution making Illinois a State. This final step was the result of many compromises and one falsified census; but nonetheless, Illinois had now reached adulthood in the American family. For the time being, the seat of government remained in Kaskaskia, and the first Governor, Shadrach Bond, a nephew of one of the original English-speaking settlers in Illinois, selected Pierre Ménard for his Lieutenant-Governor. This was a calculated move; a special provision had been inserted in the Illinois Constitution, tailoring the eligibility of the position to Ménard's recent naturalization. From his first day in Illinois, he had proven extremely helpful to American interests and his elevation was the reward. The Ménards, the Chouteaus, and some others were success stories, the exceptions among the French of the ancient *Terre des Illinois*. They were the businessmen familiar with the vocabulary of investments—capitalization, collaterals, dividends—and able to speak entrepreneurial language with the newcomers. Ménard had elegance, perhaps even "class;" his house, still standing today, demonstrates his refined taste, but his main asset was an ability to fit in. Tradition has reported the kindness he extended to the Indians camping at his door during their journey into exile. In the end, kindness mattered little; like Auguste Chouteau, Pierre Ménard had taken a primordial role in convincing the Indians to relinquish their ancestral lands, and to submit to the future imposed on them by the victorious Americans.

For the majority of the French populations, in Detroit, in Vincennes, in Mackinac, in Illinois and across the Mississippi, adaptation to life within the United States presented many problems not unlike those encountered by any immigrant from overseas who must cope with a foreign language and operate in an alien environment. To the powerful newcomers, the French culture and way of life were objects of scorn. Read the nineteenth-century writers who chronicled the aftermath of the French period in the heart of North America and you will find a unanimously negative, even hostile assessment of the French and their stubborn attachment to traditional ways. In particular, their closeness to the Indians was, to American eyes, an obvious sign of backwardness. The *Metis* (a French word meaning "mixed-blood") were a constant reminder of the sinful ways of the French in the view of the puritan-minded pioneers. The fact that there were French individuals such as Antoine Ouilmette, who lived with a Potawatomi wife on a parcel of land north of Chicago, or the Mackinac Langlade clan, who mixed with abandon with the Indians, was incomprehensible to them. Once the Louisiana Purchase was accomplished, the West was certain to undergo considerable transformation. In the context of the last century, the American pioneers, filled with an enthusiastic spirit of development, had neither the interest nor patience for any excessive baggage from the past. When the forests were cut down, the prairie turned over, and the Indians driven away, the communities the French had created from the Great Lakes to the Mississippi were doomed. Small in numbers and widely dispersed across a vast land, only on maps were the names to survive, a mute testimony of forgotten struggles.

NOTES

1. Captain Philip Pittman, *The Present State of the Settlements on the Mississippi; with A Geographical Description of that River, Illustrated by Plans and Draughts*, J. Nourse, London, 1772, 442-48.

2. Volney was born in Craon on February 3, 1757; made Count by Napoleon, Peer of France by Louis XVIII, he died in Paris on April 25, 1820. His complete works were published by Firmin Didot Freres, in Paris, in 1846, under the title of *Oeuvres complètes de Volney*; his observations during his journey across North America are presented in *A View of the Soil and Climate of the United States of America*, trans. C.B. Brown, Conrad and Co., Philadelphia, 1804. On the same subject, see also Gilbert Chinard, *Volney et l'Amerique*, Les Presses Universitaires de France, 1923.

3. INCLUDE (B:CH 18 NOT 2. MSS)

4. Volney, *Oeuvres Completes*, 705, trans. this author.

5. Volney, Ibid., 706.

6. Volney, Ibid., 707.

7. Professor Carl Ekberg's book, *An Account of Upper Louisiana by Nicolas de Finiels*, University of Missouri Press, 1989, is a complete and thorough analysis of the circumstances which led this French exile to leave such a vital testimony on the transitional period in Louisiana. Finiels' manuscript is kept in the Lovejoy Library of the Southern Illinois University in Edwardsville, Illinois, in the John Francis McDermott Collection. The map he drew is kept at the *Service Historique de la Marine*, Chateau de Vincennes, in France.

8. Ekberg and Foley, *Nicolas de Finiels*, 85.

9. John Jacob Astor, born near Heidelberg, Germany, on July 17, 1763, came to the United States in 1783, and soon later entered the fur business; he died on March 29, 1848, leaving a fortune estimated at twenty-five million dollars.

10. Robert Howard, *Illinois, A History of the Prairie State*, Eerdmans, 1972, 80.

11. See Charles C. Royce, ed., *Indian Land Cessions in the United States*, Bureau of American Ethnology, *Eighteenth Annual Report*, 2, Washington, 1899.

12. Solon J. Buck, *Illinois in 1818*, University of Illinois Press, Urbana, 1967, 43.

13. This event is better known as the *Coup d'etat du 18 Brumaire*. *Brumaire* was the new name the republicans gave to November.

14. Treaty of San Ildefonso, October 1, 1800.

15. See Lyon E. Wilson, *Louisiana in French Diplomacy, 1759-1804*, University of Oklahoma Press, 1934.

16. William Foley, *A History of Missouri*, Vol. I, 1673-1820, University of Missouri Press, 1971, 70.

17. Raymond Hammes, "Illinois Militiamen - August 1, 1790," *Illinois Libraries*, May 1977, Vol. 59, No. 5, Springfield, Illinois, 310.

18. Colonel James M. Rice, *Peoria City and County, Illinois*, Chicago, 1912, 123.

19. David McCulloch, *History of Peoria County*, Chicago, Munsell, 1902, 50; quoting a letter sent in by John S. Brinkley, from Potosi, Missouri, thirty-seven years later.

20. Ibid.

21. See *Decisions of the Supreme Court of the State of Illinois*, June term, 1851, at Ottawa.

22. Robert Howard, *Illinois .*, 93.

Bibliography

While a surprising number of works directly related to the focus of this book have been written, there is an even larger number on the subject of the French in North America. Obviously, it is impossible to list them all here; nevertheless, we hope that the following titles will give interested readers some useful information for further pursuit of the subject.

In addition to archival materials, rather than following the traditional approach, one that distinguishes between "primary" and "secondary" sources, we have opted to list all titles in alphabetical order by author whether they qualify as "primary source," (such as Charlevoix' *Histoire et description générale de la Nouvelle France*), or more general works, in order to facilitate their location.

Archival Materials:

Original documents can be found in the French Archives; first and foremost, in the *Archives des colonies*, series C13A, D2C, F2A, F3, and G1. These series have been microfilmed by the Library of Congress; the University of Southwestern Louisiana, in Lafayette; and the Public Archives, in Ottawa, Canada.

The *Archives du Ministère des Affaires Etrangères* (French Foreign Affairs Ministry), *Mémoires et Documents, Amérique*, in Paris, and the *Archives du Ministère de la Guerre*, located in the ancient *Château de Vincennes*, near Paris, are also important repositories of documents directly related to the French period in North America.

Of equal importance are the manuscript documents and original publications to be found at the *Bibliothèque Nationale*, in Paris. However, scholars familiar with the hallowed great hall of the "B.N." would do well to take into account its impending move to new quarters at the time of this writing.

Closer to the United States, the Canadian Archives hold important documents, particularly in the domain of local questions; (the French royal authorities took with them all other archives when Canada was surrendered to Britain). Of particular interest are the *Archives nationales de Québec*, and the *Archives judiciaires*, both in Montreal; and the *Archives de l'Archidiocèse*, in Quebec.

In the United States, rich sources of information can be found in a number of diverse depositories, such as the State Archives of New York, the Minnesota Historical Society, the Chicago Historical Society, and the Missouri Historical Society, in St. Louis. In Illinois alone there are two major depositories: the Illinois State Archives, in Springfield, and the Illinois Historical Survey, at the University of Illinois, in Urbana. The Randolph County Courthouse, in Chester, Illinois, is the jealous keeper of the well-known Kaskaskia Manuscripts for 1721-1765, but these manuscripts are also available on microfilm. It would be remiss not to list among the depositories the Newberry Library, in Chicago, which in addition to a number of ancient maps, also holds original editions of books and manuscripts for the French period (particularly in the Edward E. Ayer Collection), as well as a History of the Iroquois Archive at the D'Arcy McNickle Center for the History of the American Indian. Finally, one can also find almost inexhaustible sources for a plethora of research subjects in each state, in addition to Illinois and Missouri, whose territory was once part of the French colonial empire of North America, including: the Indiana State Historical Society Library and the Indiana State Library; the Michigan Pioneer Historical Society; the Ohio Historical Society; the Pennsylvania State Archives; and the State Historical Society of Wisconsin.

To examine what often appears to be a maze of sources, it is advisable to initially arm oneself with reliable guides, either general ones, such as Henry Putney Beers, *The French in North America: A Bibliographical Guide to French Archives, Reproductions and Research Missions*, published in Baton Rouge, Louisiana, in 1967; and the *Guide des Sources de l'Histoire des Etats-Unis dans les archives françaises*, published in Paris, in 1976; or those restricted to one particular area, such as Marie-Antoinette Menier's *Inventaire des Archives Coloniales: Correspondence à l'arrivée en provenance de la Louisiane*; or, the *Inventory of the County Archives of Illinois, Peoria County*, Illinois Historical Records Survey, completed by the W.P.A. and published in Chicago, in 1942. More recently, in 1982, Glen Conrad and Carl A. Brasseaux, respectively Director and Assistant Director of the Center for Louisiana Studies at the University of Southwestern Louisiana, in Lafayette, published a very useful volume entitled *A Selected Bibliography of Scholarly Literature on Colonial Louisiana and New France*.

Under the same category of "path-finder," also falls Francis Paul Prucha's*Bibliographical Guide to the History of Indian-White Relations in the United States*, published by the University of Chicago Press in 1977; the *Dictionary Catalog of the Edward E. Ayer Collection of Americana and American Indians in the Newberry Library*, published in Boston, in 1961; and Jean-Jacques Messier's *Bibliographie relative à la Nouvelle-France*, Montreal, 1979.

Printed Sources:

Abbott, John S.C. *The Adventures of the Chevalier de La Salle and His Companions*, New York, 1875.

Adams, Diane L. *Lead Seals from Fort Michilimackinac, 1715-1781*, Mackinac Island, 1989.

Allain, Mathé. "Plus ça change, plus c'est la même chose: Premier Acte, Cadillac and Duclos," *Proceedings of the Twelfth Meeting of the French Colonial Historical Society, Ste. Genevieve, May 1986*, New York, 1988.

Alvord, Clarence Walworth. *Cahokia Records, Illinois Historical Collections*, Springfield, 1907.

———. *The Mississippi Valley in British Politics*, Cleveland, 1917.

———. *The Illinois Country, 1673-1818*, Springfield, 1920.

Alvord, Clarence Walworth and Clarence Carter. *The Critical Period, 1767-1769*, Springfield, 1913.

———. *The New Régime, 1765-1767*, Springfield, 1913.

Andreas, A.T. *History of Cook County, Illinois*, Chicago, 1884.

Angle, Paul M. and Richard L. Beyer. *A Handbook of Illinois History*, Springfield, 1943.

———, ed. *Prairie State, Impressions of Illinois, 1673-1967, by Travelers and Other Observers*, Chicago, 1968.

Arnold, Morris S. *Colonial Arkansas, 1686-1804, A Social and Cultural History*, Fayetteville, Arkansas, 1991.

Axtell, James. *The European and the Indian, Essays in the Ethnohistory of Colonial North America*, New York, 1981.

Baker, George A. *The St. Joseph-Kankakee Portage*, South Bend, Indiana, 1899.

Bald, Clever F. *Michigan in Four Centuries*, New York, 1961.

Ballance, Charles. *History of Peoria, Illinois*, Peoria, 1870.

Bamford, Paul Walden. *Forest and French Sea Power, 1660-1789*, Toronto, Canada, 1956.

Barr, Keith L., Jerry J. Moore and Charles L. Rohrbaugh. *Intensive*

Archaeological Explorations for Peoria's 18th Century French Village, Normal, 1988.

Baudry des Lozières, Louis Narcisse. *Second Voyage à la Louisiane,* Paris, 1803.

Baugy, Louis Henri de. *Journal d'une Expedition Contre les Iroquois en 1687,* Paris, 1883. Trans. and ed. Nathaniel S. Olds, Rochester, 1930.

Baylis, Clara K. "The Significance of the Piasas," *Transactions of the Illinois Historical Society for the Year 1908,* Springfield, 1909.

Beckwith, Hiram W. *The Illinois and Indiana Indians,* Chicago, 1884.

———, ed. *Collections of the Illinois State Historical Library,* Springfield, 1903.

Belting, Natalia Maree. *Kaskaskia Under the French Régime,* New Orleans, 1975.

Bernard, Jean F., ed. *Relations de la Louisiane et du Fleuve Mississippi,* Amsterdam, 1720.

Biggar, Henry Percival. *The Early Trading Companies of New France,* Toronto, 1901.

Billon, Frederic L. *Annals of St. Louis in its Early Days under the French and Spanish Dominations, 1764-1804,* St. Louis, 1886.

Blanchard, Raoul. *Le Canada français, Province de Québec,* Montreal, 1960.

Blegen, Theodore C. *The Voyageurs and Their Songs,* St. Paul, Minnesota, 1966.

Borgia-Steck, Francis. *The Jolliet-Marquette Expedition, 1673,* Quincy, 1928.

Bossu, Jean-Baptiste Homère. *Nouveaux Voyages aux Indes Occidentales,* Paris, 1768.

———, John Foster, trans. and ed. *Travels through that part of North America formerly called Louisiana,* London, 1771.

———. *Nouveaux voyages dans l'Amérique septentrionale,* Paris, 1777.

Boucher, Philip P. *Les Nouvelles Frances, France in America, 1500-1815, An Imperial Perspective,* Providence, Rhode Island, 1989.

Bourée de Poney. *Notice sur la vie et les relations de voyage du Capitaine Jean-Baptiste Homère Bossu,* Châtillon-sur-Seine, 1852.

Breese, Sidney. *The Early History of Illinois from its Discovery by the French in 1673 until its cession to Great Britain in 1763, including the Narrative of Marquette's Discovery of the Mississippi,* Chicago, 1884.

Bridges, Roger D., ed. "John Mason Peck on Illinois Slavery," *Journal of the Illinois State Historical Society,* Springfield, 1982.

Briggs, Winstanley. "A Most Peculiar Institution: Slavery in French Colonial Illinois," paper presented at the *Illinois History Symposium*, Springfield, 1986.

Brodhead, J.R. *Documents Relative to the Colonial History of the State of New York*, Albany, 1856-1887, 15 vols.

Brown, Margaret K. and Lawrie C. Dean, eds. *The Village of Chartres in Colonial Illinois, 1720-1765*, New Orleans, 1977.

Buck, Solon J. *Illinois in 1818*, Chicago, 1967.

Buisseret, David, ed. *From Sea Charts to Satellite Images, Interpreting North American History through Maps*, Chicago, 1990.

———. *Historic Illinois from the Air*, Chicago, 1990.

Caldwell, Norman Ward. "The Chickasaw Threat to French Control of the Mississippi in the 1740s," *Chronicles of Oklahoma*, 1938.

———. "The French in the Mississippi Valley, 1740-1750," *Illinois Studies in the Social Studies*, vol. XXVI, 27, Urbana, 1941.

Carter, Clarence Edwin. *Great Britain and the Illinois Country, 1763-1774*, Washington D.C., 1910.

———. *The Correspondence of General Thomas Gage with the Secretary of State, 1763-1775*, 2 vol., New Haven, 1931.

Caruso, John Anthony. *The Mississippi Valley Frontier: The Age of French Exploitation and Settlement*, New York, 1966.

Champagne, Roger J. "Political Conditions in Illinois, 1763-1787," *Illinois History*, vol. 29, number 7, Springfield, 1976.

Chapais, Thomas. *Jean Talon, Intendant de la Nouvelle France: 1665-1672*, Paris, 1904.

Charlevoix, Father de. *Histoire et description générale de la Nouvelle France avec le Journal Historique d'un voyage fait par ordre du Roi dans l'Amérique Septentrionale*, Paris, 1744.

Chinard, Gilbert. *Volney et l'Amérique*, Paris, 1923.

Chouteau Papers. MSS, Missouri Historical Society, St. Louis.

Clément, Pierre. *Lettres, Instructions et Mémoires de Colbert*, Paris, 1861-1873, 7 vols.

Clifton, James A. "Chicago, September 14, 1833: The Last Great Indian Treaty in the Old Northwest," *Chicago History*, 86-97, Chicago, 1980.

Collet, Oscar W. *Notes on Parkman's "Conspiracy of Pontiac"*, St. Louis, 1882.

Collot, Victor. *A Journey in North America, 1796*, Florence, 1924.

Conrad, Glenn R. and Carl A. Brasseaux. *A Selected Bibliography of Scholarly Literature on Colonial Louisiana and New France*, Lafayette, Louisiana, 1982.

Cordier, L. *Les compagnies à charte et la politique coloniale sous le ministère Colbert*, Paris, 1906.

Courville, Serge. *Entre ville et campagne*, Quebec, 1990.

Cox, Isaac Joslin. *The Journeys of René Robert Cavelier Sieur de la Salle*, New York, 1905.

Craig, Oscar J. "Ouiatenon, A Study in Indiana History," *Indiana Historical Society Publications*, Indianapolis, 1898.

Curtin, Philip D. *The Atlantic Slave Trade*, Madison, 1969.

Davidson, Alexander and Bernard Stuve. *A Complete History of Illinois from 1673 to 1873*, Springfield, 1874.

Delanglez, Jean. *Frontenac and the Jesuits*, Chicago, 1939.

――――. *Life and Voyages of Louis Jolliet—1645-1700*, Chicago, 1948.

Delmas, Colonel, ed. *Conflits de sociétés au Canada français pendant la guerre de Sept Ans*, Vincennes, 1978.

Dillon, John. *History of Indiana from its Earliest Exploration b y Europeans*, Indianapolis, 1859.

Donnelley, Joseph, S.J. *Jacques Marquette, S.J.*, Chicago, 1968.

Drumm, Stella M., ed. *Journal of a Fur-Trading Expedition on the Upper Missouri, 1812-1813*, St. Louis, 1920.

Dumbar, Willis F., (revised ed., George S. May). *Michigan, A History of the Wolverine State*, Grand Rapids, 1980.

Dunn, William E. *Spanish and French Rivalry in the Gulf Region of the United States, 1678-1702*, Austin, 1917.

Eccles, William J. *Canada Under Louis XIV*, Toronto, 1964.

――――. *France in America*, New York, 1972.

――――. *The Canadian Frontier, 1534-1760* , revised ed., Albuquerque, 1984.

Edmunds, David R. *The Potawatomis, Keeper of the Fire*, Norman, 1987.

Ekberg, Carl J. *Colonial Ste. Genevieve, An Adventure on the Mississippi Frontier*, Gerald, Missouri, 1985.

Ekberg, Carl J. and William E. Foley, ed. *An Account of Upper Louisiana by Nicolas de Finiels*, Columbia, Missouri, 1989.

Ekberg, Carl and Edward B. Jelks, Terrance J. Martin. *Excavations at the Laurens Site, Probable Location of Fort de Chartres I*, Springfield, 1989.

Esarey, Louis. *A History of Indiana*, Indianapolis, 1915.

Farb, Peter. *Man's Rise to Civilization, as shown by the Indians of North America from Primeval Times to the Coming of the Industrial State*, New York, 1968.

Faribault-Beauregard, Marthe. *La population des forts français—XVIIIè siècle—*, Montreal, 1982, 2 vols.

Faye, Stanley. "The Arkansas Post of Louisiana: French Domination," *The Louisiana History Quarterly*, vol. 23, July 1943.

Flint, Timothy. *History and Geography of the Mississippi Valley*, Cincinnati, 1833, 2 vols.

Foley, William E. *A History of Missouri*, Columbia, 1971, 2 vols.

French, Benjamin F. *Historical Memoirs of Louisiana*, New York, 1846-1875, 7 vols.

French and Spanish Archives of Saint Louis, 1764-1804, MSS, Missouri Historical Society, St. Louis.

Galloway, Patricia K. "The Barthelemy Murders: Bienville's Establishment of the Lex Talionis as a Principle of Indian Diplomacy," *Proceedings of the Eighth Annual Meeting of the French Colonial Historical Society, 1982*, New York, 1985.

Galloway, Patricia K., ed. *La Salle and His Legacy, Frenchmen and Indians in the Lower Mississippi Valley*, Jackson, 1982.

Garraghan, Gilbert J. *The Catholic Church in Chicago, 1673-1871*, Chicago, 1921.

———. "The Great Illinois Village: a Topographical Problem," *Mid-America, An Historical Review*, vol. XIV, new series III, October 1931.

Gayarré, Charles. *History of Louisiana, the French Dominion*, New York, 1854-1866, 4 vols.

Gilman, Carolyn. *Where Two Worlds Meet, the Great Lakes Fur Trade*, St. Paul, 1982.

Giraud, Marcel. *Histoire de la Louisiane Française*, Paris, 1953.

Gitlin, Jay. "Avec bien du regret, The Americanization of Creole St. Louis," *Gateway Heritage*, Spring 1989.

Graham, Shirley. *Jean-Baptiste Pointe De Sable, Founder of Chicago*, New York, 1953.

Gravier, Gabriel. *Cavelier de la Salle de Rouen*, Paris, 1871.

Gravier, Henri. *La Colonisation de la Louisiane à l'époque de Law: Octobre 1717-Janvier 1721*, Paris, 1904.

Grover, Frank R. *Father Pierre François Pinet, S.J. and the Mission of the Guardian Angel, 1696-1699*, Chicago, 1907.

Guide to the Microfilm Edition of the Pierre Ménard Collection in the Illinois State Historical Library, Illinois State Historical Society, Springfield, 1972.

Habig, Marion A. "The Site of the Great Illinois Town," *Mid-America, An Historical Review*, vol. XVI, July 1933.

Hamilton, Edward P. *The French and Indian Wars*, New York, 1962.

Hamilton, T.M. and K.O. Emery. *Eighteenth-Century Gunflints from Fort Michilimackinac and other Colonial Sites*, Mackinac Island, 1988.

Hammes, Raymond. "Illinois Militiamen, August 1, 1790," *Illinois Libraries*, Springfield, May 1977.

Hand, John P. "Negro Slavery in Illinois," *Transactions of the Illinois State Historical Society for the Year 1910*, Springfield, 1913.

Harris, Norman Dwight. *The History of Negro Servitude in Illinois and of the Slavery Agitation in that State, 1719-1864*, Chicago, 1904.

Harrison, William Henry. *A Discourse on the Aborigines of the Ohio Valley*, Cincinnati, 1839.

Haydon, James Ryan. *Chicago's True Founder, Thomas J.V. Owen, A Pleading for Truth and for Social Justice in Chicago History*, Lombard, 1934.

Henripin, Jacques. *La population canadienne au début du XVIIIè siècle*, Paris, 1954.

Houck, Louis. *History of Missouri*, Chicago, 1908.

———. *The Spanish Régime in Missouri*, Chicago, 1909.

Hurlbut, Henry H. *Father Marquette at Mackinac and Chicago*, Chicago, 1878.

Hutchins, Thomas. *A Topographical Description of Virginia, Pennsylvania, Maryland and North Carolina*, original edition 1778, reprint, Cleveland, 1904.

Imlay, Captain Gilbert. *A Topographical Description of the Western Territory of North America*, London, 1797.

Indian American Revolution Bicentennial Commission. *The French, The Indians, and George Rogers Clark in the Illinois Country*, Proceedings, Indianapolis, 1977.

Innis, Harold A. *The Fur Trade in Canada*, New York, 1930.

Jaenen, Cornelius J. *Friend and Foe, Aspects of French-Amerindian Cultural Contact in the Sixteenth and Seventeenth Centuries*, Toronto, 1976.

———. *The French Relationship with the Native Peoples of New France and Acadia*, Ottawa, 1984.

Jeffrys, Thomas. *The Natural and Civil History of the French Dominion in North and South America*, London, 1760.

Jennings, Francis. *The Invasion of America, Indians, Colonialism and the Cant of Conquest*, New York, 1976.

———. *The Ambiguous Iroquois Empire*, New York, 1984.

Kalm, Peter. John R. Foster, trans. *Travels into North America, 1748-1749*, London, 1771.

Kennedy, W.P.M., ed. *Statutes, Treaties and Documents of the Constitution, 1713-1929,* London, 1930.

Knight, Robert and Lucius H. Zeach. *The Location of the Chicago Portage Route of the Seventeenth Century,* Chicago, 1928.

Laforest, Thomas J. *Our French-Canadian Ancestors,* Palm Harbor, 1984, 2 vols.

LaHontan, A.L. de l'Om Darce, Baron. *Nouveaux Voyages de M. le Baron de La Hontan dans l'Amérique Septentrionale,* La Haye, 1703.

―――. *Mémoires de l'Amérique Septentrionale, ou la suite des Voyages de M. le Baron de La Hontan,* La Haye, 1703.

Lanctot, Gustave. *Filles de joie ou filles du roi, Etude sur l'immigration feminine en Nouvelle-France,* Montreal, 1967.

Le Page du Pratz, Antoine S. *Histoire de la Louisiane,* Paris, 1758.

Lessard, René and Jacques Mathieu, Lina Gouger. "Peuplement colonisateur au pays des Illinois," 57-68, *Proceedings of the Twelfth Meeting of the French Colonial Historical Society, Ste. Genevieve, May 1986,* New York, 1988.

LeSueur, William D. *Count Frontenac,* Toronto, 1906.

Loudon, Archibald. *A Selection of Some of the Most Interesting Narratives of Outrages Committed by the Indians in their Wars with the White People,* Philadelphia, 1808.

Maccioni, Pascal. "Eléments de réflexion sur la part des phénomènes dans les causes du retrait des français de leurs colonies d'Amérique du Nord à l'occasion du Traité de Paris, 1721-1762," paper read at the Twelfth Meeting of the French Colonial Historical Society, Ste. Genevieve, Missouri, 1986.

McCulloch, David, ed. *Historical Encyclopedia of Illinois and History of Peoria County,* Chicago, 1902.

―――. *History of Peoria County, Early Days of Peoria and Chicago,* Chicago, 1904.

McDermott, John Francis. *A Glossary of Mississippi Valley French, 1673-1850,* St. Louis, 1941.

―――. *Old Cahokia: A Narrative and Documents Illustrating the First Century of its History,* St. Louis, 1952.

―――, ed. *The French, The Indians and Rogers Clark in the Illinois Country,* Indianapolis, 1977.

McKay, Betty L. *Sources for Genealogical Searching in Illinois,* Indianapolis, 1970.

McNeill, John Robert. *Atlantic Empires of France and Spain, Louisbourg and Havana, 1700-1763,* Chapel Hill, 1985.

McWilliams, Richebourg Gaillard. *Iberville's Gulf Journals,* Birmingham, 1981.

Margry, Pierre. *Découvertes et Etablissements des français dans l'Ouest et dans le Sud de l'Amérique Septentrionale, 1614-1754, Mémoires et Documents originaux,* Paris, 1876-1888, 5 vols.

Mason, G. Edward. *Illinois in the Eighteenth Century, Kaskaskia and its Parish Records, Old Fort Chartres,* Chicago, 1881.

———. *Early Illinois,* Chicago, 1890.

———, *Chapter from Illinois History,* Chicago, 1901.

Mason, Ronald J. *Great Lakes Archaeology,* New York, 1981.

Massicotte, E.Z. *Canadian Passports, 1681-1752,* new edition, New Orleans, 1975.

Matson, N. *Pioneers of Illinois, Containing a Series of Sketches Relating to Events that Occurred Previous to 1813,* Chicago, 1882.

Mereness, Newton D. *Travels in the American Colonies,* New York, 1916.

Miller, Otis Louis. Indian-White Relations in the Illinois Country, 1789-1818," Ph.D. Dissertation, St. Louis University, 1972.

Montagne, Charles. *Histoire de la Compagnie des Indes,* Paris, 1899.

Moogk, Peter N. "When Money Talks: Coinage in New France," *Proceedings of the Twelfth Meeting of the French Colonial Historical Society, Ste. Genevieve, May 1986,* 69-108, New York, 1988.

———. "Reluctant Exiles: Emigrants from France to Canada before 1760," *The William and Mary Quarterly,* 3rd series, vol. XLVI, July 1989.

———. "Manon Lescaut's Countrymen: Emigration from France to North America before 1763," *Proceedings of the Sixteenth Meeting of the French Colonial Historical Society, Mackinac Island, May 1990,* 24-44, New York, 1992.

Moore, Brian. *Black Robe,* New York, 1985.

Murphy, Robert. *Henry de Tonty, Fur Trader of the Mississippi,* Baltimore, 1941.

Nasatir, Abraham P. *Before Lewis and Clark, Documents Illustrating the History of the Missouri, 1785-1804,* St. Louis, 1952.

Neil, Edward Duffield, *The History of Minnesota: from the Earliest French Explorations to the Present Time,* Philadelphia, 1858.

Nixon, David. "New Findings about the Marquette Death Site," paper read at the Twelfth Meeting of the French Colonial Historical Society, in Ste. Genevieve, Missouri, 1982.

Norris, F. Terry. "Old Cahokia, An 18th Century Archaeological Site

Model," *Le Journal, The Newsletter of the Center for French Colonial Studies*, Prairie du Rocher, Illinois, 1984.

Nute, Grace Lee. *The Voyageur*, St. Paul, 1931.

O'Neill, Charles Edwards. *Church and State in French Colonial Louisiana: Policy and Politics in 1732*, New Haven, 1966.

Osman, Eaton G. *Starved Rock, a Chapter of Colonial History*, Chicago, 1911.

Palm, Mary Borgia, Sister. *The Jesuit Missions of the Illinois Country, 1673-1763*, Cleveland, 1933.

Papin, Théophile, ed., William Hyde and Howard Conard. "Early St. Louis," *Encyclopedia of the History of St. Louis*, St. Louis, 1899.

Paré, George. *The Catholic Church in Detroit, 1701-1888*, Detroit, 1951.

Parkman, Francis. *France and England in North America, Part 4, The Old Régime in Canada*, Boston, 1884.

———. *La Salle and the Discovery of the Great West*, Boston, 1898.

———. *Count Frontenac and New France under Louis XIV*, Boston, 1897.

———. *The Jesuits in North America in the Seventeenth Century*, Toronto, 1899.

———. *The Oregon Trail, The Conspiracy of Pontiac*, reprint, New York, 1991.

Parrish, Randall. *Historic Illinois, The Romance of the Earlier Days*, Chicago, 1905.

Pease, Theodore Calvin. *The French Foundations, 1680-1693*, Springfield, 1934.

———. *Anglo-French Boundary Disputes in the West, 1749-1763*.

Peckham, Howard H. *Pontiac and the Indian Uprising*, Princeton, 1947.

Perrin du Lac, M. *Voyage dans les deux Louisianes en 1801, 1802 et 1803*, Paris, 1805.

Petersen, Eugene T. *Mackinac Island, Its History in Pictures*, Mackinac Island, Michigan, 1973.

Peterson, Jacqueline. "Goodbye, Madoré Beaubien: The Americanization of Early Chicago Society," *Chicago History*, 98-111, Chicago, 1980.

Peterson, Jacqueline and Jennifer S.H. Brown, ed. *The New Peoples: Being and Becoming Métis in North America*, Lincoln, Nebraska, 1985.

Peyser, Joseph L. "The 1730 Siege of the Foxes: Two Maps by Canadian Participants Provide Additional Information on the Fort and Its Location," *Illinois Historical Journal*, vol. 80, number 3, 147-154, Springfield, 1987.

———. *Letters from New France, The Upper Country 1686-1783*, Urbana,

1992.

Phares, Ross. *Cavalier in the Wilderness, the Story of the Explorer and Trader Louis Juchereau de St. Denis*, Baton Rouge, Louisiana, 1952.

Phelps-Kellog, Louise. *Early Narratives of the Northwest, 1634-1699*, New York, 1917.

Phillips, Paul C. *The Fur Trade*, Norman, 1961.

Quaife, Milo Milton. "Fort Wayne in 1790," *Indiana Historical Society Publications*, vol. 7, Greenfield, 1921.

———. *Chicago's Highways Old and New, From Indian Trail to Motor Road*, Chicago, 1923.

———. *Michigan: From Primitive Wilderness to Industrial Commonwealth*, New York, 1948.

———, ed. *The Siege of Detroit in 1763*, reprint, Chicago, 1958.

Quattrochi, Anna Margaret. *Thomas Hutchins, 1730-1789*, PhD Thesis, Pittsburgh, 1944.

Reed, Charles B. *The First Great Canadian, Sieur d'Iberville*, Chicago, 1910.

Remington, Kingsbury Cyrus. *The Shipyard of the Griffon*, New York, 1891.

Reynolds, John. *The Pioneer History of Illinois*, Belleville, 1852.

———. *My Own Times*, Chicago, 1879.

Rice, Colonel James M. *Peoria City and County, Illinois*, Chicago, 1912.

Rich, Edwin. *Montreal and the Fur Trade*, Montreal, 1966.

Richard, Alden John. *General Gage in America*, Baton Rouge, Louisiana, 1948.

Robert, Jean-Claude. *Du Canada français au Québec libre*, Paris, 1975.

Roberts, James H. "The Life and Times of General John Edgar," *Transactions of the Illinois State Historical Society*, XII, Springfield, 1907.

Rochemonteix, Camille de, S.J. *Les Jésuites et la Nouvelle-France au XVIIème siècle*, Paris, 1896.

———. *Relations par lettres de l'Amérique Septentrionale, anneés 1709 et 1710*, Paris, 1904.

Russell, Donna Valley, ed. *Michigan Voyageurs From the Notary Book of Samuel Abbott, Mackinac Island, 1807-1817*, Detroit, 1982.

Salone, Emile. *La colonisation de la Nouvelle-France, Etude sur les origines de la nation canadienne française*, Trois-Rivières, Quebec, 1970.

Savelle, Max. *Empires to Nations, Expansion in America, 1733-1824*, Minneapolis, 1974.

Schlarman, J.H. *From Quebec to New Orleans*, Belleville, 1929.

Serrigny, Ernest. *Journal d'une expédition contre les Iroquois en 1687,* *rédigée par le Chevalier de Baugy,* Paris, 1883.

Severance, Frank, *An Old Frontier of France, The Niagara and adjacent lakes under French control,* New York, 1917.

Shea, John G. *Discoveries and Explorations of the Mississippi Valley, Part IV, French Historical Collection,* New York, 1852.

————. *Early Voyages Up and Down the Mississippi,* Albany, 1861.

————, ed. and trans. *First Establishment of the Faith in New France by Father Christian Le Clercq,* New York, 1881.

Smith, Alice E. *The History of Wisconsin,* Madison, 1973.

Snyder, John Francis. *Captain John Baptiste Saucier at Fort Chartres in the Illinois, 1751-1763,* Peoria, 1901.

Sulté, Benjamin. *La Noblesse au Canada avant 1760,* Quebec, 1914.

Surrey, Nancy M. *The Commerce of Louisiana During the French Regime, 1699-1763,* New York, 1916.

Surtees, Robert J. *Canadian Indian Policy, A Critical Bibliography,* Bloomington, 1982.

Tanner, Helen Hornbeck, ed. *Atlas of Great Lakes Indian History,* Norman, 1987.

Thurman, Melburn D. *Building a House in 18th Century Ste. Genevieve,* Ste. Genevieve, Missouri, 1984.

Thwaites, Reuben Gold. *Collections of the State Historical Society of Wisconsin,* vol. XVI to XX, Madison, 1902-1911.

————. *The Jesuit Relations and Allied Documents: Travel and Explorations of the Jesuit Missionaries in New France,* Cleveland, 1896-1901.

————. *Wisconsin, The Americanization of a French Settlement,* Boston, 1908.

————. *Down Historic Waterways, Six Hundred Miles of Canoeing upon Illinois and Wisconsin Rivers,* Chicago, 1910.

Thwaites, Reuben Gold and Louise Phelps Kellogg. *Frontier Defense on the Upper Ohio, 1777-1778,* Madison, 1912.

Tonti, M. le Chevalier Henri. *Dernières Découvertes dans l'Amérique Septentrionale de M. De La Sale,* Paris, 1697.

Vergennes, M. de. *Mémoire Historique et Politique sur la Louisiane,* Paris, 1802.

Villiers du Terrage, Baron Marc de. *Les Dernières Années de la Louisiane Française,* Paris, 1903.

————. *La découverte du Missouri et l'Histoire du Fort d'Orléans, 1673-1728,* Paris, 1925.

————. *La Louisiane, Histoire de son nom et de ses frontières successives, 1681-1819,* Paris, 1929.

Volney, Count Constantin de. *Oeuvres complètes,* Paris, 1846.

————, trans. C.B. Brown. *A View of the Soil and Climate of the United States of America,* Philadelphia, 1804.

Wallace, Joseph. *Illinois and Louisiana Under French Rule,* Cincinnati, 1893.

Weld, L.G. *Jolliet and Marquette in Iowa,* Iowa City, 1903.

White, Richard. *The Middle Ground, Indians, Empires, and Republics in the Great Lakes Region, 1650-1815,* New York, 1991.

Widder, Keith R. "The Persistence of French Canadian Ways at Mackinac after 1760," *Proceedings of the Sixteenth Meeting of the French Colonial Historical Society, Mackinac Island, May 1990,* 45-56, New York, 1992.

Wilson, Samuel. *The Architecture of Colonial Louisiana,* Lafayette, Louisiana, 1987.

Wilson, Lyon E. *Louisiana in French Diplomacy, 1759-1804,* Oklahoma City, 1934.

Winsor, Justin. *The Westward Movement, The Colonies and the Republic West of the Alleghenies, 1763-1798,* New York, 1897.

Wolf, John B. *Louis XIV,* New York, 1968.

Woodford, Frank. *Yankees in Wonderland,* Detroit, 1951.

Wright, J. Leitch, Jr. *Britain and the American Frontier,1783-1815,* Athens, Georgia, 1975.

Zay, E. *Histoire Monétaire des Colonies Françaises d'après les Documents Officiels,* Paris, 1892.

Zeuch, Lucius H. *The Location of the Chicago Portage Route of the Seventeenth Century,* Chicago, 1928.

Index